UNIVERSITY OF SOUTHAMPTON DEPARTMENT OF ARCHAEOI

CELTI
(Peñaflor)

The Archaeology of a Hispano-Roman Town in Baetica
Survey and Excavations 1987-1992

Simon Keay,
John Creighton and José Remesal Rodríguez

Oxbow Books

Southampton University Department of Archaeology Monographs are published by
Oxbow Books, Park End Place, Oxford OX1 1HN

© *Simon Keay, John Creighton and José Remesal Rodríguez 2000*

ISBN 1 84217 035 X

A CIP record for this book is available from The British Library.

This book is available direct from

Oxbow Books, Park End Place, Oxford OX1 1HN
(Phone: 01865–241249; Fax: 01865–794449)

and

The David Brown Book Company
PO Box 511, Oakville, CT 06779, USA
(Phone: 860–945–9329; Fax: 860–945–9468)

or from our website

www.oxbowbooks.com

Printed in Great Britain at
The Short Run Press
Exeter

Contents

Appendices (continued)

List of Figures

Chapter 3

Chapter 4

Chapter 10

Introduction

Rationale

It has long been known that Andalucía in Southern Spain has a rich archaeological record for much of antiquity. Much attention in recent years has been focused upon the impressive Copper Age complexes of El Argar and Los Millares, while important new discoveries have been made at the coastal Phoenician colonies and the indigenous cultural complex of Tartessos. For the Roman period, however, archaeological research has not yielded such spectacular results. The discovery of bronze municipal charters at Osuna and Malaca in the late 19th century, buttressed by excavations at Italica, Baelo and Munigua, awoke great expectations about the archaeological potential of the region for the study of Roman towns, which were never realised. Similarly, Ponsich's great survey of Roman rural settlement in the lower Guadalquivir valley created a framework for archaeological research which has never been properly fulfilled. Subsequent research into Roman towns has been piecemeal and many of the larger questions remain to be answered (Keay 1998). At the same time, the archaeological heritage of the region, like that in so many parts of southern Europe, has come under increasing threat. The renewal of regional infrastructure during the 1980s and 1990s and quickening desertification has led to increasingly rapid destruction of Roman urban sites and their hinterlands.

It is against this background that this project was conceived. It was clear that key questions about the character of urban settlement in the Roman province of Baetica could only be answered by excavation. Little was known about the origin of Roman towns, their degree of continuity from the late Iron-Age, their economic and social development during the early Empire and their transformation during late antiquity (Fig. 1). At the same time it was clear that the large area and deep stratigraphy of many Baetican town-sites meant that traditional sondage-style excavations would not be sufficient to provide answers to these kinds of questions. As a result, considerable thought was invested in finding a site which would have:

1. A good epigraphic and historical record.
2. A key central location to ensure that results from the project would be of regional significance.
3. A considerable extent of open-area uncluttered with post-Roman and modern buildings to permit unrestricted access to Roman and earlier levels.
4. A good stratigraphic sequence stretching between the later bronze-age and late antique period and which would be susceptible to open-area excavation.

Peñaflor, the site of ancient Celti, was a major settlement which answered all of these requirements (Fig. 2). In addition, it was also a site which in the mid 1980s was under threat of destruction by the widening of the Córdoba to Sevilla TGV. Indeed, in many ways, the site was emblematic of the frustrating threats and challenges that confront many Roman town sites in southern Spain. In developing the original project-design for this project, it was realized that it was not enough simply to conduct an excavation within the town. The excavated area needed to be fully contextualized into the rest of the site's topography and, consequently, would also need some clearly defined methodological aims. Consequently, the final report would not simply be a report on the excavations and survey carried out by the team, but would provide the impetus for a full consideration of the history of the town within the broader social and economic history of Roman Baetica. In short, Peñaflor would be a much-needed type-site for the development of Roman towns in the lower Guadalquivir valley. Consequently, the fieldwork attempted to gauge:

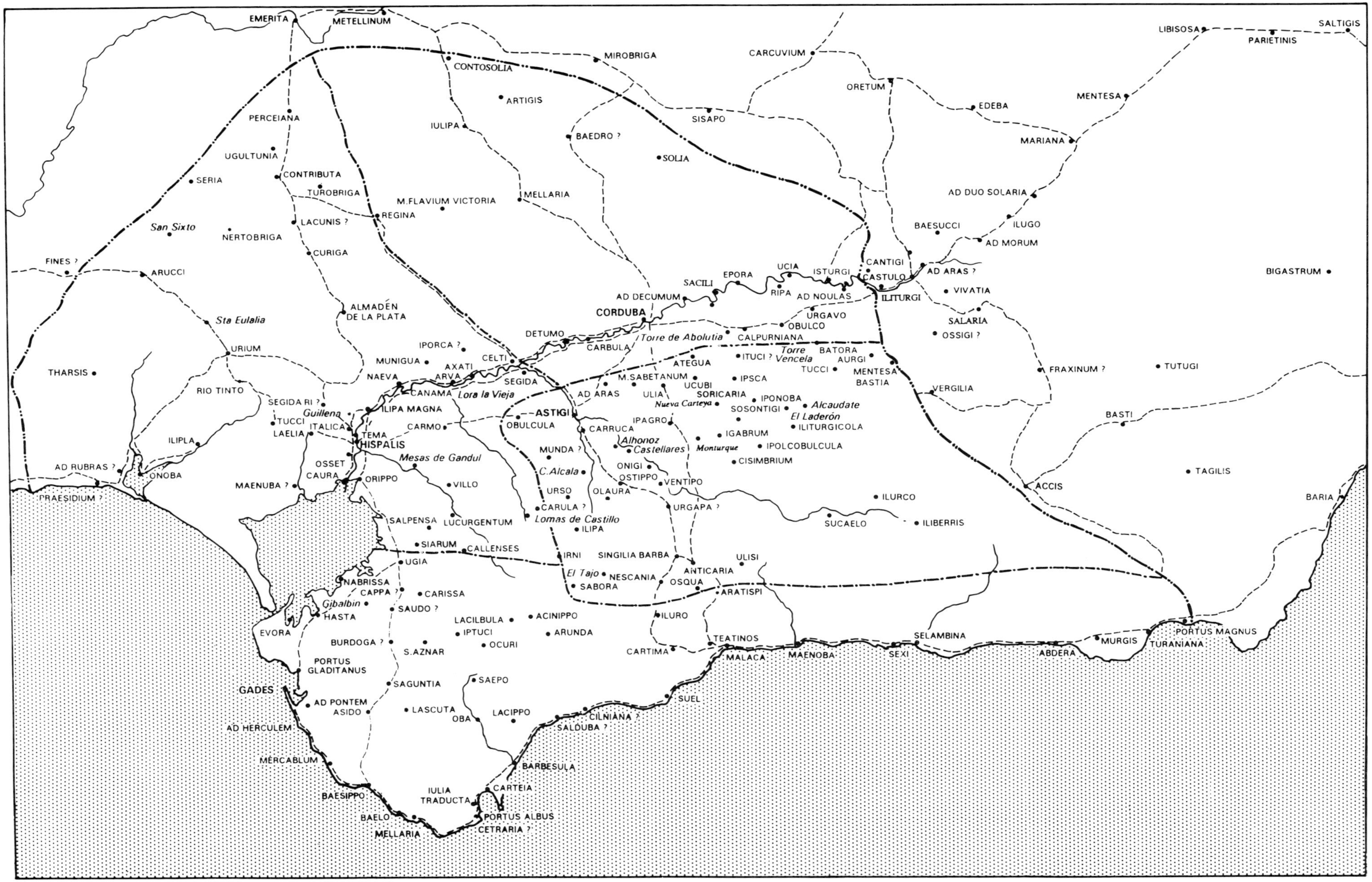

Fig. 1. The Roman Province of Baetica

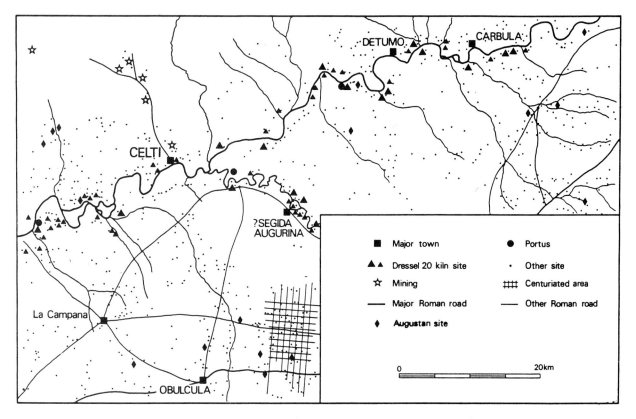

Fig. 2. The environs of Celti during the Roman Period

1. The date and cultural context for the first establishment of the site.
2. The date by which the settlement began to assume urban functions and signs of organized planning.
3. The regional context of the site and its relationship to contemporary Phoenician and Carthaginian settlements.
4. The impact of the Rome upon the town following the conquest of southern Spain in the later the 3rd and earlier 2nd centuries BC.
5. The Romanization of the town during the late Republican and early imperial periods.
6. The role of the town in the economy of the province, with particular respect to the production and export of olive oil in Dressel 20 amphorae.
7. The ways in which the town may have responded to the broader social, cultural and economic transformation of the province during the late Roman and germanic periods.

However, these could only be satisfactorily achieved by means of a fieldwork strategy, which included the following techniques:

1. Open-area excavation in conjunction with full topographic and systematic surface survey.

2. An integrated programme of environmental and faunal sampling.

This book is part of a broader programme of publication for the project. This book forms the main part of the British publication. It is intended to provide an overview of the project as a whole but excludes some of the more detailed analyses and appendices which are accessible in a linked web-site based at the University of Southampton (http://www.arch.soton.ac.uk/research/Penaflor/). In this way, the detailed ceramic data from the survey, the context list, matrices and the ceramic typology and fabrics do not form part of this publication but can be accessed by means of the web. The web-pages are organized in the following way:

Text and Illustrations

W/*Chapter 1:* Site Matrices
W/*Chapter 2:* The Ceramic Typology
W/*Chapter 3:* Spatial Modelling of Pottery, Bone and Metalwork by Phase

Appendices

W/*Appendix 1:* The Context List
W/*Appendix 2:* The Pottery Fabrics

W/Appendix 3: Weights of all Pottery from the Excavation

W/Appendix 4: Data from the Surface Survey

Reference in this volume to the Chapters and Appendices which appear in the Web-site is denoted by the letter W: hence W/Chapter or W/Appendix.

The published volume and Web-based material was collated, translated (Chapter 8) and edited by Simon Keay. Individual sections of text were authored by individuals whose names have been abbreviated in the following manner:

ACK (Anthony King, Department of Archaeology, King Alfred's College, Winchester)

ARS (Ana, Romo Salas, C/- San Clemente 17, Sevilla)

AW (Anthony Waldron, Institute of Archaeology, UCL)

CC (César Carreras, Universitat Oberta, Catalunya, Spain)

CV (Christian de Vartavan)

DJ (David Jordan, Terra Nova Limited, Brecon)

EP (Elizabeth Pye, Department of Conservation, Institute of Archaeology, UCL)

FM (Federica Massagrande, Department of Archaeology, University of Southampton)

JC (John Creighton, Department of Archaeology, University of Reading)

JR (Jane Reed, Department of Archaeology, University of Cambridge)

JRR (José Remesal Rodríguez, Departmento de Historia Antigua, Universitat de Barcelona)

KK (Kathryn Knowles, Department of Archaeology, University of Southampton)

KW (Kate Wilson, English Heritage)

MA (Marguerite Attree, Department of Archaeology, University of Southampton)

MJ (Martin Jones, Department of Archaeology, University of Cambridge)

MH (Martin Henig, Institute of Archaeology, University of Oxford)

MR (Miguel Ribagorda)

SG (Sheila Gibson, Institute of Archaeology, University of Oxford)

SK (Simon Keay, Department of Archaeology, University of Southampton)

The Spanish publication will comprise a similar text, but with a CD-Rom rather than a linked web-page. This is largely because it is hoped that the ceramics will provide an indispensable tool for other archaeologists working in the lower Guadalquivir valley and that a CD-based publication of this will make it more accessible to archaeologists in the field than if it is published in a web-page. The text will essentially be the same as that published in English. It is hoped that this book will be published in later 2000/earlier 2001.

Acknowledgements

The project would like to acknowledge generous financial support from The Society of Antiquaries of London, The British Academy, The Royal Archaeological Institute, the National Geographic Society, The University of Southampton and the Institute of Archaeology (UCL). Logistical support was provided by the Antonio Pozanco León, Ilmo Delegado of the Delegación Provincial de Cultura (Sevilla) de la Dirección General de Bienes Culturales of the Junta de Andalucía, Juan Antonio Suarez Japón, Ilmo Consejero of La Consejeria de Cultura, Sr. Don Moíses Ruiz, Alcalde of the Ayuntamiento de Peñaflor, Fernando Fernández Director del Museo Arqueológico de Sevilla. Key moral support was always freely given by José Manuel Rodríguez Hidalgo (Delegación Provincial de Cultura de Sevilla), Fernando Amores Carredano and Victor Hurtado Pérez of the Departamento de Prehistoria I Arqueología of the Universidad de Sevilla. We are also very grateful to Professor John Wilkes of the Institute of Archaeology (UCL) for refereeing this book for publication, particularly at such short notice, and making a number of helpful suggestions. In addition, Professor John Richardson kindly commented upon an earlier draft of Chapter 9. In the field, special thanks are due to Mary and Tony Morse for their careful management of the catering throughout many hot and difficult months. Nick Bradford supervised the day to day management of the work-force, assisted by Carlos Romero Moragas, Jeremy Taylor, Henry Stevens and César Carreras. The workforce involved students from the Department of Archaeology of the University of Southampton, the Departamento de Prehistoria I Arqueologia de la Universidad de Sevilla and the Institute of Archaeology (UCL) who are too numerous to mention, but included Toby Driver, Yöelle Carter, Antonio Perez Paz, Alvaro Jiménez, Olga Viñuelas, Nina Keay, David Rance, Ranjan Jayawardena and Ana Romo Salas. At Southampton, Sophie Jundi, Nick Bradford and Kathryn Knowles assisted in the production of the artwork. We would also like to thank José Carranza Cruz and José Luis Meléndez for permission to study and publish their inscriptions. Last, but not least, we would like to express our thanks to the people of Peñaflor for their generosity and forbearance during our six seasons of work in their village.

Photographic acknowledgements: *Figs. 1.1b and 1.4:* Junta de Andalucía. Consejería de Obras Publicas y Transportes. Instituto de Cartografia de Andalucia. *Fig. 1.9:* Museu D'Arqueologia de Catalunya. Barcelona.

Chapter 1
Background to the Site

Simon Keay

Abstract

This Chapter provides an introduction to the site of ancient Celti (Peñaflor). It begins by analyzing its central position in the heart of the lower Guadalquivir valley, as well as its surrounding resources. It then reviews historical references to the town from the Roman through into the Medieval period. The latter part of the Chapter is concerned with the archaeological evidence from the town. This starts with a brief description of the archaeological remains at the site which are still visible today. It then goes on to describe the ways in which the archaeological heritage of the site has suffered from destruction and agricultural work and concludes with a brief analysis of recent archaeological work.

Location and Geographical Background

The archaeological site of Peñaflor (Provincia de Sevilla) lies immediately to the west of the village of the same name, on the north bank of the river Guadalquivir at UTM 30 STG 928761 (IGM 1: 50,000 Sheet 14–38[942]). It is mid-way between Sevilla, which lies nearly 70km to the west, and Córdoba which is to be found nearly 60km to the east (Fig. 1.1a, 1b and 1c).

The Guadalquivir valley, which today embraces an area of 58000km², is in origin a geosyncline between the older Precambrian massif of the Sierra Morena to the north and the younger Cordillera Sub-Bética to the south (Fig. 1.2). From the Tertiary period onwards, it was infilled with a range of secondary sediments and subsequently cut into by the meandering course of the Guadalquivir itself. This river, which is 657km long, rises in the Sierra de Cazorla (Jaén) to the east and today flows into the Atlantic just to the north of Cádiz. It drains the valley by means of a large number of tributaries, including the Guadaira, Huesna, Bembezar, Corbones and the Genil, the latter of which bore water from the Cordillera Sub-Bética a long way to the south-east. The meandering course of the Guadalquivir in the lower valley has varied quite considerably since antiquity, although its precise

development is not entirely clear (generally, see Drain *et alii* 1971). River action is heaviest in the period between Autumn and Spring, when it receives a large amount of run-off from the Sierra Morena, periodically flooding some of the lower-lying adjacent areas. Downriver from Palma del Río, the average volume of flow is in the region of 164m³/s. In summer, by contrast, the river is relatively quiet and bears very little water (García-Baquero López 1990, 45–57).

Peñaflor lies close to the intersection between the Guadalquivir and the Genil at a relatively narrow point in the river valley, near the modern town of Palma del Río (Fig. 1.3). The site itself covers a low-lying plateau at the western edge of a large outcrop of Ordovician schists and metamorphosed limestone with occasional basalt intrusions (IGME 76). This is one of a number of similar outcrops which are to be found along the north bank of the Gudalquivir and which mark the site of such ancient settlements as the Castillo de Lora (Axati), El Castillejo (Arva) and Alcolea del Rio (Canama). They mark the southernmost outcrops of the underlying metamorphic and igneous rocks of the Sierra Morena which, in turn, is a southward extension of the Spanish Meseta to the north. It seems likely that these outcrops have largely

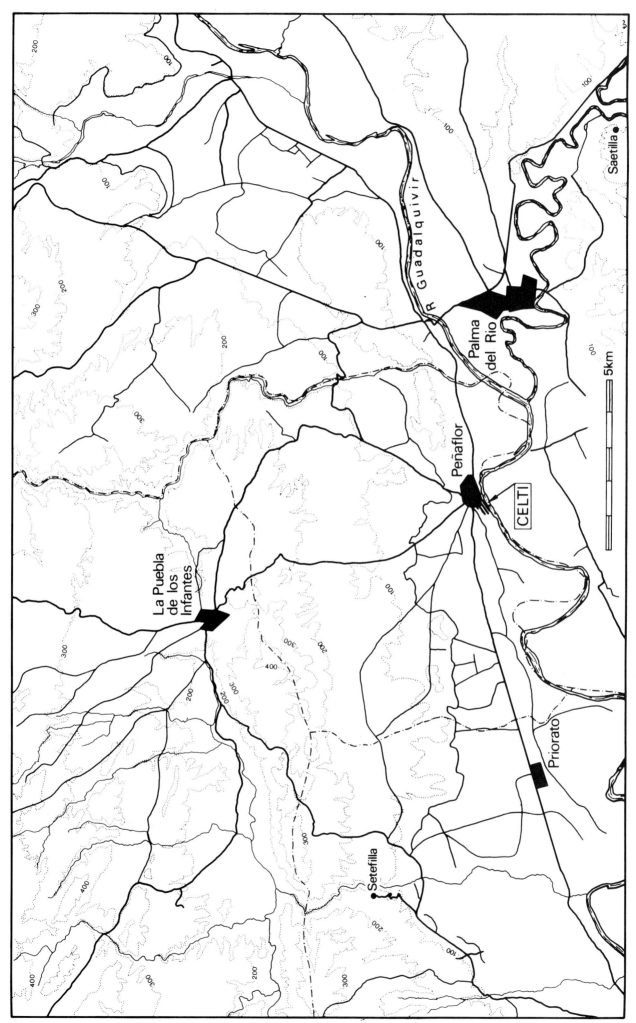

Fig. 1.1a. Map of the immediate region of Peñaflor

Fig. 1.1b. Aerial Photograph of Peñaflor and its immediate region: the line of the Roman aqueduct from the Castillo de Almenara to the site is marked by white arrows (Junta de Andalucía. Instituto de Cartografía: Hoja 942. October 1991)

Fig. 1.1c. View of the site of Celti from across the Guadalquivir to the south: Peñaflor lies immediately to its east

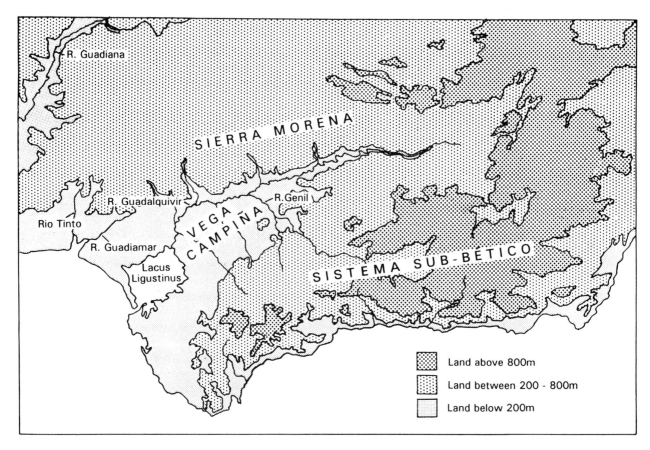

Fig. 1.2. The Topography of the Lower Guadalquivir Valley

conditioned the meandering of the Guadalquivir since antiquity to the present-day, preventing any movement northwards. They would also have ensured that any settlements located upon them would have been safe from the periodic floods of the river.

The region has excellent potential for agricultural production. The rich alluvial soils of the valley floor and in the terra-rossa soils of much of the first river terrace to the north are extremely fertile and well-adapted to most crops on an annual rotation (including cotton, maize, sunflowers and beetroot). The soils in the foothills of the Sierra Morena further north are better suited to dry-farmed crops on an annual cycle, particularly olives, admixed with some pasture. The Sierra Morena itself is largely covered by dry-scrub, maquia and oak trees. The agricultural richness of this region is tempered by the Mediterranean-Continental climatic regime of the region. The soils of the river terraces to the south of the Guadalquivir border the flat-lands of the Campiña and are best adapted to dry-farming and key cereal crops (De la Rosa and Moreira 1987, 58–64 and Map 3). On account of its inland location, the region is subject to quite cold winters (between 8 and 10 degrees), but extremely hot summers,

particularly over the months of June, July, August and part of September, when the average summer temperatures are in the region of 28 degrees but can rise to over 50 degrees. The area is very flat and shut off by mountains to the north and is one of the hottest regions in peninsular Spain. Rain is rare and most common in autumn and early spring (600–700mm). Aside from agriculture, the Peñaflor region is well-placed to benefit from transhumance from the valley floor to the Sierra Morena in the summer months and vice-versa in the winter, as is well documented by historical and contemporary sources. Finally, the Sierra Morena are also a key resource for a range of key metals and stone. In the stretch of the mountains that lie within the province of Sevilla, iron, copper, lead, limestone, marble and volcanic rock are quite common (Cano García 1998, 59–62; Domergue 1987).

Historical Background to the Site

The principal area of the ancient site covers 23.6 Ha (Fig. 1.4 and 1.1b). It is defined by the Guadalquivir to the south, the Arroyo Moreras to the east, the Arroyo Majuelo to the west and to the north by

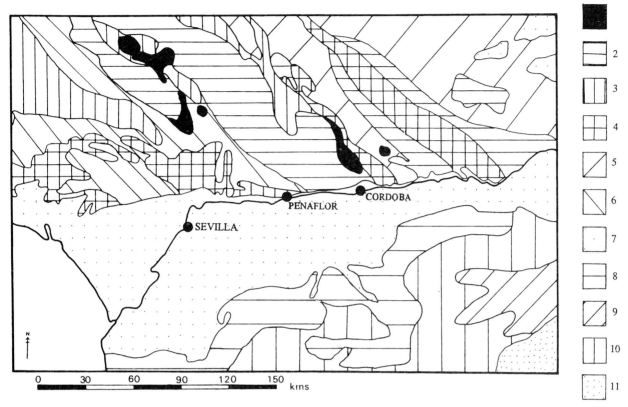

Fig. 1.3. The Geology of the Region. The numbers to the right of the map refer to the following classes of rock: 1)Volcanic rocks; 2)Cambrian deposits; 3)Schist; 4)Granite; 5)Marine sediments; 6)Silurian sediments; 7)Glacial and Post-Glacial sediments; 8)Eocene deposits; 9)Upper Jurassic sediments; 10)Lower Jurassic sediments; 11)Schists

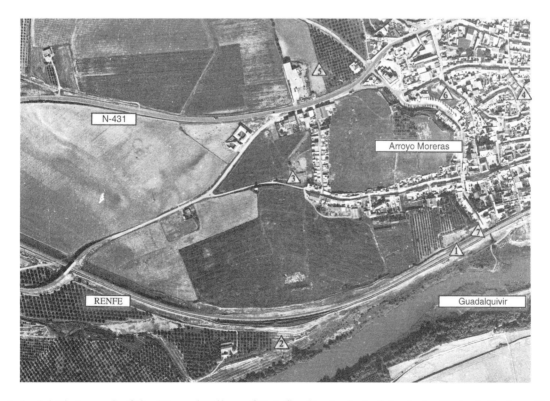

Fig. 1.4. Aerial Photograph of the Site and Village of Peñaflor (Junta de Andalucía. Instituto de Cartografía. Hoja 942 pasada 5 October 1991)

the Almodóvar to Lora del Río road (N-431). Traditionally, the archaeological remains at Peñaflor have been identified with the Roman town of Celti. This has been suggested from successive analyses of the literary sources and, to some degree, by the epigraphic record from the site and its region. For example, 'Pop. Celti' was inscribed on a tile found at Palma del Rio (Cean Bermúdez 1832, 275), while the names Celtitana (CIL II 2332 = CILA 2.1 176 = Chapter 8 nos. 8 and 14) and Celtitanus (CIL II 2326 = CILA 2.1 165 = Chapter 8 no. 5) appear upon inscriptions from Peñaflor. Although the question is not definitively resolved, the identification of Celti with Peñaflor is now generally accepted; this matter is discussed further elsewhere in this volume (see Chapter 8).

The town of Celti is only mentioned rarely in the ancient sources. Its significance as a name is unclear, although it is doubtful that it signifies the presence of a "Celtic" population at any time in its history (see Chapter 10). The earliest reference to it is to be found in Pliny the Elder (*NH* 3, 11). Following a discussion of the conventus Astigitanus, Pliny lists Celti as the first in a list of cities of the conventus Hispalensis. It is then followed by Axati, Arva, Canama, Naeva, Ilipa, Italica and Hispalis – before Pliny proceeds to list other towns in the conventus. The subsequent surviving sources date to the late Empire. The first is to be found in the late 3rd century Antonine Itinerary (It. 414, 5), in which *Celtici*, along with Carmane (Carmo), Obucula (Obulcula), Astigi and Regiana (Regina) are mentioned as stops along the road from Hispalis to Emerita Augusta (*Item ab Hispali Emeritam*: Roldán Hervas 1975, 61–2). The 7th century AD Ravenna Cosmographer (Rav.IV.44, 315, 2) is the later source and mentions *Celtum* amongst the masiones Regina, Astigin (Astigi), Obucula and Carmona (Carmo) along the road which runs from Augusta Emerita (Mérida) to Hispalis (Roldán Hervas 1975, 130). The latest reference to the town dates to AD 619, and concerns a discussion in the II Hispalensian Council of AD 619 between the bishops of Astigi and Corduba about a basilica and as to whether it lay in the jurisdiction of either Regina or Celti (Vives 1963, 185).

The site then slips from the historical record until AD 1249, when a manuscript, now lodged in the Archivo Histórico Nacional (Ladero Quesada & Jiménez González 1976), records the mention of a *Castillo de Peñaflor* as one of several castles donated to the Order of Saint John of Jerusalem by King Fernando III, in recognition of their assistance during the reconquest of the Guadalquivir valley from the Moors (for the reconquest of Andalucía, see González Jiménez 1988). The *Castillo* is mentioned again in another manuscript dated to

between AD 1465 and 1469 (Ladero Quesada 1973, 95). By the early 17th century, Peñaflor is known to have been an important ancient settlement (Rodrigo Caro 1634, 3, 98–9, 101, 215–6), while visits to the site and the discovery of ancient buidlings, inscriptions and artefacts are recorded by such people such as Flores (1752, 60–1), D. Agustín Cean Bermúdez (1832, 275–277), Ambrosio de Morales (undated, Fig. 12-24-1-B-1 folios 127,128, 129, 130) and Luís María Ramírez y Las Casas-Deza (1844). It was also mentioned by Delgado (1871–1876) as the possible source of native bronze coins bearing the legend CELTITAN (Fig. 1.5a and 5b).

a

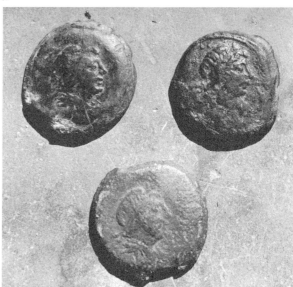

b

Fig. 1.5a and 1.5b. Obverses and reverses of CELTITAN bronze coins

Little more is heard of the site until the end of the 19th century. By this time, however, research into the antiquity of the Roman period in southern Spain was sufficiently advanced for scholars to be aware of the possible connection between Peñaflor and Celti. This was fuelled by Hübner's publication of Roman inscriptions from Peñaflor in the second volume of the Corpus Inscriptionum Latinarum (CIL II. 1236, 1514, 2304, 2326, 2327, 2329, 2330, 2331, 2332, 2333, 2334, 2335, 2336, 5539, 5540, 5541 and 5542: restudied with more recent texts by González 1991; see however Chapter 8 of this volume) between 1869 and 1892. A few years later, the archaeological potential of the site was demonstrated by George Bonsor (1899, 100; id.1901, 835–57; id.1931, 19–21). He described the remains of a river port and the cyclopean structure of the Higuerón, a family tomb or columbarium in the Cortinal de las Cruces (see also Chapter 8), a mosaic in the Calle de San Pedro, column bases and capitals, the remains of buildings in the "Pared Blanca" field, the impluvium of a Roman house with 4 columns and tank, "visigothic" lead coffins and pottery kilns, as well as the remains of an aqueduct at the Fuentes de Almenara, 3.5km to the north of the village (Bonsor 1899, 100; id. 1901, 837–57; 1931, 19–21; see also Clark Maxwell 1899). Bonsor also made the important link between the site of Peñaflor and the production of olive oil amphorae, which came to be known as the Dressel 20. The archaeological remains at the site were also alluded to by Fernández Casanova (1909, 68).

The site has been subsequently mentioned by a number of distinguished scholars, such as Serrano Ortega (1911, 10–19, 133–34), Thouvenot (1940, 45, 248, 297, 398, 481, 487, 500, 522, 533, 542), García y Bellido (1960, 191–2) and Tovar (1974, 158ff) who built upon earlier published work and dicussed ancient sources and known standing structures. Vives (1924–1926), Guadán (1969) and Villaronga (1979; 1994) periodically returned to the theme of the CELTITAN coins, continually suggesting that they be associated with Celti of the classical sources and, therefore, Peñaflor. More recently, however, enquiry has focused upon the town's role in the economic structure of the Roman province of Baetica. This has built upon the traditions of Bonsor's earlier work, Thevenot's study of the involvement of the Aelii Optati in the trade of olive oil – a family which may have originated in Peñaflor (Thevenot 1952; see also Chapter 8), and Callender's synthesis of amphora stamps (1965). Lorenzo Abad Casal's synthesis on the Guadalquivir (1975, 71, 112–114, 123) was a useful update of earlier work by Bonsor and Clark Maxwell although it had little to add that was specifically new about Celti. Ponsich's account

(1979, 101–4) was a useful summary of ancient and more recent references to the town, together with information on newly discovered Dressel 20 amphora stamps from the town and the discovery of rural sites and villae in its hinterland, in the context of his survey of the lower Guadalquivir valley. The theme of stamped Dressel 20 and their manufacture at the site has been revisited by a number scholars subsequently, most notably Chic (1985).

Visible Ancient Remains at the site

There is little to be seen of Celti today. Within the confines of the ancient town, the most celebrated monument is without doubt the Higuerón (Figs. 1.4.1 and 1.6). This is a large bastion-like structure built from cyclopean masonry, which sits on the banks of the Guadalquivir in the south-eastern corner of the site close to the mouth of the Arroyo Moreras; it has been interpreted variously as a Turdetanian fortification, quay or bridge abutment (for example: Ponsich 1979, Abad 1975, Chic 1978 and Remesal 1991). Further along the river front towards the south-western limit of the site, Dressel 20 amphora kilns have been located at Las Piedras Negras and were excavated at El Cortjillo (Figs. 1.4.2 and 1.7) in 1986 (infra). Further to the north, a short distance below the highest point of the La Viña field, semi-circular and rectangular tanks had been exposed through agricultural work over the years: these were fully excavated during the course of this project (Figs 3.10 and 3.12 bottom). Further north again, immediately to the south of the pig-sties at the south-eastern corner of El Calvario hill, the remains of a polychrome mosaic have been discovered (Fig. 1.4.3). To the east of the town, a mausoleum – the Cortinar de las Cruces – is preserved in the Calle Blas Infante no. 7 (Fig. 1.4.4); it was originally reused as a small chapel and is now a private house. Elsewhere in the village, there are inscriptions and column capitals built into the houses. Outside the town are the remains of a Roman aqueduct which can be traced from its source at the Castillo de Almenara, to the Arroyo de Almenara, the Fuentes de Almenara, the canal de Bembazar and the carretera de las vegas de Almenara (Fig. 1.1.b). Its precise point of entry to the ancient town is not known, although somewhere along the line of the modern Calle Calvario would seem likely. This runs up the north side of the town and reaches a maximum height of 73.35m, a little lower than the highest point in La Viña to the south (75.14m). Very recently, a curved stone structure has been discovered a short distance to the north of the east–west N-431 road (Fig. 1.4.5).

Fig. 1.6. The monument of El Higuerón

The only others structures in the town date to the post-Roman period. There is a small building, presumably of medieval date (Fig. 1.4.6), surrounded with high walls behind the parish church of San Pedro Apostol and close to the junction of the Calle Torno Iglesia and the Calle las Cuevas. This sits on top of a small rocky outcrop and would have watched over the Almodóvar to Lora del Río road, now the N-431, which ran a short distance to the north. This may perhaps be identified with the Castillo de Peñaflor mentioned in 15th century manuscripts [above: p. 6]. The remains of a bridge, perhaps of Medieval date, close to the junction of the Arroyo Moreras and the Higuerón may have been related to this (Fig. 1.4.7). Otherwise, there is the Parish Church of San Pedro, which was built between 1780 and 1801 on the ruins of an earlier Mudéjar church destroyed in the earthquake of 1755 (Morales *et alii* 1982, 394–402). There is also the church of the old Convento de San Francisco (Pascual Madoz 1849, 781) – otherwise known as the Iglesia de San Luís and which is dated to the second half of the 18th century (Morales *et alii* 1982, 401–2), together with the 18th century Ermita de San Crispulo y Restituto in the village (Pascual Madoz 1849, 781, Morales *et alii* 1982, 405), and the Ermita de Nuestra Señora de la Encarnación: originally constructed in 1766–1768 (Morales *et alii* 1982, 404–5). Outside the village, less than 1

Fig. 1.7. View of a section cut through a Dressel 20 kiln at El Cortijillo: the collapsed dome on the floor can be clearly seen

kilometre to the west lies the Ermita de Nuestra Señora de Villadiego (Morales 1982 *et alii*, 404–5), on the site of some kind of Roman site and at which are to be found a number of inscriptions and architectural fragments (Ponsich 1979, 95 nr.72).

Destructive Work at the Site

For many years, Peñaflor has been the victim of destructive activity, at times threatening the very survival of the site. In this sense, Peñaflor is symptomatic of the treatment that many Baetican towns have received over the years. At the very least, these would have been small-scale sondages dug when house foundations were excavated. These might have been the circumstance of occasional finds such as those reported in the leisure magazine *Semanario Pintoresco Español* in the mid-nineteenth century (Ramírez y Las Casas-Deza 1844). Sadly, however, the first "excavations" at the site can only be described as destructive. These were undertaken during the construction of the Seville-Córdoba railway which was opened in 1859. A wide cutting separated most of the town from El Higuerón, Dressel 20 kilns and other elements of the river port. There is little doubt that irreparable damage was caused to the southern sector of the site although there are no records of what was destroyed. It is possible, however,

that two white marble statues of standing women (Fig. 1.8: now in private possession in the C/-Guzman el Bueno nr.2 in Sevilla) may have come to light during this work. Fernández Chicarro suggested that they came to light in the Pared Blanca as a result of works for the railway in 1865. As the Pared Blanca field lies at some distance from the Railway Line one can only assume that they were actually found in the La Viña field.

The next recorded act of destruction took place in the early 1970s. It is recorded that the western part of the ancient town was used as a quarry for rubble to shore up the bridge which carried the Camino Viejo de Sevilla over the Railway Line: a substantial amount of this came from the El Camello property at the western edge of the site. The discovery of cremation burials, early imperial epitaphs and lead sarcophagi of "early Christian" date over the years suggest that this may have been a Roman cemetery (Ponsich 1979, 105). Clearly, therefore, the El Camello property is of considerable importance. Indeed, an aerial photograph of Peñaflor taken in 1990 reveals a number of large circular structures (Fig. 2.1b.L) which may perhaps be mausolea. In this context, it would be interesting to know whether the carving of a stone lion of Roman Republican date, which is now conserved in the Museu Arqueològic de Barcelona (Fig. 1.9: discussed in Chapa 1985, 112–4) and which is known to have come from Peñaflor, derived from this part of the site. Although its precise provenance and

Fig. 1.8. Two white marble statues from Peñaflor now in private ownership.

Fig. 1.9. Stone Lion from Peñaflor now in the Museu Arqueològic de Barcelona (Inv: M.A.B. 19879)

date of discovery is unknown, it clearly belongs to a Turdetanian funeral monument of 2nd or 1st century BC.

At some stage in the early 1980s, a small warehouse was built on the north-western side of La Viña immediately adjacent to the camino de Pared Blanca (Polígono 8, Parcela no. 41). Sadly, however, there is no record of the damage that this may have caused to underlying archaeological remains. An even more serious threat developed in 1986 and 1987. The south part of the La Viña field was threatened by the construction of the final stretch of the Madrid to Seville TGV, as part of regional developments in the run-up to EXPO '92 at Seville. This would have required quarrying away a major sector of the La Viña field and adjacent land to the east, lying to the north of the old RENFE line in order to straighten its curve; this would have involved the destruction of some 14000m² of the ancient town. To achieve this, the *Ministerio de Transportes, Turismo y Comunicaciones* intended to compulsorily purchase 14620 m² of the ancient city. During preparatory work, a cutting 100m long by 3m high was made (parcel 48a of polígono 9), destroying over 1000m² of archaeological remains dating to between the 8th century BC and the 4th century AD. In the end, however, the threat was averted, although the remains are exposed today and have been open to erosion and metal-detectors. During the later 1980s works in the vicinity of the Polideportivo c.1/2 km to the north of La Viña revealed a

Turdetanian burial, comprising a cremation in a decorated ceramic funeral box placed within a large storage jar. Oral tradition in the village makes it clear that lead coffins and tegula burials are known to have been discovered in this area in the past, even though there is no archaeological record. The most recent threat to the site comes from the frequent use of metal-detectors. The site has long been, and still remains, a target for treasure-hunters. Indeed, the site was frequently pitted by metal-detectors during the excavations by this team and is one of the reasons why coins and other significant metalwork were rare discoveries.

Archaeological Work at the Site

Until the late 1970s, this site had never been the object of any serious archaeological excavation. Despite its rich archaeological potential, work here had been episodic and never published. This period ushered in a phase of rescue work to gauge the archaeological potential of the site in the face of the threat of the expansion of the modern village of Peñaflor. Unfortunately, all of this remains unpublished. The only part of the site not sampled by excavations was the the field of La Viña, the largest open expanse of the ancient site. Nevertheless it was the object of a collection of surface materials by the *Delegación Provincial de Cultura* in 1987/1988.

In 1979, agricultural work at the site of "El Tesoro" farm on the SW outskirts of Peñaflor uncovered fragments of coloured *opus sectile* mosaic with geometric pattern and a fragment of a white marble statue. In this and the following year, rescue excavations were undertaken by Fernando Fernández and Javier Verdugo (Museo Arqueológico de Sevilla) in an attempt to gauge the archaeological potential of the site. These revealed that the site was both deeply stratified and that significant structural remains were still in-situ. Indeed, there is every reason to believe that the low plateau of the site was in large measure a man-made tell. In the El Calvario field on the north-western side of the ancient town, sondages were dug down to bedrock (Fernández & Verdugo 1980). Carbon 14 samples from close to bedrock at the deepest points of the site (5.10m) yielded dates of 580 BC (Teledyne Isotopes 2530 ± ?80 BP) and 330 BC (2540 ± 330 BP: 590± 330 BC) (Fernando Fernández, Personal Communication). Further rescue excavations were undertaken at the bottom of the slope on the northern edge of the El Calvario field by Larrey Hoyuelos in 1987, an area which was shown to lie outside the ancient settlement (Larrey Hoyuelos 1990). In the following year, further excavations by Fernández and Verdugo were undertaken in the Huerto de Pepe Higueras, to the east of La Viña (Fernández & Verdugo 1980), where the remains of a Roman *domus* were uncovered. In the Pared Blanca, rescue excavation was undertaken by Asumpción Blanco in 1986 (unpublished). Little is known of the results, although they were re-analyzed in a subsequent excavation by Pérez Paz (Delegación Provincial de Cultura de Sevilla) in 1989 (Pérez Paz 1989). Three trenches (X, Y and V) were opened in a north–south direction. The results were important in that they identified the scarp and the possible line of a town wall, which defined the northern edge of the town. Ceramics suggest that the wall may have been built at some time between the late 7th/early 6th centuries BC, and reinforced during the second half of the 6th and first half of the 5th centuries BC. This was separated from buildings of uncertain function to the south by a perimeter road. Excavations at El Cortijillo in the south-western corner of the site to the south of the Seville-Córdoba railway line by Asumpción Blanco in 1986 uncovered the remains of Dressel 20 kilns and a pottery dump (Blanco Ruiz 1987). These continued in use until the middle 3rd century AD, after which time the site was abandoned and used for occasional tile burials.

The Legal Status of the Site and Protection Measures

The 1979 and 1980 excavations clearly demonstrated the archaeological potential of the site and led to the purchase of 179750 m² in the properties of La Viña, El Calvario and La Pared Blanca by the Consejería de Cultura de la Junta de Andalucía. The largest of these was the field of La Viña (96500m²: polígono 8, parcel 49), which covered much of the southern side of the ancient town down to the line of the Sevilla-Córdoba railway line. The smaller fields of La Pared Blanca (55000 m²: polígono 8, parcels 45, 46, 47 and 48) and El Calvario (28250 m²: polígono 8, parcels 43 and 44) covered most of the northern sector of the site and were divided from each other by the Calle de Calvario and flanking housing. The aim of this purchase arrangement was to ensure that all of these properties were "Freed Areas" (Zonas Liberadas) and, thus, exempt from further agricultural work. Areas that lay outside the original built-up area of the ancient town lay in land with a different use-classification; the Cortinar de las Cruces mausoleum in the town falls within an "Urban" zone, while cemetery areas to the west and north of the town are in a "Rural" area.

In recognition of its long-standing perceived importance, the site was declared to be of Public Utility (Utilidad Publica) in 1973 and the "incoado expediente" for the town as a *Bien de Interés Cultural* was issued on the 18th February 1987 by the *Dirección General de Bienes Culturales de la Consejería de Cultura* (B.O.E. 103, 30 Abril 1987). This aimed to ensure that the site was subject to the provisional protection normally ensured for sites which had been confirmed as scheduled (a *Bien de Interés Cultural*: *Ley del Patrimonio Histórico Español* 13/85, artículo 11). This declaration covered the archaeological zone delimited by the N-431 to the north, the arroyo Morenas to the east, the Guadalquivir to the south and specific properties to the east. In particular it comprised land parcels 35–36–37–38–39–40–41–42–43–44–45–46a–47–48–49–50–56–57–58 of polígono 8, and 43–44 and 48a of polígono 9 on the *Mapa Topográfico Parcelario* of the *Instituto Geográfico Catastral* (Término Municipal de Peñaflor). It also included all the urbanized properties to the west of the arroyo Morenas between the N-431 and its junction with the Gaudalquivir: specifically the Morera, San Pedro, and Calvario streets as well as part of the Arroyo street and the Avenida de Andalucía. The site was finally scheduled as a *Bien de Interés Cultural* on the 18th January 1994.

Chapter 2
The Surface Survey

Simon Keay and John Creighton

Abstract

This chapter presents the results of a detailed analysis of the topography of ancient Celti. It starts from the premise that any excavation at a major complex site such as this needs to be set in its full site context. The analysis begins with a detailed topographic study, as a result of which, a preliminary interpretative model is proposed. It then proceeds to analyze the results of a geophysical survey, which attempted to elucidate the planning and organization of two key sectors, La Viña and the Pared Blanca fields. It concludes with a detailed systematic surface survey, which attempted to the map the distribution of surface pottery and construction material by date and function. This is complemented by the in-depth analysis of two more focused surveys (Platforms 1, 2 and 3), upon the basis of which an interpretation of the western part of the site is suggested.

The Aims and Overall Strategy (SK)

One of the underlying aims of this project was to use the results of limited archaeological intervention at Peñaflor to write an archaeological history of the site to answer a series of key cultural questions (Introduction). Moreover, given the paucity of archaeological work at many Roman towns in the region, Peñaflor had the potential of acting as an urban "type-site" for the lower Guadalquivir valley. However, like many other ancient urban sites in southern Spain, this was no straightforward task. The estimated urban area was large and previous archaeological work at the site had been episodic and had achieved little more than revealing a long occupational sequence. Moreover, there was an administrative constraint. Contingent upon the Consejería de Cultura of the Junta de Andalucía's *"Plan General de Arqueología (1986)"*, a new planning framework for research projects (*actividades sistemáticas*) was introduced in 1987. Each new project was permitted a maximum period of six years activity, within which excavation/survey and finds work alternated from one year to the next.

It was thus clear that considerable thought was needed about how best to extract the maximum amount of information from this large and complex site within the constraints of available time and budgetary resources. In many ways, Peñaflor epitomises large multi-period sites in Andalucía. Traditional archaeological approaches to these had usually involved the excavation of deep and narrow sondages, which provide the chronological sequence for a very small part of the site but tell us little about the its overall development. It rapidly became clear that the only way in which meaningful results could be extracted from the site would be through undertaking open-area excavations (Chapter 3). Notwithstanding this, however, these could only ever shed light upon a limited area of the site. Consequently, complementary strategies were required to contextualise the open-area excavation within the rest of the site. The first of these was to produce a topographic plan of the site and to plot the location of key surviving archaeological remains. However, standing structures were very rare, scattered across the site and on their own could tell us but little about the layout or development of the ancient settlement. Thus, it was decided to precede the open-area excavations by a systematic surface survey of all accessible parts of the sites. Previous work in Italy (Walker 1984–5) and in Greece (Bintliff and Snodgrass 1988a) had shown that the the collection of surface-materials from large urban sites allowed the the extent, chronology and internal organisation of sites to be gauged with some degree of success. The approach adopted at Peñaflor (Keay *et alii* 1991) represented a development of this technique. The intention was to learn sufficient from surface and subsurface remains to:

i) make an informed choice about where to excavate within the site

ii) target the excavation to answer specfic questions about the site

iii) be able to relate these to the rest of the town

Consequently, the strategy employed was to undertake an integrated programme of systematic surface collection and geophysical survey.

The Topographical Survey
(SK and JC) (Fig. 2.1a)

The intention of the topographic survey was to build up a picture of the basic shape and structure of the site of ancient Celti. The plan eventually produced (Fig. 2.1a) was achieved by means of a detailed contour survey of the La Viña, El Calvario and Pared Blanca fields carried out by a team of three people with an Electronic Distance Meter (EDM). It covers the main area of the site, but excludes a substantial area to the east, which was either built-up, of difficult access or was under private ownership. The limits of the ancient settlement to the north-west and west were not readily apparent and the team took surface materials, such as pottery and construction material, as a guide. All surface undulations and upstanding remains, and the position of mosaic floors, the position of early excavations and the limits of the ancient site

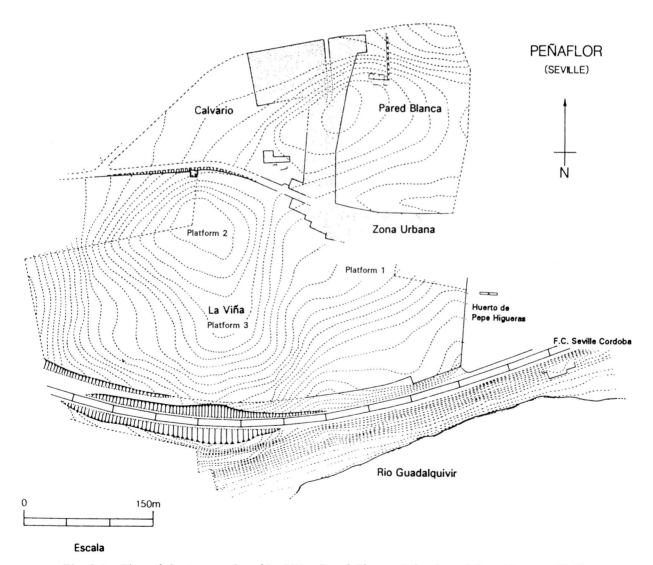

PEÑAFLOR
(SEVILLE)

N

0   150m

Escala

Fig. 2.1a. Plan of the topography of La Viña, Pared Blanca, Calvario and Pepe Higueras Fields

within the three fields were carefully recorded. Readings were taken at variable spacing, depending upon the micro-topography, with the aim of being able to reconstruct contours at 10cm intervals across the majority of the site. These revealed a coherent set of topographical units formed by terraces and cuttings. Furthermore, the depth of stratigraphy was assessed by examining the modern railway cutting and earlier excavation records, and plotting the location of outcrops of natural rock. Zones of geomorphological change could be analyzed against this survey. For example, the height of the Roman amphora kilns on the banks of the Guadalquivir (Chapter 1) were an important index of the ancient course of the river.

Preliminary model (Fig. 2.1a and 1b)

These data were used to propose a model for the broad outlines of the topography of the ancient settlement (Fig. 2.1a). Our survey work confirmed the traditional view that it was demarcated by the river Guadalquivir to the south and the arroyo Majuelo to the west.

The limit to the north and east was harder to elucidate since El Calvario and Pared Blanca fields had not been ploughed for many years at the time of the survey and surface materials were thus invisible. Nevertheless, the excavation by Pérez Paz (Fig. 2.1b.A) made it clear that, to the north, it probably ran along the 70m contour in the Pared Blanca parallel to the N-431 Almodóvar to Lora del Río road. To the north-east, the limit of the site is surely to be identified with the sharp scarp which is visible from the Plaza de Pablo Iglesia (Fig. 2.1b.B) and continues southwards as the eastern edge along the Calle Arroyo down to the Guadalquivir (Fig. 2.1b.C). The limit of the settlement to the west is imperfectly known. However, it is likely that it coincides with the steep break of slope which runs in a gentle arc from the junction of the N-431 and the old Camino de Sevilla down towards the Guadalquivir, close to the amphora kilns at El Cortijillo. Inspection of surface materials, which are dense on the slope itself (see, for example Fig. 2.14) showed that they rapidly disappeared at the bottom. The southern edge of the site, which lies between the El Cortijillo kilns and El Higuerón is

Fig. 2.1b. Aerial Photograph of La Viña, Pared Blanca, Calvario and Pepe Higueras Fields (Junta de Andalucia. Instituto de Cartografía. Hoja 942 pasada 5. October 1991)

clearly marked by a very steep break of slope. The total area circumscribed within these limits was approximately 26.34 Hectares. The only feature of note outside the built up area of the site was a concentration of circular structures revealed by aerial photography. These lie a short distance to the north-west of the site and immediately to the south of the Almodóvar to Lora road (the N-431: Fig. 2.1b.L): their date is uncertain.

Within this area, the site took the form of a natural 'theatre' opening south-eastwards towards the Guadalquivir. The most prominent feature of the site is high ground above 70m (above sea-level) which curves around from the south-west of the site a short distance to the north of the Guadalquivir, to the north-eastern corner. It is interrupted by a saddle or gentle depression through which runs the modern Calle de San Pedro (Fig. 2.1b.D). To the south-west (La Viña field), at the highest point of the site, this reaches 75.14m (Fig. 2.1b.E), while to the north-east (La Pared Blanca) it reaches 73.35m (Fig. 2.1b.F); to the north-east immediately above the Calle Arroyo it descends to c.60m (Fig. 2.1b.G). Within this enclosed area the land drops away towards the river, gradually at first (66m adjacent to the Ermita de la Encarnación: Fig. 2.1b.H) down to 40m by the banks of the Guadalquivir. In crude terms, therefore, the site inclines gently down towards the river.

It is possible that part, or all, of the site may have been walled in the protohistoric period. The clearest evidence is provided by the Higuerón (Fig. 2.1b.I: Fig. 1.6), which lies down by the river at the south-eastern corner of the settlement. Although opinions about the function of this enigmatic structure have varied considerably (Chapter 1), it can be argued that it may have acted as a defensive bastion. It makes little defensive sense today, given its closeness to the river. However, it is not impossible that the ancient course of the river lay some distance further to the south of where it is today, which would have meant that there would have been some rationale for a defensive circuit running along this part of the site. Another piece of evidence for ancient defences is provided by the possible stretch of walling revealed by Pérez Paz (Fig. 2.1b.A). If the north and south sides of the site were defended, then it would seem likely the circuit continued along the western side. By contrast, the sheer scarp may have rendered artificial defences to the east unnecessary.

Within the site, the micro topography and the alignment of the few remaining walls suggested that the predominant road network was oriented around a north-west to south-east axis. These were visible in the angle formed by the Calle San Pedro and the Calle Calvario at the lowest point of the 'saddle' (Fig. 2.1b.D) and immediately in front of farm buildings on the north side of La Viña field (Fig. 2.1b.J). This alignment was shared by the *opus signinum* basins in the La Viña field (Chapter 1) and the *domus* excavated in the property of Pepe Higueras in the south-eastern corner of the site (Fig. 2.1b.K). There were also clear indications of a discrete series of terraces, some of which were substantial enough to have belonged to public buildings, whilst the nature of surface finds suggested that others indicated residential housing.

On the basis of the above results and earlier knowledge, a tentative interpretation of surface topography of the ancient town could be put forward. It probably consisted of:

a. Cemetery Areas to the north, west and east
b. A core area of 26.34 Hectares within which there was:
   – an elevated area in the western part of La Viña which may have housed public buildings overlooking the Guadalquivir: this was later identified as Platforms 2 and 3.
   – a possible forum area immediately to the east of the 'saddle' in the central part of the site (La Viña) (Fig. 2.1b.D): this was later identified as Platform 1.
   – a river port along the Guadalquivir, lying between the Higuerón (Fig. 2.1b.I and 1.4.1) and the kilns at El Cortjillo (Fig. 1.4.2).

Available evidence suggests that within this area the road-system was oriented north-west/south-east. It would be tempting to suggest that the modern Calle de San Pedro lies along the line of the main east–west road of the ancient settlement and that the Calle Calvario lies along the line of a key north–south road. However, these roads runs at an angle to the known orientation of ancient buildings and the buildings flanking the roads were built in the earlier part of this century. Moreover, it is possible that the alignment of the Calle San Pedro may have been predicated by the position of the Ermita de la Encarnación, which was built in the 18th century (Chapter 1).

The Geophysical Survey of La Viña and La Pared Blanca (DJ)

Aims

The first step in testing this model was to conduct a geophysical survey in two key areas of the site. A cursory consideration of surface pottery suggested that there may have been a palimpsest of occupation levels at the site: consequently, the intention was to map only those structures buried up to a depth of two metres. Any attempt to record those lying at a greater depth would have led to a more cluttered and less comprehensible picture. The intention was then to 'calibrate' these results by undertaking systematic surface survey at the site and, eventually, excavation. It should be stated at this point that the dry surface conditions at the site meant that there was no guarantee that geophysics would be successful at Peñaflor.

Method

The site lies on several interlocking spurs overlooking the river Guadalquivir. The bedrock is basalt which is overlain, in places, by recent river deposits ranging from coarse gravels to silts and clays. Archaeological remains are found in soils developed both on the basalt and on the alluvium. The soils therefore have three "parent" materials: basalt, alluvium and archaeological remains – all of which have a significant influence on the local geophysical properties. This is most significant given that the individual geophysical properties of each are very different. The site has strong relief, including steep slopes falling south to the river and to the east, and gentler slopes descending north and west. Thus, it is to be expected that erosion and colluviation may have been very active in removing archaeology-rich material from the higher parts of the site and re-depositing it over other archaeological remains downhill. The depth of soil above the remains and the degree of damage caused by erosion can therefore be expected to vary inversely across the site.

The survey concentrated in the field of La Viña and the work here was carried out (1988 and 1989) under conditions which were less than ideal (Fig. 2.2a and 2.2b). In 1988, the soil was compacted and very dry, greatly reducing the resistivity contrast between archaeological remains and their surroundings. In the following season, much of the site had been planted with cotton and was fre-

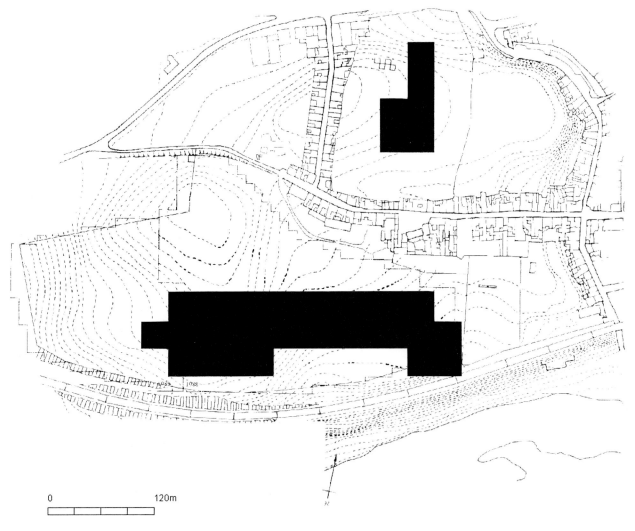

0   120m

Fig. 2.2a. Location of the Resistivity Survey area within La Viña and La Pared Bianca

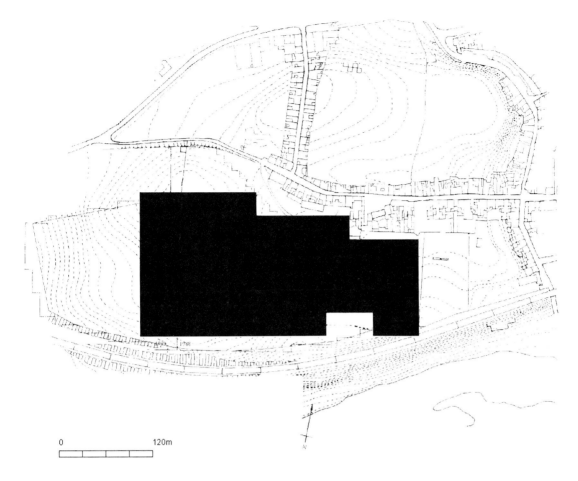

Fig. 2.2b. Location of the Magnetometry Survey area within La Viña

quently irrigated. These small, tough and bushy plants are grown in ridges of soil and need to be irrigated periodically. The plants and ridges often impeded the progress of the survey across the site while the irrigation caused complex surface resistance anomalies, which made deeper archaeological features difficult to detect. Other problems were caused by high temperatures (often up to 42 degrees C) and the great diurnal temperature range caused the fluxgate gradiometric magnetometers to produce readings which "drifted" rapidly. These could only be corrected by careful handling and frequent correction by an experienced geophysicist. Subsequent mathematical treatment of the data was able to improve the results. A smaller portion of the survey was undertaken in the Pared Blanca field during April (1989). Here the conditions were better and the soil was covered in thin grass, ensuring that the results were much improved.

Survey Methods

Two quite different survey methods were chosen because, while both are efficient ways of detecting buried archaeological remains, they provide complementary information. Test surveys at the site showed that both methods could give useful geophysical images of the remains, despite the difficult conditions discussed above. Preliminary magnetic survey scans showed that the magnetometer was able to detect very small magnetic anomalies produced by the buried buildings at Peñaflor. However, it also indicated that these signals were heavily masked by the magnetic noise produced by ceramic and other debris in the soil.

Prior to the beginning of each survey, the field was divided up into a 30m grid by a number of fixed pegs hammered into the ground; this also served for the subsequent systematic surface survey. The geophysical survey then proceeded on the basis of systematically recording many readings within this 30 metre grid: a total of 291600 were taken throughout the survey. This large number was dictated by taking a small sampling interval with the aid of computer-based systems.

RESISTIVITY

A small and light resistivity meter (the Geoscan

RM4) was favoured for this survey because it took accurate readings rapidly and it can be easily transported in the field. The twin-electrode array, with an electrode separation of 0.5 metres, was adopted: this was easy to use and sensitive to buried remains to a depth of about 1.5 metres. Deeper structures were ignored in subsequent analysis owing to the possibility of confusing archaeological and geological effects. Readings were taken by the resistivity meter when two electrodes were inserted into the soil at each survey point of a 1 × 1 metre grid within the broader site 30m × 30m grid. The resistivity meter itself was connected to a datalogger in the field from which the results are periodically passed to a larger field-computer for storage and processing during the survey. This enabled the results of the survey to be reviewed on a daily basis and, thus, allowed techniques to be improved and any problems solved. Subsequent computer analysis in the UK transformed the raw survey results from each 30m square into an image of the buried structures once the survey was completed. It then combined them all into a single large image and removed any intereference caused by agricultural work and other modern activity.

MAGNETOMETRY

The magnetic survey was carried out using a fluxgate gradiometer, the Geoscan FM18, which took about 6 readings per second (adjustable by the operator). The FM18 has a precision of 0.1 nano Tesla (nT) and at Peñaflor was able detect archaeological magnetic anomalies as small as 1 nT. This is better than is possible with proton magnetometers not only because the FM18 is more precise but because it takes many more readings. A high reading density makes it possible to detect the patterns of weak archaeological anomalies against the normal "noise" produced by the soil.

In the field, the FM18 sampled by taking readings at every 0.25 metres north–south and 1m east–west within the 30 metre grid squares. The measurements shown on the accompanying images thus show deflections in the local magnetic field rather than the absolute value of the field itself. This has the advantage that the magnetometer is insensitive to very large magnetic background variations and to fluctuations in the earth's magnetic field with time. It is important to bear in mind, however, that the images produced by the magnetometer represent the way in which buried objects – including archaeology – cause the earth's magnetic field to bend, rather than the absolute value of the field itself.

As with the resistivity survey, the results of the magnetometer survey were passed to a field-computer so that it was possible to gain an immediate impression of the buried remains. The data were then processed in a larger computer by combining the results from individual survey blocks, removing instrument drift and carrying out the necessary filtering. However, both the resistivity and the magnetometry data were processed as little as possible since excessive treatment can produce convincing "archaeological anomalies" which do not actually exist. It is better practice to produce good results in the field rather than to try to correct deficiencies later.

Results

Both the resistivity and magnetometer data are complex and contain a great deal of information, some of which is difficult to interpret. The images printed here (Figs 2.3–9) can only reproduce part of this detail and most of the interpretation was carried out from the computer screen which is

N

0   30m

Fig. 2.3. Raw Resistivity: La Viña

capable of much higher resolution. The interpretation of the magnetic data is less clear than the resistivity – as is almost always the case – and some of the anomalies are hard to define precisely. In these cases the intention has been to reproduce faithfully the broad structure of the anomalies.

The soils and rocks at the site have a variable natural background magnetic susceptibility. Ceramic debris and human activity – principally burning – have increased this and the resulting local magnetic field immediately above the ground is very disturbed. This is common to many archaeological sites but we may conclude that, given the extent of the disturbance, archaeological remains are distributed throughout the area surveyed. We note, however, that the slope immediately to the east of the highest point in La Viña (see Fig. 1.4E) had much less magnetic "noise" than elsewhere and we conclude that the archaeological remains here are more deeply buried. The high concentration of archaeological remains encountered in many parts of the site, however, made it difficult to

distinguish individual structures, especially since the excavations revealed that some buildings were constructed of limestone, which has a low magnetic susceptibility.

La Viña (Figs 2.2a and 2b)
The geophysical survey sampled a large part of La Viña. This was done while the field was under cotton, which considerably complicated access. Nevertheless, the resistivity image succeeded in defining much of the structure of the buried site (Fig. 2.3–5) in the western part of the field. This is an exposed position, which has been quite heavily eroded. Three positive, linear anomalies define an area in which smaller anomalies abound; the latter were identified as walls and drains. All of the larger, and some of the smaller, resistivity anomalies have an associated positive magnetic anomaly which suggests that they were probably ceramic structures. The most obvious interpretation for the large anomalies are roads, which produce a resistance anomaly, with underlying tile drains, producing

0   30m

Fig. 2.4. Filtered Resistivity: La Viña

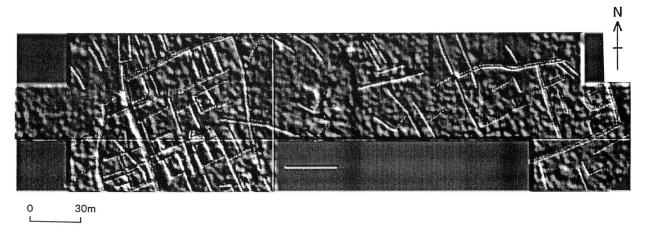

0   30m

Fig. 2.5. Resistivity Interpretation: La Viña

the magnetic anomaly. The bulk of the magnetic anomalies are narrow, linear structures which closely follow the pattern of the smaller resistivity anomalies (Fig. 2.6–7) These are most likely to be walls which have magnetic ceramic built into them. The smaller, linear anomalies form a dense grid which represents a complex of buried buildings. Within this grid are areas of high, disturbed magnetic anomalies which are probably due to a high concentration of ceramic debris.

In the eastern part of La Viña greater soil depth has meant that results were less clear. However it has also probably ensured that archaeological remains are better preserved than those to the west. The strong, local positive anomalies which are present are probably caused by ceramic debris, most

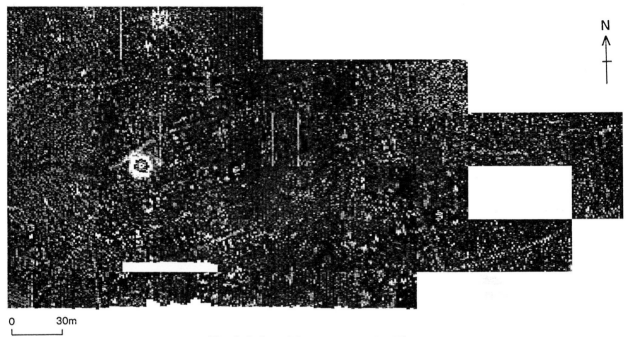

0   30m

Fig. 2.6. Raw Magnetometry: La Viña

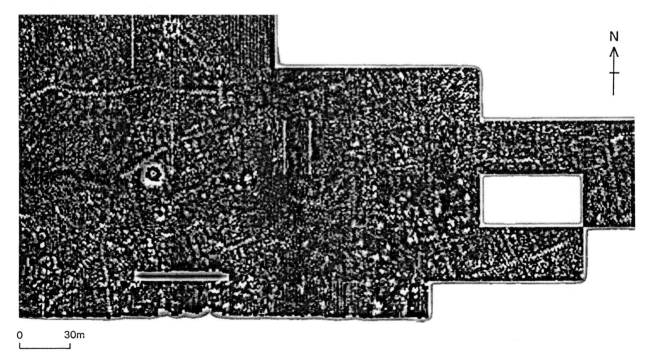

0   30m

Fig. 2.7. Filtered Magnetometry: La Viña

of which will have an archaeological origin. There are also large numbers of very strong but very local (less than 1 metre across) positive and negative anomalies, most of which are to be explained by modern metal debris near to the surface. At the eastern edge of the field, however, the survey did record a number of large, positive, linear anomalies which probably represent large walls but may prove to be metalled roads. The most easterly of these, which turns northwards at the eastern limit of the survey, is a very substantial structure with a strong, positive magnetic anomaly. North of this are a number of similar, strong anomalies – both magnetic and resistive – also representing substantial structures.

All the above magnetic anomalies are seen through a background "noise" caused by small fragments of magnetic material in the soil and by the slight instability of the magnetometer itself. All soils are slightly magnetised by the earth's magnetic field and also contain very small amounts of magnetic material. The very variable effect created by this is detected by the magnetometer as a background "noise" underlying all other anomalies. Soils which incorporate the remains of human activity, tend to be slightly more magnetic than normal and the enhanced background "noise" can be recognised by surveyors with experience. The whole of the area surveyed contains some of this kind of variation. The magnetic anomalies corresponded well to those produced by the resistivity meter and together facilitate our interpretation of the site. Thus, walls visible on the resistivity plot but not on the magnetometry image are most likely to be built of stone and to contain no ceramic element.

LA PARED BLANCA

The resistivity survey of this area identified a very high density of buried remains (Figs.2.8–9). These are mostly stone or ceramic walls represented by positive, linear, resistivity anomalies. Between the walls are areas of much lower resistivity, suggesting rooms and open areas. To the north is a strong positive anomaly about 5 metres wide running east–west which clearly corresponds to the large wall found during the 1989 excavation by Pérez Paz. It has a broader negative anomaly further north still, corresponding to the deeper soil found on the down-hill side of the wall. The resistive anomalies of the Pared Blanca seem to have a number of orientations which suggests, perhaps, a number of construction phases. The density and clarity of anomalies in this area is greater than in La Viña, making their archaeological interpretation more difficult. A magnetometry survey of this field was not attempted.

OVERALL INTERPRETATION (Fig. 2.10) (SK, JC, DJ)
The image presented by both geophysical surveys

suggests that the topography of ancient Peñaflor was structured by a well-defined street network. This appears to be more regular in the western part of the site where a large stone building with complex internal divisions occupies what appears to be an *insula* block. Different road alignments are visible down the hill to the west, the east and north. Here there appear to be other square buildings and enclosures. A major axial road may run from the 'saddle' between the high points in La Viña and La Pared Blanca down to the port area by the river.

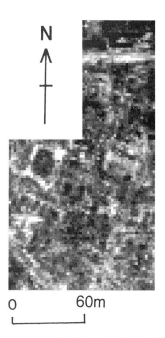

Fig. 2.8. Raw Resistivity: Pared Blanca

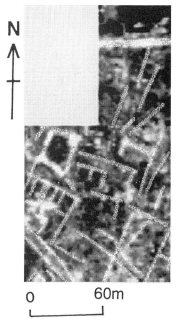

Fig. 2.9. Resistivity Interpretation: Pared Blanca

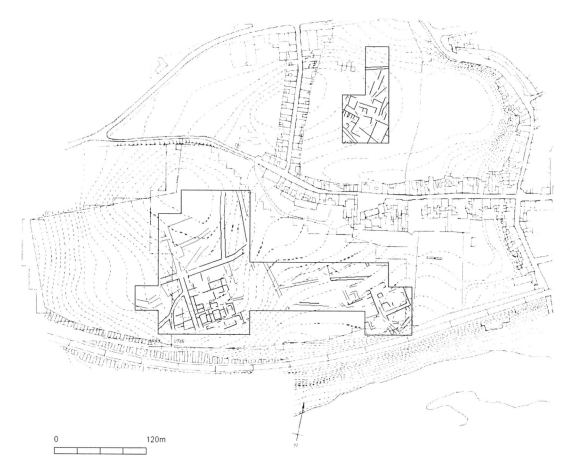

0   120m

Fig. 2.10. Interpretation of Restivity and Magnetometry on Topography

The Systematic Surface-Survey (JC)

The systematic surface survey was undertaken in order to map broad changes in the functional and chronological nature of the ceramics and other material culture distributed across the site. It was planned from the beginning as being complementary to both the topographic survey of the site and the geophysical surveys. The survey focused upon the fields of La Viña and El Calvario; La Pared Blanca had not been worked in many years and little surface material was visible, while the Huerto de Pepe Higueras was not accessible at the time of survey. The data which supports the analyses presented in this chapter are accessible in W/Appendix 4.

The overall 30×30m survey in La Viña and La Pared Blanca (W/Appendix 4.1)

SAMPLING STRATEGY (Fig. 2.11–12a and 12b)
The density of surface material in La Viña and El Calvario was so great that normal fieldwalking would not have been appropriate. There was simply too much material for a representative sample to be collected by conventional line-walking and the quantities of material would have been far beyond the resources of the project to process. Instead, team members were allocated a 3m square randomly located within each of the 30m squares of the site grid and were given 20 minutes to collect as much pottery and other material as possible (Fig. 2.12a). In this way, a 1% sample of surface materials was recovered. The use of the same 30m grid meant that the surface survey collection could be directly related to the geophysical results. La Viña was walked in 1988 and Calvario in 1991; the dry and extremely compacted nature of the fallow ground in La Pared Blanca meant that this was unsuitable for fieldwalking. A different approach was developed for ceramic column segments, which were quite common on the site. A 1% sample of these would not have revealed their patterning over the site, so a more comprehensive approach was required for these. Thus, a special line-walking survey of La Viña and El Calvario was carried out for these in 1988 and 1989, with team members recording the number of fragments in every 10m².

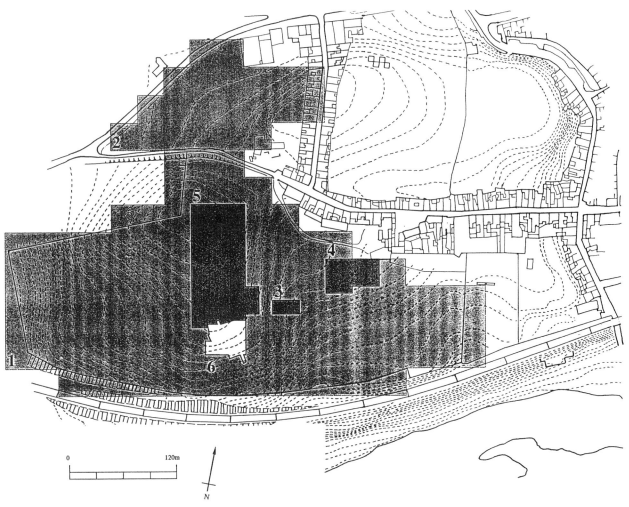

Fig. 2.11. La Viña and El Calvario. Location of General and Detailed Surface Surveys. The different surveys are as follows: 1) 1988 Survey of La Viña; 2) 1991 Survey of El Calvario; 3) 1988 Survey of La Viña: Calibration Area; 4) 1991 Survey of Platform 1; 5) 1991 Survey of Platforms 2 and 3; 6) Area of Excavation

CALIBRATION EXERCISE

Four team members were used in an attempt to minimise variability between individuals. However it was still considered likely that there would be some collection biases between different team members. Thus a calibration exercise was undertaken to measure it. A coherent block of 50 squares (30 × 15m) was analysed (Fig. 2.11: Area 3; Fig. 2.12a) to look for any variability in the collecting habits of individuals in adjacent squares. The results of this calibration exercise are shown in W/ Appendix 4.1.2, 4 and 6. There were no marked differences between the collection of different individuals or if there are, they are minimal in comparison to the overall site variability.

DISTRIBUTION OF MATERIAL BY DATE (Figs 2.13–17)

The surface material collected was divided up into three rough chronological periods: Iberian (Turdetanian)/Roman Republican; Early Empire; and Late

Empire. In 1988, when La Viña was walked, the dating of much of the pottery was poorly understood. Subsequently, the stratified groups from the excavation enhanced our understanding of the material considerably. However, it led in this first surface collection exercise to a significant proportion of the pottery being classified as 'unidentified' as far as its date was concerned. This problem was rectified by the time of the El Calvario collection in 1991, by which time it was recognized that many of the coarsewares could be ascribed to the Early Empire. Strictly speaking, therefore, the two data sets are not comparable.

In an ideal situation, one might expect Late Roman surface materials to dominate the surface remains, with progressively less of Early Imperial and Iberian (Turdetanian)/Roman Republican date. However, it must be remembered that this is a multi-period site, which has been subject to considerable post-depositional activity. Thus, the

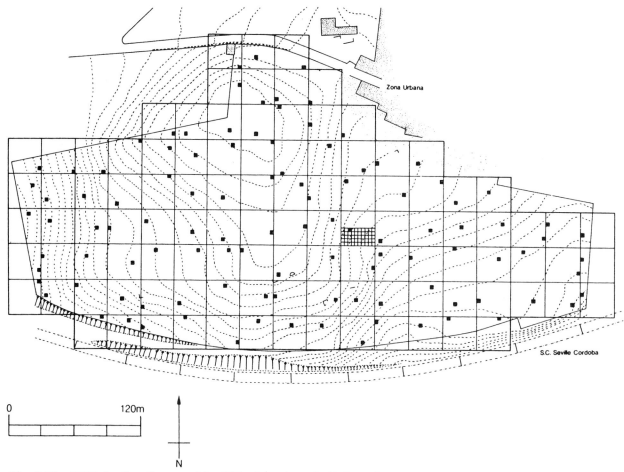

Fig. 2.12a. 1988 Surface Survey of La Viña: Location of 1% Sampling Units and Calibration Area (gridded)

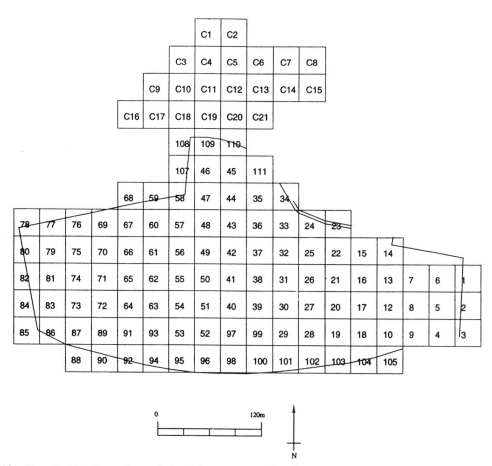

Fig. 2.12b. Key to the Location of the 30m squares in the 1988 Survey of La Viña and El Calvario

interpretation of surface distributions is fraught with difficulties. Complementary erosion and colluvation can at once reveal and mask early strata. Thus, the 'presence' and 'absence' of early material may in fact be due to the disturbance of early layers or the sealing of earlier layers by later occupation.

The distribution of Iberian/Roman Republican material (Fig. 2.13–14) concentrated upon the southern and north-western slopes of La Viña, with a more generalized scatter found in El Calvario to the north. Although it was rare in the eastern part of La Viña, excavations on the land of Pepe Higueras to the east showed that there was a considerable build up of deposit here, masking earlier layers. The concentration of material on the slopes could be interpreted as the product of colluviation and the removal of later layers to reveal earlier deposits. However it is perhaps better explained as being brought to the surface when later terraces for buildings and house platforms were excavated.

By far the most common material was pottery of Early Imperial date (Figs 2.15). This was distributed over most of the site, although it thinned out at the western fringes. The distribution maps reveal two areas of above average density. The first was in the southern part of La Viña, in the region where the geophysics suggested that an axial road led southwards across the site down to the area of the river port. The second was in El Calvario. This was walked in 1991, by which time the pottery was known sufficiently well for the abundant coarse-wares to be ascribed to the Early Imperial period. By contrast with both preceding periods, material of Late Imperial date (Figs.2.16 and 2.17) was sparse; no square yielded more than 5 fragments of pottery. While this material was attested in most parts of the site, its distribution was patchy with some slight concentrations on the eastern side of platforms 2 and 3 and on the northern side of platform 4.

DISTRIBUTION OF MATERIAL BY FUNCTION
a. Pottery
Whilst only a proportion of the pottery could be ascribed to a specific chronological period, all of it could be divided into simple functional groupings of fineware, coarse ware and amphorae. The finewares were the most common (Figs 2.18 and 19). Because the great majority of these were of Turdetanian/Roman Republican date, their pattern

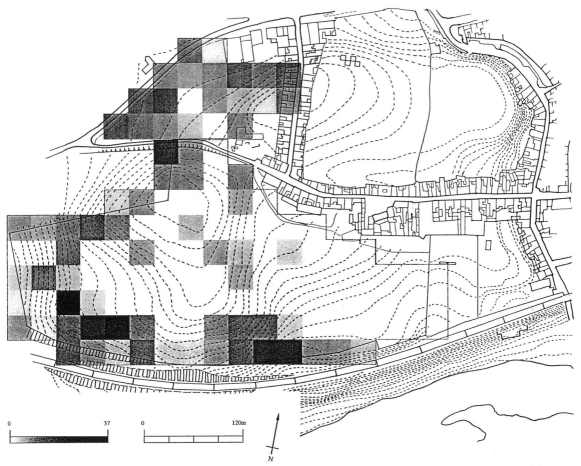

0   37   0   120m   N

Fig. 2.13. 1988 Surface Survey of La Viña and El Calvario. Density of Iberian and Roman Republican pottery expressed in counts: maximum density of 37 sherds per 3 metre square

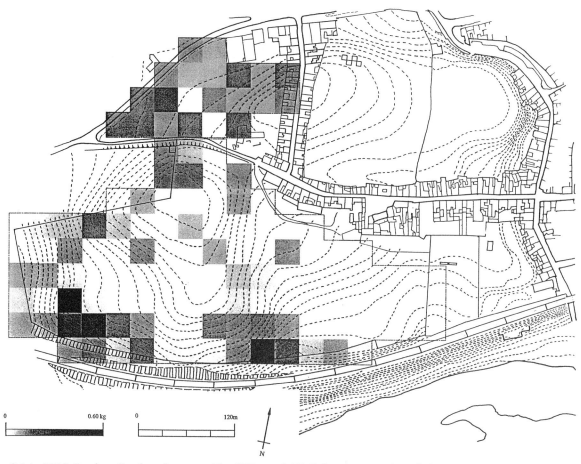

Fig. 2.14. 1988 Surface Surface Survey of La Viña and El Calvario. Density of Iberian and Roman Republican pottery expressed in weights: maximum density of 0.60kg per 3 metre square

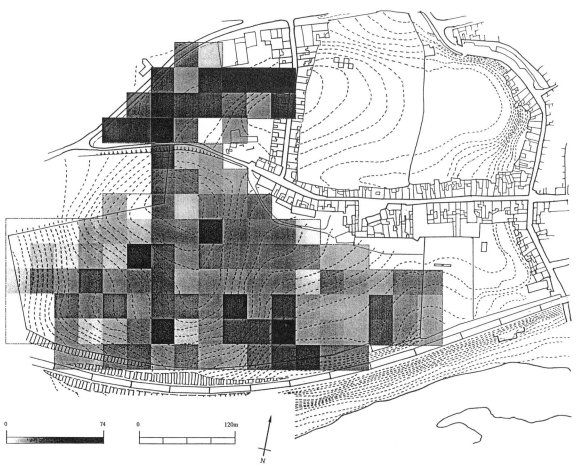

Fig. 2.15. 1988 Surface Surface Survey of La Viña and El Calvario. Density of Early Imperial Pottery expressed in counts: maximum density of 74 sherds per 3 metre square

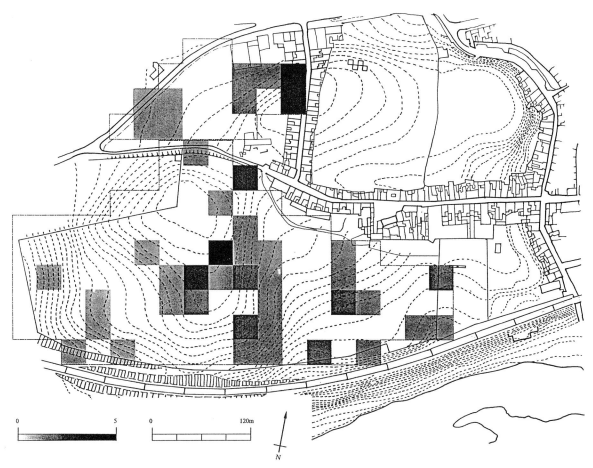

Fig. 2.16. 1988 Surface Survey of La Viña and El Calvario. Density of Late Imperial Pottery expressed in counts: maximum density of 5 sherds per 3 metre square

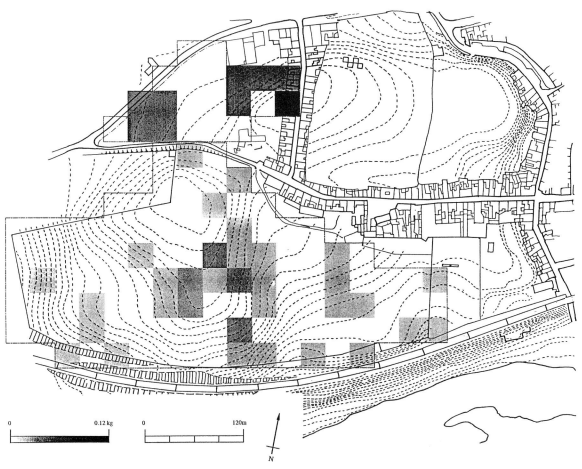

Fig. 2.17. 1988 Surface Survey of La Viña and El Calvario. Density of Late Imperial Pottery expressed in weights: maximum density of 0.12kg per 3 metre square

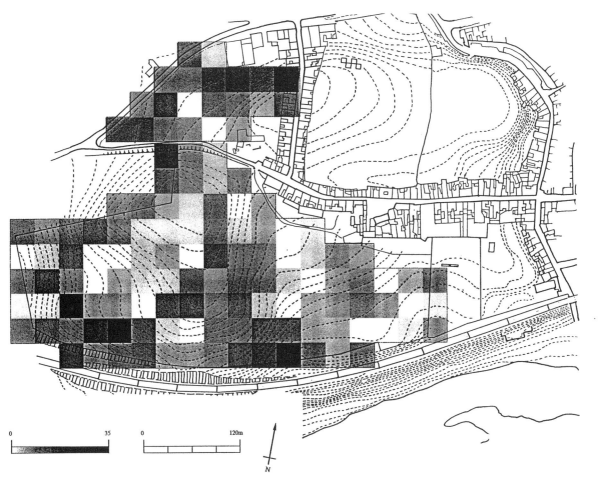

Fig. 2.18. 1988 Surface Survey of La Viña and El Calvario. Density of Finewares expressed in counts: maximum density of 35 sherds per 3 metre square

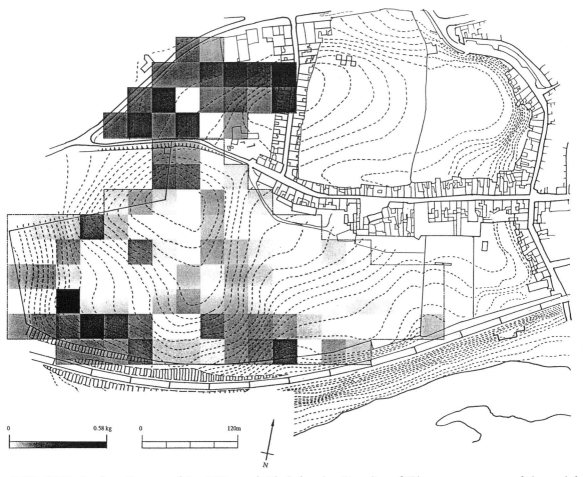

Fig. 2.19. 1988 Surface Survey of La Viña and El Calvario. Density of Finewares expressed in weights: maximum density of 0.58kg per 3 metre square

of distribution resembled that of Turdetanian/ Roman Republican pottery, appearing on hill slopes where early deposits may have been disturbed during terracing of the site. The coarseware distribution (Figs 2.20 and 2.21) resembled that of Early Imperial pottery, with a dense presence across most of the site and a particular concentration along the line of the suspected axial road running southwards down to the river port; they tailed off towards the western edge of La Viña. The amphorae exhibited a similar pattern (Figs 2.22 and 2.23), with a broad overall distribution and a definite concentration along the line of the road leading down to the river. The majority of identifiable amphora fragments were Dressel 20s (see W/Chapter 2: Type 20) and, thus, of Early Imperial date.

The interpretation of the surface distributions of pottery by function is difficult. Individually, these three functional types demonstrate little more than the coincidence of dense amphora and coarse ware concentrations on the lower slopes of La Viña as it approaches the river. However, a significant pattern does emerge when the data are combined. In Fig. 2.24 the different proportions by weight of each category of pottery across the site were plotted: this was later refined by calculating densities in terms of octiles. Both methods highlighted a high proportion of finewares on the NW facing slopes of

the site and a concentration of amphorae and coarsewares in the low-lying areas near the river.

b. Construction material

Much of the material encountered during the surface was construction material of one variety or another. The quantification of brick and tile did not produce any discernable patterning in surface distributions at this level of resolution. However, analysis of the marble (Fig. 2.25) from La Viña was more successful and highlighted a concentration in the eastern part of the site along the line of the supposed axial road which ran down to the river. Even more successful was an attempt to plot the distribution of ceramic column segments (Fig. 2.26). There were distinctive concentrations on the eastern side of the site, particularly on the top of platform 2 and for a stretch of 100m along the southern side of platform 1; they were completely absent from the western area. It is possible that the latter alignment may have represented a colonnade along the south side of platform 1.

CONCLUSIONS (JC, SK)

Relatively little could be deduced from the analysis of the distribution of surface materials by their broad chronology. This is a complex multi-period site and the survey only collected 1% of visible

Fig. 2.20. 1988 Surface Survey of La Viña and El Calvario. Density of Coarsewares expressed in counts: maximum density of 84 sherds per 3 metre square

Fig. 2.21. 1988 Surface Survey of La Viña and El Calvario. Density of Coarsewares expressed in weights: maximum density of 1.11kg per 3 metre square

Fig. 2.22. 1988 Surface Survey of La Viña and El Calvario. Density of Amphorae expressed in counts: maximum density of 65 sherds per 3 metre square

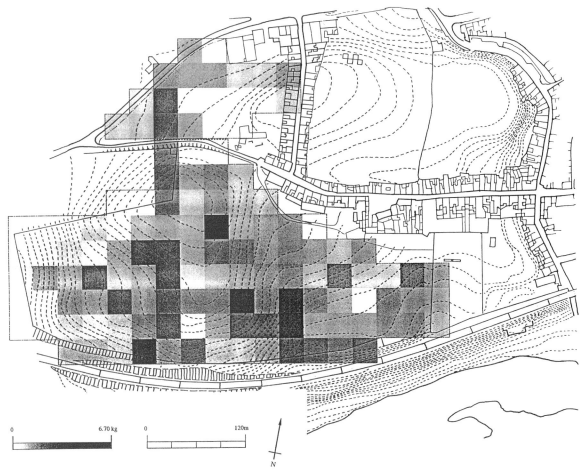

Fig. 2.23. 1988 Surface Survey of La Viña and El Calvario. Density of Amphorae expressed in weights: maximum density of 6.70kg per 3 metre square

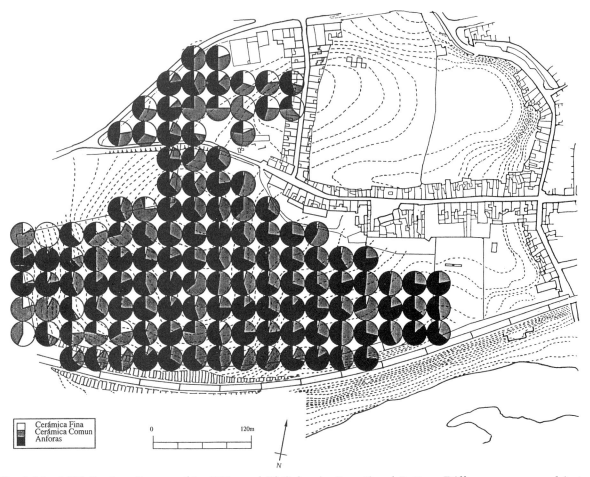

Fig. 2.24. 1988 Surface Survey of La Viña and El Calvario: Functional Pottery Differences expressed in terms of the total weight of pottery per 3 metre square

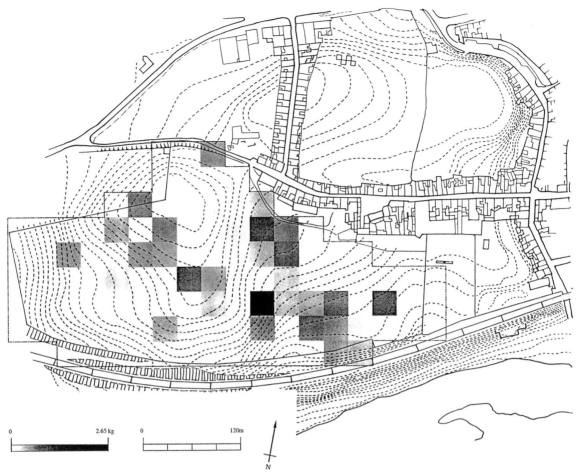

Fig. 2.25. 1988 Surface Survey of La Viña and El Calvario. Density of Marble expressed in weights: maximum density of 2.65kg per 3 metre square

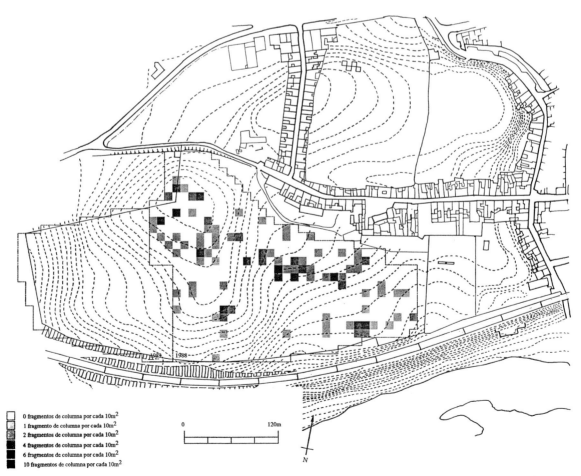

0 fragmentos de columna por cada 10m²
1 fragmento de columna por cada 10m²
2 fragmentos de columna por cada 10m²
4 fragmentos de columna por cada 10m²
6 fragmentos de columna por cada 10m²
10 fragmentos de columna por cada 10m²

Fig. 2.26. 1988 Surface Survey of La Viña and El Calvario. Density of Column Segment expressed in counts: densities expressed in terms of 0, 1, 2, 4, 6 and 10 pieces per 3 metre square

surface material. There is little to be said of material dating to the Iberian (Turdetanian)/Roman Republican period, except that it seems to have a broad constituency across the site, which suggests that early occupation within the confines of the archaeological site at Peñaflor was quite extensive. In those places where it does occur, it has either been brought to the surface through the erosion or destruction of later, Roman, phases or is in a residual context with later, Roman, material. Its gradual disappearance at the eastern end of the site is harder to explain. Early Imperial material was far more common because it was closer to the surface and the layers from which it derived had been more heavily disturbed than those of the preceding period. Pottery was also probably produced in much greater quantity than it had been previously. The rarity of Late Imperial material may be explained by the fact that it was intrinsically rarer than that of the Early Imperial period. It is also possible that since Late Imperial coarsewares are poorly understood, some of these may have been ascribed to the Early Imperial period.

Analysis of the distribution of pottery by function highlighted a concentration of largely Early Imperial finewares on the NW facing hillsides. This distinctive means of rubbish disposal might have been the by-product of purely residential occupation. The concentration of amphorae and coarse wares in the lower-lying slopes near the river could be taken to suggest that there may have been a dump near the port. Here, larger pottery vessels could have been broken-up as foodstuffs were decanted from their original containers into smaller vessels and sold in the town. An alternative interpretation is that the amphora sherds represent mid-imperial walls constructed from amphora sherds: a technique which was attested during the excavation (Chapter 3). A final possibility is that all of this material accumulated through erosion of the higher ground to the north and west.

The construction material showed a fairly even scatter of marble across the site, but a particular concentration on the top of Platform 3 and in lower eastern part of La Viña. This was shared by the quarter column segments. The distribution of both these classes of material, however, was distinct from that of the finewares. The former may be indicative of fine decorated buildings disturbed by the plough, while the latter may be reflect the accumulation of rubbish in abandoned houses.

The detailed survey of platform 1:
The Platform Survey (JC) (W/Appendix 4.2)

The 1% surface survey described above was intended to shed light upon the chronology and the possible existence of functional zones in the town. However, the wide spacing of the squares made it impossible to sample all the buildings revealed by the geophysical surveys. Consequently, other forms of surface collection were devised to enhance our knowledge of two specific areas

PLATFORM 1 AT THE CENTRE OF THE TOWN
During the systematic collection of column segments discussed above, it was suggested that an alignment of segments might represent a colonnade along the southern edge of platform 1 (Figs. 2.11 and 2.27). This platform (c. 230 × 120m) ran to the south of the modern buildings along the northern side of La Viña between the entrance to the field and the Ermita de la Encarnación. This large area occupied a distinctive position at the centre of the town, overlooking the land sloping down to the river port. It was thought that it might mark the site of a complex of public buildings. In an attempt to test this hypothesis, construction material from a sample area within the platform was collected to see whether the distribution of construction debris related to any distinctive geophysical features and whether the architectural scheme could be ascertained without excavation. If it proved successful, a larger survey was planned for a future season.

It was decided to retain part of the procedure used for the 1% surface survey. In all, one hundred and twenty 3x3m collection units were established within the same 30m grid that had been used previously, although only 50% of the squares were actually sampled. A team of 13 people was used and one person collected the material from each square for a 10 minute period. All construction material from each square was identified and divided into tile, brick, marble and column segments. It was then counted and weighed on site and then discarded in its original square.

Some patterning in the material was apparent (Fig. 2.27). The brick concentrated on an alignment towards the edge of the terrace and on the slope to the SE. There was also a trace of an alignment at right-angles to this. The tile distribution revealed a similar pattern although it was less clear. The column segments clustered on the lower slope of the edge of the terrace, possibly indicating the presence of a portico or colonnade on the southern edge of the platform. The marble fragments hinted at an alignment at right-angles (as with the brick and tile) and a concentration to the east. This survey was only suggestive of building alignments, a situation which could perhaps be remedied with a larger sample and survey area. Nevertheless it does underline the potential of quantifying surface building material from complex urban sites such as these.

Topography & Geophysics

Collectors (13 people, A-M)

											A	B	C	D	E	F	G	H	I	J
A	B	C	D	E	F	G	H	I	J											
											A	B	C	D	E	F	G	H	I	J
A	B	C	D	E	F	K	H	L	J											
											A	B	C	D	E	F	G	H	I	J
A	B	C	D	E	F	K	H	L	J											
											A	B	C	D	E	F	G	H	I	J
A	B	C	D	E	F	K	H	L	J											
											A	B	C	D	E	F	G	H	I	J
A	B	C	D	E	F	K	H	L	J											
A	B	C	D	M	F	K	H	L	J											
A	B	C	D	M	F	K	H	L	J											

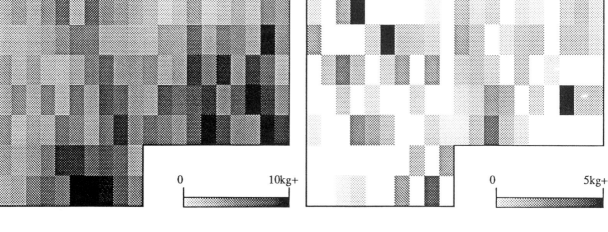

Brick

0   10kg+

Marble Fragments

0   5kg+

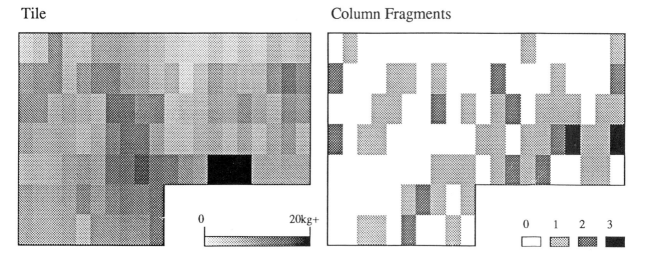

Tile

0   20kg+

Column Fragments

0   1   2   3

Fig. 2.27. 1990 Construction Material Survey of Platform 1

B. PLATFORMS 2 AND 3
ON THE CREST OF THE WESTERN HILL

A second construction material survey was carried out during 1991. It should be pointed out that this survey was undertaken after the excavations had begun. The area chosen for this was on the western hill of La Viña a short distance to the north of that part of the site that had been excavated during the course of 1989 and 1990 (Fig. 2.11). The aim of this survey was to enhance our interpretation of the excavation and, by implication, the most prominent platforms on the site. In 1992, following the completion of the survey, the excavation was enlarged so that it included the southern part of the survey area.

In the light of the earlier survey of Platform 1, a number of changes were made to the collection technique. First, all the 3m squares were to be investigated rather than half of them. Secondly, in an attempt to avoid creating a collection bias of construction material relative to small pieces of ceramic, there were separate collections for each category of material. Thus, the first 10 minutes were dedicated to the collection of construction material (building debris and decorative elements) alone. A further five minutes were given to collection of *diagnostic* pottery for dating purposes only: in practice this usually meant any finewares and amphora rims. In this way it would be possible to distinguish the latest material in each area.

Over 22 tonnes of material were collected, sorted, counted and weighed from 990 squares (an area of 8910m²). All the material was discarded back into the square from which it came, with the exception of the fragments of diagnostic pottery. The full data are presented in W/Appendix 4 (section 4.3.1–18).

Construction material

Tiles	7050	2,791.5 kg	Fig. 2.37	W/Appendix 4.3.17 & 4.3.18
Brick	42062	6,343.8 kg	Fig. 2.28	W/Appendix 4.3.1 & 4.3.2
Cobbles	6697	2,035.4 kg	Fig. 2.31	W/Appendix 4.3.3 & 4.3.4
Limestone	24497	10,334.7 kg	Fig. 2.30	W/Appendix 4.3.9 & 4.3.10
Greenstone	1049	514.2 kg		W/Appendix 4.3.7 & 4.3.8
Total	81355	22,019.6 kg		

Decorative elements/flooring

Column Segments	146	115.9 kg	Fig. 2.36	W/Appendix 4.3.5, 4.5.6
Marble	409	136.4 kg	Fig. 2.35	W/Appendix 4.3.11 & 4.3.12
Opus signinum	504	125.0 kg	Fig. 2.33	W/Appendix 4.3.13 & 4.3.14
Opus spicatum	457	57.3 kg	Fig. 2.32	W/Appendix 4.3.15 & 4.3.16
Tesserae	890	35.0 kg	Fig. 2.34	W/Appendix 4.3.19 & 4.3.20
Wall plaster	73	6.7 kg		W/Appendix 4.3.21 & 4.3.22
Total	2,479	476.3 kg		

Latest diagnostic pottery in assemblage

Fig. 2.37   W/Appendix 4.3.23

RESULTS
Construction Material (Fig. 2.28–37)
The clearest distribution patterns came from the

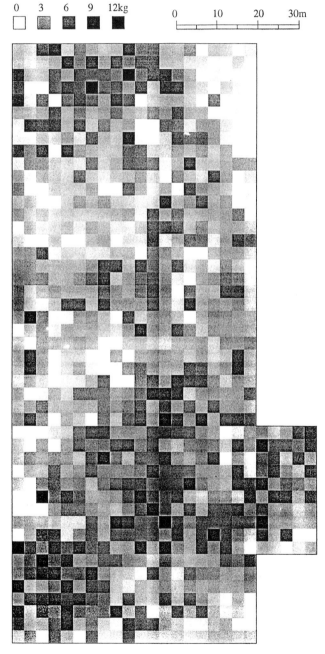

Fig. 2.28. *1991 Survey of Platforms 2 and 3. Density of bricks expressed in weights*

flooring materials (*opus signinum, opus spicatum* and tesserae: Fig. 2.32, 33 and 34). This was perhaps to be expected. Individual rooms in a building might have undifferentiated construction materials like brick and tile for their walls and roofs, although one might anticipate different kinds of floor surfaces within individual buildings. However, some individual patterning was evident in the former.

Analysis of the construction material was aided by observations from the excavation (see Chapter

3). Four types of construction technique had been observed during the 1989 and 1990 seasons:

1) Construction from large blocks of limestone.
2) Walls from mortared limestone rubble
3) Column sub-plinths made from limestone rubble with several fragments of greenstone
4) Foundation walls made from water-worn cobbles.
5) It should be noted that the existence of walls of brick, tile or amphora on the site were only

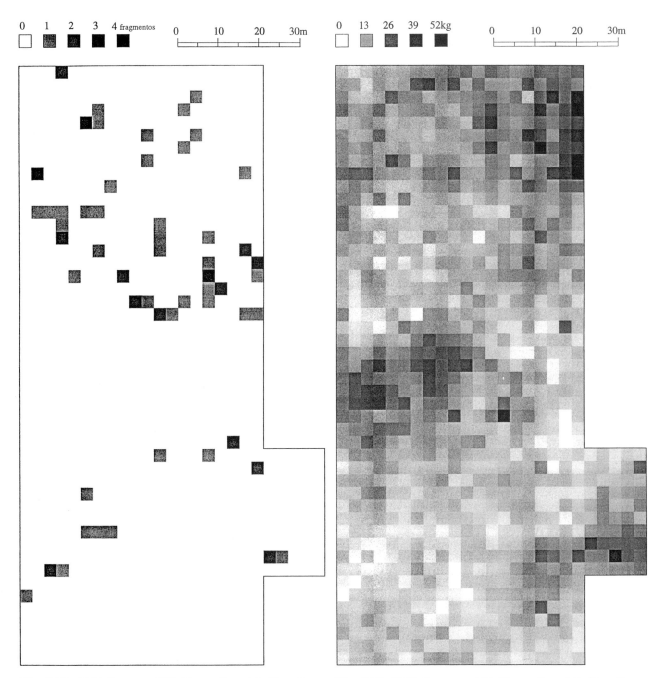

Fig. 2.29. 1991 Survey of Platforms 2 and 3. Density of concrete expressed in weights

Fig. 2.30. 1991 Survey of Platforms 2 and 3. Density of limestone expressed in weights

revealed after the completion of the survey, during the 1992 excavation season.

The distribution plots were all examined against an overlay of the basic geophysical results and the topography. Initially, few direct correlations were observed. For example, the distribution of tesserae appeared to cross a roadway and not respect any of the hypothesised walls. However a comparison of all the plots revealed a series of discreet anomalies (Fig. 2.38). These are now discussed in a sequence running from north to south.

A) A cluster of brick and *opus signinum* (c.30×25m) existed at the north end of the survey (Fig. 2.38: 12). This was in a dominant position on the crest of platform 2, overlooking the site from the north-west. No clear geophysical features appeared to relate to this.

B) South of (A) was a large spread (c.50x20m) of *opus spicatum* (Fig. 2.38: 11). The extent of this

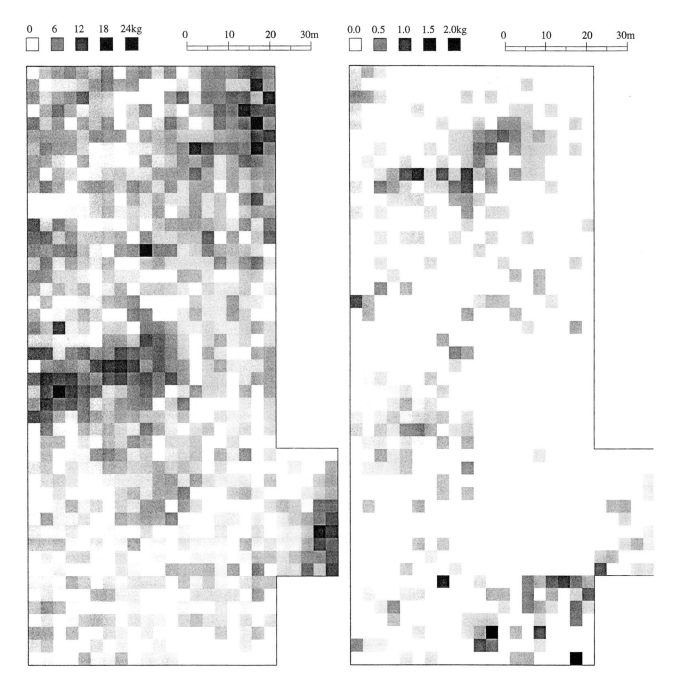

Fig. 2.31. 1991 Survey of Platforms 2 and 3. Density of cobbles expressed in weights

Fig. 2.32. 1991 Survey of Platforms 2 and 3. Density of opus spicatum fragments expressed in weights

hinted at the existence of a large open area. No clear geophysical features could be related to this.

C) On the eastern side of a possible road was a combined concentration of limestone and water-worn cobbles (Fig. 2.38: 13). These two types of construction material frequently cropped up in unison. The survey only clipped the edge of this feature, although it hints at a structure with a unity of construction that was over 30m in length along one side. Parallel to this some c.30m

to the east, the remains of a long wall were revealed by the plough providing some cor-roboration to the alignment provided by the geophysics and distribution plots.

D) A possible roadway curving round the con-tours of platform 2 was suggested by the geophysics (Fig. 2.38: 9). This was borne out by the survey, which revealed a concentration of brick and tile along its course. It is possible that this may have represented the remains of boundary walls on either side of the road. No

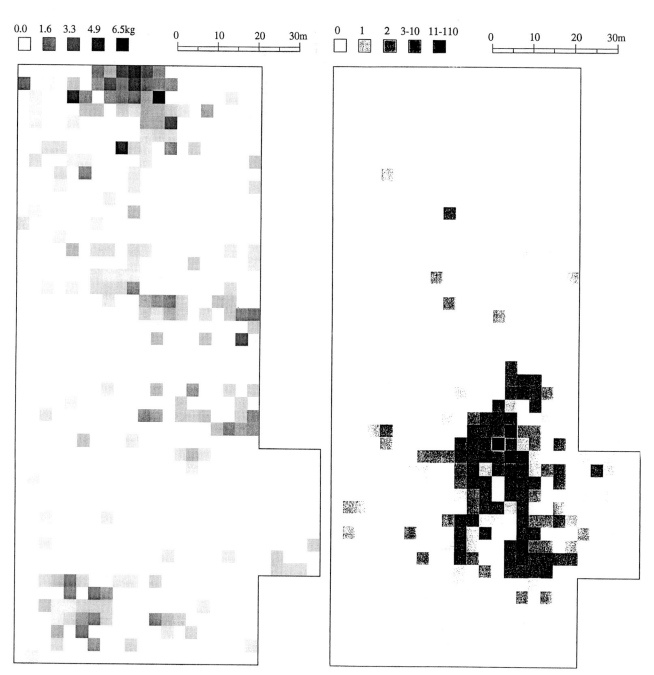

Fig. 2.33. 1991 Survey of Platforms 2 and 3. Density of opus signinum fragments expressed in weights

Fig. 2.34. 1991 Survey of Platforms 2 and 3. Density of tesserae expressed in weights

other material clustered here nor did the geophysics reveal traces of any flanking buildings.

E) Within a triangle defined by several possible roadways was revealed a cluster of limestone and cobbles (45x20m) with an *opus spicatum* floor offset to the SW. This contrasted with the materials on the south side of the road (Fig. 2.38: 7).

F) Within a triangular area to the south of (E) was a concentration of brick and tile, together with column segments and tesserae (Fig. 2.38: 6).

This points to the existence of a range of buildings.

G) South of (F) and the main SW/NE road and on the northern side of the *insula* block revealed by the geophysics and examined by the excavation was a distinctive rectangular area (c.15 × 40m: Fig. 2.38:5). This showed up well in the geophsyics and was dominated by brick, tile and tesserae; column segments were absent.

H) SE of (G) was another limestone and cobble scatter (c.15x10m: Fig. 2.38:1)

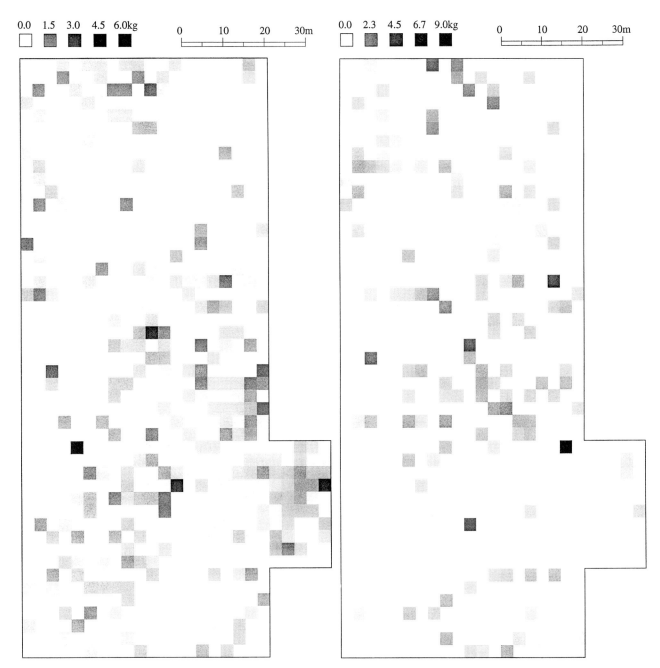

Fig. 2.35. 1991 Survey of Platforms 2 and 3. Density of marble fragments expressed in weights

Fig. 2.36. 1991 Survey of Platforms 2 and 3. Density of column segments expressed in weights

I) South of the large brick building (Fig. 2.38: 5) was an alignment of column segments (Fig. 2.38: 4).

J) South of the column segment alignment was an area of *opus spicatum* flooring (Fig. 2.38: 2).

K) To the west was a discrete cluster of brick and *opus signinum* (Fig. 2.38: 3) which did not clearly correlate with any of the geophysical anomalies, except that it was confined within the *insula* by the NW/SE road.

There were two additional areas which can can be characterised by an absence of construction material (Fig. 2.38: 8 and 10) and geophysical anomalies. The reason for these in such a prominent location is not clear.

Pottery

The latest pottery collected from each square was analyzed and a distribution map plotted (Fig. 2.39). No significant patterning was detected. There was slightly less material to the NW and some of the latest came from the central eastern area, but any hopes that the material might date the build up of rubbish in disused houses were not fulfilled.

Overall Interpretation (SK)

The ancient settlement at Peñaflor had a distinctive topography on a natural prominence on the north bank of the river Guadalquivir. It took the form of a natural "theatre" with high ground to the west, north and east and low ground dipping down towards the river to the south. In this way, the main part of the site is open towards the Guadalquivir and is "shut-off" from the hinterland and Sierra Morena to the north. This topography is relatively common at protohistoric and Roman sites in western Andalucía. One might cite for example, La Torre de Aguila (Utrera: ancient Siarum), El Casar (El Coronil: ancient Salpensa) and the central portion of Las Cabezas de San Pedro (Fuentes de Andalucía), to name but a few (Keay, Wheatley and Poppy 2000: see also Fig. 10.1). Previous excavations at the site (Chapter 1) suggest that topography may have developed as a result of accumulated occupation debris, akin to a middle eastern tell; a good parallel is to be found at the protohistoric site of El Cerro Macareno, located a short distance to the north of Seville.

The maximum area of ancient Peñaflor was approximately 26.34 Hectares. The systematic surface survey has shown that much of this area was occupied throughout the Turdetanian, Roman and Late Roman periods. The post-depositional

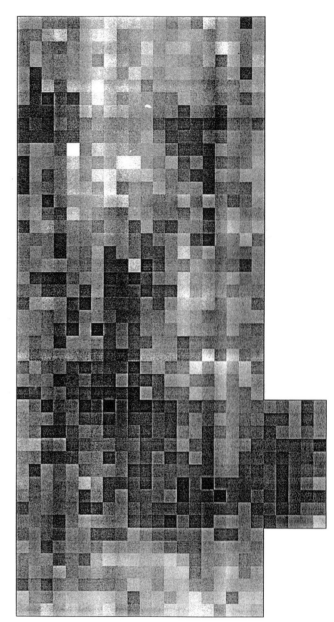

Fig. 2.37. 1991 Survey of Platforms 2 and 3. Density of tegulae expressed in weights

processes which generated much of this material make it difficult to ascribe the extent of occupation in any one of these periods. However, it is possible to suggest that it might have been localized at different points during the late Bronze and Early Iron Ages and that the settlement only began to coalesce as a single unit during the Turdetanian Iron Age. The whole area was occupied during the Early Imperial period, with evidence of a

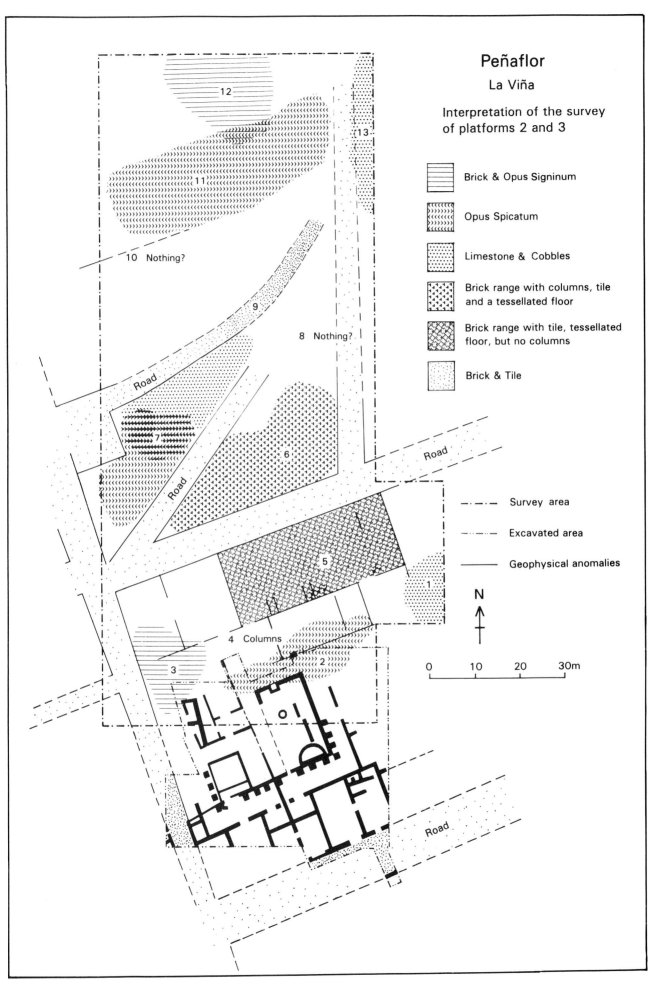

Peñaflor

La Viña

Interpretation of the survey
of platforms 2 and 3

Brick & Opus Signinum

Opus Spicatum

Limestone & Cobbles

Brick range with columns, tile
and a tessellated floor

Brick range with tile, tessellated
floor, but no columns

Brick & Tile

10 Nothing?

8 Nothing?

4 Columns

—··—··— Survey area

—···—···— Excavated area

——— Geophysical anomalies

N

0   10   20   30m

Fig. 2.38. Interpretation of 1991 Survey of Platforms 2 and 3

0   10   20   30m

None   BC   e.1st   l.1st   e.2nd

l.2nd   e.3rd   l.3rd   e.4th   l.4th

e.5th   l.5th   e.6th

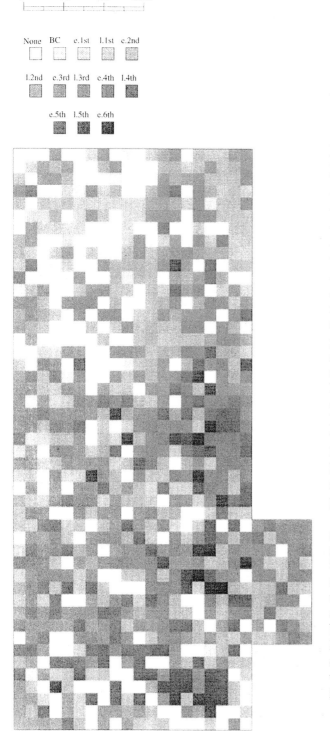

Fig. 2.39. 1991 Survey of Platforms 2 and 3. Distri-
bution of dated pottery expressed in counts

contraction towards the centre of the settlement during the Late Empire.

The structures revealed by the geophysics lie in the uppermost 1.5m of archaeological deposit and are, thus, most likely to be of Early or Late Imperial date. Street alignments conform to the topography and differ at the western and eastern sides of La Viña, suggesting that they were the result of accumulated urban development. Moreover, the grid-like arrangement or 'insula' at the highest point of the site (Fig. 2.10), points to the replanning of this area at some stage in the town's history. This is clearly a focal point in the topography of the town, given that it commands a dominating vista over the whole town, northwards towards the Sierra Morena and down towards the Guadalquivir. This argument is strengthened by the fact that it encloses what is clearly a 'public' building and, if the proposed interpretations are correct, is adjacent to other substantial buildings. It is not impossible, therefore, that this was one key area of public buildings. Another probably lay on flatter ground down the hill towards the east. The available geophysics and results of earlier excavation suggest that much of the town to the north in La Pared Blanca and the Pepe Higueras property comprised residential areas with, in the Pared Blanca at least, an irregular street-grid. By contrast, the lower lying areas of La Viña and the land adjacent to the Guadalquivir seem to have been areas concerned with the transhipment and manufacture of Dressel 20 olive amphorae and pottery.

It is clear that the careful integration of topography mapping, systematic surface survey and geophysics can make a significant contribution to the understanding of complex urban archaeological sites of this kind. In particular, it provided a general understanding of the archaeological site of Peñaflor as a whole. The interpretation ventured here should be regarded as little more than a hypothesis. However, it did raise a number of archaeological questions which could only be answered by excavation. It was in this context that the choice of area for excavation was made.

Chapter 3
The Excavations

Simon Keay and John Creighton

Abstract
This Chapter describes in detail the open-area of a key area of ancient Celti. In all some twelve phases of activity are outlined, beginning with some ephemeral late Bronze Age structures of uncertain character, and evidence for some significant urban changes in the Augustan and Julio-Claudian periods. The most important phases, 7 and 8 see the construction of a major public building in the Neronian/Early Flavian period and its replacement by two houses in the early third century AD. The site is demolished in the early fifth century AD (Phase 9), although there are traces of a later building (Phase 10) in the north-eastern sector of the site.

3.1 Selection of the Area for Excavation (SK)

The integrated programme of topographical work, systematic surface survey and geophysics discussed in the previous chapter made a major contribution towards our understanding of the topography of ancient Celti and key research questions addressed by this project. However, the resultant urban model needed to be tested by excavation. Our challenge was to select a place for open area excavation at a point which had:

1. A full stratigraphic sequence
2. The potential to shed light upon the internal organization of the site and its political and cultural history throughout the Roman period
3. The potential to calibrate the results of the surface survey.

This was not a straightforward matter. One of the most difficult problems was deciding where to excavate. One constraint was that our time was limited. Given the constraints of *the Plan General de Arqueología* (1985), which only permitted an excavation season every other year for six years, we could only count upon about three and one half months in total. Another was that earlier excavations and our topographic survey had made it clear that parts of the site were deeply stratified. It

was also likely that access to early levels would be difficult in those areas where there were large stone Roman buildings, while late levels would have all but vanished from places where erosion or deep ploughing had been acute. Furthermore, in order to maximise the value our results, it made sense to excavate in a part of the site that had not been hitherto touched: this ruled out the Pared Blanca and the Huerto de Pepe Higueras fields even though their results were still unpublished. This only left El Calvario, La Viña and the land between the railway line and the Guadalquivir. The former was ruled out on the grounds that it was too small for a large open-area excavation, particularly since a pigsty occupied much of the ancient site enclosed within the field. The latter was impractical since the land sloped very steeply down to the river and had probably been disturbed when the railway line was cut. La Viña was, therefore, the only realistic proposition. However, it was the largest surviving expanse of the ancient town and little was known about it apart from a few surviving walls, two *opus signinum* lined tanks and, of course, our own systematic surveys. The area eventually chosen seemed well able to satisfy the three conditions mentioned above. It was located in what may have been an area of public buildings in the town. Moreover, it was hoped that the clarity of the geophysics at this point might prove helpful in the final interpretation of the excavated sequence. These advantages outweighed some of the more obvious limitations. Not least of these was the fact that this part of the site had been quite heavily ploughed – and still was prior to excavation – but it was felt that this might provide a good index of the rate of destruction in the more prominent and exposed parts of the site.

Nearly all excavations at protohistoric and Roman town sites in the lower Guadalquivir valley have taken the form of small sondages or, more rarely, to have been with the use of box-trenches. This has minimised the conclusions that can be drawn from them which, in the end, amount to little more than occupational sequences of one tiny part of a much larger site. The considerable size of the ancient settlement at Peñaflor and the kinds of questions being posed by this project demanded that a large open-area be excavated. In 1989, a relatively small area was selected; it lay across the most clearly defined rooms in the large complex defined by the geophysics and incorporated the two opus-signinum lined tanks which were still visible above ground. This area was considerably enlarged in 1991.

There were three major difficulties encountered during the excavation seasons. For financial and logistical reasons the excavation seasons always had to take place between late June and early August, when the daily temperatures often reached over 43 degrees C by midday. This meant that by 10 o'clock in the morning most archaeological surfaces had dried out and that colour and texture differences in the soil were almost impossible to detect. By midday, therefore, dust had become a major problem on the site. The second difficulty was that the site had been very heavily plough-damaged, rather more than had been anticipated. Ploughing had removed nearly all late Roman structures while those of late 1st century AD date were removed down to the level of foundations. This ensured that for the Roman period there was little stratigraphic cross-linking across the site and that the occupational sequence that was eventually produced owed much to structural analyses. Deposits of earlier periods, however, did survive and reached a maximum depth of about 3m. Given this degree of plough damage and the dryness of the site it was sometimes difficult to be sure that individual contexts were properly defined or had been removed in their entirety. In an attempt to remedy all of these problems a site specific context sheet was developed (Fig. 3.1).

The best strategy for establishing the stratigraphic sequence at the site was to create a series of mini-sequences at key points and to cross-link these with the bridging stratigraphy that did exist. Thus, the structural report which follows is organized around an overall phase by phase site discussion (3.2). This is complemented by an area by area discussion (W/Chapter 1). The areas for the latter discussion are based upon the mini sequences mentioned earlier. The report concludes with a discussion of the dating of the site phases (3.3).

3.2 Overall Phase by Phase Site Discussion (JC)

This section of the structural report discusses the interpretation of the evidence on a phase by phase basis. This is followed by detailed plans of each area (Figs. 3.10–3.17), whose descriptions and matrices are in W/Chapter 1.

The Twelve Main Phases of Activity

The structural sequence was divided up into twelve main phases of activity with a series of sub phases. These can be summarised as follows:

P1   Early features in Area A: Undiagnostic strata
P2   Early features in Area A: Two parallel walls
P3   Early features in Area A: Hearth
P4   Early features in Area A: Postholes
P5   Early features in Area A: Three walls
P6   A series of walls in Area A & B
P7   The "public building"
    P7a   Levelling up prior to construction
    P7b   Construction of the "public building"
    P7c   Adaptations to the building
P8   The Double Courtyard House
    P8a   Double Courtyard house construction
    P8b   Addition of water features to both courtyards
    P8c   Refurbishment of existing features
P9   Robbing
P10   Late building in the NW corner of the excavation, Area J
P11   Modern features
P12   Surface strata disturbed by agriculture

The phasing of the site was established entirely on structural grounds. The dating of the ceramics was not used as the primary basis for phasing any of the contexts, not least because of the high degree of residuality of earlier ceramics in later deposits (see section 3.3 at the end of this chapter).

Much of the report is taken up with describing phases 7 and 8. These remains were extensive, even though there had been a significant amount of robbing, both in antiquity and, more recently, through plough damage. Due to the scale of these remains, excavation down to the earlier deposits

Peñaflor (La Viña)

X:	Area/*Sector*:	Context No.:
Y:	Height/*Altitud*:	*Contexto*:

Finds/*Hallazgos*

- ○ Pottery/*Cerámica*
- ○ Human Bone
  Hueso Humano
- ○ Animal Bone
  Hueso Animal
- ○ Marble/*Mármol*
- ○ Building Material
  Material de construcción

Other/*Otra*:

Small Finds
Hallazgos especiales

Stratigraphic Relationships
Conexiones Estratigráficas

Underlies/*Por debajo de*...:

Cut by/*Cortado por*:

- - - - - - - - - - - - - - - - - - - -

Equal to/*Igual a*:

Similar to but.../*Parecido pero*...:

- - - - - - - - - - - - - - - - - - - -

Overlies/*Por encima de*...:

Cuts/*Corta*:

Type of feature
Definición del Contexto

Cut/*Corte*: ○

Layer/*Estrato*: ○

Structure/*Elemento*: ○

Preliminary Matrix
Matrix Preliminar

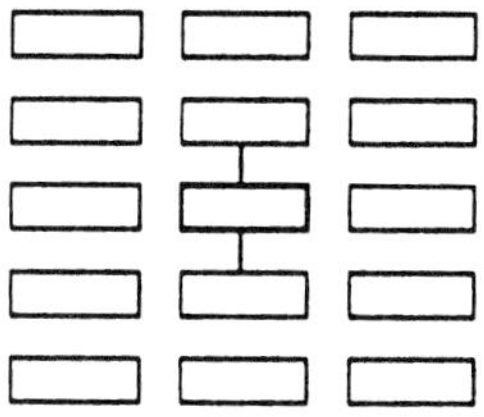

Soil Description
Características de la Tierra

Texture/ *Textura*:
Colour/*Color*:
Stones / *Piedras*:
Number / *Número*:   <1   1-5   5-15   15-35   35-70   >70%
Shape / *Forma*:   (A)   (S-A)   (S-R)   (R)
Size / *Tamaña*:   (2-6mm)   (6-20mm)   (2-6cm)   (6-20cm)   (20-60cm)   (60cm+)
Boundary / *Lindero*:
Definition / *Definición*:   (0-2mm)   (2-10mm)   (1-5cm)   (>5cm)
Form / *Forma*:   Smooth/*Llano*   Wavy/*Ondulado*   Artificial/*Artificial*
   Irregular/*Desigual*   Broken/*Imperfecto*
Other Comments/*Otra*:

Samples Taken
Muestras Escogidas

Unit Description
Descripción Del Estrado/Elemento:

Length/*Largo*:	cm	Proportion Excavated:	%
Width/*Anchura*:	cm	*Percentajo excavado*:	
Depth/*Profundidad*:	cm		
Diameter/*Diámetro*:	cm	Method of Excavation:	
Volume/*Volumen*:	cm^3	*Método de Excavacíon*	

Dating Evidence
Criterios para Fechar

Phase:
Fase:

Interpretation
Interpretación

Plan Nos.:	Section Nos.:	Photographs/*Fotografías*	Date/*Fecha*:
Nº de Plano:	*Nº de Sección*:		Initials/*Responsable*:

Fig. 3.1a. Excavation Recording Sheet

Peñaflor (La Viña)

Context No.:
Contexto:

Fig. 3.1b. Excavation Recording Sheet

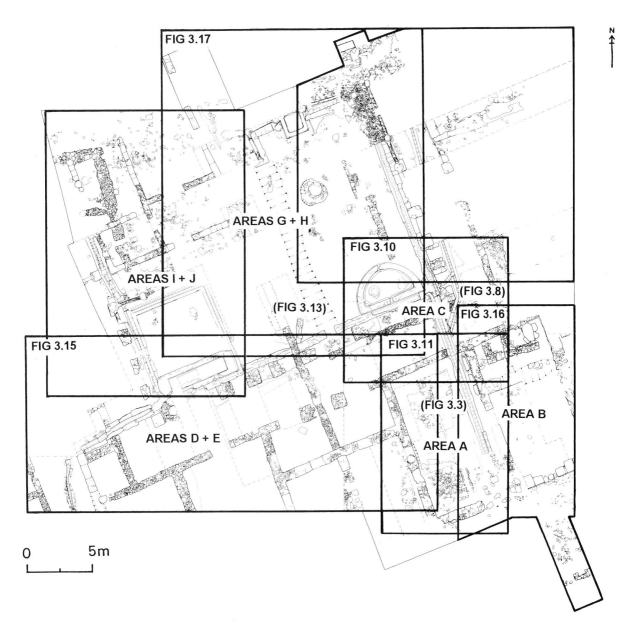

Fig. 3.2. Plan Showing the Location of Areas A–J and Corresponding Plans, as well as the Position of More Detailed Plans (in parentheses)

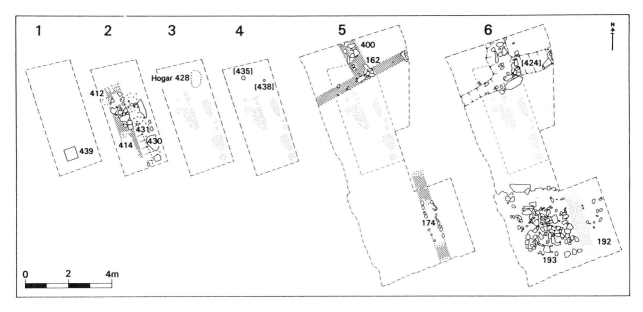

Fig. 3.3. Plan Sequence of Phases 1–6

of P1–6 was restricted to the interior of some of the larger rooms of the phase 7 "public building" complex.

Conventions

All the features on site were given one numerical sequence. A list of all these and supporting matrices, together with site plans showing spot heights are to be found in Appendix W/Ch.1. An analysis of the dating of occupation phases follows at the end of this chapter. The contexts were designated as either structures, layers or cuts. In the text cut numbers can be distinguished by the use of square parentheses [000], whereas structures and layers are all designated by round parentheses (000). On the matrices, a further distinction has been made with only the structures being placed in round parentheses. With the significant amount of robbing on the site, sometimes it was useful to give a number to a structure which was known to have existed, but which had been entirely robbed away. A case in point would be a lead pipe, whose outline survives intact, but which itself has been robbed away. In order to show such features in the matrix and discuss their phasing, nominal context numbers were allocated to them. These are indicated by single quotation marks: '000'.

Phases 1–5 (Figs.3.2, 3.3, 3.11, 3.27 and matrices in W/Chapter 1)

On the southern side of the "public building" colonnade was a large room delimited by walls (125) (36) (224) (240) (4) and (233). Here, the contemporary ground surface was levelled up to the height of the portico by the dumping of earlier material; whereas that of the adjacent rooms, by contrast, was excavated away to a lower level to ensure access from the street to the south. This arrangement ensured the survival of earlier deposits underneath the dump, and one of the priorities of the excavation was to examine these in order to obtain a long environmental sequence. During the process of excavation, the area open to view became increasingly restricted. Whereas the room was 79m² large, only 40m² of P5–6 were visible, 9.00m² of P2–4, and at the bottom only 0.25m² of P1 could be excavated. Consequently, the greater the depth the harder it was to interpret the structures.

PHASE 1: UNDIAGNOSTIC STRATA

The earliest deposit investigated was context (439). This was a small area of 0.50x0.50m. The deposit in itself had no form or structure, other than being sealed by P2.

PHASE 2: TWO PARALLEL WALLS

Above a preparation layer of small pebbles (429), two walls were constructed which ran parallel to each other. One was composed of irregular sub-angular limestone rubble (412), the second comprised a line of blue metamorphic rocks about 1m to the east (414). Around both of these was a gravel/cobble floor (430/431).

PHASE 3: HEARTH

Sealing the P2 cobbles was another floor layer (433) on top of which was a spread (428) which showed significant signs of burning.

PHASE 4: POST-HOLES

Cutting into the P3 burnt deposit were two post-holes [435] & [438]. Whatever kind of activity these represent, they came to an end with their back-filling (346 & 347) and the area being sealed under a layer of melted mud-brick.

PHASE 5: BUILDING

From P5 onwards the area accessible on the excavation enlarged from around 9m² to 40m². With this it becomes possible to make more sense of the structures excavated. In this phase two main series of walls were revealed. In the northern part of the area there was a T-junction of dry-stone and mud-brick walling which was subsequently robbed away in P6. A short stretch of the lower stone courses remained (400 & 162), as did some blocks of mud-brick (426). Contained within the angle of these walls was a small burnt area, which may be the remnants of a hearth (427). To the south was another wall of a rather different construction comprising mud-brick (174) with a cobble facing on either side. Excavation did not continue down here, so it is impossible to say if this is a foundation level or whether the cobble facing would have been visible above-ground. It is not clear whether the walls share exactly the same alignment. The subsequent robbing in Phase 6 meant that the precise orientation of the northern walls is obscure. Nonetheless, both could have been contemporary in stratigraphic terms.

PHASES 6A–D (Figs 3.2, 3.3, 3.4 and 3.11)

In this phase, the P5 building in Area A was comprehensively robbed out, marking a new phase of activity. No evidence for later structures was found in this area. Instead, the P5 features were covered with layers associated with the levelling for the construction of the P7 "public building" complex. In Area B immediately to the east, some structures – which undoubtedly would have formed part of the same complex – did survive to a higher level without being robbed away or removed during

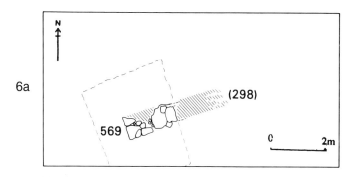

6a

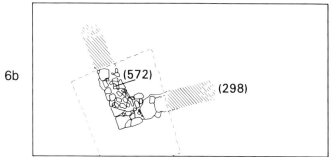

6b

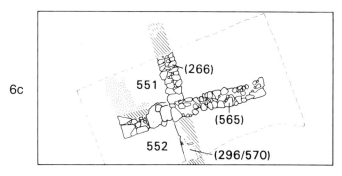

6c

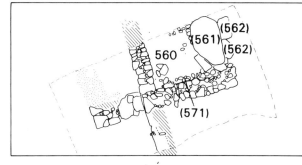

6d

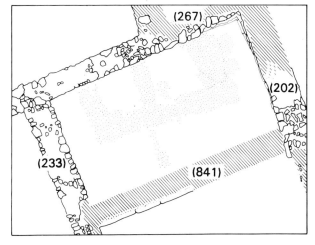

7a–b

Fig. 3.4. Plan Sequence of Phases 6a–7a/b

levelling for the "public building". This adjacent area was too small to make a great deal of sense out of the few walls that remained. Nevertheless their stratigraphic sequence did suggest that the building had been modified on a number of occasions: these are discussed below as sub-phases a–d. It is not possible to ascribe function or status to this building since so little survives. However, it may have had some architectural embellishments. A number of limestone column drums were found reused in a wall (36) of P7 (Fig. 3.21) which may have derived from the demolition and robbing of the P6 building.

Area A: Robbing of P5 structure
The P5 buildings were comprehensively robbed. A robber trench [424] cut away most of the northern walls. The southern wall was also demolished and rubble was scattered on either side of the wall (192,193).

Robber trench of northern wall:
Cut: [424] and fills: 188, 403, 404, 417, 421, 423, 425
Southern area rubble:
To the west of the wall 193 and to the east of the wall 192

Area B: A sequence of walls (Figs. 3.4 and 3.16)
In the area 531–538E / 474–480N a series of stone walls survived. They have all been treated as sub-phases of 6 as they all built upon one another on the same alignment, unlike the remains from Area A where each phase was radically different from the last.

Phase 6a: One wall
This consists of one dry limestone wall (298) running E–W. To the west of this the strata (569) and (576) were excavated to recover dating material.

Phase 6b: Two walls
Wall (298) continued in use while wall (572) was constructed at right-angles constructed to it.

Phase 6c: Two crossing walls
Wall (298) probably went out of use. It was covered by a spread of material (551), which appeared to underlie part of a new north–south wall (266). This new wall comprised three elements; a limestone base: 266 and 570, with mud-brick on top: 296. Its construction was contemporaneous with the eastward extension of wall (298) with (565).

Phase 6d: Two crossing walls and a large slab
At the eastern end of wall (565) a new feature is added; this comprised a series of deposits covered by a large stone slab (561). The latter rests on a series of large limestone blocks on the east (562), and on a series of cobbles to the south and west (568). Directly beneath the stone was a silty loam deposit.

PHASE 7A AND 7B: "PUBLIC BUILDING" CONSTRUCTION
Areas A, B, C, D and E, F, G and H, I and J

(Figs. 3.2, 3.4, 3.5, 3.8, 3.11, 3.12, 3.13, 3.14, 3.15,
3.16, 3.17, 3.18 and matrices in W/Chapter 1)

Phase 7 marked a radical change on the site with
the construction of a large building with a central
square surrounded by a portico which has been
identified as a public building, and possibly the
"forum" of ancient Celti (see discussion in Chapter
9). This large building (28.50m wide) was terraced
into the southern side of the hill overlooking the
Guadalquivir. Some areas were built up with
levelling deposits to create rooms at a higher level,
while others were scoured out to allow for the

construction of lower rooms. Later demolition, robbing and more recent ploughing activity has
ensured that in most parts of the southern area of
the "public building", walls have been destroyed
to the level of their footings; the only substantial
walls to survive enclose the west and northern sides
of the lower rooms. In the northern area of the
"public building", any surviving walls and floors
were sealed beneath Phase 8 deposits and were not
excavated.

Changes in ground level:
Upper and lower level rooms
The large scale of this building required a sub-
stantial remodelling of the site before construction

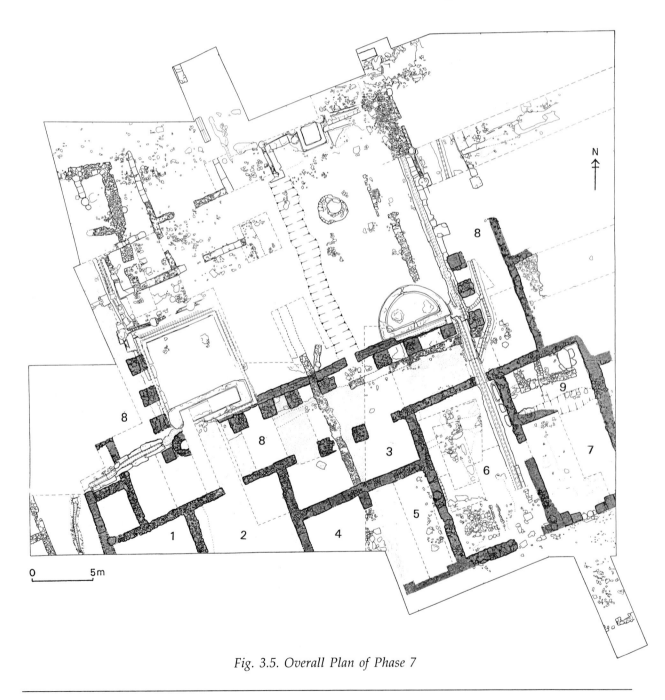

Fig. 3.5. Overall Plan of Phase 7

could commence. Work began with the demolition and robbing of many of the earlier structures and the recuperation of masonry for reuse in the new "public building" walls. This would have been followed by the adaptation of the hillside site for the construction of the horizontal "public building" platform, portico and row of rooms which ran along its southern side. While the platform could be accommodated on the hillside, the ground fell away quite steeply to the south. This meant that the road level which defined the southern side of the complex was almost one storey (at least 2.21m) below the level of the square at the heart of the "public building". There were two possible solutions to this problem. The rooms of the southern range could either be built upon huge dumps retained behind strong terrace walls, or be founded upon rooms at a lower level carved out of the hillside. In the end, both strategies were employed. In some areas huge dumps did manage to raise the level of the ground (Rooms 2, 3 and 8), whilst in others lower levels were scoured out (Rooms 1, 4, 5 and 7).

Initially, the creation of these dumps was defined as P7a. It is thought that some time would have to have elapsed before the new surface had settled and was stable enough for building work to have commenced. This began (P7b) with the digging of construction trenches, which would have cut into the earlier P7a layers. Whilst this is borne out on stratigraphic grounds, it is clear that some of the final layers of levelling were laid down *after* some of the walls had been constructed, presumably acting as final preparation layers which would have evened up the settled ground before the floors were laid. Thus, the division between P7a and 7b is somewhat artificial even though they are facets of the same process, namely the construction of the "public building".

The dumps were fairly amorphous, both in terms of the debris itself and the waste material they contained, with much being derived from decomposed mud-brick. Excavations at different points of the site revealed that in many areas they were capped by white mortar-rich layers several centimetres thick. These were not flat surfaces laid as preparation for a floor, but frequently undulated and were often discontinuous. Around column foundation (135) in Area D an almost conical sheet of this material had been rammed against the stonework. Sometimes these mortar-rich layers preceded the construction of the "public building" walls. For example, one of them (40) is cut by the construction trench [39] of wall (36), which divided rooms 3 and 6. Often, there were superimposed series of these layers, as can be seen (Fig. 3.19) in a series of sections running north–south across the portico of the "public building" (Area E). The

most likely interpretation of these layers is that they were laid to help consolidate the levelling dumps. Thus, the extra packing around column foundation (135) is suggestive of the extra care that was taken to ensure that important structures were solid and well-bedded.

There remained nothing of the floor of either the portico or the upper rooms, and their height could only be gauged by assuming that it lay above the level of the white mortar layers. It is assumed, without firm proof, that they were all at the same level. The apparent absence of a threshold block seemed to rule against access to the portico from Room 6 although it did seem possible from Room 3. By contrast, structures survived far better in the lower rooms. In Area B, cut [842] was dug into the terrace and earlier phases as part of construction work for creating the northern wall of the lower Room 7. On the southern side of this room, fronting onto the roadway, was a doorway c.2.5m wide, flanked by solid limestone blocks. It is not clear whether this entrance was intended to facilitate communication between this lower room and the upper level through Room 9. There were no traces of masonry steps or fixtures for wooden steps leading up from one to the other, although the latter might not have survived the later disturbance to this area. The safest conclusion would be that this room was a self-contained *taberna*. However, the overall architectural scheme suggests that it did provide access up to the portico (Chapter 9). There was some floor level information from this room. Adjacent to the entrance was a small patch of surviving preparation material for a floor (255/283), though most of this was robbed away at a later date.

Rooms 4 and 5 presented a similar problem. Both were at the lower level and at least one had an opening onto the street. At first glance it is perhaps tempting to see these two rooms as small *tabernae*. However, the difference in height between the floor of Room 5 and that of the "public building" portico (a minumum of 1.57m) meant that the space in the *taberna* would have been quite cramped. Since both were aligned with the central north–south axis of the "public building" it seems more likely that the rooms facilitated access to Room 3 and the "public building" portico by means of a monumental staircase. However no traces of any staircase was found in Room 5 – although excavation here was limited – and Room 4 was never excavated.

Levelling dumps:
Area A: (151), (159), (160), (161), (166), (167), (172), (173), (175), (176), (182), (186), (187), (220), (406), (410), (411), (413), (415), (416) & (422); Area B: (262), (263) & (299); Area C: (31), (645), (647), (648) & (652); Area D:

(134), (141) & (244); Area E: (330), (335), (336) & (353); Area H: (133), (142), (143), (144), (148) & (203)

Mortar rich layers:
Area A: (40) & (150); Area B: (268); Area C: (115), (116), (646); Area D: (122) & (328); Area E: (328), (329), (333) & (334); Area H: (116)

Room 1
Excavation of lower room: [842]; Remains of the floor: (255) & (283)

The construction of the building
and construction techniques
The walls of the "public building" themselves were not all constructed in the same manner. There were clear differences in technique depending upon the visibility and structural function of the walls. There were three main wall types:

a. Mortared limestone rubble (Fig. 3.20)
b. Large masonry blocks (Fig. 3.23)
c. A mixture of the two (Fig. 3.22)

In areas where the "public building" walls were designed to make a strong visual impression, large limestone blocks were used. On the western side of the building the external wall (52) was made of large rectangular limestone blocks, just as were the flanking sides of the entrances to the lower Rooms 7 and 5 (Room 7: (259); Room 5: (96) and (98)). In these cases the dressed stone was presumably used for show, however solid blocks were also used at the lower level of the retaining wall (841) between low level Room 7 and upper level Room 9. Here the weight of the earth would have required a substantial wall to hold it back: pressure would have come southwards from the levelling layers of Room 9, but also there would have been lateral pressure eastwards from the adjoining Room 6. In this context, the use of such materials would have been entirely appropriate.

In situations where there were differences in level on either side a wall, a combination of solid limestone blocks alternating with short stretches of mortared limestone rubble was used. This may be a local version of *opus africanum*. The sections of limestone rubble in amongst the solid blocks would have made the wall slightly flexible and better able to withstand slight shifts from the settlement of the newly levelled deposits upon which much of the building was constructed.

Both of these techniques are clearly visible in the section along the western wall of Room 6 (Fig. 3.20). The southern stretch (224/177) shows the alternate block and mortared rubble construction whereas the northern stretch (36) is of limestone rubble. This change coincides with the change in level of the rooms behind the wall. The southernmost stretch of the wall (224/177) separates the

void of Room 5 to the west from the dump of Room 6; by contrast its northern stretch (36) needs to hold nothing back since it lies between two rooms on the same level: rooms 3 and 6. All other internal walls with no retaining function were constructed of mortared limestone rubble.

Solid limestone bocks:
External walls/thresholds (52), (97), (98) & (259), internal retaining wall (841)

Mortared limestone rubble:
(36), (125), (233), (267), (310), (338), (339), (340), (341), (351), (361),

Alternating blocks and mortared rubble:
(96), (111/112/225/238), (224/177), (235), (240/4) & ?(202)

Construction trenches:
[179] for wall (177); [39] for wall (36) & [408] for wall (4)

The Colonnade
The sides of the square of the "public building" itself were defined by a colonnade. Its position is marked by 17 square foundations which were located at 2.5m intervals around its west, south and eastern sides; none of the column plinths, bases or shafts survived. The column foundation presumably carried on northwards along both sides of the square although the excavation did not continue deep enough to reveal them. The column foundations measured approximately 1.00m square and were normally composed of large angular pieces of limestone (0.20–0.30m) and occasionally incorporated fragments of greenstone. The column foundations at the south-east and south-west corners were of a different construction technique. The former (140) was composed of larger limestone pieces, while the latter (321) was a single large solid limestone block. These differences are probably to be explained by the additional solidity that they would have afforded, each ensuring that the columns which they supported would have been able to bear the weight of the north–south and east–west stylobates. Moreover, as there was a small well (357) adjacent to (321) it may well be that it was also intended to prevent any subsidence.

The spacing between the columns is by no means perfectly regular, with those along the east–west portico being the most irregular. It is possible that whilst the foundations were irregularly placed, the plinths and columns themselves were positioned more precisely, but that would be an unusual form of construction. There were two other column foundations of similar size framing the entrance to Room 3. However, it is noticeable that these were sited in such a way as to block the intercolumnations between the foundations of the portico of the "public building" (311), (318) and (28). This would have had the effect of obscuring the view of the open square from Room 3 and vice versa (see Chapter 9 for the possible significance of this).

Not a single column plinth or base was found in-situ. However, the excavations did uncover a column base in a later robber trench along the line of wall (177) (Figs. 3.20 and 5.39a & b). While there is no evidence to formally relate this to the column foundations described above, both its size and stylistic date suggest that this may have derived from the portico of the "public building" (further discussion in Chapter 9).

Colonnade:
Column foundations (anti-clockwise): Area I: (806), (809), (368), (369), (346); Area E: (321), (320), (308), (309), (311); Area H: (318), (319), (117); Area A: (241), (139/205), (140/206), (217), (680)

Entrance to Room 3:
Column foundations: Area D: (135) & (317)

The well at the SW corner (Area D and E)
In the south-western corner of the square, a cistern or well was constructed between two of the columns of the south portico. This was only excavated to the depth of three courses of stone facing. It was roughly circular with an internal diameter of c.0.90m. The facing stones (357) went back c. 0.20m, behind which was other stone packing (363) which would have been inserted as the well was lined. The chronological positioning of this well is difficult. The solid corner limestone column foundation (321) abutted the stone packing, which could suggest that the packing (and therefore well) was later. Also, the top of the surviving part of the well was still above the height of some of the levelling up layers for the "public building", so it is unlikely to be an earlier feature. It is just possible that it might belong to P8a although it must pre-date P8b: the packing behind the well-lining is sealed by the concrete (359) surrounding the lead pipe which drains the rectangular pool of P8b. The well has been interpreted as P7ab on the basis that it would be difficult to imagine a well being dug between two upstanding columns, and it is therefore assumed that it must have been integral to the original design and construction of the "public building". The well could have continued in use right up until the end of Phase 8c. There is no evidence one way or the other. Eventually it was filled and became disused (358).

Well:
Area E: facing stones (357), well pit packing (363)

The eaves drip gully
The inner edge of the square of the "public building" was defined by a series of large oblong rectangular limestone blocks, which ran in front of the column foundations. They directly abutted their inner faces and were, thus, later in construction terms although they were also part of the same architectural project. Some of these had been robbed away in later phases, but many remained in-situ. The surface of these was very degraded. A longitudinal depression ran along their upper face, details of which had been removed by recent plough action. Fortunately three of these blocks were removed from their original location in Phase 8b when the semi-circular pool was constructed: they were re-deposited (675) in the cutting of a new outflow drain (221). These blocks were far better preserved than those still in-situ and had a gentle U-shaped gully carved along their upper face. The best interpretation of these is that they served as a gully to catch rainwater off the "public building" portico, channelling it to the SW corner of the square from whence it was removed by another drain. A similar feature defined the northern edge of the forum at Singilia Barba (El Castillón, Antequera, Málaga) [personal observation: SK].

Limestone eaves drip gully:
In situ: (301) & (25); redeposited: (675)

Opus signinum drain
running down the eastern portico
Running down the eastern portico was a well constructed *opus signinum* drain which continued in use through into P8b. The entire structure was about 0.70m wide, though the drain itself was 0.16m wide and 0.22m deep. It sloped down to the south, draining water away from an unknown source to the north. The stratigraphic evidence suggests that this drain could either have been constructed during this phase, or later, in P8a. Where it passed through the south-eastern corner of the portico, its tile covering was intact (239). This was sealed in position by a white mortar rich surface (232) which was characteristic of other similar deposits relating to the construction "public building" (see above). There was no dating evidence from the layers sealed by this deposit which would negate the idea that this drain was part of the original construction of the "public building".

N–S corridor drain:
Drain: (631/108/114), tile cover (239), white mortar seal (232)

Waste drain running through Room 6 (Fig. 3.8)
The water collected in drain (25) had to be removed somehow. Its angle of slope suggests that

it would have flowed downwards to the southern corner of the square. It is probable that a north–south drain would have existed during this phase, removing the water down through room 6 and out into the street. The evidence for this is indirect as any such drain was totally removed in Phase 8b when the entire drainage system in this area was lowered to allow for the insertion of the semi-circular tank discussed below. However, another indication that there must have been one comes from another *opus signinum* drain (108/114). This drain carried waste water down under the eastern portico. At its southern end it bent round as if to meet another drain, though the precise join was lost when the original drain was removed and a new lower drain was inserted in P8b.

Wall decoration
The only walls which survived above foundation level were those of the two lower rooms excavated: Room 1 and Room 4. Within Room 7 the north and south walls were built of large limestone blocks (c. 1.10 × 0.50 × 0.50m or similar). No traces of any surface treatment were found on these. However the side wall (235) was a different matter. This was made from alternating blocks and mortared limestone rubble, so some kind of surface treatment to cover this up may have been deemed desirable. This was rendered (843). There were three holes in the rendering, but none of these suggested any particular fittings or function. In Room 5, large sheets of painted wall plaster were found to have sheared away from the walls. It is suspected, however, that these relate to the redecoration of these rooms during phase 8, to which belongs all the other stratified painted wall plaster on the site (further discussed in Chapter 7).

Other features
Only one further feature is perhaps attributable to the construction of the "public building". In the eastern half of the open square, a well [844] was constructed. In stratigraphic terms this could either date to the "public building" horizon or to P8a. Since it would seem unlikely for a cistern to have been constructed in the middle of a "public building", this has been allocated to Phase 8a.

PHASE 7C: ADAPTATIONS TO THE "PUBLIC BUILDING"
There was very little evidence for subsequent modifications to the "public building". At some stage a number of features were cut through the floor of Room 7 (Area B), which was subsequently robbed, to reveal patches of a yellow mortar rich preparation [261]. Many of these features were small post-holes, although some were larger perforations or spreads of material. None of them

exhibited any obvious shape or pattern. Chronologically, all of this could date to any time between the initial construction of the "public building" in P7ab and the disuse of the Room 7 at the end of P8c/beginning of P9 when it was backfilled with dumped material. Thus, P7c has been created to take account of the possibility that this activity took place before the re-use of the "public building" as a double courtyard house in P8 (see below).

The robbing of the floor: (283/255): [261]
Features cut into the floor: [261], [272], [277], [280], [281], [282], [284], [285] & [288]

PHASE 7–8: THE BUILDING
ON THE OTHER SIDE OF THE ROAD (AREA D AND E)
The western side of the "public building" was defined by a north–south road. On its western side lay another building, a small portion of which was excavated. This comprised an external (55/73) and an interior dividing wall (74). The room was filled up with rubble including an almost intact pottery vessel (71). It is virtually impossible to date although it clearly post-dated the laying out of the road (P7ab). Thus, although it could have been built at any time during P7 or 8, it has been placed in the latter.

PHASE 8A: DOUBLE COURTYARD BUILDING
(FIGS.3.2, 3.6, 3.8, 3.10, 3.11, 3.12, 3.13, 3.14, 3.15, 3.16, 3.17, 3.24 AND MATRICES IN W/CHAPTER 1)
The new building: reuse of the "public building"
At some stage prior to P8a the "public building" ceased to be used as such and was demolished. It was replaced by a large new building constructed within what remained, converting the site into one or two houses surrounding a pair of courtyards, one larger than the other. The new building re-used many of the elements of the "public building", but ignored many others. The extensive destruction of the uppermost levels of the site by post-Roman activity has destroyed so much of the ancient structure and linking stratigraphy, that it is not clear how much of the "public building" was incorporated into the new house. The only surviving P8 structures lie to the north of the line of the old east–west "public building" portico and impeded access to earlier "public building" levels – even though these may have been obliterated when the house was built. Down-slope to the south, levels of P8 and the preceding "public building" phase had been eroded away. Nonetheless, it seems likely that many P7a structural walls were incorporated into the new building although the original columns had been robbed away.

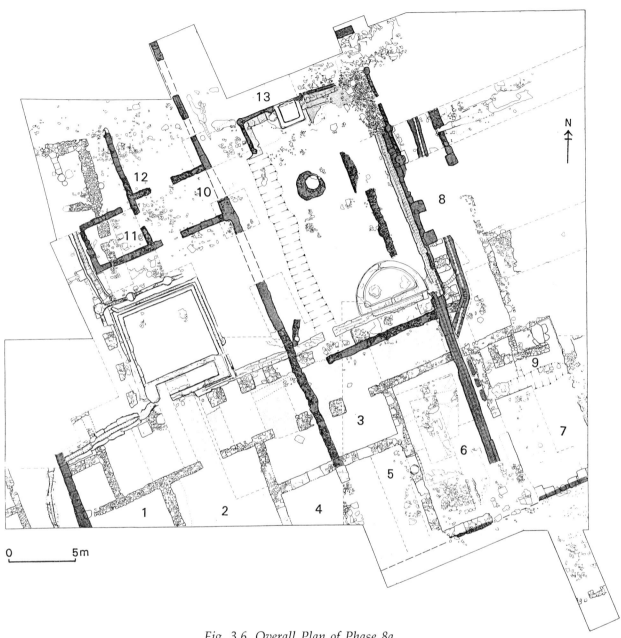

Fig. 3.6. Overall Plan of Phase 8a

Two areas of the old "public building" square remained open, while a series of rooms encroached upon the rest. This had the effect of transforming the whole area into a large eastern rectangular courtyard and a smaller western square courtyard. These two courtyards were separated by a long north–south wall, which continued the alignment of the P7a wall dividing Rooms 4 and 5 (96). This wall may have divided the block into two totally separate houses, or there may have been a passage from one side of the house to the other. No evidence for a doorway was found.

Construction techniques

The new building was made from almost anything which was to hand. There are sections made from mud brick, limestone blocks, mortared limestone fragments, bricks, and even Dressel 20 amphora sherds. There was no obvious structural rationale behind this variation in construction technique. Unlike the "public building", however, all of these walls were faced with a plaster finish to give the impression of a uniform facade.

A good example of the variable construction technique is the wall which proceeds north from the north west side of the small courtyard (383/384/385/386) at the western side of the site (Fig. 3.12). All the walls in this vicinity were c.0.50m wide. In certain places there were gaps in the walls which are probably to be interpreted as doorways. The wall plaster survived intact in many places demonstrating these walls survived well above foundation level. In no case, however, was an intact floor found – even when excavation continued below what could reasonably be expected to have been the height of the ancient floor-level. At best, floor make-up deposits were capped with a final preparation layer, even though this had subsequently been robbed away. In Area I, for example, the surviving ground level of the "public building" had been raised significantly by the dumping of layer (796) which was about 0.40m thick in places.

In the central part of the site, the main north–south dividing wall (775/773/772/[782]/381/212) was again built by using a range of construction methods, including mudbrick (773) in solid limestone block foundations (772). As in other areas, however, this wall was faced with a uniform layer of wall plaster (774). The southern stretch of this included the use of unmortared round water worn cobbles. These were never found in anything other than foundation levels for walls: a similar construction technique can be observed in the early to mid 2nd century AD Casa de la Exedra at Italica (S. Keay: personal observation). In the south of Area H, where the cobble wall started to survive to above foundation level (just before it was robbed out by trench [782]), it was capped with mortared limestone. The longest stretch of wall with a water worn cobble foundation was the new wall in the eastern area (28). Excavations here revealed that it had a narrow construction trench c.0.50m deep. At the bottom of this was a mortary layer (211), whilst above were unmortared tightly packed cobbles (28).

All of the new walls survive on the northern part of the excavation. To the south of the old "public building" colonnade, erosion has meant that none of these levels survived. It is probable that here many of the old walls remained in use. In what had been Room 7 of the "public building", the features cut into the floor may belong to this phase, though their positioning in the structural sequence is ambiguous.

New walls
Cobble wall: Area C & E: (28); Area D, E & H (212)
Limestone blocks: (386), (516), (538), (539 – with some amphorae), (775), (772)
Mudbrick: (773), (657)
Mortared limestone fragments: (384), (532), (535),
Brick: (383)
Amphora sherds: (385), (531), (533), (536), (540), (541), (542), (546)

The larger courtyard
(Areas G and H; I and J; F; Figs. 3.12, 3.14, 3.17)
The two new courtyards are the most outstanding features of this phase. The largest was in the eastern portion of the P7 "public building" square (Fig. 3.29). A line of eight columns was constructed on the east and west side of the courtyard; further columns ran along the northern side. Column spacing was precise and along the middle of the eastern side provided a gap for an entrance into the open courtyard. By contrast there was no evidence for columns along the south side and instead a plain wall (28) marked the edge of the courtyard.

The eastern side of the portico had the potential of reusing some of the "public building" column foundations, and it seems likely that for the first four columns this was indeed the case. Where both layers remained intact, a new P8a sub-plinth (715) was placed on top of the old "public building" foundation (680), and one can presume that similar sub-plinths once existed on the other two foundations (217) and (140) (Area C). The columns themselves remained intact in a number of places, though some had been robbed out, including many of those along the western colonnade. Most were made of stone, although one was made of mud-brick (722) (Fig. 3.24). It is just possible that this mud-brick column may have been a later replacement, though there was no evidence for repair to the screen between this and the columns to the north and south.

Screens were erected between the columns and, in the main, they were made from mortared limestone fragments with stucco facing. There were usually several layers of stucco facing moulded over both these and the columns themselves.

Colonnade
Colonnade foundation (clockwise): Area G: (790), (827), (826), (825), (824), (829), (830)
New limestone plinths for new columns: Area F: (639), (742), (716) & (715)
Colonnade columns (clockwise): Area G: (845), (750), (753), (829); Area F: (666), '668', (744), (722)
Screens between the columns: Area G: mortared *limestone:* (709), (759/760),(667), (669), (743); stone (821)
Stucco on screens: Area G: (819), (820), (710); Area F: (636), (637), (661)

The portico itself was covered with a tile roof. Much of this was to collapse in P9. However in the north-east corner of the portico (Area F) a different kind of rubble was found from the P9 abandonment. Here, large chunks of *opus signinum* ceiling (658) had collapsed onto a stone floor (659), suggesting that the house may have had an upper storey (further mentioned in Chapter 9).

Little excavation took place to the east of the

portico, although that which did revealed a new doorway with a new threshold stone (613), and a series of new tangential walls running off to the east (603), (606) & (607). These were not excavated, so that little form or structure can be made of them beyond noting that like nearly every other wall of this phase, they too were faced with painted wall plaster. Within the eastern portico, the north–south drain originally constructed for the "public building" (P7a) remained in use. This is assumed because it was certainly functioning in P8b when its outflow was altered in a series of changes necessitated by the insertion of a new semi-circular pool.

Portico
New doorway/threshold stone through wall (606): (613)
New tangential walls to (606, 613): (603), (606), (607)
Collapsed Ceiling: (658)
Stone floor: (659)
Eastern portico drain (continuing in use): Areas C & F: (631/108/114)

There were a number of features of note within the courtyard, including the cistern (see below) and the two stretches of 'wall-footings' (737) and (746). The latter ran parallel to the long side of the courtyard and only survived to the thickness of one course. They could not be related to anything else in terms of structure or form. They must predate P8b as (746) was cut by the construction of the semi-circular tank. They could just belong to P7c, representing late activity within the "public building" square, or they could represent an early feature within the courtyard.

Features within the courtyard
Two walls within the courtyard: (737) & (746)
Opus signinum surface appearing in the cistern section, possibly the original surface of the courtyard: (730)

The most distinctive feature of this new building, particularly in P8b when it was enhanced, was its provision for water. The first facility was a drain, which has been detected running down the eastern side of the courtyard. Presumably this carried rainwater run-off from the roof of the eastern courtyard. It had a stone foundation (670/725/673), stretches of which may have been part of the original "public building" portico eaves gully. The drain was sealed by an *opus signinum* lining (671), while further layers point to its continued use during this and subsequent phases (P8b and 8c). Water carried by the drain followed the incline of the hill-slope down to the south-east corner of the courtyard to the same point where water had been drained away from the square of the original P7b "public building". It is believed that the same outflow drain functioned in this phase: however it does not survive since it was replaced in P8b. Thus, water from the courtyard would have joined

that from the portico drain (631/108/114) and would have exited downhill through Room 6.

Provision also needed to be made for rainwater that would have accumulated in the courtyard after heavy autumn, winter and spring rainstorms. A large cistern [844] in the middle of the courtyard would have fulfilled this function and, presumably, stored water. It had a narrow neck that opened into a bell-shape and was at least 1.50m deep. Unfortunately it was not possible to reach bottom and calculate its full capacity since the excavation proved hazardous. Nevertheless, it was clear that it had a reasonably long life: it went through two main phases of construction and had several facings. The first construction phase could be related to P8a and the second to P8b when the floor level was raised by about 30cm. At the top of the first phase cistern linings (731/726) were traces of an *opus signinum* floor, sealed by the later raising of the top of the cistern. It is thought that this may be the only remaining trace of the original P8a flooring of the courtyard square. If this is the case, then relative levels would suggest that water from the interior of the courtyard would slope down a gentle gradient into the top of the cistern, hence its interpretation as a cistern rather than a well.

Water features
Courtyard Drain on the inside of the courtyard: formed by an *opus signinum* lining (671) on top of a line of stones (673) and the colonnade foundation (670) & (725), end based on foundations (30) & (34).
Cistern: Cut [844], first cistern lining (731) & (726).

The smaller courtyard (Area I and J, Fig. 3.12)
The smaller courtyard was relatively unadorned (Fig. 3.33). No columns or water features can be allocated to this phase. All that survives is the slight trace of a plain tessellated pavement running north–south down the centre of the square. This was sealed beneath the P8b open gully.

Interior features of the small courtyard
Tessellated pavement in small courtyard: (835)

Wall decoration
One of the most visible differences between P7 and 8 was the use of painted wall plaster. On virtually every wall traces of wall plaster survived and all of it was painted. This is discussed separately in Chapter 7.

In situ wall plaster given context numbers
(534) Area J&H: On south side of wall (533/532/531), multiple layers, almost 0.05m thick
(537) Area J: South side of wall (538/536/535)
(654) Area F: South side of wall (657)
(656) Area F: East side of wall (657)
(657) Area F: North side of wall (657)

(771) Area H: North face of wall (546)

(774) Area H: East face of wall (775/772)

(836) Area J: North face of wall (536) & west face of wall (540)

Dumps including lots of wall plaster from abandonment P 9, but deriving from 8a or b:
(99), (100), (121), (136), (711), (794), (795), (833), (789)

PHASE 8B: ADDITION OF WATER FEATURES
TO BOTH COURTYARDS
(FIGS.3.2, 3.7, 3.8, 3.10, 3.11, 3.12, 3.13, 3.14, 3.15, 3.16, 3.17, 3.24 AND MATRICES IN W/CHAPTER 1).

The Principal Changes
The building was refurbished in P8b. The main changes entailed a radical alteration in the use and

movement of water in both courtyards. In the eastern one, the cistern was altered and two tanks, or pools, were added: one took the form of a small square and the other that of a larger semi-circle. These additions involved major changes in the waste-water outflow from the square (from which the chronology of these separate features can be established). In the smaller courtyard a rectangular pool was added, and the entire courtyard was surrounded by an open water-course, and colonnade with screens (just as the larger courtyard had been decorated in P8a).

The large courtyard (Areas G and H; F)
The greatest changes took place in the large rectangular courtyard. The mouth of the cistern

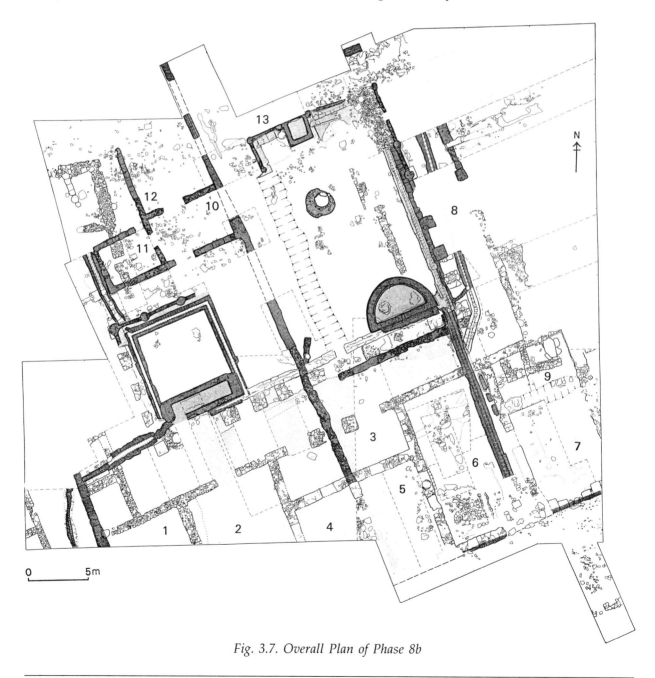

Fig. 3.7. Overall Plan of Phase 8b

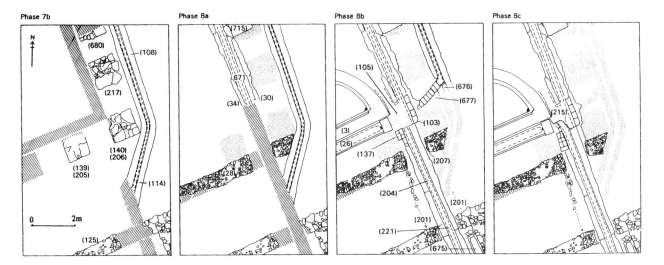

Fig. 3.8. Detail of the Development of Drain Area

[728] was raised, a square (703) and semi-circular (3) pool were added and various repairs carried out.

(a)   In P8a the cistern probably collected water draining from the courtyard. In P8b the original courtyard surface was raised about 30cm (728) and a new surface was laid (818). Also entering the cistern now was the U-shaped profile of a gully, lined with *opus signinum* (733). This entered from the side of the cistern facing the SW corner of the courtyard. The gully itself was not excavated, but the presence of another feature (312) on a direct alignment with this in the south-west corner of the courtyard (Fig. 3.13) suggested that it carried water. This comprised a short stretch of concrete, within which were set the traces of a narrow pipe and a large oval depression. The interpretation of this is not obvious. However, since the alignment of the two was related and the concrete was at a higher level than the cistern, it seems likely that rainwater flowed from this feature into the cistern. The main problem with this interpretation is that the diameter of the pipe would have been insufficient to carry much storm water. An alternative is that the pipe carried water under pressure, pumped up from the cistern, to service the water shoot in front of the semi-circular pool (discussed below). However, this fails to explain the size or function of the *opus signinum* drain running into the cistern.

Cistern and related features
New opus signinum *drain entering it from the south:* Cut [736], foundation (735), *opus signinum* (733)
Feature in south-west corner of courtyard including a pipe on alignment with drain (733): (312)

Levelling up to new courtyard level in vicinity of cistern: (728)

(b)   On the north side of the square a small square tank, or pool, lined with *opus signinum* was added: it measured 2.00 × 2.00m on the outside, 1.28 × 1.28m on the interior and was 0.37m deep (703) (Fig. 3.32). Like each of the three pools added during this phase, the interior corners at the base and the sides had quarter circle bevels. The pool was inserted slightly clumsily between two P8a columns and was not perfectly aligned or central to the courtyard. All of this suggests that this pool was a secondary addition. There were no traces of a water supply for the pool, which probably lay in the unexcavated area to the north. However, there was an outflow hole about half-way along its eastern side. Water would have flowed through this onto the *opus signinum* surface of the courtyard square (818) and eastwards to join the P8a north–south drain (673), which was relined during this phase (672). The flow was contained between the stone footing of the east–west wall and a small *opus signinum* ridge running east–west. The new *opus signinum* surface of the square (818) and its make-up deposit (832), only survived as a small patch at the north end of the courtyard. Its gentle slope ensured that it drained rainwater within the courtyard to its edge, joined the waste water from the square pool, and that together it all flowed clockwise round the courtyard in the north–south drain (673). There were traces of another floor to the west of the pool (823) at a higher level. Because the two surfaces did not join up it was impossible to tell how water flowed around this area of the courtyard. One further water feature could be seen in this area. There was a small slot for a pipe in the floor (818) heading down south to the semi-circular pool (3). This is mentioned below.

Square water tank: (703)
New lining of inner courtyard drain: (672)
Interior courtyard surface, east of square water tank, with moulded ridges on the north edge: (818)
Levelling up to new courtyard level in vicinity of (818): (832)
Interior courtyard surface, west of square water tank: (823)

(c)   In the south-east corner of the courtyard a second pool was added (3) (Fig. 3.31). This was semi-circular in shape with quarter-circle bevels on all edges, and was larger and deeper than the first pool (703). In its western corner of the pool two steps were provided in order to allow entry; this may have facilitated periodic maintenance or might suggest that it was perhaps used as a plunge-bath. There were two possible traces of a water supply to the pool. In the centre on both the northern and southern side there had been some robbing in P9, presumably to remove lead fittings which have now disappeared: '229' and '227'. In both cases the robbing had cut significantly into the wall of the pool. Heading towards the northern fitting '227' were traces of a pipe in the courtyard floor heading from the square pool (703) on the northern side of the square. The height difference between the bottom of the square (703) and the semi-circular pools (3) was sufficient to allow water to flow from the former to the latter; indeed the two may represent fittings for fountains, though this is only speculative. On the other hand, the cistern (731) in the middle of the courtyard may have been the water source. A definitive answer is difficult in light of the fact that most of the *opus signinum* surface of the courtyard had been robbed out together with traces of other possible pipes. The out-flow from the pool (3) ran into the south-east corner of the courtyard.

(d)   To the south of the pool (3) was a higher level sloping trough running west to east. This would have provided a continuous stream of water and might possibly have acted as an overspill for the pool. It is also possible that it may have been fed by a lead fitting. The evidence comprises a small cutting [118] into the earlier limestone wall (25), as if to take a pipe, and the robbing of the western side of the feature where such a lead pipe would have entered [678]. Again the waste water from this would have flowed out into the south-east corner of the courtyard.

Semi-circular pool: construction trenches [18] & [47]; construction trench fills (19) & (46); pool (3)

Pipe on southern side of pool: '229' robbed in action [228]
Pipe on northern side of pool: '227' robbed out in action [226]
Pipe to trough on south side of pool: cut [118] into limestone blocks (25), then robbed out in action [678]

(e)   Elsewhere within the courtyard a number of small repairs were undertaken. At some stage, a stretch of the inter-columnar screens on the northern side collapsed and was replaced. It is possible, but not certain, that the original columns were stone-cut; in any event one of the new columns was made from mud-brick (722). In addition, several layers of stucco could be found on most of the screens, suggesting that some redecoration may have taken place during this phase. Finally, a small hole was cut into one of the screens [665] for no obvious purpose.

Repair to screen (759/760): New screen (751), new wall plaster facing (752)
A hole cut into screen (639): [665]
Note: mudbrick column (722) may be a replacement from this phase and some of the P8b layers of stucco may come from redecoration during this phase.

Waste water from the large courtyard
(Area C, Figs. 3.8, 3.10)
The waste water from the square pool and rainwater from the courtyard was channelled into the north–south drain (673) on the east side of the courtyard and, hence, down to the south-eastern corner. Here in P8a it had met with the colonnade drain (108/114/631) and their joint waters flowed southwards through Room 6 and out of the building. The south-east corner of the courtyard also acted as the collection point of waste water from the semi-circular pool and the water shoot on its south side, and from the *opus signinum* floor of the square itself.

It would have been possible for the original drain running down through Room 6 to have remained intact if the semi-circular pool had not been added. However, since the plug-hole for this was much lower than the existing drain, the original outflow drain for all the waste water from the building had to be lowered. The original drain was removed, a deeper trench excavated [201/157/189] and the new drain was inserted (204/221/191). The capacity of this new drain is uncertain as its walls were robbed in antiquity. To the north only its "U" shaped *opus signinum* base survived. Further down to the south a few tiles survived on either side of the drain, suggesting that it had tile "walls". These survived to two courses at one point, suggesting that the drain measured at least 0.22m deep by 0.15m wide. When the new drain was installed, three large limestone blocks were inserted into the side of the construction trench (675). Close inspection of these revealed that they were re-used drain mouldings from the run-off drain (25) of the P7 "public building" colonnade. Presumably they were removed when the semi-circular pool (3) was constructed.

As the trench for the new drain (204) leading south from the semi-circular pool (3) was cut, it severed the line of the old north–south portico drain (108/114/631). This was now altered to curve round between two of the old "public building" column foundations, and to dip down to the new lower level with a new extension (677). The water flow along the old drain line was blocked off by the insertion of a tile (676). At its new low level it was joined by waste water from the pool (3) and the trough (26) at a nodal point beneath the *opus signinum* flooring of the courtyard (105). The upper surface of the same floor acted as a catchment for the water from the courtyard gully and the courtyard surface itself, which then cascaded down into the lowed drain (204/221/191). The detail of this junction of five water-sources is complicated, but clearly demonstrates which water features were contemporaneous that they went out of use at different stages (i.e. P8c).

Water sources joining in Area C:
1. Water from the N–S drain down the east side of the courtyard: Stone foundation (34) & (36), lining (672)
2. Water from reused *opus signinum* drain down eastern portico: (108/114/631) now blocked off by (676) and redirected down (677)
3. Semi-circular plunge-bath: (3)
4. Water shoot on the front of the plunge-bath: (26)
5. Water from off the *opus signinum* flooring of the square: (105)

New lower drain through Room 3 in Area A
Construction trench of drain: [189], [157] & [201]
Opus signinum *drain:* (191)

The smaller courtyard
(Area I and J, Fig. 3.12)
The smaller courtyard on the western side of the site also underwent significant changes. In P8a there had only been evidence for a tessellated pavement running from north to south through an otherwise empty yard. In P8b, however, a small square area was defined by columns and linked by screens at its south end. This was enhanced by the provision of a channel to carry water on the north, west and east sides and a long rectangular pool to the south.

A. These new water features were fed by a new *opus signinum* channel (393), which ran parallel to the P8a wall (383, 384, 385, 386) to intersect with the north-west corner of the garden. The insertion of this channel was clearly secondary in the construction process, as can be demonstrated by traces of the points of contact on the wall. Moreover, the existence of a construction trench [803] showed it had not been in position when the new floor level (796) was laid down. At some stage between these adaptations and the original construction, an area to the west of the wall (383, 384, 385, 386) exhibited traces of burning (389) as well as small features that were cut into the original ground level. At the same time a new mortar-rich surface was also laid down (800 & 502). This was fairly level and was presumably the preparation for a floor that has since been robbed away.

Water supply feeding the water feature (Area I and J)
Opus signinum *drain:* construction trench [803]; *opus signinum* (393); construction trench fill (797)

B. The channel described above fed a square enclosure which has been identified as a small formal garden and which was defined on three sides by an open water channel. Nothing is known about the arrangement of its interior on account of later robbing. The construction of this feature necessitated cutting [373] through three earlier column bases to the west (368), (369), (346) and the addition of a colonnade with linking screen along the northern side. At its north-western corner, the foundation of one of the P7 "public building" columns (809) was reused with the addition of a solid limestone block (808) and column base (367). Further to the east, the adjacent column (525) was intact, whereas only the impression in *opus signinum* '524' of its neighbour remained. Linking screens about 0.15m wide were built between these columns. They comprised mortared limestone fragments (807, 396) coated with multiple layers of rendering (503, 811), sometimes as many as five. Their full height is difficult to estimate although at the least they were higher than the top of the column bases.

C. There is no evidence for the re-use of any of the P7 column foundations on the southern side of the courtyard during this phase. One of them (320) hardly survived at all, though the damage here could have occurred at a later date. However, this does not rule out the possible existence of smaller and more ephemeral columns with screens akin to those on the northern side of the courtyard; unfortunately, later robbing removed everything here down to the level of P7 foundations.

New colonnade and water feature (Area I and J)
Construction trench: [373]
Columns: (367), (525), '524'
Screens between columns: (807), (396)
Stucco on screens: (503), (811)

D.   At the south end of the formal garden was a rectangular pool (300), which undoubtedly acted as its focus. Its southern side abutted the limestone eaves drip (301) of the old P7 "public building", while the upper face of the drip was lined with *opus signinum* and acted as the south stretch of the open channel which surrounded the other three sides of the garden.

Rectangular pool (Area D&E)
Rectangular pool: (300)

E.   The water was drained out of the complex via a tripartite drain. First, a lead pipe (376) set in concrete (359) took the water out underneath the portico. The lead pipe had been robbed out, but its impression remained. This indicated that it had a diameter of c. 0.18–0.20m and slotted into a collar with a bevel of 15mm. After passing beneath the portico, the pipe joined drain (360), a deep U shaped channel, until it passed under wall (351) and into another more rectangular channel (355), where there was evidence for a tile covering. At this point the entire channel was 0.60m deep and 0.40m wide. It then passed beneath the external wall of the building (52) and out into a purpose built drain (54) running down the street. Beneath wall (52) there was a 0.30m remaining stretch of lead pipe (376), robbed in antiquity [377]: it was c.0.20cm diameter and c.8mm thick. In the street, the drain (54) measured c.30cm wide and 0.35–0.40cm deep, had a tile covering (57) and was set in a construction trench [58].

Outflow drain from pool
Lead pipe (376) set in concrete (359), joining drain (360), and then channel (355) after which it passes out under wall (52) into street drain (54); this has a construction trench [58], drain walls (54), construction trench fill (59) and tile covers (57).

PHASE 8C: REFURBISHMENT
(FIG. 3.2, 3.7, 3.8, 3.10 AND MATRICES IN W/CHAPTER 1)

Drainage Problems
(Area C)
Five sources of waste-water coincided in the south-east corner of the larger courtyard. At times, the volume of water may have exceeded the system's capacity to drain it away and caused it to back up into the courtyard and cause localised flooding. It may have been in recognition of this, or perhaps because of changes elsewhere, that one of these water sources was taken out of use. The drain (631/108/677) which passed down the north–south corridor on the eastern side of the courtyard was blocked off at the junction with the other outlets by a wall of tiles (215). In order to bring this about, the *opus signinum* floor of the upper

level drain had to be cut away here [126]. At around the same time, the drain was filled in (632). Similarly, at this time or later, a white mortar surface (664) was laid over the floor of the corridor above this now decommissioned drain; this had the effect of sealing it at points where the tile covering had been removed.

Opening of opus signinum *floor (105) to facilitate repairs to drainage system:* [126]
Blocking off of drain (677): (215)
Filling of disused drain (677): (632)
White mortar layer sealing drain (631) (without drain cover): (664)
Drain (631) fill: (632)

Refurbishment of the Pools and Water Features
(Areas C, D and E, G and H, I and J)
(Fig. 3.2, 3.7, 3.10, 3.12, 3.15, 3.17 and matrices in W/Chapter 1)
The square, rectangular and semi-circular pools, or tanks, were all relined. The top surface of that on the semi-circular pool survived intact in a number of places (2) to reveal a red painted surface. This was not the only refurbishment to have taken place and many of the other water features were re-lined or repaired. For example, the *opus signinum* lined water channel on the south side of the rectangular pool was resurfaced (302). The most extensive alterations took place on the water channel that fed the north-west corner of the formal square garden. First, its junction (393) with the garden was reconstructed at some point [810]. Secondly, the *opus-signinum* water-feed was entirely re-lined with tiles and a new series of tile covers placed on it (mortar 802, tile-lining 801, covers 394). As far as the garden enclosure itself was concerned, the original inter-columnar screen (834) was repaired at about this time, but with a core of tile (396) rather than limestone rubble, a difference which was masked by a new layer of rendering (397).

Area G
Relining of the square water tank (703): (822)
Area C
Relining of the semi-circular pool (3): (2)
Area E
Relining of opus signinum *drain (303):* (302)
Repair at the point where the water feed (393) enters the small courtyard water feature: Repair cut [810];
New replacement screen (396); New rendering (397)
The water feed was also relined with tiles: tile-lining (801), retained by mortar (802), sealed by tile covers (394)

PHASE 9: ROBBING
After the P8 buildings fell down or were demolished, rubble accumulated and the walls were then

robbed systematically. This ensured that very little survived above foundation levels. Evidence for this process is now discussed area by area.

Area A
(Fig. 3.2, 3.10, 3.17 and matrices in W/Chapter 1)
The main drain which removed waste water from the eastern side of the building filled up with sediment and was then systematically robbed. Its floor was made from *opus signinum*, while its walls were of mortared tiles which could easily be removed intact. As a result virtually all of them had been removed in antiquity.

Drain fill: (194)
Robber trenches: [195] [155]
Robber trench fills: (154), (181) & (196)

Area B
(Fig. 3.2, 3.16, 3.19, 3.23 and matrices
in W/Chapter 1)
The lower level Room 7 was filled up with different kinds of debris. First, the doorway was blocked with reused column drums and other rubble (Figs.3.19 and 3.34). Then, a range of material was tipped down into the room from its northern side, suggesting there was no wall of any height at this stage between Rooms 9 and 7; the tip lines were clearly visible (Fig. 3.18). The main bulk of this dump was quite uniform, although the top-most levels included major concentrations of pottery, tile and *opus spicatum*. Elsewhere, there was systematic wall-robbing. Thus, robber trench [297] is a record of the removal of the upper levels of wall (841). There was similar activity with robber trench [269] and wall (267), as well as at other stretches of wall in the area.

The aim of demolishing these standing walls and backfilling the deep room may have been part of a broader project to create a level surface for a new building. But if this was the case, erosion and deep ploughing has removed any surviving evidence.

Column blocking the SE "public building" entrance: (258)
Lower room in-fill: (247), (252), (253), (254), (264), (265), (553), (554), (555), (556), (557), (558)
Upper room fills: Rubble (248), *Opus spicatum* (246), Pottery & brick (245)
Robber trenches: [297], [269]

Area C
(Fig. 3.2, 3.10, 3.17 and matrices in W/Chapter 1)
The semi-circular pool had been fitted with a number of lead water pipes, all of which were robbed out [678], [226] and [228] during this phase. The absence of *opus signinum* in most of the courtyard floor is witness to the thoroughness of

the ancient robbing. Indeed, its presence in this area can only be inferred from a jagged offset running around the curved base of the semi-circular pool [106], which marked the point of breakage during robbing (visible in Fig. 3.31), as well as the broken "edge" [43] where the courtyard floor had been cut away from the lining of the drains in the south-east corner.

Robbing out of lead fittings: [226], [228] & [678]
Robbing of opus signinum *floors:* [43] & [106]

Area D
(Fig. 3.2, 3.15 and matrices in W/Chapter 1;
see also Chapter 7)
The lower level Rooms 4 and 5 opening onto the southern street had been faced with painted wall-plaster, presumably in P8a or b. At some stage this sheered off the wall in large sheets (99), and the rest of the room was filled with a rich reddish matrix, possibly melted mud-brick, mixed with substantial quantities of more fragmentary painted wall plaster; possibly (though not definitely) from the same room. Further west the western wall of the P7/8 buildings was robbed, and the drain running down through the street silted up.

Wall plaster sheering off walls in Room 4: (99)
Fill of road drain: (56)
Robbing of western wall of the "public building" (52): [76]

Area E
(Fig. 3.2, 3.15 and matrices in W/Chapter 1)
In the vicinity of the small square courtyard all the watercourses filled up with sediments (500, 354, 372 & 332) and various rubble deposits spread over the area (504 & 350). The lead pipes which had taken water away from the rectangular pool were robbed out [377].

Drain fills: (332), (354), (372) & (500)
Rubble deposits: (350) & (504)
Robbing of lead pipes: [377]

Area F
(Fig. 3.2, 3.14, 3.17 and matrices in W/Chapter 1)
An area was excavated to the east of the main N–S portico and semi-circular pool. It rapidly became clear, however, that the inner courtyard drain became filled up with sediment. Apart from this, many other areas were less well understood, largely because the excavation only reached the surface of the archaeological strata by the time the final season of excavation drew to a close. One of the structures revealed was a stone rubble layer against wall (604). This is probably best interpreted as the collapse of the wall during phase 9. To the east of this were uncovered layers containing wall plaster out of its original context,

which were again suggestive of a Phase 9 abandonment or demolition deposit.

A second and narrower extension was excavated eastwards half-way up the line of the eastern portico. Shortage of time meant that there was time to do little more than remove unstratified material and define the uppermost surface features. However, several robber cuts were distinguished. Of these, [617] seems to cut the wall (606), and [619] cuts through the mortar surface (616).

The portico itself eventually collapsed, probably through decay and collapse rather than systematic demolition. It fell down leaving rubble deposits, such as (614), on the inside of the portico, and extensive tile-rich debris on the inside of the courtyard (723, 741 etc.). A similar process is suggested for the ceiling in the north-eastern corner of the portico. Here, large fragments of *opus signinum* (658) had collapsed directly onto a stone floor (659), with only a small deposit (660) accumulating beforehand.

Superficial deposits in extension east of semi-circular pool and portico: (600), (601), (641), (609), (623) & (624)
Robber trenches in second eastern extension: [617], [619]
Rubble deposits from the collapse of the portico: (614), (723), (741)
Collapsed opus signinum *ceiling:* (658)
Filling of inner courtyard drain (672): (749)

Area G
(Fig. 3.2, 3.14, 3.17 and matrices in W/Chapter 1)
Within the courtyard the cistern went out of use. Limestone blocks from standing structures were robbed out and the cistern and associated drain were filled in. Much of the interior of the courtyard was covered by rubble which derived from the collapse of the portico. It mainly comprised tiles, and was densest along the line of the portico on the eastern side of the courtyard (723, 833, 744, 741). Within the rubble was a column drum with a stucco facing (813 on 812), possibly from the colonnade. By the square pool was the lower half of an amphora, possibly a Type 20/Dressel 20 (755). It is possible that this relates to the use of the courtyard, rather than its abandonment.

The western side of the courtyard, however, did not gradually decay and collapse, it was deliberately demolished. The entire portico was systematically robbed away [708] and no traces of rubble from the collapse of the portico remained.

Cistern robbing [732] and fills (758), (757), (756), (727), & silting up of drain (733) which ran into it: (734)
Tile rubble from the collapse of the colonnade: (723), (833), (744), (741);
Column out of situ: drum (813), stucco facing (812)
Amphora: (755)

Robber trenches:
1. *The western colonnade:* [708]
2. *The area in front of the cistern, possibly looking for lead:* [706]
3. *Floor level (818):* [679]

Area H
(Fig. 3.2, 3.12, 3.17 and matrices in W/Chapter 1)
A large proportion of the main north–south dividing wall was robbed away, as was the adjacent portico (discussed under Area G).

Robber trenches: i.e. western portico wall [782]; western colonnade [708]

Area I
(Fig. 3.2, 3.12 and matrices in W/Chapter 1)
The drains filled up (500, 395) and rubble layers covered various areas (798, 799, 504). The painted wall plaster on some of the walls sheared off. For example, wall (536) had painted wall plaster on its southern face (537). This slumped to create a dump at the base of the wall (795), which contained other forms of rubble including an out of situ column drum, probably of the type which had graced the northern side of the square water feature.

Drain fills: (500) & (395)
Rubble layers: (798), (799), (504)

Area J
(Fig. 3.2, 3.12 and matrices in W/Chapter 1)
Wall plaster started to shear off the walls, giving rise to dumps of wall plaster itself and other wall detritus. Thus, feature (547) was a dump of tiles, while (520) and (521) were two column drums out of situ, and (794), (795) and (545) were piles of wall plaster. The interior of one room was excavated, revealing fills (762) and (788), within which were a couple of amphorae; one of these was largely intact (792, fill 793; Fig. W/Chapter 2.86.4).

Dump of tiles: (547)
Out of situ column drums: (520), (521)
Dumps of wall plaster: (794), (795), (545)
Room fills: (762), (788) including amphora (792, fill 793)

PHASE 10: LATE STRUCTURE
(FIG. 3.2, 3.9, 3.12, 3.35 AND MATRICES IN W/CHAPTER 1)
Part of a dry stone wall building was found in the north-west corner of the site. It was built from material robbed from earlier buildings, including dressed stone and column segments. Its alignment was totally different to any other structure on the site and could only have been constructed after all the walls in the vicinity from Phase 8 had been demolished.

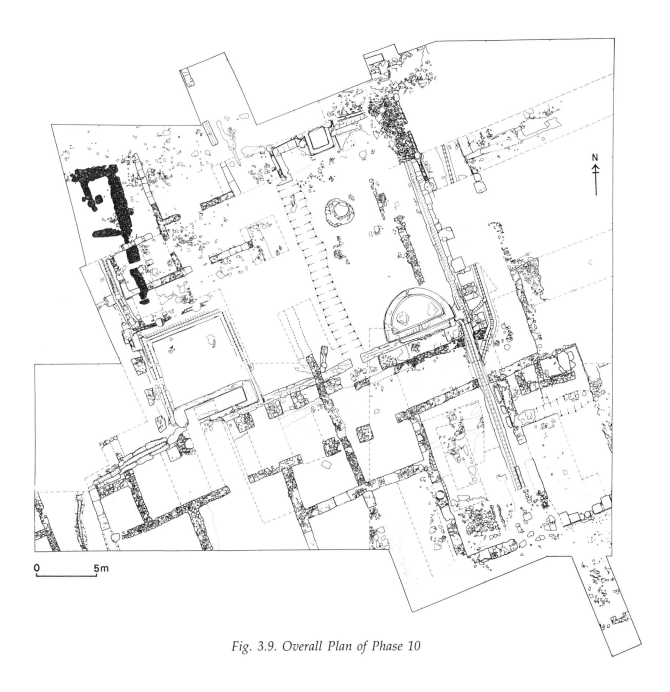

Fig. 3.9. Overall Plan of Phase 10

The plan of this building was only partially recovered. It comprised several blocks of walling constructed from limestone rubble (838, 837, 514, 839, 549), one post-hole with post packing, and a solid wall constructed of re-used rectangular limestone blocks, terminating in a couple of re-used column drums (548). If there were any other structures of the same date elsewhere north of the East–West "public building" portico it is expected that evidence for them would have survived, so the absence here of anything is possibly real. However the absence of any structures to the south of this line could be misleading since all later layers, including those of P8, have

been eroded away by colluviation aggravated by ploughing.

Late building structural elements:
Building constructed from limestone rubble: (838), (837), (514), (839), (549)
Posthole with post packing: (840)
Reused column drum: (548)

PHASE 11: MODERN ACTIVITY
There were some traces of modern activity on site:

Area B (Fig. 3.2 and matrices in W/Chapter 1)
Some of the robbing on the site took place much more recently than Phase 9. Several holes could

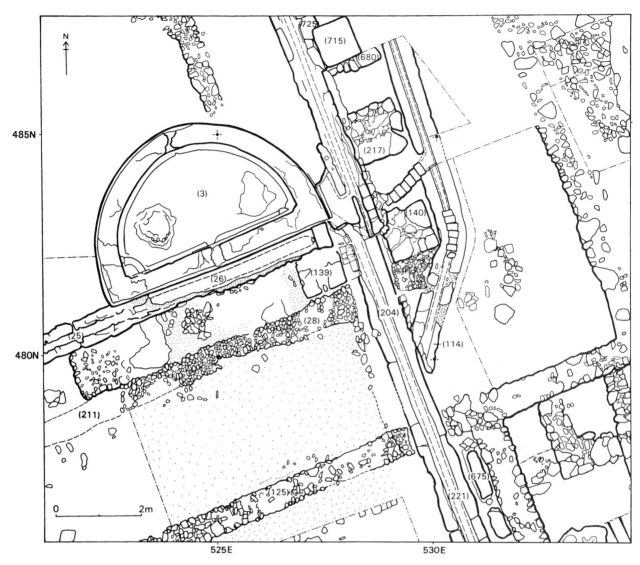

Fig. 3.10. Detail 1of Site Plan Area C with layer numbers

be seen cutting down from very high up, down to the SE entrance which was constructed of very large limestone blocks.

Robber trenches: [77], [78], [79]

Area C (Figs. 3.2, 3.10 and matrices in W/Chapter 1)
The semi-circular pool remained upstanding right up until the beginning of the excavation. It was found to have been filled with modern rubbish, including barbed wire. At the base of the pool had been cut a deep hole unrelated to any obvious robbing activity. This was also filled with modern barbed wire.

Hole cut into the bottom of the semi-circular pool: [42]

Areas D & G (Figs. 3.2, 3.13, 3.15 and Matrices in W/Chapter 1)
Across the site the remains of two live tree holes

were also found, demonstrated by roots remaining in situ.

Area D: Olive tree hole: (51)
Area G: Olive tree growing in cistern [844]: hole [713], fill and roots (714)

Phase 12: Superficial layers
Phase 12 was the number given to all the uppermost strata on the excavation, and most were largely surface layers disturbed by modern agriculture.

Area A: (11), (13), (38), (45), (152), (153), (180), (412)
Area B: (5), (145), (146), (236) & (295)
Area C: (11), (15), (21), (24), (37), (200) & (605)
Area D: (11), (12), (14), (50), (306), (322), (325), (326), (331), (343), (349)
Area E: (305), (306), (307), (322), (323), (326), (349), (364), (382)
Area F: (602), (605), (628), (651)
Area G: (628), (700), (763), (766)

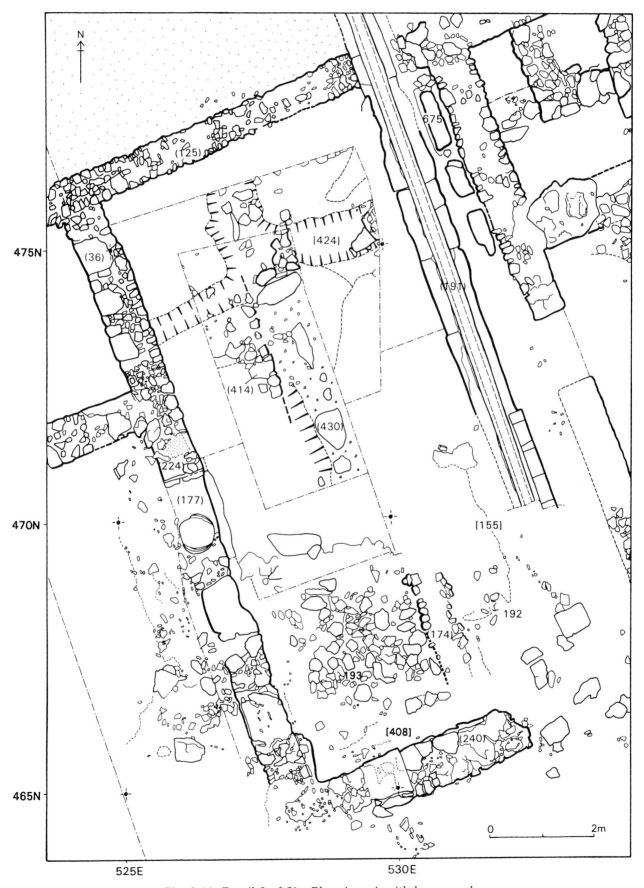

Fig. 3.11. Detail 2 of Site Plan Area A with layer numbers

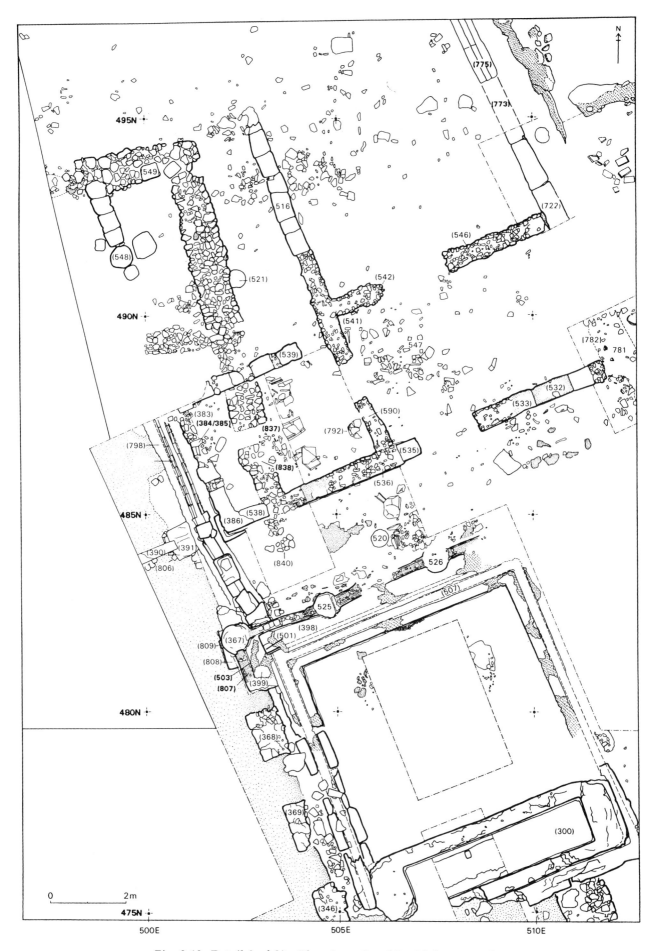

N

495N

(549)

(548)

516

(521)

490N

(542)

(541)

(539)

547

(775)

(773)

(722)

(546)

(782)

781

(533)

(532)

(383)

(384/385)

(837)

(838)

(798)

(386)

(538)

(840)

(390) (391)

(806)

(809) (367)

(808)

(503)

(807) (399)

480N

(368)

(369)

(590)

(792)

(535)

(536)

520

526

525

(501) (398)

(507)

(300)

(346)

485N

0   2m

475N

500E   505E   510E

Fig. 3.12. Detail 3 of Site Plan Areas I and J with layer numbers

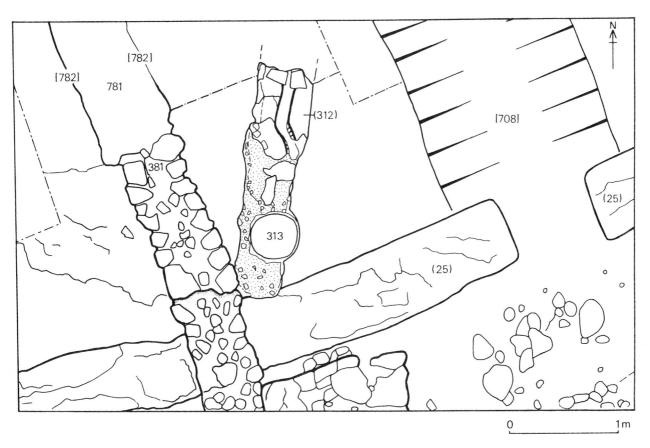

Fig. 3.13. Detail 4 of Site Plan within Area G and H with layer numbers

Area H: (11), (12), (15), (16), (22), (27), (305), (315), (718), (761), (765), (767), (768), (778)
Area I: (366), (382) & (530)
Area J: (513), (515), (517), (518), (530), (545)

3.3 Dating of the Site Phases

The Dating of the Structural Phases (SK)

The site was initially phased on the basis of the stratigraphic evidence. Once this had been established, the ceramics were used to assign chronological dates to each of the phases. This was not an easy task, given that there was a very high degree of residuality amongst the material (Figs. 3.25 and 3.26). Coins and other metalwork had little value as chronological indicators. The pro posed dating of the structural phases is presented below. It is based upon an analysis of all relevant ceramics and small finds. It will be noted that there is reference to the detailed and the general quantification. The former corresponds to those layers whose pottery was quantified in terms of EVEs (see W/Chapter 2) and counts/weights (see Appendices 1 and 2: generally, see W/Chapter 2). The

latter, by contrast, refers to all other layers at the site: these were smaller or less well dated deposits and were the subject of a less detailed analysis (see W/Chapter 2). In both cases, specific classes of ceramic were referred to in abbreviated form:

TSI: Terra Sigillata Italica
TSI Local: Local Terra Sigillata Italica
TSH: Terra Sigillata Hispanica
TSSG: South Gaulish Terra Sigillata
TSCLA: Terra Sigillata Clara A (African Red Slip Ware)
TSCLC: Terra Sigillata Clara C (African Red Slip Ware)
TSCLD: Terra Sigillata Clara D (African Red Slip Ware)
ACW: African Cooking Ware (Cerámica Cocina Africana)
ACW Imit: Local African Cooking Ware (Cerámica Cocina Africana)

The layers in which the pottery was found was signified by a number or numbers in brackets: thus (419), or (419, 420 and 421).

Phase 1
There were no finds from this Phase which, on

Fig. 3.14. Detail 5 of Site Plan Area F with layer numbers

stratigraphic evidence, must date to some time before Phase 2.

PHASE 2
The detailed pottery quantification (W/Chapter 2) revealed the presence of Cerámica Bruñida Type 6 (414) and particularly Type 11 (432), which suggests that this phase may date to the pre-Tartessian Late Bronze Age (Bronce Final) of the 9th to the beginning of the 8th century BC. No intrusive Roman material was discovered amongst the ceramics from any of the contexts assigned to this phase.

PHASE 3
The detailed pottery quantification (W/Chapter

2), revealed the presence of Cerámica Bruñida Types 1, 6 (428) and 14 (433). In addition, there was one EVE of Cerámica Fina Iberica Type 9 (433). This suggests that this phase may date to the Orientalizing period of the 8th to 7th/6th century BC. There was no later, Roman, material present in these deposits.

PHASE 4
The detailed pottery quantification (W/Chapter 2) revealed the presence of Cerámica Bruñida Types 3, 6, 8, 11, 13 and 14 (419), as well as Cerámica Bruñida a Torno Types 1, 2 and 4 (419), suggest that this phase may date to some time between the 6th and 5th centuries BC. There was

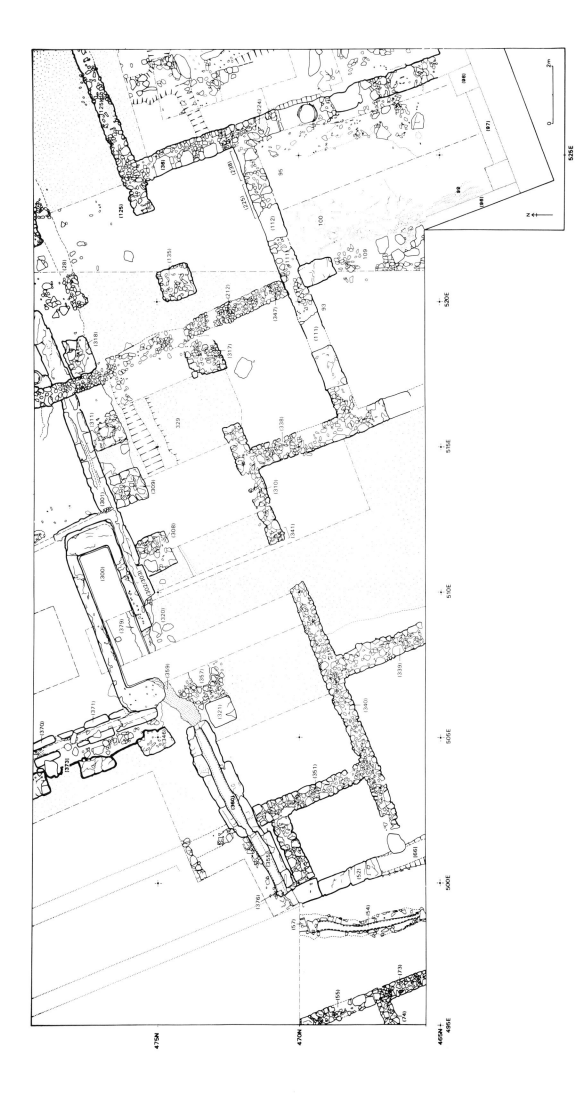

Fig. 3.15. Detail 6 of Site Plan Areas D and E with layer numbers

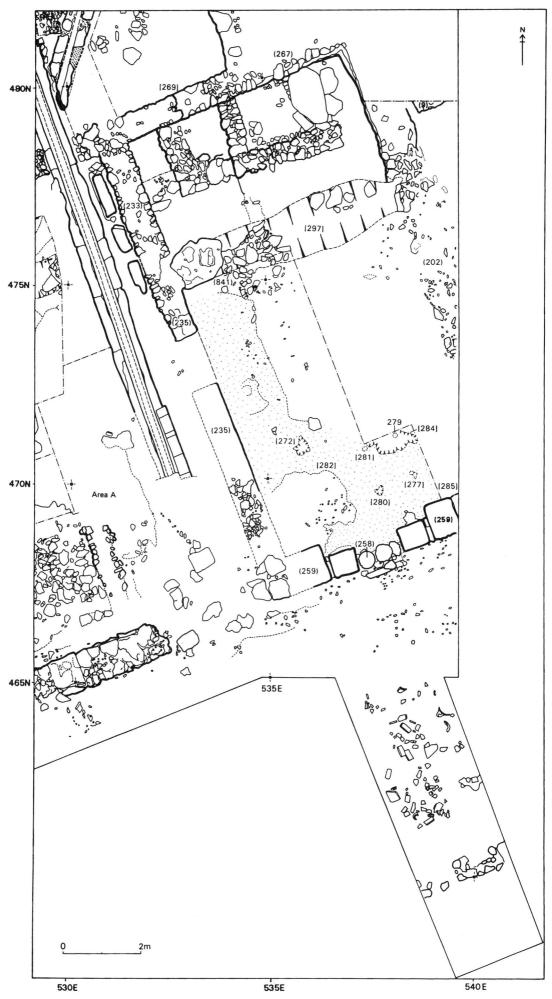

Fig. 3.16. Detail 7 of Site Plan Area B with layer numbers

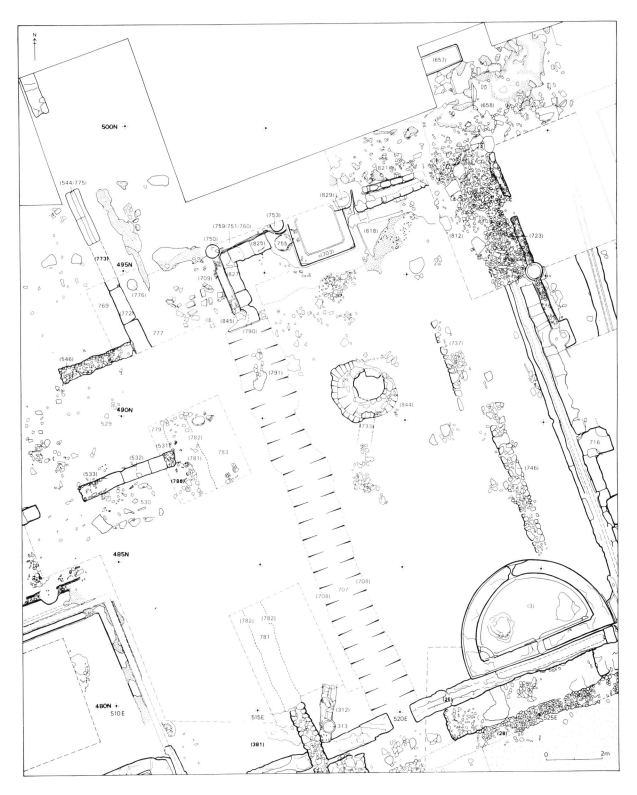

Fig. 3.17. Detail 8 of site plan Areas G and H with layer numbers

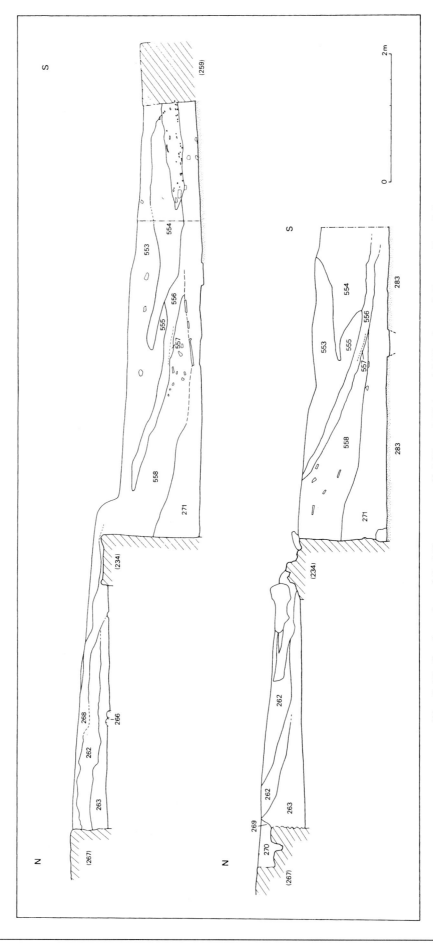

Fig. 3.18. Sections 2 and 3: NS across wall 267 and 234 and 259, through Rooms 7 and 9

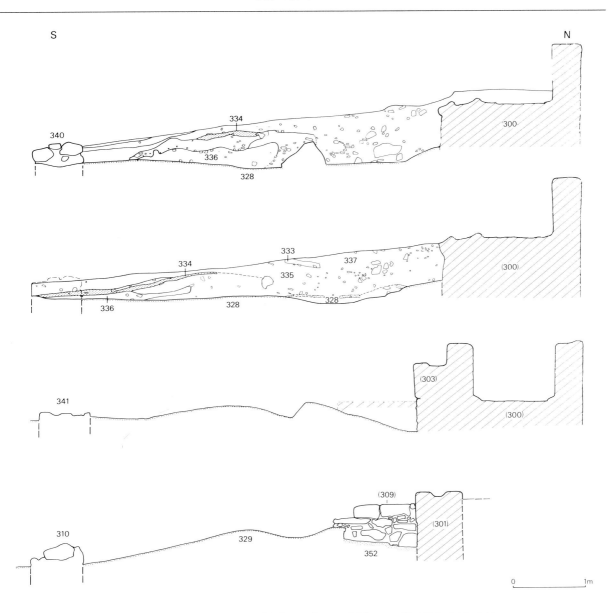

S   N

Fig. 3.19. Sections 4 to 7: NS from cistern 300 to walls 310, 340, 341

no later, Roman, material from this or the more general quantification.

PHASE 5

Analysis of the Turdetanian pottery present in the detailed quantified data (W/Chapter 2) suggests that this phase may date to some time after the mid 1st centuries BC and before the early 1st century AD. Support for this date comes from one fragment of a Type 14/Haltern 70 amphora (405) and some sherds of miscellaneous coarseware (401 and 405). Similarly, TSI local and miscellaneous Roman amphora was present amongst material from the general quantification (174 and 197). Sherds of TSSG (introduced during the reign of Tiberius) and Type 20/Dressel 20 amphorae (introduced during the reign of Tiberius) were absent

from all contexts of this phase. By contrast, one sherd of TSCLA was present in 174. This might suggest that this phase date to some time after the introduction of Sigillata Clara in the early Flavian period. However, this is highly unlikely and this pottery was almost certainly intrusive, given that the layers of subsequent phases were uncontaminated and probably Augustan in date.

PHASE 6

Analysis of the detailed pottery quantification from Phase 6 layers suggests an Augustan date. This included TSI Local Forms 14 and 17 (Augustan/Tiberian and some time after 20BC: 403), sherds of Barniz Negro (404 and 417) and cerámica común (403, 404 and 421). Moreover, one should note that TSSG (introduced during the reign of Tiberius) and

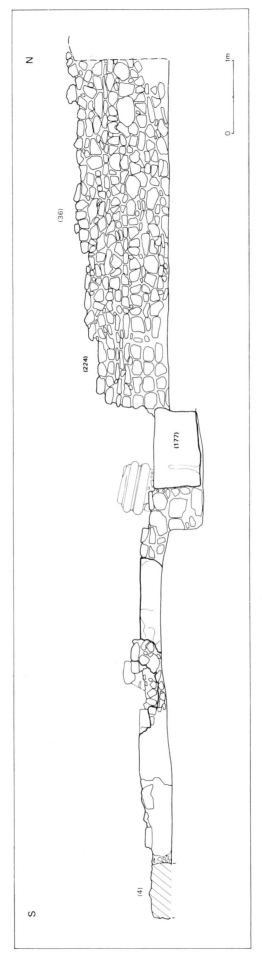

Fig. 3.20. Section 8: NS from wall 125 to 238 across 36, west side of Room 6

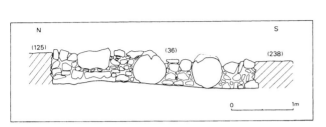

Fig. 3.21. Section 9: WE from wall 36 across 238, 225, 112 and 111

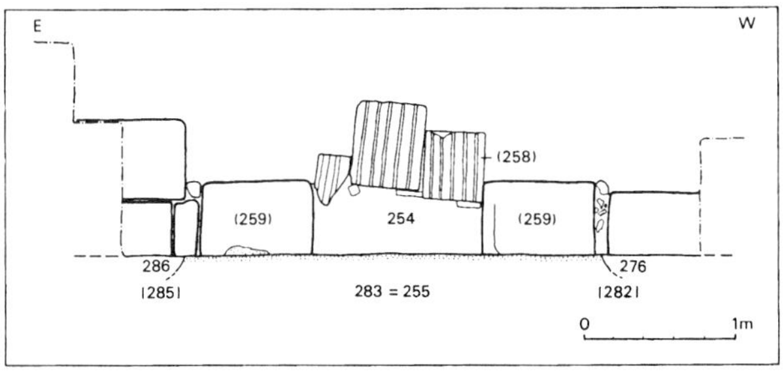

Fig. 3.23 Sections 11–13 along wall 36 and door-blocking 258

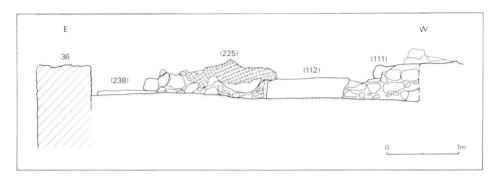

Fig. 3.22. Section 10: WE across doorblocking 254, 259 etc.

Type 20/ Dressel 20 amphorae (introduced during the reign of Tiberius) were absent. One sherd of TSI Local Form 17 (after 20 BC: 192). In *grosso modo*, therefore, Phase 6 is stratigraphically, if not temporally, later than Phase 5.

PHASE 6A
Analysis of the detailed pottery quantification from this sub-phase suggests a date between the Augustan and Claudian periods. This included TSI Local Form 10 (between the Augustan and Claudian periods: 569), as well as fragments of Type 14/Haltern 70 amphorae: 569), Paredas Finas (569) and Cerámica Común (569). Sherds of TSSG (introduced during the reign of Tiberius) and Type 20/ Dressel 20 amphorae (introduced during the reign of Tiberius) were absent. Nothing relevant was discovered in the general quantification. Thus, Phase 6 in *grosso modo* is stratigraphically, if not temporally, later than Phase 5.

PHASE 6B
There were no finds from this sub-phase which must, therefore, date to some time between Phases 6A and 6C.

PHASE 6C
This included TSI Local Forms 9 (circa Augustan/ Claudian period: 551), 10 (circa Augustan/Claudian period: 551) and 15 (Claudian/Neronian period: 269, 551), as well as sherds of Type 14/Haltern 70 amphorae (551) and two side sherds of Baetican Garum amphorae (dateable generically to between the end of the 1st century BC until the late 2nd century BC: 551). It should be noted that there was no TSSG (introduced during the reign of Tiberius) or Type 20/Dressel 20 (introduced in the Tiberian period) amphorae. All of this suggests a date stratigraphically, and perhaps temporally, later than Phase 6a.

PHASE 6D
Analysis of the detailed pottery quantification from this sub-phase suggests a date between the Augustan and Claudian periods. It included the Type 14/Haltern 70 amphora (mid 1st century BC to mid 1st century AD: 560, 564 and 575), although there was no TSSG (introduced during the reign of Tiberius) or Type 20/ Dressel 20 amphorae (introduced during the reign of Tiberius). Nothing relevant was discovered in the general quantification, apart from a Type 1 lamp (563) which is dated to between the Augustan and Claudian periods. All of this suggests a date stratigraphically later than Sub-Phase 6c and either contemporary or later in chronological terms.

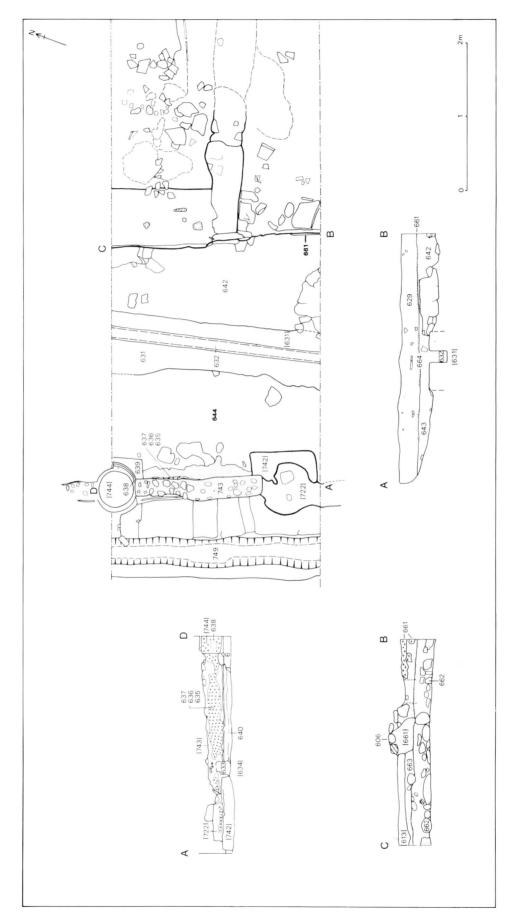

Fig. 3.24. Section 14 and corresponding plan for to show relationship between drain 631 and portico wall 743 at the eastern edge of site

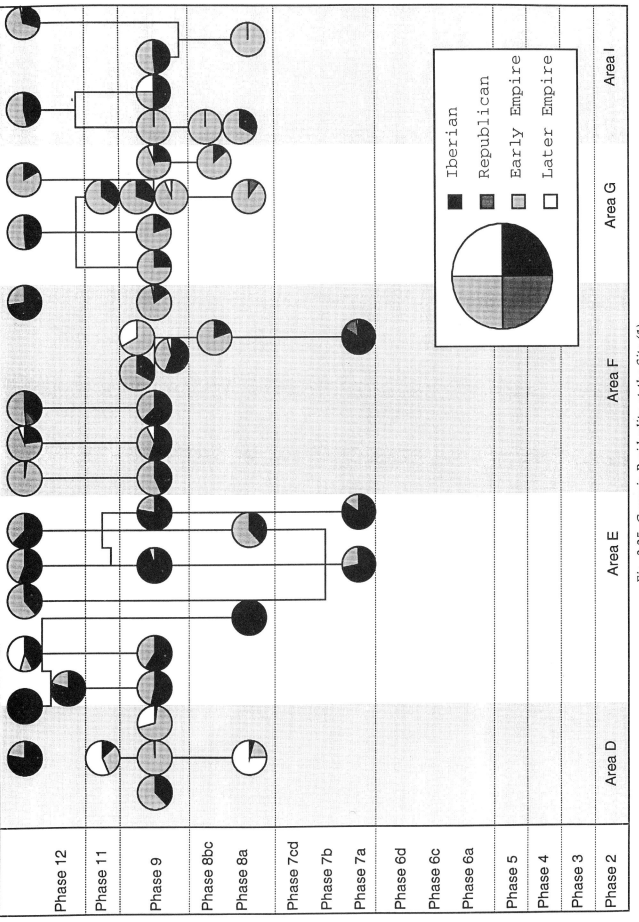

Fig. 3.25. Ceramic Residuality at the Site (1)

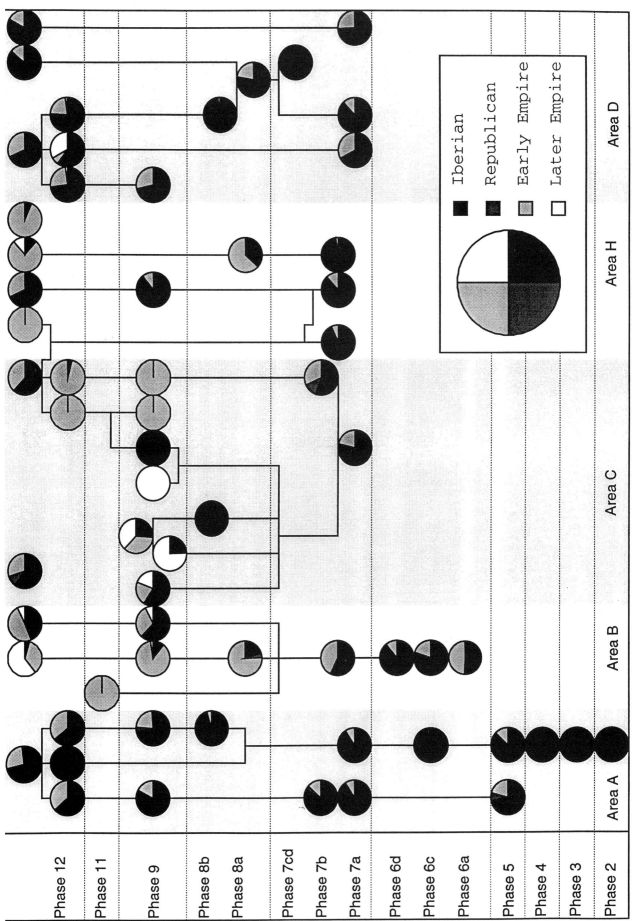

Fig. 3.26. Ceramic Residuality at the Site (2)

Fig. 3.27. General Photograph of the Excavations (Area A): View north over Room 6 towards the open square (top of picture)

Fig. 3.28. General Photograph of the Excavations (Areas A, C, D and E): View westwards over Phase 7a south colonnade (Room 8), with open square (right) and Rooms 7, 6, 5, 4, 3, 2 and 1 (left).

Fig. 3.29. General Photograph of the Excavations (Area G and H): View southwards over the garden of the eastern Phase 8a and 8b house. The cistern lies at the centre, the portico robbed-out in Phase 9 to the right and semi-circular water-tank in the background.

Fig. 3.30. General Photograph of the Excavations (Areas G and H, I and J): View southwestwards over the western Phase 8a and 8b house. The portico robbed-out in Phase 9 lies to the left and the small square garden in the centre background.

Fig. 3.31. General Photograph of the Excavations (Area C): Detail of the semi-circular tank and its junction with the main north–south drain of the eastern Phase 8b house.

Fig. 3.32. General Photograph of the Excavations (Area G and H): View northwards of the northern sector of the easternmost Phase 8b house. Cistern mouth visible at centre, with square tank in backgound.

PHASE 7

Within Phase 7 there were three clearly defined structural sub-phases whose dating evidence is discussed immediately below. However, given the robbing and plough damage to the upper levels of the site, many layers could not be specifically assigned to any of these sub-phases. Consequently, they have been assigned to broader horizons within Phase 7, or between Phases 7 and 8 and sometimes between Phases 7 and 9.

Main Structural Phases

PHASE 7

Phase 7a

Analysis of the detailed pottery quantification from this phase suggests that it may date to some time immediately prior to, or during the initial years of the Flavian period. A key consideration must be the absence of any sherds of TSCLA, which was first manufactured from the Flavian period onwards (Hayes 1972). By contrast the earliest forms (Hayes 3A and 3B) are present at other neighbouring sites in the Guadalquivir valley, such as Munigua (Mulva), Italica and Orippo (Dos Hermanas) (Alonso de la Sierra 1998, 240ff). The latest pottery present at Peñaflor in contexts of this phase includes TSI Local Forms 8 (263: some time after the middle Augustan period), 9(262, 263: Augustan/Tiberian), 10 (262, 406: Augustan/Claudian), 11 (173, 263, 335, 406: Claudian/Neronian), 13 (262, 652: Claudian/ Neronian), 14 (173, 335, 406, 645, 647: Augustan/ Tiberian), 15 (647: Claudian/Neronian) and 18 (406: Augustan/Claudian); TSH Type 10/Dr.29 (AD 50 to 60/70: 263). Also present were Paredas Finas forms 4 (second half of the 1st century AD: 647) and 7 (between AD 40 and 90: 406), Lamp type 3 (late 1st century BC or Cladian/Neronian date: 173) and amphora types 14/Haltern 70 (mid 1st century BC to mid 1st century AD: E.172, 173, 262, 263, 299, 336, 406, 410, 415 and 652), 15 (late 1st century BC to late 1st/early 2nd century AD: E.647), 20/Dressel 20 (early 1st century AD to mid 3rd century AD: 335 and 336) and 22 (Flavian to 3rd century AD: 335). It is also important to note that this is the first phase in which appear imitation Rojo Pompeiano vessels (173, 262, 263, 410 and 647), which date largely to between the Augustan period and the later 1st century AD, as well as African Cooking Ware Type 5 (Tiberian period to the 2nd century AD: 262). One should also note the presence of examples of Cerámica Común types IA (336), IC (647) and 3 (263) , all of which appear at some time after the middle of the 1st century AD onwards.

The Neronian/early Flavian date proposed for this phase is supported by the range of ceramics

Fig. 3.33. General Photograph of the Excavations (Area I and J): View southwards over the drain leading south to the square garden of the westernmost Phase 8b house. Phase 10 wall runs parallel to the drain to the left.

noted in the general quantification. The latest pottery dated type attested is a TSH Type 4/Drag.37A (31: between AD 60/70 and the 2nd century AD). Otherwise TSSG is attested (31, 128, 133, 143 and 151), Type 20/Dressel 20 (299), as well as TSI (186), TSI Local (31, 40, 128, 133, 142, 143, 144, 151, 159, 172, 173, 175, 176, 186 and 299), Paredas Finas (128, 144, 160, 176 and 299) and Rojo Pompeiano (176).

The only evidence which runs counter to the suggestion of the proposed date consists of one example of a Type 23/Dressel 23 amphora (415: late 3rd to late 5th/early 6th centuries AD) and an Antoninianus of Claudius II (AD 268–270: 336). Given that the overwhelming majority of the ceramic evidence points to an early Flavian date, it seems reasonable to suggest that both of these are intrusive.

Phase 7b

From the general quantification there is a fragment of TSSG Type 14 (134) of the first half of the 1st century AD in a context of this Phase in association

Fig. 3.34. General Photograph of the Excavations (Area B): Phase 9 blocking of Room 7.

with TSI Local and Paredas Finas. In addition there is also TSI, TSI Local, Paredas Finas and Rojo Pompeiano (37); TSI Local, Paredas Finas (141). All of this is consonant with a start date of some time at, or shortly after, Phase 7a – in other words towards the start of the Flavian period.

Phase 7c
There was no dating evidence from this sub-phase although it clearly post-dates the initial early Flavian date for the construction of the complex.

BROADER PHASE 7–9 HORIZONS
Phase 7a–9
An analysis of the detailed pottery quantification points to the presence of sherds of Type 20/Dressel 20 (Tiberian period to the middle 3rd century AD: 337), Type 14/Haltern 70 (mid 1st century BC to the mid 1st century AD: 337),Type 19/Dressel 2–4 (mid 1st century BC to mid 1st century AD: 337), Type 22/ Gauloise 4 (between the Flavian period to the 3rd century AD: 337), as well as Rojo Pompeiano Type 1 (Augustan period to the late 1st century AD: 337). TSI Local and Dr.20 (601); TSSG and Rojo Pompeiano (641) were discovered in the general quantification. All of this suggests a date of some time after the beginning of the Flavian period. A Julio Claudian/ Flavian coin of 1st AD date (641) was also found.

Phase 7b–8a
The latest pottery from this Phase came from the

general quantification and consisted of TSCLA Type 7/Hayes 17Var (48: second half of 2nd AD). Other pottery present in contexts of this phase included TSI Local, TSSG and Paredas Finas (20) in the general quantification. This horizon must, therefore, date to some time in the second half of the second century AD.

Phase 7b–9
Sherds of TSI Local and Paredas Finas (348) were discovered in the general quantification. This horizon must, therefore date to some time around the same horizon as 7b–8a.

PHASE 8
Within Phase 8 there were three clearly defined structural sub-phases whose dating evidence is discussed immediately below. However, given the robbing and plough damage to the upper levels of the site, some layers could not be specifically assigned to any of these sub-phases. Consequently, they have been assigned to the broader horizon of Phase 8 (below).

Phase 8a
From the general quantification, the later pottery includes TSCLA Type 4/Hayes 9A (60, 61, 68: AD100–160 +), TSH Type 1 (second quarter 1st to early 2nd AD: 44), ACW Type 4 (Hayes 196: 728, 747: mid 2nd to mid 3rd AD), as well as Type 20/ Dressel 20 amphora side sherds (early 1st to the

Fig. 3.35. General Photograph of the Excavations (Area I and J): View eastwards showing the Phase 10 wall (running diagonally across the picture) cutting walls of the Phase 8 house (bottom left).

mid-3rd centuries AD) being used as part of the construction material for walls 541, 542 and 546. However, the key piece of dating evidence is clearly the TSCLC1 sherd: it comes from the make-up of a mudbrick column (722). It was just a small body-sherd splinter whose original form cannot be determined. However it can provide a *terminus post quem* for the construction of the column. The C1 production began around AD 200 (Hayes 1972, 290–290) and so, given that the vessel had been around for a while before it was broken and included in the make-up of the column, it seems licit to suggest a date in the course of the first half of the 3rd century AD.

Phase 8b

From the general quantification, the later pottery includes TSH Type 1 (second quarter of the 1st to early 2nd centuries AD: 728), Type 4 (between AD 60/70 and the 3rd century AD: 728), ACW Type (Hayes 196: mid 2nd to mid 3rd centuries AD), as well as miscellaneous sherds of Type 20/Dressel 20 (728 and 797). Given the date of Phase 8a, this phase must date to well into the 3rd century AD at the earliest.

Phase 8c

The latest pottery from the general quantification in these layers comprises fragments of Type 20/

Dressel 20 amphorae (632). This phase must date to some time after Phase 8b.

Phase 8

There is very little from the detailed or general quantification of relevance for this horizon; most ceramics seem to be residual. The exceptions from the former were side sherds of Type 20/Dressel 20 (271) and Garum (271) amphorae. Nevertheless the dating for the Phases 8a, b and c suggests a 3rd century AD date. This would appear to be supported by the evidence of a bronze coin (271: Lab. no. 6658D). It was issued under Commodus in AD 190/191, but its squareness suggests that it had been in circulation some time before it was lost, possibly during the earlier 3rd century AD.

PHASE 9

The latest pottery from site came from contexts in the detailed quantification, and comprised Imitation TSCLC3 Type 13/Hayes 50A (127, 129, 723: AD 230/240 and 325) and Type 13/Hayes 50B (723: AD 350 – 400), TSCLC2 Type 13/Hayes 50A or B (149, 253: AD 230/40 to AD 400), TSCLD Types 14/Hayes form 58A (265: AD 290/300–375), 15/Hayes 59B (247 and 557: AD 320–420), Imitation Type 16/Hayes 61A (705: AD 325 – 400/425), Type 17/Hayes 61B (762: AD 380/90–450), Type 19/Hayes 67 (247: AD 360–440), Type 22/Hayes 78 ?(265: AD 360–

440), Type 24/Hayes 94? (53: between AD 360/440 and the 6th century AD), Cerámica Vidriada Type 3 (707: 4th century), and late Roman amphorae Type 23/Dressel 23 (741: earlier 3rd and middle 5th AD), 25/Africana IIA (762: late 2nd and 4th to 5th centuries AD), 26 (762: AD 230 and first quarter of the 4th: Africana IIC), 28/Keay XIX (723: 4th or 5th centuries AD), 31/Keay I (553 and 741: late 2nd/early 3rd and late 3rd/early 4th AD), and 32/Keay LIV (553: late 4th to late 6th AD). From the general quantification, the latest pottery included TSCLD Type 24/Hayes 94 (53: early 7th century AD?), as well as other sherds of TSCLD and imitation in a range of contexts (247, 629 and 758) and TSCLC and imitations (53, 127, 129, 149, 208, 245, 380, 749 and 758). The only other dating evidence consists of an Antoninianus of Gallienus from 707 (Lab no. 6658A) dating to AD 253–268 and an illegible AS of 1st century AD date (707: Lab no. 6655).

A consideration of all of the above data suggests a date at some time in the first half of the 5th century AD at the earliest – although if the identification of the Hayes 94 (Type 22) is correct (Fig. 47.24) then an early 7th century date might be possible.

PHASE 10

This must post-date the previous period. However, there was no accompanying ceramic or numismatic evidence to give a firm idea of date. Consequently, all that can be said is that it dates to some time after the first half of the 5th century AD.

PHASE 11

As this post-dates Phases 9 and 10 it must clearly date to some time after the first half of the 5th century AD. There is no ceramic evidence from the site of this chronological horizon. However, the presence of a possible fragment of TSCLD Hayes form 107 (AD 600–650) from the "Platform" Survey (T3B.76: Fig. 47.22), to the north of the excavated area, suggests that it may have dated to within the Byzantine period.

PHASE 12

This dates down to the present-day.

Conflation of the Broad Phases

On the basis of the Phasing the following broad chronological horizons of occupation can be proposed:

Phase 2	The late Bronze Age period
Phase 3	Some time after the Late Bronze Age and the 6th/5th centuries BC
Phase 4	The 6th/5th BC
Phases 5, 6, 6a	The Augustan period
Phases 6c, 6d	The Julio-Claudian period?
Phases 6c/7a and 7a	Between the Neronian and the beginning of the Flavian periods.
Phases 7b and 7c	Between the late 1st and late 2nd centuries AD
Phase 8a and 8b	Some time in the earlier 3rd century AD
Phase 9	Some time after the early 5th AD +
Phase 10	Some time after the early 5th century AD +
Phase 11	Between some time after the early 5th and the 7th centuries AD ?
Phase 12	Down to the present day.

Chapter 4
The Ceramics: A Summary

Simon Keay and Ana Romo Salas
with a contribution by Kathryn Knowles

Abstract

This Chapter presents an overview of the pottery from the surface survey and excavations at Peñaflor. It is complemented by a detailed typological analysis (W/Chapter 3). In essence, it seeks to characterize the principal Turdetanian and Roman ceramic productions from each phase of the site's occupation, and to set these in their regional contexts. This is aided by some low level quantitative analysis (Appendices 1 and 2). The size and integrity of the deposits ensures that the ceramics from Phases 7 and 9 are the most important. From this evidence, it is clear that throughout the history of the site, local production of pottery played an important role in the economic and cultural history of the site and while imported pottery was clearly present it was often imitated rather than being imported in volume.

Introduction

The aim of this Chapter is to present an overview of the pottery from the surface survey and excavations at Peñaflor undertaken between 1987 and 1992. Pottery was abundant at the site and, in the first instance, provides the information necessary for dating the sequence of occupation attested at the site (Chapter 3). Traditionally, this has been achieved by a consideration of the finewares and better known imported ceramic types, since there are few comprehensive published ceramic sequences from the lower Guadalquivir which would allow the evidence of locally produced pottery to be taken into account. In an attempt to remedy this, a detailed typology of all the pre-Roman and Roman pottery from the excavations and survey was produced and is presented elsewhere (W/Chapter 2). At the same time, pottery can also be used as an index of economic behaviour and social attitudes. For example, the fluctuating balance of imports to locally produced ceramics through time can contribute to our understanding of the changing economic role of the town. Alternatively, changing dining habits and preferences for particular kinds of imported foodstuff can also be gleaned from broad-brush analyses of the ceramics.

However, this is not without its pitfalls. There are few precedents for this kind of analysis at Roman sites in the lower Guadalquivir valley and, consequently, few sites with which Celti can yet be directly compared. Moreover, the chronological scope for this kind of analysis at Celti is constrained by the limited number of phases where there is sufficient well-dated material to allow meaningful analyses to be undertaken: 6–6d, 7a and 9. Finally, the relative uniformity of the geology in the region makes it difficult to distinguish local and regional ceramic products (see discussion in Appendix W/App. 2). Nevertheless, taken as a whole, the pottery from the excavations and survey at Peñaflor provides a starting point for analyzing material from an urban site in the middle Guadalquivir valley between the 9th century BC and the 5th century AD.

The following section attempts to highlight significant points about the volume of pottery present in each phase, as well as comments about certain classes of pottery. It should be read in conjunction with the ceramic typology (W/Chapter 2). In this discussion, most emphasis is upon local production rather than imports, since the chronology and typology of many of the latter is well established, while our knowledge of the former, particularly for the Roman period, is poor. Throughout, reference is made to specific phases, whose chronology is discussed in Chapter 3, but which can be summarized as follows:

Phase 2	The late Bronze Age period
Phase 3	Some time between the Late Bronze Age and the 6th/5th centuries BC
Phase 4B	The 6th/5th BC
Phases 5, 6, 6a	The Augustan period
Phases 6c, 6d	The Julio-Claudian period?
Phases 6C/7a and 7a	Between the Neronian and the beginning of the Flavian periods.
Phases 7B, and 7C	Between the late 1st and late 2nd centuries AD
Phase 8a & 8b	The earlier 3rd century AD
Phase 9	Some time after the early 5th AD +
Phase 10	Some time after the early 5th century AD +
Phase 11	Between some time after the early 5th and the 7th centuries AD ?
Phase 12	Down to the present day.

Pre-Roman and Turdetanian Pottery (ARS and SK)

The evidence from the excavations at Peñaflor points to a vigorous tradition of local pottery production throughout the pre-Roman period that continues well into the Roman imperial period. The size of surviving deposits, however, means that the most meaningful data comes from the later phases (see the quantified deposits in Appendix 1 and 2). Consequently, therefore, much of our information for pre-Roman pottery is drawn from early Roman levels (Fig. 4.1, 4.2 and 4.3), and care has to be taken to ensure that due consideration is given to the possibility of individual ceramic types appearing in residual contexts.

A rapid glance at the counts and weights totals from quantified totals suggests that exotic imports are extremely rare, such as very occasional *gris emporitana*, which is germane to the east coast of Spain. Indeed, the early phases are dominated by a limited range of locally produced pottery. Most of the pre-Roman amphorae discussed in the typology (Types 1, 2, 3, 4, 5, 5, 6 and 7) seem to be local or regional imitations of well-established Phoenicio-Punic types, the production of which was established at Phoenician and Punic centres around the western Mediterranean. It is quite possible that many of these types may have been manufactured in the region of the Phoenician colony at Gadir.

The largest body of material is the painted *cerámica fina ibérica*, whose types fall into a compre-

hensive developmental sequence with new types and decorative schemes dating first appearing in dated contexts from the 6th/5th century BC onwards (Phase 4). One of the important advances offered by this material is evidence for its continued production well into the imperial period (Fig. 4.4; see also Keay 2000 for a preliminary discussion of the implications). Indeed, a number of forms are only attested for the first time in 1st century AD and later levels. This suggests, therefore, that the Turdetanian ceramic tradition does not disappear as quickly or as completely as has been previously thought. This has important implications for our understanding of the cultural history of the site (Chapter 10). However, its significance may be compromised to a limited degree by the small size of many of the earlier deposits and the large-scale residuality of Bronze and Iron Age pottery in deposits of Phases 5 and 6.

This apparent continuity of Turdetanian pottery into the Roman imperial period was examined more closely, by analysing the frequency of individual forms at different periods through time: these are listed by type (see W/Chapter 2) and expressed in EVEs (Fig. 4.4). Wherever forms are attested in early Roman contexts at Peñaflor, care has been taken to record dated parallels at other sites in the region.

1) *Cerámica Fina Ibérica* types which seem to originate during the Turdetanian period:
   Types 1B, 1C, 1D, 5B, 6 and particularly 9A and 9B

2) *Cerámica Fina Ibérica* types of Turdetanian tradition which disappear during Phases 6–6d:
   Type 6 appears in Phase 4 and effectively disappears in Phase 6
   Type 7E appears in Phase 6d alone

3) *Cerámica Fina Ibérica* types which appear at Peñaflor and which may be local variants of late date:
   Subtype 1G: the clearest traditional type which appears at Peñaflor alone and in Late Imperial contexts
   Subtype 1I: appears at Peñaflor alone in contexts dating to early and late imperial dates

4) *Cerámica Fina Ibérica* forms which appear at Peñaflor from early or late imperial dates onwards but are not exclusive to Peñaflor:
   Early Empire: 2A, 2B, 2C, 7C, 8A, 11, 12, 13, 15A, 15B, 18, 19 and 20
   Late Empire: 4B/C and 8E

Painted surface decoration of the *cerámica fina ibérica* is one of its distinguishing characteristics. A range of different designs, usually in abstract form, appear on the pottery from the 6th century BC onwards. At Peñaflor, evidence from the

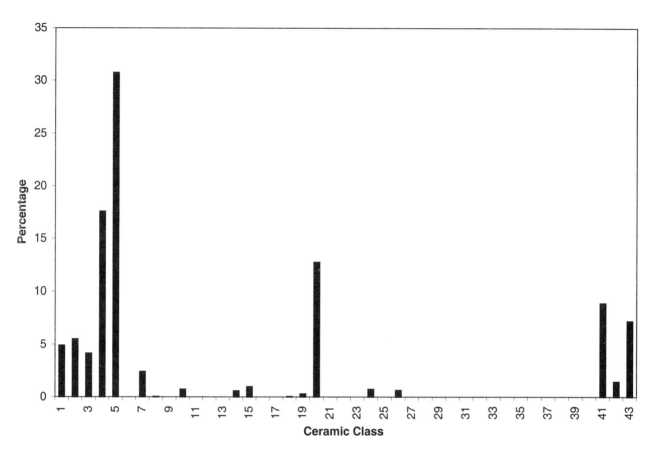

Fig. 4.1. Graph showing percentages of weights of all pottery from Phase 6–6d. The key to the ceramic classes for this and Figs 4.2 and 4.3 is as follows:
1) Cerámica Bruñida; 2) Cerámica a Torno Bruñida; 3) Cerámica a Mano; 4) Cerámica Fina Ibérica (Painted); 5) Cerámica Fina Ibérica (Plain); 6) Gris Emporitana; 7) Anfora Prerromana; 8) Campaniense; 9) Campaniense Regional ; 10) Anfora Republicana; 11) Anfora Punica; 12) Comun Italica; 13) Lamps; 14) Terra Sigillata Italica; 15) Terra Sigillata Italica Local; 16) South Gaulish Sigillata; 17) Terra Sigillata Hispanica; 18) Rojo Pompeiano; 19) Paredas Finas; 20) Haltern 70 amphorae; 21) Dressel 20 Amphorae; 22) Dressel 2–4 amphorae; 23) Dressel 28 amphorae; 24) Garum Amphorae; 25) Gauloise 4 amphorae; 26) Otra Anfora; 27) Anfora Egipcia; 28) Terra Sigillata Clara A; 29) Imitation Terra Sigillata Clara A; 30) Terra Sigillata Clara C; 31) Imitation Terra Sigillata Clara C; 32) Terra Sigillata Clara D; 33) Imitation Terra Sigillata Clara D; 34) Indeterminate Terra Sigillata Clara; 35) Miscellaneous Terra Sigillata; 36) Cerámica Vidriada; 37) Cerámica Cocina Africana; 38) Imitation Cerámica Cocina Africana; 39) Anfora Gaza; 40) Anfora Bajo Imperial; 41) Cerámica Común: Imported and Local; 42) Dolia; 43) Sin Identificar (unidentified)

quantified deposits suggests that this practice begins to decline from the Augustan period (Phase 6) through until the mid/late 1st century AD (Phase 7a: Figs. 4.4 and 4.5), but that it seems to become popular again from the later 2nd century AD onwards (Phase 8). More specifically, types 7A, 7B, 7C, 7D, 8C, 8D and 10 which appear as un-decorated from the Augustan period, are only decorated in late imperial contexts.

This trend in changing surface treatment of *cerámica fina ibérica* may reflect a gradual roman-ization of taste in pottery decoration. This growing preference for "plain" forms might be part of a change in personal taste, as individuals responded to the introduction of new ceramic types, such as

the *Terra Sigillata Italica Local* (see below), by moving away from the more regionally specific decorated forms. It is also possible, however, that the domin-ance of decorated over undecorated *cerámica fina ibérica* may be an illusion brought about by the small sample size in the earlier phases.

Definition of Production Areas

This has been long recognized as an important issue but one that holds out little hope of resolution with our current data sets. For much of the pottery, the fabrics are all too similar and for the *cerámica fina ibérica* in particular, the material is too fragmentary to allow for the kind of typological and statistical

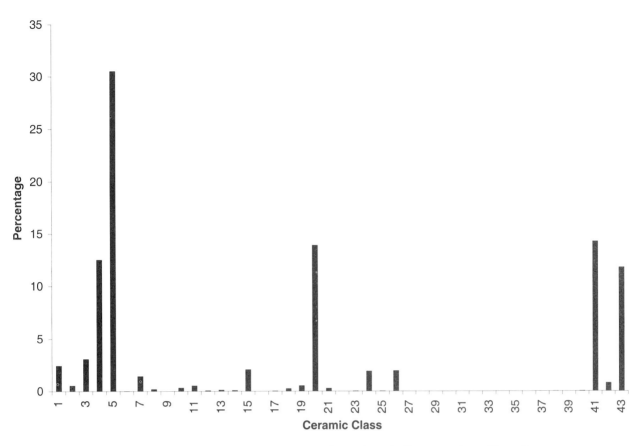

Fig. 4.2. Graph showing percentages of weights of all pottery from Phase 7

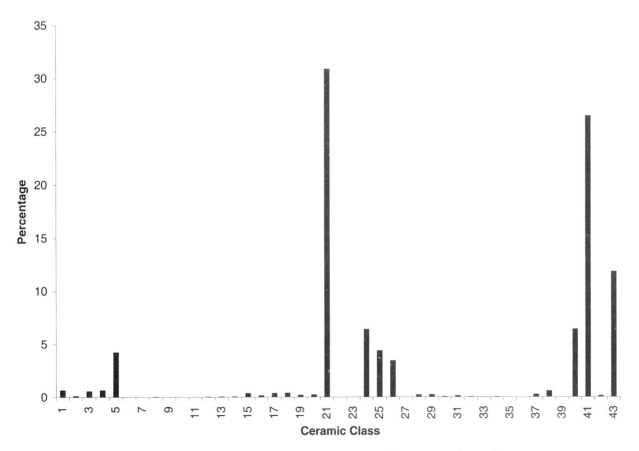

Fig. 4.3. Graph showing percentages of weights of all pottery from Phase 9

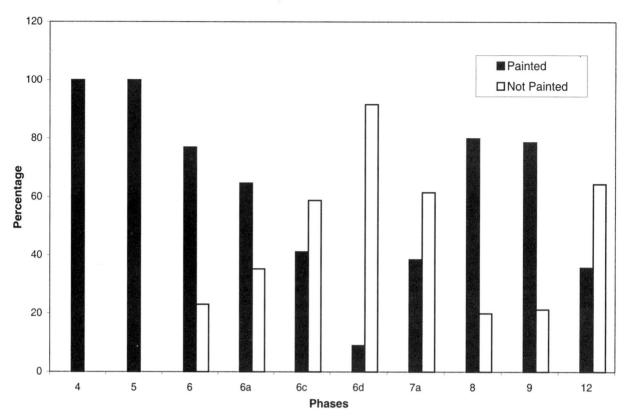

Fig. 4.4. Table showing the occurrence of Cerámica Fina Ibérica *types in the main site phases: Occurrence of Types and Phases*

analysis undertaken by Juan Periera in eastern Andalucía (Pereira 1988). Nevertheless an attempt was made to do this by subjecting several samples of *Cerámica Fina Ibérica* to thin section analysis (W/ Appendix 2). This suggested that most of the more typical fabrics (F.2, 3, 4 and 9) could have been local to the Peñaflor region and regions of similar lithology, although it is possible that some varieties of these (F.3) came from a more distant source. The best results from thin-section analysis came from the *cerámica bruñida* and *cerámica a mano*, suggesting that these were manufactured in the foothills to the north of Peñaflor: indeed an origin in the vicinity of the protohistoric site of Setefilla is not impossible.

Roman Pottery *(SK)*

Ceramics of Roman Republican Date

In practice, it will be clear from the foregoing section that the vast majority of pottery in circulation during the Republican period (late 3rd to late 1st centuries BC) will have been locally produced. However, imported Italic material, together with the occasional fragment of North African "Punic" amphorae (bodysherds only), was also present although always in very small quantities (see Appendices 1 and 2). This is to be partially explained by the lack of Republican contexts but is also a feature of other local sites, and may reflect a genuine rarity in the region. This stands in stark contrast to the large volumes of imported Italic amphorae, *Campaniense, Paredas finas* and *Cerámica Común Itálica* which appears at sites along the east coast of Spain (see the recent summary in Molina Vidal 1997). There is very little to be said about the volume of any of these since they occurred so rarely in the quantified deposits, and usually in residual contexts alone.

Definition of Production Areas

The main characteristic of this material is that despite its rarity, a number of the "Italic" types present seem to be local or regional imitations. Thus, the Black Gloss pottery included the standard central Italian A (F.112) and B (F.113) fabrics, as well as possible local productions (F.114 and F.2) in Type 7 and a miscellaneous base (Fig. W/ 2.36.12). Similarly, it is likely that Paredas Finas Type 1 and possibly 2 were imported, while Type 8 was probably a local production. The same is true of the Italic wine amphorae. Type 9 (Greco-Italic)

	4	5	6	6a	6c	6d	7a	8	9	12
IA					3/1		3/8	4/0	1/0	6/0
IB		1/0	4/0	1/0			2/2		1/0	3/0
IC		3/0	1/0				7/5		4/1	1/0
ID		1/0		1/1	1/1		3/2			2/0
IE				2/1	2/1	0/1	1/2		1/0	0/2
IFa				1/2	0/2		3/2		3/0	1/0
IFb			1/0		3/2	0/1	5/4		9/0	1/2
IFc		1/0	3/0		1/4	0/1	7/8		4/0	1/1
IG									6/0	
IH					0/1		2/0			
II							0/3		4/1	1/3
2A							1/0		3/0	2/0
2B					0/4				0/1	
2C							0/1		2/0	
3									0/1	
4A					3/0	1/0	2/1		2/0	
4B									1/0	
4C										0/3
5A			1/0				6/0		0/1	1/2
5B	1/0		0/1						1/0	
6	1/0	1/0	1/0							0/2
7A				0/1	1/2		0/3		3/0	0/1
7B				0/1		0/1	0/15		3/0	0/7
7C					0/1		0/8		2/0	0/5
7D					0/1		0/2		5/0	0/4
7E						0/1				
8A							1/0		2/0	
8B			1/1		0/1		0/7		0/14	0/4
8C						0/2	0/13		1/0	0/14
8D						0/2	0/1		6/0	0/2
8E							1/0			
9A	3/0	2/0	0/1		2/0	0/1	6/2		4/0	4/0
9B	1/0	1/0	2/1	1/0	2/2		10/2	0/1	9/5	6/6
9C					0/2		8/11		9/0	6/4
9D					2/1	0/1	7/5		4/0	0/1
10			0/1				0/1		1/0	
11							2/0			
12							1/2		1/0	1/1
13					1/0		1/2			0/1
15A							0/1			
15B							1/0			1/0
18					0/1		0/2			0/1
19							0/2			0/1
20							3/0			
21							0/1		0/1	
Tot	6/0	9/0	10/3	11/6	21/30	1/11	74/118	4/1	92/25	37/67

Fig. 4.5. Graph showing the proportion of painted to plain Cerámica Fina Ibérica *pottery through time*

and examples of Type 10 (Dressel IA) and 11 (Dressel IB) were probably manufactured locally, with only one example of Type 10 being imported from Italy. In a sense, this is not unexpected given the recent discovery of stamped Greco-Italic amphorae being manufactured at the kilns of Torre Alta (San Fernando) in the vicinity of Gades (Perdigones Moreno & Muñoz Vicente 1990; De Frutos Reyes & Muñoz Vicente 1994).

Ceramics of Early Imperial Date

An analysis of the percentages of counts and weights (Appendix 1 and 2; Figs. 4.1 and 4.2) reveals that a very wide range of material was circulating at the site, reflecting the inclusion of Celti into the broader commercial circuits of the western Roman Empire. At around the Neronian/early Flavian period (Phase 7a) there was still a heavy preponderance of ceramics in the Turdetanian tradition, together with some Roman inspired forms, such as local Type 14/Haltern 70

amphorae and imitation *Terra Sigillata Italica Local* and imported *Terra Sigillata Sudgallica, Terra Sigillata Hispanica* etc.

By the late 2nd/early 3rd centuries AD (Appendix 1 and 2) the picture has changed, even though the sample size is smaller. The proportion of ceramics in the Turdetanian tradition has dropped, while pottery in the Roman tradition is more abundant than in the previous period. The standard range of imported finewares and amphorae are present, together with a large amount of Type 20/Dressel 20 olive oil amphorae and locally produced coarsewares; this is unsurprising given the presence of kilns in the town itself (Chapter 1). A key characteristic of this period, however, is the imitation of established Roman finewares and coarsewares: *Sigillata Clara A* and *Ceramica Cocina Africana* – either locally or in the region.

DISCUSSION OF DIFFERENT CERAMIC PRODUCTIONS

Sigillata Italica Local
One of the key local productions is without doubt the *Sigillata Italica Local*. This has been known since the late 1960s when it was first found at Baelo (Domergue 1969). It was readily recognized on the basis of its distinctive flakey matt orange slip and micaceous fabric. It has been labelled as "imitaciones de cerámica aretina", "cerámica de barniz rojo julio-claudio" and "cerámica bética de imitación tipo Peñaflor." It has been identified at Munigua (Villanueva del Rio y Minas, Sevilla) (Vegas 1973) and again at Baelo (Remesal Rodríguez *et alii* 1975), as well as at sites in the province of Málaga (Serrano 1988), in the Julio-Claudian wreck at Port-Vendres off the coast of south-west France (Colls *et alii* 1977) and, in the opinion of the writer, at excavations in the hinterland of Emporiae (Empùries), in north-eastern Spain (Sanmartí Grego 1974–1975), and possibly Narbonne (Passelac and Sabrié 1986). Most recently, it has been documented in modest quantity at the excavations of the early Imperial villa at Cercadillas in Córdoba (Moreno Almenara 1996, 114–121).

The most important study was undertaken by Federico Martínez Rodríguez (1987), of which only a summary was later published (Martínez Rodríguez 1989). This was a comprehensive study of known find-spots up until the 1980s, which proposed the division of production into four distinct groups:

Type I (with subtypes): Cups imitating *sigillata italica* and *sigillata sudgálica* prototypes
Type II (with subtypes): Cups imitating *sigillata sudgállica* prototypes
Type III (with subtypes): Bowls and platters imitating Pompeian Red Ware prototypes

Type IV: Bowl or cup imitating *Paredas Finas* forms

Martínez Rodríguez's study suggests that despite the wide distribution area of this pottery, its core area was the lower Guadalquivir valley. He records fragments at Celti, Astigi (Écija), Munigua (Castillo de Mulva) and Italica (Santiponce), and in lesser volume at Olivar Alto (Utrera), Orippo (Torre de los Herberos, Dos Hermanas), Las Canteras (Alcalá de Guadaira), Hispalis (Sevilla), Irni (Los Baldios, El Saucejo), Urso (Osuna), Laelia (Cerro de las Cabezas, Olivares), Mesa de Villaverde (Villaverde), Munigua (Castillo de Mulva), Arva (El Castillejo), Axati (El Castillo, Lora del Rio), Carmo (Carmona) and Verdeja I (Marchena). Furthermore, in a recent survey by the writer, its presence has been attested at Basilippo (Cerro del Cincho, El Arahal), Munda (Alto de las Camorras), Ventipo (La Atalaya Chica, Casariche), Casablanca (El Coronil), Cerro de las Cabezas, Carruca (Cerro de les Cosmes), Cerro de San Pedro (Fuentes de Andalucía), Cerro del Cincho, Ilipla Minor (Cortijo de Repla), El Guijo, Olaura (El Hachillo, Lora de Estepa), Laelia (Sobarbina, Los Olivares) and Siarum (Torre del Aguila, Utrera).

All previous studies have been based upon relatively small quantities of material from single sites. Site specific typologies have been proposed, while there have been attempts to refine the chronology of production. There have also been attempts to locate the centre of production. Suggestions for the latter have ranged from Celti (Peñaflor) and Los Villares de Andújar to Emporion and Narbo. However, Celti is the only site at which wasters have been attested (Amores & Keay 1999). These were discovered by chance in the vicinity of the railway cutting at the southern edge of La Viña field: this area is close to the Type 20/Dressel 20 kilns of El Cortijillo (Chapter 1; Fig. 1.7). The thin section analysis (W/Appendix 2) of material from these excavations does not argue against this. Moreover, the repertoire of material from excavations is very broad, particularly when compared to those from sites like Córdoba (Moreno Almenara cit.), Emporion (Sanmartí cit) or Narbo (Passelac & Sabrié 1986 Fig. 3). They run from imitations of some of the earliest plain and stamped italian sigillata forms through to the limited imitations of *paredas finas* and *sigillata sudgallica* noted by Martínez Rodríguez, as well as some new forms (W/Chapter 2). The manufacture of the pottery itself is also fairly homogeneous, with only two fabrics being noted.

As with the Turdetanian ceramics, the pottery from a selected range of deposits was quantified by EVEs in an attempt to guage the life-span and frequency of individual types (Fig. 4.6). As with the Turdetanian pottery, however, the sample size for the earlier periods makes it difficult to produce substantive conclusions. A review of this suggests that only Types 9, 10 and 14 are attested in the Julio-Claudian period (Phase 6c) and continue into the Neronian/Flavian period (Phase 7a). The forms attested in Phase 9 were almost certainly residual.

Terra Sigillata Hispanica
This class of pottery was manufactured at a number of centres within the Hispanic provinces between the 1st and 3rd centuries AD, but particularly in central Tarraconensis and in eastern Baetica (most recently, see Roca Roumens & Fernández García 1999). The greatest challenge in studying this material is distinguishing between these production areas on the basis of fabrics. Lack of first-hand familiarity with kiln samples of these – particularly the Baetican fabrics – made this a difficult task and it was decided not to attempt to subdivide the fabrics. Nevertheless, the general impression gained from the Peñaflor material is that much of it originated from the kilns around Tritium Magallum (Tricio) in northern Tarraconensis, rather than from those in Baetica. There was little point in undertaking any EVEs analysis of this pottery, since most of it came from residual deposits.

Imitation Terra Sigillata Clara A
Analysis of quantified sherd counts and weights (Appendices 1 and 2) suggests that imitations of regular *Sigillata Clara A* forms were quite common, pointing to a continuation of the regional tradition of imitating imported Roman pottery that began with the *Terra Sigillata Italica Local*. Types 6/Hayes 14, 7/Hayes 17Var, 8/Hayes 23A, 9/Hayes 23B, 10/Hayes 27 and 11/Hayes 32 were all produced

	2	3	4	5	6	6a	6c	6d	7a	8	9	12
3									1			
5									1			
6									1			
7											2	
8									8	1		
9							1		3		1	
10						1			3			
11									7		1	1
12									1			3
13									3			
14				1					12		3	5
15									1		1	
18									2			
23											1	
25												1

Fig. 4.6. Table showing the occurrence of Terra Sigillata Italica Local *types through time*

in either F.15 or 61. It is unclear whether this pottery was produced at Celti, although the fabric is macroscopically similar to that of the *Sigillata Italica Local*. However, the relatively uniform geology in the region suggests that production at other sites is also possible: indeed a kiln producing TS Clara of 1st to early 3rd century AD date has been reported in the vicinity of Marchena (Romero 1987). Local productions of Hayes forms 14A and B, Hayes 23B and Hayes 27 have also been attested at Cercadillas in Corduba (Moreno Almenara and Alarcón Castellano 1996, 77–80). No attempt was made to gauge the relative frequency of different types, since they mostly ocurred in residual contexts.

The Coarse Wares

Amongst the coarse wares, the most distinctive productions are the local imitations of imported pottery. The best known are the *Rojo Pompeiano* (Types 1/Aguarod 6, 2/Aguarod 4 in F.15 and 18) and *Cerámica Común Africana* (Types 1/Hayes 181, 2/Hayes 182, 3/Hayes 197, 4/Hayes 196 in F.18, 32 and 61). The former first appear in a Julio-Claudian context (Phase 6A: Appendices 1 and 2) but are most common from the Flavian period onwards. The latter are not attested in Neronian/early Flavian contexts (Phase 7a), suggesting that they appeared alongside regular productions in the course of the 2nd century, and are first found on the site in residual early 5th+ century AD contexts (Phase 9).

The range of productions included within the *Cerámica Comun Corriente* is best appreciated by comparing the percentages of EVEs from quantified deposits (Fig. 4.7) of the Neronian/early Flavian period (Phase 7a). Quite a wide range of forms are attested although the commonest were the open platters Type 7A and the large thick-walled bowls Type 20. Although Type 17 appears to be the commonest it should be remembered that this is a 'composite' type. The best defined of these early productions is without doubt the kitchen ware Type 5A, which was produced in a range of fabrics (including F.1, 5 and 66), perhaps pointing to a number of different production areas locally and in the region. Analysis of parallels indicates that these forms were all manufactured between the late 1st century BC and the 5th century AD, suggesting that there was little typological change in the course of the Roman period. Other well-defined productions include Types 3 and 14B.

The Amphorae

Analysis of typology and fabric has pointed to quite a wide range of amphora production in the region – possibly a continuation of the earlier tradition of manufacturing Turdetanian and Dressel I amphorae.

Type 14/Haltern 70

Amphorae of this type first appear in an Augustan context and are by far the most common amphora type in contexts of the early Flavian period (Appendices 1 and 2). Two different fabric groupings were identified here. One of these is similar to the local Dressel 20 fabric as well as that of neighbouring kiln of La Catria where the production of Type 14/Haltern 70 amphorae has been attested (Carreras 1994). This suggests that Type 14 amphorae were manufactured in the vicinity of Celti.

Type 19 /Dressel 2–4

These are comparatively rare at the site and only appear in a context dating to between the late 1st and late 2nd century AD, residually in Phase 12 and from the surface survey (W/Chapter 2). The

	2	3	4	5	6	6a	6c	6d	7a	8	9	12
IA									1		1	
1B											1	
1C									1			
1D												1
1E											1	
2									1		1	
3									2		8	1
4B											1	
5A									3		8	
5B											4	
5C											4	
6A											9	1
6B										1	1	
5/6										1	6	
7A									7		4	
8									2		1	
9									3		1	
10									1		3	3
10A											7	
11											1	
12												6
13									1			
14A											1	
14B							1		2		8	4
15											2	
16									1		1	1
17						1	2		20		3	5
6/17									4		1	
18											5	3
19									1		1	2
20									8		7	2
21												6
23											1	
24									1			1
26									1			
27A								1			2	
27B											2	
27C											2	
28									3	1	1	
29										1	1	
30A											1	
31									1		1	
32									2			

Fig. 4.7. Table showing the occurrence of regional Cerámica Común Corriente *pottery through time*

rarity is curious given that the fabrics suggest that the type was produced in southern Spain (see also Beltrán 1977).

Type 20/Dressel 20

Celti was a manufacturing centre of Dressel 20 amphorae. Kilns have been located at El Cortijillo at the south-western edge of the site (Chapter 1), and at La Botica, Cortijo de Mallena, Cortijo de María, Cortijo de María II, Berro II, El Tesoro and Cortijo del Instituto in the broader region of the town (Ponsich 1979, 83–109: see also Chapter 10). However, it should be pointed out that so far only a few stamps have definitely been associated with production centred at the town. This suggests that it was one of the smaller producers along the Guadalquivir. Type 20/Dressel 20 sherds were common at the site – to the point where part of the Phase 8 house was built from large quantities of body sherds. The production of Type 20/Dressel 20 amphorae is generally acknowledged to begin at around the Tiberian period – preceded by the manufacture of the Augustan Oberaden 83 (Peacock and Williams 1986). Quantification of its occurrence at the excavations at Peñaflor, however, suggests that it was not being manufactured or used here until at least the Flavian period. This suggests that the maximum period of production was the second and possibly the third century, although the lack of pre-5th century AD deposits of a sufficient size does not allow this to be confirmed. It is also borne out by the evidence of olive stones (Chapter 6) and the fact that stamps which can definitely be associated with the town of Celti are dated towards the middle of the 2nd century AD.

Lamps (KK)

Three lamp fragments in the catalogue with their narrow ridged shoulders, deep decorated discus and volute nozzle (Loeschcke type I, Deneauve type IV) can be dated to between the late first century BC and the late first century AD. The fragmentary nature of each lamp makes it difficult to classify or date them precisely. However, it is probable, given the better quality of these pieces, that they may be Italian imports, although such assumptions should be treated with caution because petrological examination has not taken place (see also comments in W/Appendix 2: Fabric 3). A fourth fragment, with its plain wide shoulder and ring handle is a form common in the late first century to second century AD (Loeschcke type V or VII). Unfortunately the nozzle and discus are absent from this lamp preventing a close determination of type. Macroscopic examination of this fabric suggests that the lamp is likely to be of local manufacture. It is equally difficult to establish a precise typological

classification for lamp Type 5 with its elaborate shoulder and discus decoration. This is because the absence of such diagnostic features as a nozzle places it anywhere between Loeschcke Type IV and VIII (late 1st to mid 3rd centuries AD). However, it is possible to suggest that the later the date of the lamp, the greater the likelihoood that it is a Spanish copy. Lamp Types 6 – 8 are elaborately decorated shoulder and discus fragments. Comparison with examples found on sites around Spain reveal that they may have a form similar to Deneauve type VIIIB, common from the late second to mid third century AD onwards. The late second to third century date and the coarseness of the fabric suggests that these fragments are likely to have had a Spanish provenance.

Determination of the provenance of the illustrated lamp fragments from the site have been based on the accepted premise that lamps manufactured in Italy were generally of a better quality and workmanship than their provincial copies: it was not possible to conduct a thin-section analysis of these pieces. On this basis, lamp fragments 1–3 have been assigned a possible Italian provenance; however it must be remembered that recent publications have recognised that local provincial lamp manufacturers could produce very convincing copies of Italian originals (Knowles 1994).

Ceramics of Late Imperial Date

An analysis of the counts and weights (Appendix 1 and 2) suggests that by the early 5th century AD, ceramics of Turdetanian tradition had long since ceased to be manufactured and are only present as a small residual tail. The assemblage is large, dominated by Type 20/Dressel 20, cerámica común corriente, late imperial amphorae, rare sigillata clara C and D (and local imitations) and some residual early imperial amphorae and finewares. Imported material is present although it is still difficult to gain any sense of its proportion relative to local production, since contemporary products are still difficult to separate out from residual productions of earlier periods. The ceramics from Phase 12 were not considered, since some of the deposits were 'open-ended' and included unstratified material.

Sigillata Clara C and Imitations

Analysis of the EVEs from quantified deposits suggests that this was less common than Sigillata Clara D. The imitation of such forms as Types 13/ Hayes 50A and B (F.61) points to the continuation of the tradition of ceramic manufacture in the Celti region. Similar imitations of Hayes 50 have been attested at Corduba (Moreno Almenara and Alarcón Castellano 1996, 77–80).

TSCLD AND IMITATIONS

There is a reasonably good range of forms from the site. However, the most interesting discovery was imitation of Types 16/Hayes 61A and 17/Hayes 61B in fabrics 4A and 61. These are difficult to distinguish – particularly when the slip has been removed and raises the question as to how far imitation *sigillata clara D* bodysherds are missed during classification, and hence underestimated in the analysis of the ceramics from this and other excavations.

CERÁMICA COMÚN CORRIENTE

Given the high degree of residuality at this site through all periods, one of the greatest difficulties in this period is trying to establish how far pottery is contemporary with the phase and to what extent it may be residual. Consequently, it has not been possible to distinguish late productions of *cerámica común corriente* with any confidence. Nevertheless analysis of the EVEs from quantified deposits suggests that Types 5A, which was attested in the earlier Phase 7a, 5B and 5C were amongst the commonest form in 5th century AD (Phase 9) contexts (Fig. 4.7). As there are paralells for these forms in mid to late imperial contexts, it is unclear whether any of these were actually produced in the early fifth century AD. Types 3, 6, 10, 20 and 27 were all well represented in this phase. Analysis of published parallels for all these, however, suggests that only Type 20 may have been manufactured in the late imperial period and that even here, too little is known of the overall shape of this type to be sure that it is not a composite "type".

LATE ROMAN AMPHORAE

Dressel 20 and Dressel 23

This is the period in which the largest volume of Dressel 20 amphorae are attested and there is little doubt that all of this must be residual. As is well known, the Type 23/Dressel 23 replaces this towards the later 3rd century AD (Keay 1984). At Celti, examples of this are rare and only appear in this context and in a contaminated early Flavian deposit.

African Amphorae

A range of Tunisian amphorae of 2nd to 4th century AD were present in contexts of this Phase. Noticeably absent, however, were the typical 5th century types – viz. 27 and 33 – which only appeared in the surface survey. One important discovery was that of a Type 25 amphora in what is clearly a local or regional fabric, (F. 2), the same as that in which the Type 14/Haltern 70 amphora was produced. Given the fact that production of the latter has been attested at the local kiln of La Catria (Carreras forthcoming) there is every reason to suspect that manufacture of the Type 25 represents a continuation of the regional amphora production Type 14-Type 20–Type 25. It should be noted, however, that the fabrics of the Types 14 and 25 and the Type 20 are different in terms of hardness and fracture – something which may be ascribable to the need to produce amphora (Dressel 20) to carry a liquid with a higher specific gravity. One should also note that other imitation African amphorae have been discovered in the Palaeochristian cemetery at Tarragona (Keay 1984), suggesting that these, like the Type 23/Keay 23 were distributed quite widely in the west Mediterranean region.

Eastern Mediterranean Amphorae

These were absent apart from a possible fragment of a Gazan and an Egyptian amphora (Types 30 and 32 respectively), both of which may have been residual.

Chapter 5
Finds other than Pottery

Simon Keay
with two contributions from Martin Henig

Abstract

This Chapter analyzes the finds other than pottery from the excavation. It begins by pointing out that the distribution of these across the site tells us little about the way in which any of these finds were used in antiquity, on account of the very extensive ploughing and robbing of the site – particularly in recent years – and the action of metal-detectors. This is followed by a catalogue of the most signficant pieces of metalwork, followed by descriptions of all the Roman coins, architectural fragments and inscriptions. This is to be complemented by a tabulated list of all small finds (Appendix 3).

Introduction

The excavations at Peñaflor revealed an interesting range of small finds in metal, glass, pottery and stone. However, the value of the small finds in quantitative terms has been severely compromised by sustained metal-detecting at the site in recent years. The field of La Viña has long been recognised as a valuable resource by metal-detecting enthusiasts in the region: indeed, the site was quite frequently combed for metal-finds on a daily basis during the field-seasons. This has seriously affected the uppermost levels of the site: given the unequal survival of Early and Late Imperial levels across the site on account of sustained ploughing over the years, the contextual value of small finds, particularly those recovered from P7a to P12 contexts, will have been compromised. Given the overall project priorities and constraints of time and manpower, it was thus decided at an early stage not to sieve excavated deposits for small finds.

The value of the small finds is further limited by the nature of the stratigraphic sequence at the site. The pre-Neronian/early Flavian (P2–6) and late 2nd/early 3rd century AD (P8) levels were all small with few finds, whereas those of the early 5th century AD onwards (P9–12) contained large amounts of residual material. In principle, therefore only the small finds from P7a had any value

as an assemblage. However, the importance of these is compromised by the high degree of residuality suggested by the ceramics (Chapter 3), the fact that the distribution of small finds across the site was generated by the dumping of construction material and later robbing, and occasional contamination.

Overall Patterning of Finds from Excavated Contexts

An analysis of the occurrence of small finds in excavated contexts across the site allowed a few conclusions to be drawn (Appendix 3). In general terms, it is noticeable that there are very few small finds prior to the Neronian/early Flavian period (P7a). This patterning is probably more real than apparent, since these deposits were mostly too deep for conventional metal-detectors, although it should be remembered that the contexts themselves were much smaller than those of subsequent phases. The finds are principally formless pieces of iron, together with iron nodules, the occasional iron nail and pottery counters. In the Neronian/early Flavian period (P7a), all of these continue to be present together with other finds, such as fragments of copper and bronze and lead flashings from the construction of lead-pipes associated with the P7a buildings, a residual bronze fibula, a bronze stylus or pin and glass. Finds are relatively rare prior to the construction of the Phase 8a houses and then increase in volume during Phases 9 and 12. During these periods, the same range is present, together with bronze coins, bronze door-locks, furniture studs and handles etc.; many of these presumably derive from the demolition of the Phase 8a/8b house in the early 5th century AD. Of all these finds, the most significant for the site are perhaps the small iron nodules, which first appear in a Phase 5 context and continue to be present in all subsequent phases; only 1 fragment of copper slag was found (E.306: Phase 12). The spatial distribution of metalwork, pottery and other finds is briefly considered in W/ Chapter 3, and suggests that it was largely generated by post-depositional activity and has little to tell about the primary functions of different parts of the site throughout its history.

Catalogue of Significant Finds

Metalwork

a. This is a small bronze figurine of a bearded male (Fig. 5.1), who holds one arm across his forehead while the other is behind his back. The head, with its long hair and beard is that of a Barbarian, Celt or German. The nearest parallels are to be found at Segobriga (Cabeza del Griego, Cuenca: AAVV 1990, 268 no. 197) and from Vienna in Austria (Fleischer 1967, 148–9 no. 200). Unlike these, however, the Peñaflor example wears not a pair of trousers, like one of the active enemies of Rome, but short trunks which suggest that he may have represented a gladiator (Fleischer cit. 147–148 no. 198). A date around the second century AD is perfectly acceptable for this piece (MH).
Height: 6.0cm

Width: 2.7cm
Context: E.51 (Phase 11)

b. This is a circular bronze lock plate with an "L" shaped hole for the key crudely cut into the plate just off-centre (Fig. 5.2). Only the 'obverse' face was decorated, with a series of concentric circles. Bronze-studs, as well as the holes for those that were missing, ran around the edge of the plate. The large size of this lock-plate suggests that it came from a door.
Diameter: 16.4cm
Thickness: 0.3cm
Context: E.271 (Phase 8)
Parallels: The nearest parallels come from the sites of Szekszárad (Gáspár 1986, 71–4 and Taf.CCCXVIII No. 946), possibly dated to the 4th century AD and undated examples from Györ (Gáspar 1986 Taf.CXCIX No. 742), Szonbathely (Gáspár 1986, Taf. CXCVIII No. 965) and Szöny (Gáspár 1986, Taf. CCIV No. 1056), in Hungary.

c. This is a circular bronze lock-plate (Fig. 5.3) with an "L" shaped hole for the key crudely cut into the plate just off-centre (marked by a small depression). On the 'obverse' face, the outer edge of the lock-plate was decorated with an outer beaded edge, a narrow band of a running-scroll infilled with niello, and two sets of concentric circles. The lock plate was attached to the main body of the lock by four nails (?) whose holes are visible. In addition there four bronze studs were fixed to the plate – of which only two survive. The reverse face of the lock-plate is plain.
Diameter: 9.1cm
Thickness: 0.075cm
Context: E.257 (Phase 12)
Lab No. 6532
Parallels: None known.

d. This is a copper patera (Fig. 5.4) with round, shallow, bowl with gently everted sides and out-turned lip, with the site of the handle attachment visible: the handle itself has been lost.
Maximum Width: 11.7cm

  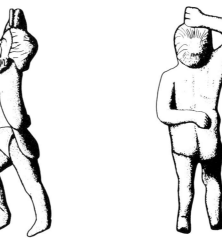

5.1-E51

0   1cm

Fig. 5.1. Bronze Statuette

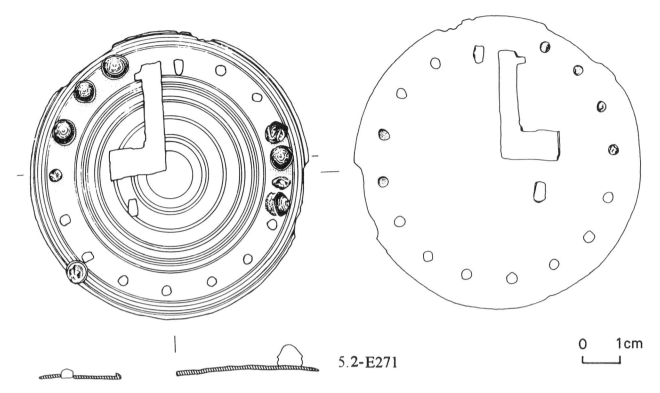

5.2-E271

Fig. 5.2. Plain Bronze Door Lock Plate

0   1cm

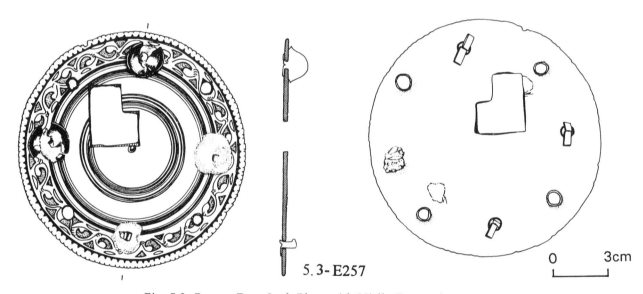

5.3-E257

Fig. 5.3. Bronze Door Lock Plate with Niello Decoration

0   3cm

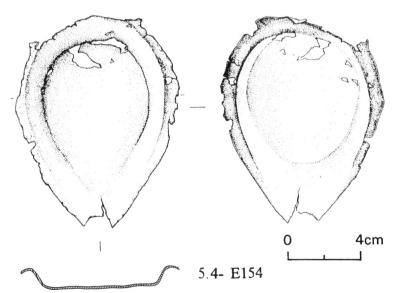

5.4- E154

0   4cm

Fig. 5.4. Copper Patera

Depth: 1.3cm
Context: E.154 (Phase 9)

e. This is a bronze fibula (Fig. 5.5) with a humped 'shaft' decorated with a simple beaded line, a complex spring-like hinge, a long and straight clip and a rectangular clasp.
Length: 6.9cm
Height: 2.4cm
Context: E.336 (Phase 7a)
Lab No: 6391
Parallels: In some ways this is similar to the Acebuchal fibula discussed by Ruiz Delgado (1989, 139–153 and Fig. 15.II) and dated to between the mid 7th and the end of the 6th centuries BC. However this example lacks the characteristic upward projection at the end of the clasp.

f. A pointed bronze stylus or pin (Fig. 5.6) with a thickened bevel at the centre and which terminates in a rounded finial.
Length: 14.1cm
Maximum Thickness: 3.1mm
Context: E.416 (Phase 7a)
Lab No: 6531

g. This is a simple undecorated bronze ring (Fig. 5.7).
Diameter: 2.75cm
Thickness: 0.35cm
Context: E.50 (Phase 12)
Lab No. 6533

h. This is a plain curved bronze strip handle turned up at each end (Fig. 5.8).
Width: 7.1cm
Thickness: 0.17cm
Context: E.257 (Phase 12)
Lab No: 6397

i. This is a small and deformed hollow bell-shaped stud with a vertical iron fixture attached to the inside (Fig. 5.9). Similarity to the studs on the large bronze-lock plate (above, no. 2) suggest that it may have been

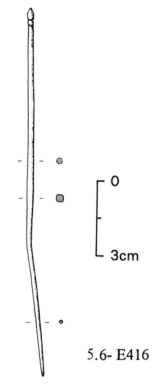

5.6- E416

Fig. 5.6. Bronze Stylus or Pin

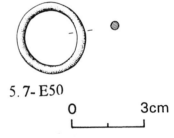

5.7- E50

Fig. 5.7. Bronze Ring

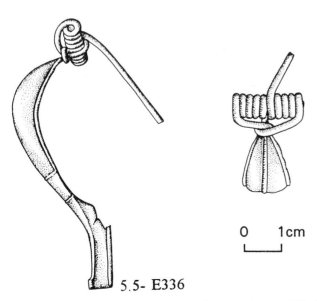

5.5- E336

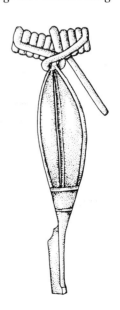

Fig. 5.5. Bronze Fibula

used to affix a door lock.
Maximum Width: 1.9cm
Maximum Height: 1.1cm
Context: E.271 (Phase 8)
Lab No: 6671

j. This is part of a deformed hollow bronze stud in the shape of an inverted bowl (Fig. 5.10). Similarity to the studs on the large bronze lock plate (above, no. 2) suggest that it may have used to affix a door lock.
Width: 1.7cm
Height: 0.6cm
Context: E.728
Lab No: 6671

k. This is a cracked hollow bronze stud in the shape of an inverted bowl (Fig. 5.11): a complete version of the preceding piece. Similarity to the studs on the large bronze-lock plate (above no. 2) suggest that it may have been used to affix a door lock.
Width: 2.0cm
Height: 0.5cm
Context: E.728 (Phase 8b)
Lab No: 6657

l. This is part of a bronze disk (Fig. 5.12) decorated on its upper face by three concentric circles and a central hole, while its lower face is plain.
Width: 3.9cm
Thickness: 0.1cm
Context: E.755 (Phase 9)
Lab No: 6659

m. This is a small bronze pin with a cone-shaped point (Fig. 5.13) that probably fitted a thin wooden shaft.
Length: 6.5cm
Maximum Width: 0.5cm
Context: E.257 (Phase 12)
Lab No: 6398

n. This is an irregularly shaped lead (Fig. 5.14) object with three pointed studs and a central cavity partially obscured by a rounded stud.
Maximum Width:
Maximum Thickness: 3.2cm
Thickness: 0.2cm
Context: E.260 (Phase 12)
Lab No: 6536

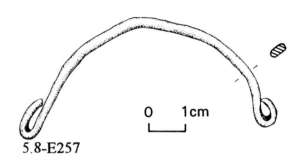

5.8-E257

Fig. 5.8. Bronze Handle

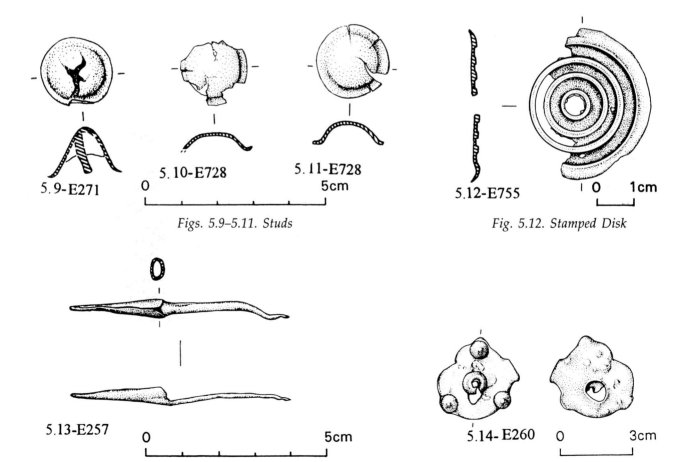

5.9-E271   5.10-E728   5.11-E728   5.12-E755

Figs. 5.9–5.11. Studs   *Fig. 5.12. Stamped Disk*

5.13-E257   5.14-E260

Fig. 5.13. Pin   *Fig. 5.14. Lead Object*

o. This is a round bronze stud (Fig. 5.15) whose upper face is distinguished by two concentric ridges between which there are traces of red enamel: there is a hole at the centre of the stud. The underside of the stud is slightly recessed.
Diameter: 2.00cm
Thickness: 1.5cm
Context: E.354 (Phase 9)
Lab No: 4535

p. This is a plain bronze handle with circular section (Fig. 5.16).
Width: 5.4cm
Height: 3.5cm
Context: E.700 (Phase 12)

q. This is a thin bronze disk with upturned edge and a central projection (Fig. 5.17).
Width: 5.70cm
Height: 0.2cm
Context: E.271 (Phase 8).

r. This is a plain iron strap with simple hinge and three (?) studs holding front and rear sections together (Fig. 5.18).
Width: 5.0cm
Height: 5.9cm
Context: E.271 (Phase 8)
Comment: This and the iron strap (Fig. 5.19) were found in association with the lock plate (Fig. 5.2).

s. This is part of what appears to be a hinge or corner strap for a box (Fig. 5.19).
Width: 4.9cm
Height: 4.0cm
Context: E.271 (Phase 8)
Comment: This and the iron strap (Fig. 5.18) were found in association with the lock-plate (Fig. 5.2).

Glass

Almost all the glass was very fragmented and the majority of it came from contexts of Phases 9 and 12 that were probably residual. Consequently, only a small selection is illustrated here.

a. Small open transparent grey/green glass bowl with simple beaded rim (Fig. 5.20).
Rim Diameter: 9.8cm
Context: E.728 (Phase 8b)
Parallels: None known.

b. Shallow open grey/green glass bowl with everted rim with out-splayed tubular rim (Fig. 5.21).
Rim Diameter: 12.1cm
Context: E.265 (Phase 9)
Parallels: Broadly similar parallels have been discovered in contextxs of the late 4th/early 5th century AD at Luni, Italy, and in a context of AD 440/450 at Tarragona (Benet I Arqué & Subias Pascual 1989, Fig. 9.16). In Britain, similar shapes are attested in 2nd to 4th century AD contexts (Cottam & Price 1998, Fig. 44).

c. Closed grey/green glass bowl with 'folded-over' rim (Fig. 5.22).

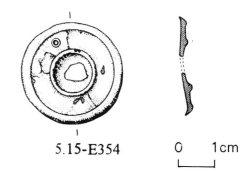

5.15-E354   0   1cm

Fig. 5.15. Enamelled Stud

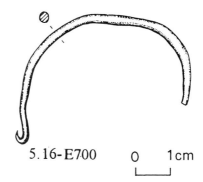

5.16-E700   0   1cm

Fig. 5.16. Bronze Handle

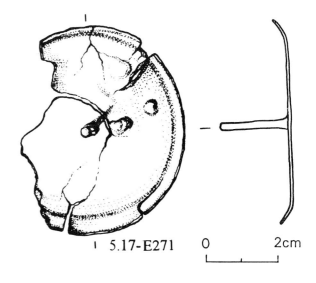

5.17-E271   0   2cm

Fig. 5.17. Large Bronze Stud

Rim Diameter: 14.6cm
Context: E.788 (Phase 9)
Parallels: None known.

d. Shallow grey/green glass cup with outsplayed rim with interior ledge (Fig. 5.23).
Rim Diameter: 14.1cm
Context: E.788 (Phase 9)
Parallels: A similar, but smaller, shape was discovered in a context of AD 440/450 at Tarragona (Benet I Arqué & Subias Pascual 1989, Fig. 9.18).

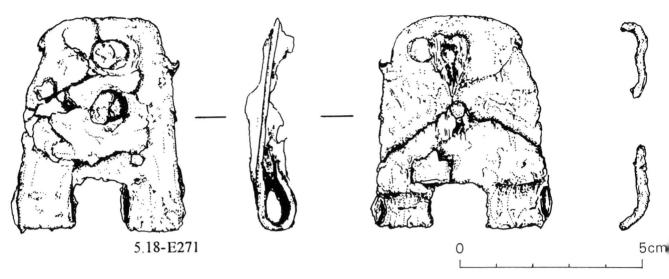

5.18-E271   0   5cm

Fig. 5.18. Iron Strap/Hinge

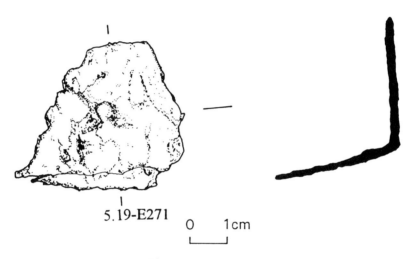

5.19-E271   0   1cm

Fig. 5.19. Iron strap

e. Small convex grey/green glass cup with simple rim (Fig. 5.24).
Rim *Diameter:* 6.0cm
Context: E.265 (Phase 9)
Parallels: None known.

f. Wide grey/green rimmed glass beaker or bowl with overhanging edge (Fig. 5.25).
Rim *Diameter:* 12.3cm
*Context:*E.265 (Phase 9)
Parallels: This may be equated with the beaker Isings 106 variant c, which appears in contexts of the 4th to 6th centuries AD (Isings 1957). Alternatively, it can be taken to resemble the bowls which have been discovered in contexts of the late 1st to late 2nd and the mid 4th to early 5th centuries AD in Britain (Cottam & Price 1998, Figs.13.c and d, and 54 respectively).

g. Small closed grey/green glass beaker or jar with simple everted rim (Fig. 5.26).
Rim *Diameter:* 4.0cm
Context: E.788 (Phase 9)

Parallels: This may be equated with Isings 4, a beaker which appears in contexts of the late Augustan or Tiberian periods (Isings 1957, 21 Fig. 4). However, it also resembles a jar discovered in a context of AD 440/450 at Tarragona (Benet I Arqué & Subias Pascual 1989, Fig. 9.51), although other 1st to 3rd century AD parallels are known.

h. Open grey/green glass bowl with flat base and offset running around the outside (Fig. 5.27).
Rim *Diameter:* 15.9cm
Context: E.264 (Phase 9)
Parallels: This may be identified with Isings form 23, which is dateable to the 1st and 2nd centuries AD (Isings 1957, 39 Fig. 23). Similar shapes are known from contexts of AD 43 to 60/65 in Britain (Cottam & Price 1998, Fig. 10).

i. Bodysherd of grey/green glass with lattice decoration (Fig. 5.28).
Context: E.264 (Phase 9)
Parallels: None known.

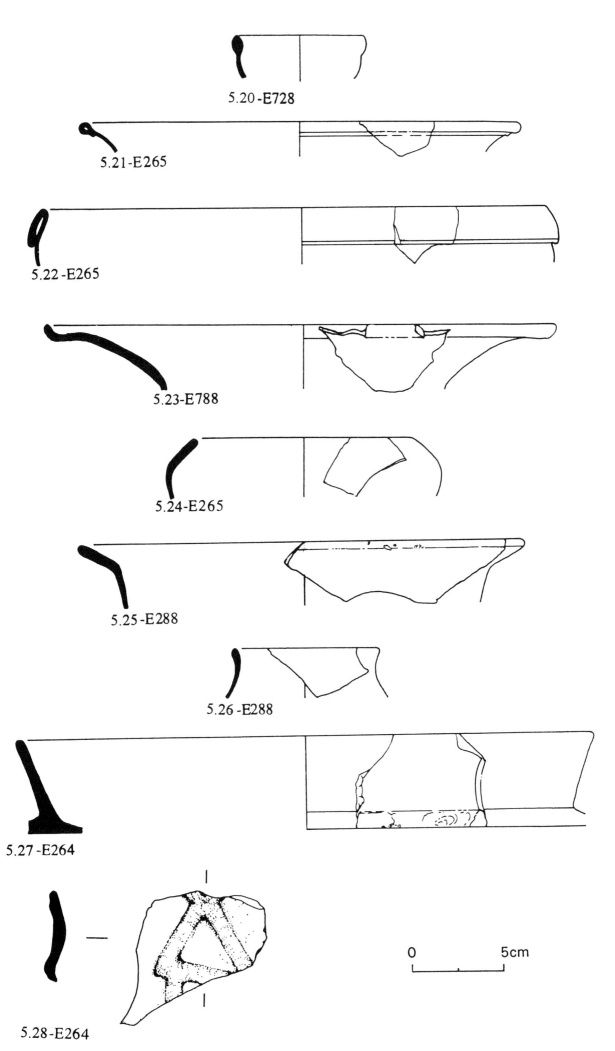

5.20 - E728

5.21 - E265

5.22 - E265

5.23 - E788

5.24 - E265

5.25 - E288

5.26 - E288

5.27 - E264

5.28 - E264

0   5cm

Fig. 5.20–28. Glass Fragments

Jewellery

a. This is a translucent chalcedony intaglio depicting Victory pouring out a libation from a jug into a patera (Fig. 5.29).
Height: 2.0cm
Width: 1.5cm
Context: 1988 Surface Survey
Parallels: This is an Augustan type and the piece can be paralleled by a green emerald in Berlin (Furtwängler 1896: 110 no. 2324), although the image is here reversed. This subject is very much consistent with Augustan propaganda, making allusion both to military victory and religious renewal – a "political" imagery which, as Zanker (1983: Chapter 7) points out, was taken into the private sphere (MH).

Marble Fixtures

a. Squared handle fragment from a white marble mortarium (Fig. 5.30).
Wall Thickness: 1.5cm (maximum)
Context: E.707 (Phase 9)

b. Simple mortarium with a shallow bowl and simple handle, made from whitish marble interlaced with greyish veins (Fig. 5.31).
Width: 29.0cm (including handle)
Height: At least 4.3cm
Wall Thickness: 1.7cm (maximum)
Context: E.741 (Phase 9).

c. Simple white marble mortarium with a shallow bowl and simple handle (Fig. 5.32)
Width: 38.5cm (estimated)
Height: 9.7cm (minimum)
Thickness: 4.2cm
Context: E.707 (Phase 9).

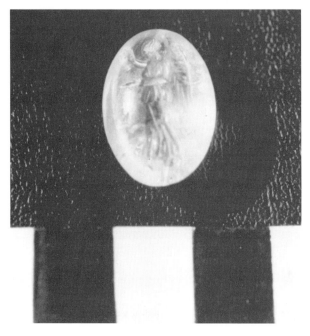

Fig. 5.29. Intaglio

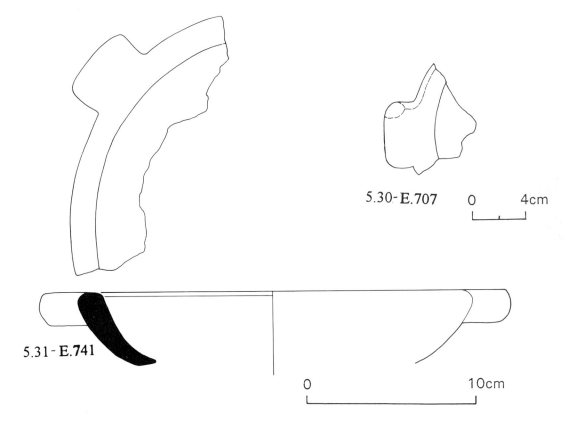

5.30- E.707   0   4cm

5.31- E.741

0   10cm

Fig. 5.30–31. Mortaria

Ceramic Objects other than Pottery

a. Circular loom weight with two holes for attachment (Fig. 5.33).
Diameter: 14.2cm
Thickness: 5.2cm
Fabric: F.17
Context: E.153 (Phase 12)

b. Partially complete rectangular loom weight with a hole for attachment (Fig. 5.34).
Width: 7.0cm
Height: 10.2
Thickness: 3.5cm
Fabric: F.17
Context: 1988 Systematic Surface Survey (P/88/99A)

c. The upper section of a rectangular brick, with traces of stamped decoration on the interior (Fig. 5.35).
Thickness: 5.6 cm
Fabric: F.17
Context: 1988 Systematic Surface Survey P/88/??

d. Part of the centre of a brick decorated with a flower-shaped stamp (Fig. 5.36).
Thickness: 3.4 cm
Fabric: F.17
Context: Ermita de Villadiego, to the west of Peñaflor.

e. Fragment of a brick with a simplified flower shape stamped within a square cartouche (Fig. 5.37).
Length: 8.0 cm (surviving)
Thickness: 5.0 cm

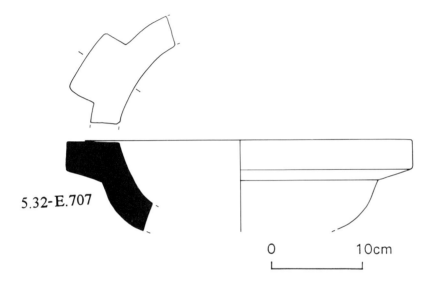

5.32-E.707

0   10cm

Fig. 5.32. Mortaria

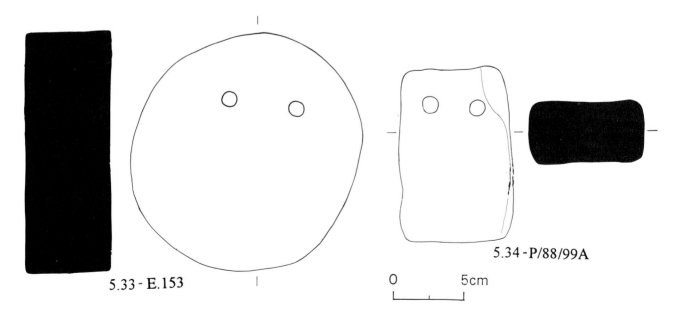

5.33-E.153

5.34-P/88/99A

0   5cm

Fig. 5.33–4. Loom Weight

Fabric: F.17
Context: 1988 Systematic Surface Survey (P/88/46)

f. Complete brick with stamped decoration consisting of a spoked wheel within a square cartouche (Fig. 5.38).
Width: 26.4cm
Length: 38.8cm
Thickness: 6.2cm
Fabric: F.17
Context: 1987 Topographical Survey

Roman Coins (Unillustrated)

A total of 16 Roman coins were discovered during the excavations.

a. *Bronze*
Obverse: Head of Janus
Reverse: Very worn prow of ship: before, L. Below (R)OMA.
Diameter: 2.7cm
Denomination: As
Axes: 12 o'clock
Mint: Rome
Reference: As RRC 117B/1
Date: Some time after 206–195 BC
Year: 1989
Context: E.119 (Phase 8a)

b. *Bronze*
Obverse: Head of Janus
Reverse: Illegible
Diameter: 3.1cm
Denomination: As
Mint: Rome
Date: Republican
Year: 1990 (Lab no. 6392B)
Context: E.315 (Phase 12)

c. *Lead*
Obverse: ??Lower part of a figure standing on flat surface
Reverse: ? A D or AP
Diameter: 1.00cm
Denomination: Lead token
Axes: 10 o'clock
Mint: Not Known
Reference: There is no published parallel in Casariego, Cores and Pliego 1987.
Date: These coins are dated generically to the 1st century BC (Casariego, Cores and Pliego 1987, 161–2).
Year: 1992 (Lab No. 6660)
Context: E.762 (Phase 9)

d. *Bronze*
Obverse: Illegible Head of Augustus (l)
Reverse: Laurel Wreath enclosing legend IVLIA TRAD
Diameter: 2.5cm
Denomination: As
Axes: 9 o'clock
Mint: ? Iulia Traducta
Reference: Villaronga 1979, 268 no. 1014.
Date: Augustan.

Year: 1989
Context: E.13 (Phase 12)

e. *Bronze*
Obverse: [......]CAESAR[....], Male Head (r), possibly Claudius
Reverse: Totally illegible
Diameter: 2.6cm
Denomination: As
Date: Julio-Claudian period
Year: 1992 (Lab No. 6663)
Context: E.641 (Phase 7a–9)

f. *Bronze*
Obverse: Indistinct
Reverse: Indistinct
Diameter: 2.3cm
Denomination: Halved coin
Date: Usually date to early Imperial period
Year: 1992
Context: E.513 (Phase 12)

g. *Bronze*
Obverse: Head (l)
Reverse: Illegible
Diameter: 2.00cm
Denomination: As
Mint: Rome ?
Date: ?1st century AD, possibly a Flavian Emperor
Year: 1992 (Lab No. 6655)
Context: E.707 (Phase 9)

h. *Bronze*
Obverse: Illegible, Bearded head of Commodus (r)
Reverse: Illegible but [M.COMM.ANT.P.FELIX AVG. BRIT.P.P.], Apollo standing front, head (r), with l hand holding lyre and plectrum supported on column; on either side SC
Diameter: 2.65cm
Denomination: As (squared)
Axes: 12 o'clock
Mint: Rome
Reference: RIC III.588
Date: AD 190/191
Year: 1992 (Lab No. 6658D)
Context: E.271 (Phase 8)

i. *Brass*
Obverse: Illegible
Reverse: Illegible
Diameter: 2.35cm
Denomination: As
Date: Early Imperial ?
Year: 1992 (Lab No. 6667)
Context: E.554 (Phase 9)

j. *Bronze*
Obverse: IMPGALLIENUSAUG, Radiate bust of Gallienus (r)
Reverse: SALUSAUG, Aesculapius standing (l) (holding serpent on staff)
Diameter: 2.1cm
Denomination: Antoninianus
Axes: 4 o'clock

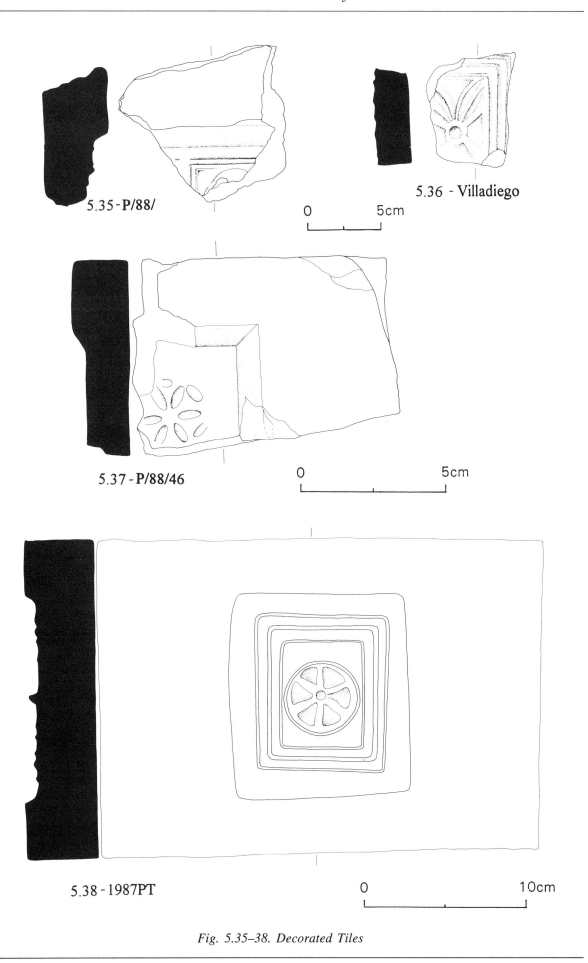

5.35 - P/88/

5.36 - Villadiego

0   5cm

5.37 - P/88/46

0   5cm

5.38 - 1987PT

0   10cm

Fig. 5.35–38. Decorated Tiles

Mint: MP
Reference: RIC IV.1.511b
Year: 1992 (Lab. No. 6658A)
Context: E.1 (Phase 12)

k. *Bronze*
Obverse: Cut down in size: no traces of lettering survive
Radiate bust of Claudius (r)
Reverse: (consecrat)IO
Flaming Altar with garland
Diameter: 1.25cm
Denomination: Antoninianus
Axes: 12 o'clock
Mint: Rome
Reference: As RIC IV.1.259ff
Date: AD 270.
Year: 1990 (Lab No. 6534)
Context: E.336 (Phase 7a)

l. *Bronze*
Obverse: IMPCCLAUDIUSAUG
Radiate bust of Claudius (r)
Reverse: VICT/ORIAAUG
Winged Victoria standing (l) holding palm (l) and wreath (r)
Diameter: 2.00cm
Denomination: Antoninianus
Axes: 1 o'clock
Mint: Rome
Reference: RIC V.1. 103
Date: AD 268/270
Year: 1992 (Lab No. 6666)
Context: E.700 (Phase 12)

m. *Bronze*
Obverse: [..cl] AUD [ius......] AUG
Bearded head of Claudius with diadem (r)
Reverse: [?fides exerci...]
Female figure standing (r) holding two ensigns, one transverse.
Diameter: 2.1cm
Denomination: Antoninianus
Axes: 6 o'clock
Mint: Rome ?
Reference: RIC IV.1.34.
Date: AD 268/270
Year: 1992 (Lab No. 6662)
Context: E.1 (Phase 12)

n. *Bronze*
Obverse: DNVALEN/SPFAUG: Diademed bust (r)
Reverse: (securitas)./REIPUBLICA(E): Winged victory advancing (l), holding ?sceptre (r) palm (l).
Diameter: 1.8cm
Denomination: AE3
Axes: 12 o'clock
Mint: Unclear
Reference: As LRBC II.82ff
Date: AD 364–7
Year: 1992 (Lab No. 6670)
Context: E.700 (Phase 12)

o. *Bronze*
Obverse: Male Head (r)
Reverse: Illegible

Diameter: 2.5cm
Denomination: As
Date: Early Imperial
Year: 1992 (Lab No. 6668)
Context: E.700 (Phase 12)

p. *Bronze*
Obverse: Illegible
Reverse: Illegible
Diameter: 2.00cm
Denomination: AE3
Date: Roman, possibly from a regional Baetican mint
Year: 1990 (Lab No. 6399)
Context: E.260 (Phase 12)

Architectural Fragments

Architectural pieces at the site were rare. Apart from the occasional fragments of *opus spicatum* bricks, quarter column segments, tesserae and marble (Appendix 5), the following pieces of note were discovered:

a. Double torus column base (Fig. 5.39).
Width: 0.75m
Surviving Height: 0.38m
Material: Whitish marble.
Context: Directly overlying the north–south wall 177 (Fig. 3.25).
Parallels: The on-site context suggests that the column base was re-deposited at its find-spot during the demolition and robbing of the site, during Phase 9 or subsequently. However, dated parallels make it clear that it was originally installed in the early imperial period. This column base is part of a well-known group in which the upper torus is slightly narrower than the lower one, which sits directly on the column support without a stylobate (Jiménez 1975, 266–9). The origin of these is to be sought in Italy in the later Republic. In Hispania, they have been attested on sites from the Augustan through to the Flavian period. In southern Spain, they are known at the Temple of Diana at Emerita Augusta (Mérida), which is dated to the Augustan period (Trillmich *et alii* 1993, Taf.46), at Carmo in a structure dating to the early decades of the 1st century AD (Lineros Romero and Domínguez Mora 1987, 326–9, Lám. I), the basilica at Baelo which is dated to the Neronian period (Lancha, Le Roux and Rouillard 1983, Figs 17 and 18; Bonneville *et alii* 1982, Figs 19 and 21; Sillières 1995, 112, Fig. 58), and the Isaeum at Baelo in a context dating to the last quarter of the 1st century AD (Sillières 1997, 99 Fig. 43). Finally, other similar double torus bases are to be found at the Tumba de Servilia at Carmona, which should be dated to some time in the second half of the 1st century AD (on the basis of recent dating evidence: J. M. Rodríguez Hidalgo, pers. comm). Further north, a very similar example from the forum at Valentia has been dated to the last third of the 1st century AD (Marín Jordá *et alii* 1999, 10 and 13). The example from Celti is perhaps closest to those from the basilica at Baelo, where the upper and lower torus both have the same diameter and where the column also sits atop a solid foundation.

5.39-E.177

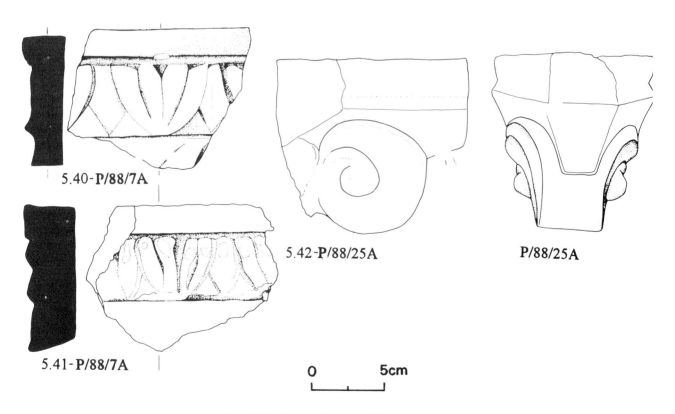

5.40-**P/88/7A**

5.41-**P/88/7A**

5.42-**P/88/25A**

P/88/25A

0   **5cm**

Fig. 5.39–42. Architectural Fragments

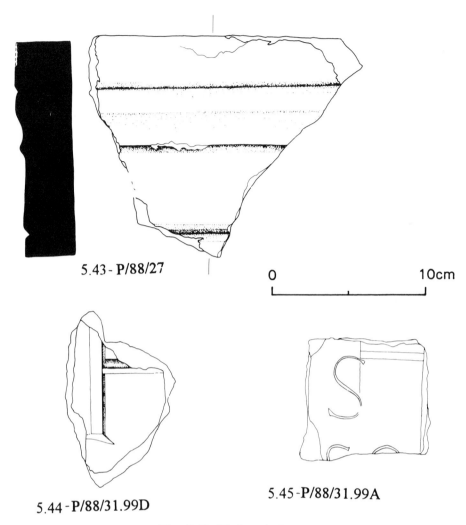

5.43 - P/88/27

0   10cm

5.44 - P/88/31.99D

5.45 - P/88/31.99A

Fig. 5.43–45. Inscriptions

b. Fragment of kymation decorated with a band of petalled flowers (Fig. 5.40).
Maximum Width: 2.6cm
Material: Coarse-grained white marble
Context: 1988 Systematic Surface survey (P/88/7A)

c. Fragment of kymation decorated with a band of petalled flowers (Fig. 5.41).
Maximum Width: 3.2cm
Material: Coarse-grained white marble
Context: 1988 Systematic Surface Survey (P/88/7A)

d. Fragment of a column capital decorated with a volute (Fig. 5.42).
Height: 10.7cm
Material: White Limestone
Context: 1988 Systematic Surface Survey (P/88/25A).
Parallels: Despite its fragmentary condition, this would appear to be part of a small-size corinthian or composite capital. Dated parallels for larger versions of this piece have been found at the Mosque of Córdoba (Márquez 1993: Lám. 65, nr.218), of Julio-Claudian date, and at the Convento de Santa Cruz at Córdoba (Márquez 1993: Lám.72, nr.237), of Hadrianic date.

Inscriptions

Very few inscriptions were found during the campaigns of survey and excavation and are listed below. Otherwise, occasional discoveries through the years have brought to light 65 inscriptions which are discussed elsewhere (Chapter 8).

a. Corniced edge of an epigraphic field: possible traces of an upright letter visible (Fig. 5.43).
Thickness of stone: 3.6cm
Material: White marble
Context: 1988 Systematic Surface Survey (P/88/27)

b. Fragment of an inscription with the following: [..] F [..] (Fig. 5.44).
Height of extent letter: 6.8cm.
Thickness of stone: 3.5cm
Material: Fine-grained white marble
Context: 1988 Systematic Surface Survey (P/88/31.99A)

c. Fragment of an inscription with the following visible: [.....] S / [...] S (?)/ [...] (Fig. 5.45).
Height of complete letter: 4.0cm.
Thickness of stone: 2.25cm
Material: White/grey marble with dark grey streaks
Context: 1988 Systematic Surface Survey (P/88/31.99A)

Chapter 6
The Environmental Evidence

Anthony King, Anthony Waldron, Martin Jones, Jane Reed
and Christian de Vartavan

Abstract

This chapter presents analyses of the environmental evidence from the site (complemented by Appendices 4 and 6). It begins with the animal bones, which point to changing husbandry practices in the region of the town from the late Bronze Age down to the late Roman period. The most salient feature is the rise in importance of pig in local diet from the Augustan and Julio-Claudian periods (Phases 5 and 6) down to the Neronian/Flavian period (Phase 7) in particular. Thereafter, pig begins to dwindle in relative importance. This trend is important for our understanding of the development of the site and is echoed in the second part of the report, where an analysis of seeds from the site points to the increasing importance of olives in the economy of the site in the period leading up to and after the Neronian/Flavian period (Phase 7). As is argued in Chapter 10, there is little doubt that these changes reflect the changing character of the economy of Celti, as it begins to respond to Roman demands for foodstuffs.

The Animal and Human Bones

The Animal Bones (AK)

A total of 2029 bones was examined, of which 1178 (58.1%) were identified to species. The remainder were allocated to size categories or parts of the skeleton (ribs, etc.) only (Appendix 4: Table 1). This is a small assemblage, capable of yielding some useful statistics, but is not amenable to detailed analysis. For the purposes of study, the assemblage has been divided into the following groups:

Phases 2–5: down to the Augustan period;
Phase 6: the Augustan and Julio-Claudian period;
Phase 7: between the Neronian and early Flavian periods;
Phase 8: early 3rd century AD;
Phase 9: some time after the early 5th cent. AD;
Phase 11: between some time after the early 5th and the 7th centuries AD;
Phase 12: down to the present day.

Only a small number of bones come from pre-Public Building phases (2–6), or from phase 11.

The methodology used in the analysis follows the usual procedures for examination of archaeo-osteological material. Bones and teeth were identified to element and species by means of comparative reference sources. Ribs and vertebrae (except atlases and axes) were not identified to species, but were allocated to size groups (Appendix 4: Table 1), as were the unidentifiable fragments. Every piece of bone, including unfused epiphyses, was counted, except where modern breakage was evident. All visible teeth in jaws were counted, and the jaws and loose 3rd deciduous and permanent molars were also determined to left-hand or right-hand sides. For limb bones, however, determinations to the side of the body were not undertaken (with the exception of dog skeleton III), since the nature of the assemblage – largely mixed food waste – reduces the significance of this information. This has had an impact on the method used for calculating the minimum number of individuals (MN), in that limb element totals (e.g. distal tibia) were simply divided by two to calculate the MN for that part of the body, and the highest element MN in each phase taken to represent the MN for the species in that phase. No attempt was made to match pairs, or to take account of age-at-death in the calculation of MN, which has had the effect of producing a slightly lower MN than would have been the case if the full methodology had been applied. For the assessment of butchery and dismemberment of the carcass, butchery marks and the part of the bone to survive were recorded. Ageing criteria followed the methods proposed in Wilson *et al* (1982), and measurements were taken according to the scheme of Driesch (1976).

Generally, the state of preservation of the bones was good, except for some contexts in Phases 9 and 12, in which the bones were very shattered and fragmentary on recovery due to adverse soil conditions. From the nature of the assemblage, it seems most likely that the bones were deposited as a result of general rubbish accumulation. Some of the bones had been burnt, probably after disposal, and a small number of the late Roman (Phases 9 and 12) bones have signs of having been chewed by dogs and rodents. With the exception of a goat horncore from phase 7 showing saw-marks for the probable removal of horn, there is no evidence of debris from industrial production, such as bone or antler working, nor is there evidence of deliberate deposition as might be associated with ritual practices. In Phases 9 and 12, a substantial proportion of the bones concentrate in and around the mouth of the well in the easternmost garden of the house complex, probably as a result of deliberate rubbish deposition to fill in the feature. This is the only marked concentration on the site, and other-

wise bones were fairly evenly scattered. In amongst the general deposits, most of which must derive from food preparation or consumption, there was an almost complete dog skeleton (E.758, phase 9) and partial remains of two others. These animals were probably dumped into the rubbish deposits.

MEAT SUPPLY: THE SPECIES REPRESENTED

The representation of the main domestic species varies from phase to phase (Appendix 4: Table 2; Figs. 6.1 and 6.2). In Phases 2–5 and 6, there are too few bones to be confident in the representativeness of the figures, but it can be seen that sheep/goat and pig are most common. Ox is also reasonably well represented, and may well have contributed substantially to the meat supply, by virtue of this species' relative size. The situation is clarified a little in Phase 7, since the group is larger, and it can be seen that ox and pig are now most common, with sheep/goat slightly less so. Horse and dog bones are also present, together with remains of hunted and trapped species (red deer, rabbit and hare). By Phase 8, pig bones are significantly more common, a matter of some interest which will be returned to below, while sheep/goat have also

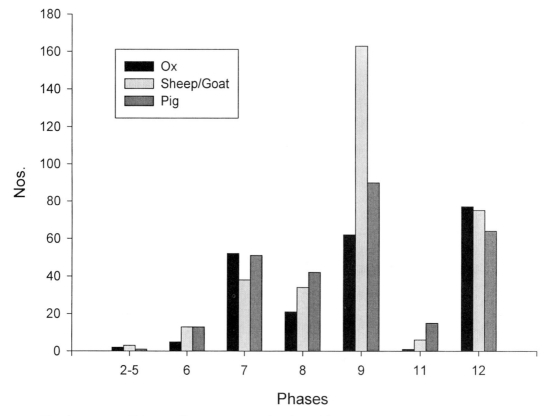

Fig. 6.1. Mammal bones, fragment count by phase (data from Appendix 4: Tables 1 and 2)

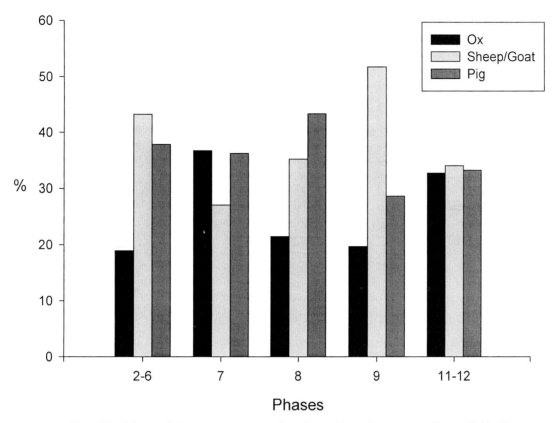

Fig. 6.2. Mammal bones, percentages by phase (data from Appendix 4: Table 2)

increased in numbers relative to those of ox. Again the figures change in Phase 9. This time sheep/ goat is significantly more common than the others, also an issue that has a wider significance, and pig and ox are roughly equal in numbers. Phase 11 is of little consequence numerically since so few bones were found, but in phase 12 a reasonable assemblage yields a picture of all three main food sources being roughly equally represented in terms of bone numbers. This phase almost certainly includes some material redeposited from earlier phases, particularly phase 9, and also some material much later than the 5th century AD, since it includes all the upper layers on the site. It is therefore probably a less reliable indicator of chronological variation than the earlier, better stratified phases.

In terms of meat supply, these figures can be interpreted for an urban site like Celti as representing the remains of food supply in the form of joints of meat or waste. Thus, the bone numbers (BN) probably give a better idea of the relative importance of these meat sources than the minimum number of individuals (MN). Nevertheless, the relative size of the animals in part conditions the size of the meat joints and discarded parts, and it is fair to say that beef may well have been much

more dominant in the meat supply than the figures in Appendix 4 (Table 2) imply.

In more detail, a small number of bones yield data on the ratio of sheep to goats. On the basis of eight horncores, astragali and first phalanges, there is a ratio of three sheep to five goats. From early Roman phases (7 and 8), all four bones indicate goat, while from late Roman phases (9 and 12), there are one goat and three sheep bones. The sample is perhaps too small to be meaningful, but hints at a predominance of goats in earlier phases, changing to a majority of sheep in later Roman times.

Similarly, it is possible to glean some information on the ratio of male to female pigs, on the basis of a small sample of ten canine teeth. In early Roman phases (6 and 7), there are two males and no females, while in later Roman phases (9 and 12) there are two males and six females. The differences may be due to the small size of the sample, but at all events, both male and female pigs represent surplus animals sent for slaughter and consumption as food. A town like Celti would be expected to be a consumer site with a different pattern visible in the pig sex ratios and other aspects of animal husbandry from a producer site such as a villa.

A small number of the pig bones is more likely to be wild boar than domestic pig, by virtue of their size: a mandible with 3rd molar erupting (Phase 6), a radius shaft and a juvenile humerus (Phase 7) and a 1st phalanx (Phase 8). Some of the other species (considered separately below) also formed a small part of the meat supply.

BUTCHERY AND PARTS OF THE CARCASS REPRESENTED

Another way of looking at the meat supply is in terms of the parts of the carcass represented (Appendix 4: Table 3). For ox, there is an interesting difference between the early Roman Phase 7 and the later Roman Phases 9 and 12. In the former, lesser quality meat (group II), cranial parts (group III) and extremities (group IV) are common, but higher quality meat (group I) is not. This may reflect the possible public nature of the excavated area at this time (see discussion in Chapter 9), with the butchery and sale of beef joints on or near the site, and the higher quality meat going elsewhere. For the late Roman phases, however, group I meat is much better represented, whilst group III is unusually low. Group IV is also more common. It is possible, therefore, that the easternmost garden of the house complex was the focus of high-status consumption of beef joints in the late Roman phases, when many bones were being dumped as food waste in or near the cistern-head. The lack of cranial parts implies that the animals had been dismembered and that bones of this group had been taken elsewhere, or that they had never been brought into the excavated area. Horncores are particularly uncommon, which may imply the removal of horns for manufacturing and industrial purposes elsewhere in Celti.

The picture for sheep/goat is less clear, since the percentages of each group are fairly consistent in all the phases represented. Groups I and II together form 50–60% of all groups throughout, showing the presence of both higher and lower quality meat debris on the site. Cranial parts are less well represented, but there is a significant increase in the number of teeth over time, relative to the number of bones overall (T/B and T/B%). This is probably due to changes in butchery practice regarding sheep/goat skull and jaws, which resulted in more loose teeth (and jaws with teeth, to a lesser extent) being scattered in the excavated area by late Roman times. Interestingly, this trend is not seen in ox or pig T/B ratios, and argues for differences in butchery practice for each species. A converse pattern to that of the teeth is noted in the sheep/goat horncores, which are more common in Phases 7 and 8 than later. This is the period when goats may have predominated over sheep (see above). One of the goat horncores has saw-marks consistent with removal of the horn, and it is possible that at this period, dismemberment of sheep and goat carcasses took place in the vicinity of the site. Taken with the T/B data, the implication for the late Roman period, however, is that the crania were more likely to have been broken up in or near the excavated area, and the horns removed elsewhere, as was noted for cattle.

The pattern for pig is variable but overall similar to sheep/goat, with the exception of the T/B pattern just noted. Groups I and II are fairly well represented, implying a range of meat joints and waste on site. Extremities are also fairly common, and are probably the result of on-site or near-site butchery and consumption of trotters. Cranial parts are generally slightly less well-represented, but the percentages are also consistent with butchery, consumption and disposal on or near the site.

All the main domestic meat species show evidence of butchery marks. For the most part, these are miscellaneous cut- or chop-marks in the vicinity of limb articulations, especially in cattle, where division into manageable joints was necessary. Cleanly chopped bones indicate the use of sharp iron tools, and saw-marks on both long-bones and horncores were noted. Many cattle long-bones were also deliberately broken up, presumably for their marrow.

AGE-OF-SLAUGHTER

An aspect of the osteological data that is related to meat supply is the age of slaughter of the animals. The expected pattern in the ancient world varies from species to species as well as between cultures; in early Imperial Roman Italy, for instance, cattle were usually slaughtered as adults at the end of their working lives, pigs were killed very young (with some adults as well) since there was a taste for young pork, and sheep/goats spread through the age range, but tending to be killed as adults (King 1994; forthcoming). The usual interpretation for sheep/goat is that a young slaughter pattern favours a milk/meat economy (usually where there is a predominance of goats), and an elderly pattern a wool economy (often the case when sheep are predominant) (Payne 1973).

In the light of these expectations, the slaughter patterns at Celti differ in some important respects, and offer the possibility of other economic and social factors at work. Generally the pattern for all species is a largely adult age-of-slaughter, but it has to be noted that the sample size is small and in places inconsistent in the conclusions that can be deduced from it.

The pattern for ox in every phase is, effectively, an adult one, with all bones except one having fused epiphyses (Appendix 4: Table 4), and all mandibles except one having adult dentition in a fairly worn state (Appendix 4: Table 5). The exceptions represent a calf of less than 10 months and a young adult of c. 2 years. The age-of-slaughter of ox, therefore, conforms with the usual pattern elsewhere, and it can be assumed that the cattle were not raised primarily for their meat.

Sheep and goat bones and teeth offer a similar picture: the epiphyses of all bones are fused, and the mandibles, with the exception of a juvenile/ sub-adult of c. 18 months from phase 7, are those of adults as well. A small number of juvenile limb bone shafts and cranial fragments were also noted, particularly from Phase 7, which are not included on Table 4. In general, the pattern is substantially more adult than might be expected, and must be the result of either the specific selection of adult animals for consumption at Celti, or a husbandry regime that reared the great majority of animals into adulthood, presumably for their wool and to a lesser extent, their milk. There is the possibility of a younger pattern of slaughter in Phase 7, which coincides with a high ratio of goats to sheep.

Pigs were slaughtered at a younger stage in their lives, on average, but the pattern is also more adult than expected. The evidence of the fusion of epiphyses shows that 33–60% of the animals survived into their third year before they were killed, with the possibility that more went into their third year in the early Roman period (Phases 7 and 8) than in the later Roman period (Phases 9 and 12). The data from the mandibles are very thin, and inconsistent with the fusion evidence in suggesting that two-thirds of the animals were slaughtered before one year old. There are three very young mandibles from Phase 9, and it may be the case that in the late Roman period there was a more juvenile bias to the slaughter pattern, but that a substantial proportion of the bones of these juveniles have not survived to be recovered. This period also sees the slaughter of more female than male pigs (see above), which may represent the killing for meat of all except breeding sows.

Whatever the exact details of the age-at-death, it remains the case that in general pigs were apparently reared for longer before slaughter than expected elsewhere, particularly in the early Roman period, when very juvenile patterns of slaughter are often seen in Roman Italy. It seems that the Italian predilection for young pork was not replicated at Celti, even if other aspects of Romanization were (see Chapter 10). It may be the case that different breeds of pig were being reared in the region, that matured more slowly than breeds in Italy.

PATHOLOGY

A related aspect to the age-of-slaughter is the health of the animals as reflected in the bone pathology. As in any mammal population, elderly animals are more likely to have degenerative joint diseases and dental problems than younger ones. This is seen to a small extent at Celti. In cattle, the animals were quite healthy, with only one foot bone from a phase 12 context showing signs of degenerative wear and associated exostosis. A couple of cattle teeth had problems of abnormal wear or calculus deposits. Sheep and goats, too, were healthy, with only dental problems noted, such as brown or silvery calculus deposits on some adult/elderly teeth, one case of abnormal wear, and about half-a-dozen adult/elderly teeth with signs of erosion or growth in the roots as a result, probably, of periodontal disease. There are no pathologies recorded for pig, denoting a very healthy herd in view of the more adult slaughter pattern noted above.

SIZES AND BREEDS

Evidence for the sizes of the domestic stock is limited, but the measurements and calculation of withers heights (Appendix 4: Tables 6 and 8) show that the cattle, sheep/goats and pigs were of average size. A small number of the pig bones are significantly larger than average, e.g. phalanx I GLpe 45mm (Phase 8): these are probably from wild boar, to judge from the metrical criteria given by Driesch and Boessneck (1976, 57–65). In comparison with other sites in the region such as Munigua, the size range of the Celti domestic stock was very similar (Boessneck and Driesch 1980), and was also broadly the same as that from the north-eastern Spanish late Roman villa at Vilauba (Girona: King 1988; archive report). Domestic stock in Roman Italy could be larger, for instance at Naples, where cattle were c. 10cm, sheep/goats c. 6cm and pigs c. 5cm higher at the withers (King 1994, Tab. 49). It is likely that the animals at Celti were essentially local breeds, but it remains to be seen whether size improvements took place in Roman Baetica as a result of Roman notions of selective breeding, or introductions of improved stock.

OTHER SPECIES

Equids are represented by both horses and donkeys, and in all probability, mules as well, although it is difficult to differentiate the latter osteologically except by means of the cheek teeth (Armitage & Chapman 1979). A mandible fragment and seven cheek teeth from a phase 7 context is attributable to horse, and other loose teeth seem more likely to be horse than mule. The majority of horse bones are from phase 7, and smaller numbers from later phases (Appendix 4: Table 1). As might be expected from an urban site, their numbers in the assemblage are low when compared with a rural site such as Vilauba villa (King 1988). Few measurements were possible, all coming from late Roman phases (Appendix 4: Table 8). They indicate animals of slightly smaller stature than those of Vilauba (King 1988; archive report) or Naples (King 1994, 402). Donkey is represented by a mandibular molar and part of a pelvis; both attributions being tentative but fairly likely. The alternative, much less likely, is that they are of small ponies of a quite different stature to the horses from the site.

There is no direct evidence that the equid bones are food waste, but it has to be noted that the bones were all disarticulated and frequently broken or shattered, and were mixed with domestic food waste. Although no butchery marks were noted, the equid bones may represent food waste if preparation methods were different from the more common domesticates.

Dog is well-represented in the assemblage, with substantial remains of a skeleton from a Phase 9 context, two very partial skeletons from phase 12, and various individual bones from these and earlier phases (Appendix 4: Table 1). Many measurements were possible from the Phase 9 skeleton, from which a calculation of shoulder height of c. 54cm was made (Appendix 4: Table 6). This is approximately in the middle of the range of 23–72cm established for a sample of Romano-British dogs by Harcourt (1974). Unfortunately, the cranium is fragmentary, but from the jaws it can be established that the dog was medium/long-snouted and in terms of appearance overall, was probably an undifferentiated breed of medium build. The other two dog skeletons are very fragmentary, one being slightly larger in size than that just described (Appendix 4: Table 6), the other being approximately the same size. A mandible from the remaining dog bones (from Phase 9) is noteworthy, since it had lost the M3 *ante mortem*. There is also a very juvenile radius from a Phase 8 context. In sum, it is likely that the dogs in the assemblage were semi-scavengers in the town, perhaps also acting as guard dogs.

The other species in the assemblage are all wild. The presence of a small number of wild boar bones has already been noted, and are presumably the product of hunting. In the case of red deer, the remains are also almost certainly the result of hunting. There is only a single antler tine (from Phase 12), all the other bones being limb bones and therefore most probably food debris. Most had been broken, but a humerus (from Phase 8) and a radius (from Phase 9) are complete, indicating that venison was possibly prepared for cooking in a different manner from beef, which

usually resulted in breakage (and chop-marks) in the ox limb bones.

Rabbit is common in virtually all phases, and although a few complete bones have a fresh appearance suggestive of modern intrusions into stratified levels, it is very likely from the broken state and appearance of the majority of the bones, that they represent food debris. Rabbits were presumably trapped, or conceivably reared in warrens, and formed a useful supplement to the meat supply. One of the rabbit bones, a pelvis from phase 7, shows a pathological condition in the form of smooth wear on the ilial side of the rim of the acetabulum, possibly caused by partial dislocation and displacement of the head of the femur. Hare is much rarer, being represented by a single broken tibia from a Phase 7 context. This was presumably a hunted species.

Another species that was probably collected and eaten is tortoise, of which three pieces of carapace were recovered from Phase 7. Wood mouse is also present in Phase 7, positively identified by a mandible and teeth. This species is found in or near human habitation, provided there is sufficient undergrowth and that disturbance is not too great. It is not, however, an indoor-preferring commensal like the house mouse. Wood mouse is the native common mouse of western Europe, unlike the house mouse, which was spreading through Europe during the Roman period, being found for instance at Pompeii in 2nd century BC contexts (King forthcoming). Another outdoor mouse species found in cultivated ground and gardens, Algerian mouse (*Mus spretus*), is currently found in the Iberian peninsula and may well have been part of Celti's regional fauna at the time. The only other small mammal bone is a tibia (from phase 12) of a rat or a similar-sized rodent.

COMPARISON WITH OTHER SITES:
CELTI AND THE AGRICULTURAL ECONOMY

There are only a few other Roman bone assemblages from Spain that can be compared with Celti (Appendix 4: Table 7; Fig. 6.3). However, there are several of pre-Roman date from Andalucía alone, which can be used to provide a background to the patterns seen during the Empire in the region. Most of these sites date to the period of Phoenician and Tartessian influence 8th–6th cent. BC, from Huelva (Belén *et al.* 1977a; Cereijo & Paton 1989; 1990), Setefilla (Estévez 1983), Castulo (Molero 1985), Castillo de Doña Blanca (Morales *et al.* 1994a), El Carambolo (Martín Roldán 1959) and Toscanos (Uerpmann & Uerpmann 1973). The data from these sites have recently been summarised and tabulated numerically by Morales *et al.* (1994b, Tab. 10.3) and will not be repeated here. For most of them, there

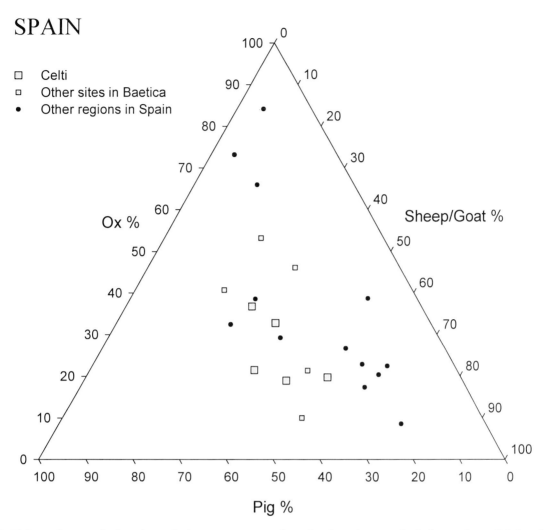

Fig. 6.3. Triangular graph showing relative percentages of cattle, sheep/goat and pig bones from Celti and other Roman sites in Baetica and elsewhere in Spain (data from Appendix 4: Table 7)

is a pattern with relatively low pig percentages, typically 20% or less (of the total of pig, sheep/goat and ox bones) with a couple of exceptions; and higher sheep/goat percentages than those of ox. Huelva, for instance, yields figures for one of the assemblages of 36.9% ox, 44.6% sheep/goat and 18.5% pig (n = 502; Belén *et al* 1977). This would imply a meat dietary pattern dominated by beef, followed by mutton/goat-meat and pork. In agricultural terms, a mixed pattern is implied, with the presence of pasture for the cattle, probably woodland for the pigs, and probably a generalised grain and animal-rearing economy. There is, however, a good degree of variability in the basic pattern, which suggests that local topography had significant influence on the economies of some sites. A good example of this is Castillo de Doña Blanca, adjacent to the coast near Cádiz. Ox and pig are both very low here, with sheep/goat percentages consequently being c. 80% of the total. Conditions were

presumably not favourable for the former, and in fact it is clear from the large quantities of fish and marine mollusc remains that much of the meat diet was derived from the sea.

It is unfortunate that the succeeding Turdetanian period has yielded very few bone assemblages. Those earlier sites with phases dated to the 5th century BC and later (e.g. Setefilla, Castillo de Doña Blanca) appear to continue their own established patterns, and it may well be the case that despite the overall diminution in settlement activity, agricultural patterns showed a continuity with previous practices. One site, Cerro Macareno (Sevilla), is interesting in showing generally increasing percentages of pig through time: Phoenician phase 13.5%, early Iberian 11.9%, Iberian 22.4%, Iberian/Roman 26.1%. There are also ox percentages at c. 46–63% and sheep/goat percentages gradually declining from 38.9% to 20.7% (Amberger 1985). This hints at changes to the agricultural economy, with less reliance on sheep/ goat and more on pig, while cattle were dominant throughout. This change may reflect intensification of production, similar to that seen in Celti's bone assemblage at a slightly later date (see below).

Another Iberian settlement of the 3rd–2nd century BC, Cerro de la Cruz (Almedinilla, Córdoba), is also interesting in having an apparently very specialised assemblage that was presumably the result of a hunting economy. There are 127 red deer bones, 36 dog bones and 16 of rabbit, compared with only 18 sheep/goat and one pig bone forming the domestic meat supply (Montero 1990).

The early phases at Celti are of this period (Figs. 6.1 & 6.2), but are too insignificant in osteological terms to allow us to establish any dietary or agricultural patterns. Phase 6, the final pre-Public Building phase (Appendix 4: Table 1), hints at a pattern with relatively few ox bones and roughly equivalent numbers of sheep/goat and pig, which may be a reflection of local conditions before Roman cultural influence became very strong at the site. Since two of the thirteen pig bones are probably of wild boar, domestic pig is marginally less well-represented than sheep/goat, but the numbers overall are too low to be able to comment meaningfully on this detail. The period 5th–1st cent. BC is obviously important for the major cultural transitions that took place, and it would be most welcome to be able to fill in the archaeozoological picture for this from future excavations in the region.

With Phase 7, and the construction of the complex tentatively identified as the forum (see Chapter 9), the influence of Roman tastes on the diet is starting to be seen. The percentage of sheep/goat is lowered, in favour of ox and pig in fairly equal proportions (resulting in an absolute predominance of beef in the meat diet). This is possibly a weak reflection of the sort of diet seen in western central Italy at this time (King 1985; 1994), but differs in having a high percentage of ox, which would be unusual in the Italian diet. The decline in sheep/goat may be significant in agricultural terms, in that it could correspond with an intensification of cropping, perhaps cash-cropping of vines and olives, that pushed sheep grazing onto more distant territory, with a lesser number, predominantly goats, kept nearby for meat and milk.

Intensification was a process at Celti that did not apparently go as far as reducing the amount of cattle pasture as well, which would have been the case with further intensification of arid-zone agriculture, since cattle compete with humans for water resources and occupy valuable land that could be used for crops. It may be interesting to note that 2nd-century levels at Munigua in the nearby Sierra Morena show very similar proportions (Appendix 4: Table 7), including a fairly high proportion of goats. In contrast, the contemporary assemblages from Lucus Augusti (Lugo), in the more humid Galician region, display a high percentage of cattle (Fig. 6.3). This emphasizes the regional nature of animal husbandry in Roman Spain and the influences of climate and topography (see Blasco 1999).

By the time of the construction of the Roman houses in phase 8, the romanization of diet and the intensification of agriculture had probably reached their apogee. Pig bones account for nearly half of the main domesticate assemblage, while ox numbers are down. Such a pattern would not look out of place in an Italian context (King 1999), and it may be the case that pigs were being raised on a commercial scale, as has been recorded in Italy at this time (at Settefinestre; King 1985). This would be a form of cash-cropping that would fit with intensive cultivation of olives, etc. A form of pig husbandry could have existed that utilised the shady conditions afforded by the cultivated trees as well as actual woodland, similar perhaps to the system used until recently in Extremadura (Parsons 1962).

An apparent chronological trend in phase 8 is the recovery in the sheep/goat percentage by comparison with the previous phase. This continues markedly in phase 9 (late Roman), in which sheep/ goat at 51.6% forms the most common domesticate, with pig and ox lower but roughly equal to each other in numerical terms. Sheep are now more common than goats. This is almost certainly not just a phenomenon of Celti alone, since it is seen elsewhere in Andalucía at Munigua, at other urban sites in Spain (Tarragona, Zaragoza, Tiermes) and indeed in many other parts of the western Mediterranean as well (e.g. Marseille, Jourdan 1976; Naples, King 1994; Setif, King 1990; see also King 1999). There seems to have been a widespread change in the late Roman period, probably towards a less intensive form of agriculture. Cash-cropping may have declined, to be replaced by ranching, pasturing, and probably a return to cultivation of grain crops that could be rotated in sympathy with animal husbandry regimes.

Not all Spanish sites reflect this change, however. Two villas in the north of the country, Vilauba (Catalunya) and Arellano (Navarra) display different patterns – the former having relatively high pig and cattle percentages throughout, and the latter high sheep/goat and ox. Both are presumably production sites in areas where the topography must have influenced local possibilities in animal rearing, and thus have affected the resulting bone assemblages. Undoubtedly many regional patterns remain to be established as further Hispano-Roman sites are examined from an archaeozoological point-of-view (see Estévez 1987 and Blasco 1999 for further regional analysis).

The final phase at Celti (12) is associated with undefined late Roman activity at the site, and any subsequent usage of it. A measure of redeposition of material from earlier strata is definitely attested, which tempers any conclusions to be drawn about the diet and agriculture of this period. All three main domesticates are represented roughly equally, with pig a little less common than the others. It is not a pattern that is easy to interpret, nor does the lack of comparative data assist. The high sheep/goat pattern of phase 9 is no longer evident, despite continuing elsewhere (e.g. Naples), and it may be that either redeposition is hopelessly confusing the picture, or that the animal economy at this time was taking on a more localised pattern as the region moved into the post-Roman era. It is perhaps not just a coincidence that the pattern resembles that of the 8th–6th century BC in Andalucía, since there could be some sort of reversion to an agricultural regime that was mixed in nature and well-suited to the type of land being cultivated. It was obviously no longer realistic to practise intensive production for export markets, as had occurred during the period of Roman rule.

A final comment on Celti in phase 12 is the apparent lack of evidence in any of the individual contexts for muslim influence on the bone assemblage, following the conquest of the region by the Arabs in AD 711. This would have manifested itself in greatly reduced or zero pig percentages, as in north African percentages of this period (King 1999). This can be clearly seen in later bone groups in the region (e.g. Las Dunas de Guardamar; Benito 1989), and would have been a highly significant conditioning factor on the animal husbandry of early medieval Andalucía.

Acknowledgements

I am very grateful to Dr Fernanda Blasco Sancho for help in finding references to Spanish Roman bone assemblages and for commenting on the text, and to the Director (Dr F. Fernández) and staff of the Museo Arqueológico de Sevilla and the Conjunto Arqueológico de Itálica (Sr. José Manuel Rodríguez Hidalgo) for providing facilities for the study of the assemblage.

The Fetal Human Bones (AW)

The assemblage from this site consisted of three fetal bones from a Phase 7a context (299). These were an intact left clavicle, the proximal two thirds of a left tibia and the distal half of a left rib, probably one of the sixth to the eighth. The clavicle measured 42.5mm and the tibial fragment measured 48.6mm. It was not possible to assign a sex to the bones and none showed any evidence of pathology.

In all probability the bones are all from the same human foetus and the length of the clavicle indicates that the age of death was between 36 and 40 weeks of gestation; the projected length of the tibia would also support this age at death (Fazekas & Kosa 1978). Thus, the foetus was likely to have been still born or to have died very soon after birth; there is nothing on the bones to help determine which of these alternatives is the most likely.

Carbonised fruits and seeds from late prehistoric and Roman Peñaflor (MJ, JR and CV)

Introduction

During the course of the Peñaflor project 62 plant macrofossil assemblages were collected through systematic flotation of excavated deposits and examined for identifiable seeds, fruits, and cereal chaff fragments. The sampling strategy was as follows. A judgmental sample of 10% was applied to most parts of the site. It was felt that this was sufficient to provide us with a framework of environmental contexts for the many later occupational phases on the site. By contrast a 100% sample was taken from sondages at the centre of the site. The aim of these was to provide a sample of environmental data from the rarer pre-Phase 7a contexts. All samples were sieved with a 500 micron mesh size, while mesh sizes of 5mm and 2mm were used on a smaller range of contexts. In the laboratory, the floats and heavy residues were examined by low power optical microscopy, and the identifications are recorded in Appendix 6. Twenty assemblages fall within Phases 1–6, eight within Phase 7, five within Phase 8, and twenty-nine within Phase 9. Our interpretation of the results is here placed in the context of an overview of contemporary archaeobotanical evidence from the Iberian Peninsula.

Identified Species (see Appendix 6)

The seeds and fruits fall into three ecological categories, food plants, weeds associated with agriculture, and perennial plants of the maquis. There are insufficient of the latter two categories to develop an extended ecological argument, beyond noting the prevalence of leguminous weeds associated with soils in which nitrogen availabity is limiting, and that the perennial fruits are all from maquis-type vegetation, the low woodland cover that established itself within southern Iberia by the Bronze Age. The single Phase 3 seed of opium poppy (*Papaver somniferum*) may reflect economic usage of this species. By the Roman period, its use for both culinary and narcotic purposes is well attested (Renfrew 1973). The remaining food plants divide up into three categories: cereals, legumes and fruit crops. These are dealt with in turn.

Hordeum vulgare L.: Hulled six-row barley
The grains are recognised as barley by their approximate symmetry in all three planes, and chisel-shaped ends. The presence of some twisted grains with angled embryos indicates the six rowed form, and evidence of dorsal ridging giving a slightly hexagonal transverse section indicates the hulled form.

Six-row barley is widespread in the prehistoric record, sometimes as the 'naked form' in which the grain is easily freed from the enclosing palea and lemma, and the 'hulled' form in which it is tightly enclosed. The crop is known in Spain from the 5th millennium BC (Hopf 1991), and continues in use through to the modern period. Throughout prehistoric Europe, the relative proportions of hulled and naked barley fluctuate both in time and space. Hopf (cit.) suggests the general transition to an emphasis on hulled barley in southern Spain did not take place until the Iron Age. While this particular fluctuation is not easy to relate to a single factor, the general point can be made about barleys as a group that they have probably the broadest ecological range of any grain crop, and are particularly tolerant of both drought and salinity.

Triticum dicoccum Schubl.: Emmer wheat
The grains are recognised as belonging to the wheat genus by their generally bulbous shape and assymetry in all three planes. Identifications of wheat grains to species are in many cases a statement of probability, and a number of grains are not taken to species level. Some however show the pronounced dorsal ridging, and flattish, almond shaped ventral surface associated with emmer wheat. Emmer wheat was grown throughout Spain from the Cardial period to at least the Roman period (Hopf 1991).

"Naked" *Triticum*
This grouping is unfortunately large, relating to a tiny number of Phase 8 and Phase 9 seeds, which are not encountered earlier. The seeds are broad, rounded, and lacking a dorsal ridge in the manner

of the hexaploid wheats, but are consistently poorly preserved such that the naked tetraploids, such as *T.durum*, cannot be excluded.

Vicia sativa L.: Vetch
These smaller *Vicia* seeds are distinguished by the wedge shape of the hilum, the length of the hilum, and the distance between the end of the hilum and the chalaza. There is no other known Spanish record of the seeds of *Vicia sativa*, which is today raised as a fodder crop, prior to a possible identification in the Roman/Byzantine levels at Cerro de la Virgen (Hopf 1991). Though it is less well studied than *V. faba*, the two species broadly share the principal nutritional and ecological characteristics cited above. It is not particularly tolerant of drought, and responds well to irrigation (Hebblethwaite 1983). Occurring as a single seed in Phase 9, it may not even be an economic plant, but instead exist as a weed in this context.

Lens esculentum Moench.: Lentil
These legumes are recognised by the characteristic lenticular shape of their cotyledons. Lentils are also recorded in Southeast Spain from Chalcolithic Campos, and Hopf (1991) suggests their main occurrence in Iberian prehistory is in Argaric sites, largely it seems on the basis of unpublished records.

Vitis vinifera L.: Grape
The seed itself has a very characteristic shape and internal form, and remains to some extent recognizable when fragmented. In general, prehistoric assemblages throughout the Iberian peninsula tend to have sparse if not infrequent records of grape, suggesting to Hopf (1991) that they were not "cultivated" until the Punic, or even Roman period (Walker 1984–5). However, recent results in the region of Huelva have been used to attest the cultivation of the vine as far back as the Chalcolithic (Stevenson 1985; id. 1985a; Stevenson & Moore 1988; Stevenson & Harrison 1992).

Olea europea L.: Olive
A large oblong seed with a rugose surface segmented by longitudinal ridges. The above comments of Hopf (1991) about grapes also apply to olives.

Discussion of the plant remains in a wider Iberian context

The existing database for Iron Age and Roman periods is not great. From the entire peninsula Hopf (1991) lists 13 Iron Age and 9 Roman sites. Amongst these, the evidence is thin, with a site with 12 species being described as "a remarkably rich assortment". To Hopf's records we can add the data from the Iron Age / Roman period site of Villaricos in Almería province, which has been intensively sampled in a manner similar to Peñaflor (Clapham, Jones, and Tenas, in press), and Torreparedones (Jones & Reed 1999). Inasmuch as one may infer contextual picture from a thin spread such as this, it is as follows.

The most widespread plants are naked wheat (*Triticum aestivum/durum*) and six-row barley (*Hordeum vulgare*). Other, less ubiquitous cereals include: einkorn (*T. monococcum*) but at only one site; emmer, more frequently further north in the peninsula along with broomcorn and finger millets, oats, and possibly rye. Perennial crops are scattered in both periods, particularly grape (*Vitis vinifera*), encountered at half the Iron Age sites. The Peñaflor data resonates with much of this, adding some legume records, particularly for the Roman period, for which Hopf has no records.

The principal pattern within the data is the marked contrast between the Tartessian / Turdetanian contexts on the one hand and those relating to the Phase 7 and Phase 8 buildings on the other. The former comprise cereals and the occasional legume, a range of annual weedy species, and a few seeds from evergreen maquis. The latter, by contrast, are dominated by olive stones. There are a few other crop plants, but weedy species are virtually absent. One of the earlier Phase 7 contexts is alone in having large numbers of grape pips. There are traces of olive and grape in the Turde-

tanian / Iberian contexts, but always in small quantities. In other words, we can contrast an earlier deposition relating to grain and pulse agriculture with a later deposition dominated by the handling of olives, and in one instance, of grapes. The scarcity of weeds and absence of chaff from the later samples would suggest that cereal crop processing was not in evidence, and such grains as are encountered reflect the importation to the site of processed crops.

The greater number of weed species from the earlier samples is less easy to interpret. These are nowhere sufficiently frequent to imply crop processing in their own right, and indeed the scarcity of chaff fragments is noticeable here. There may have simply been slightly more routes for segetal and ruderal species in the earlier phases of the site. The maquis status of the perennial seeds is not surprising. By this time the transition from deciduous to evergreen Mediterranean vegetation in southern Iberia was well established (Huntley and Birks 1983).

In summary, the broad picture is consistent with the more general one developed by Hopf (1991), though the transition to clear evidence for olive and grape cultivation does not come until the Phase 7 period, and is very clearly associated with it. This association may be a contextual one relating to the specific uses of the site, although circumstantial evidence (Chapter 10) suggests that the cultivation of olives and grapes began to become widespread in the region from the mid to late 1st century BC onwards. Hopf, however, suggests that they had a start date late in prehistory.

Chapter 7
The Painted Wallplaster

Elizabeth Pye

Abstract

This Chapter presents a detailed analysis of the wallpaster from the excavations (complemented by Appendices 7, 8 and 9). The severe plough damage to the upper levels of the site meant that this material was very fragmentary. However, in the interests of extracting as much information as possible about the character of each of the building phases at the site, great care was taken to record intelligible groups of plaster from a range of key contexts. The material from (100) was the most important of these. Overall, the study shows that the buildings of Phases 7 and 8 were decorated by high quality plaster exhibiting a range of motifs ranging from imitation marble to animal figures.

Painted Wall Plaster at Peñaflor

The use of plaster or render coatings applied to both inner and outer surfaces of walls, is a feature of the site at Peñaflor. A number of different types of wall-construction were used (mud-brick, tile, amphora-sherds, stone) most of which were apparently finished externally using a coat of rendering to provide a smooth architectural and protective finish. There were also several water features on the site, including drains, and two tanks or cisterns, all of which were created using a mix filled with coarse aggregate to provide a durable cement-like finish. The plastered surfaces of internal walls in the Phase 8 houses were apparently also decorated with wallpaintings.

Excavation during the 1989 season revealed the presence of painted wallplaster in a deep room (Room 5) in the Roman levels (95, 99 and 100; Phase 9), while subsequent excavation revealed painted plaster in many other parts of the site. The material provided an opportunity to excavate and reconstruct a sample assemblage of fragments, and to study both raw materials and manufacturing techniques. The work took place during the following excavation and study seasons at Peñaflor (1990–1993) and in the form of two programmes of analysis at the Institute of

Archaeology, University College London (UCL). A catalogue of the excavated wallplaster fragments is given in Appendix 7.

Aims

Study of painted wallplaster concentrates on two aspects: stylistic analysis and analysis of the raw materials and techniques. Stylistic analysis focuses on the types of decorative scheme and their iconography, and comparison to type material such as that from Pompeii. Study of the technology involves the examination of samples of plaster, fillers and pigments and comparison with other painted plasters, and with the information provided by the ancient writers such as Pliny and Vitruvius. Modern analytical techniques have the potential to provide further understanding of the raw materials and the nature of the painting technique.

It was hoped that study of the painted wallplaster at Peñaflor would shed light on the impact of Roman styles and tastes on house decoration in southern Spain. Excavation and reconstruction was undertaken to elucidate both the decorative schemes present, and their stylistic relationship to paintings in other Roman provinces. Analysis of the plasters and pigments was used to identify both the materials and the ways in which they had been applied. Investigation of the raw materials, structure and decorative schemes of the paintings was used to establish whether the techniques and style were conventionally Roman, or influenced by local practice.

Methods of study

The deposit of painted wallplaster discovered in 1989 was reburied at the end of the season and a group of conservators from the Institute of Archaeology, UCL joined the team in 1990 to start the process of excavation and conservation. During the 1990 season the upper layers of a large plaster deposit in (95), (99) and (100) (Phase 9) were excavated and given preliminary conservation treatment. Plaster fragments from several other contexts on the site were also excavated and recorded. Details of the excavation and conservation techniques are given in Appendix 8.

An objective of the work in 1992 was to attempt to establish the relationship of the plaster to the room, and to find out more about the structure and function of the room itself. Excavation in northern areas of the site during 1992 revealed a number of different types of wall-construction all finished with rendering, and samples were taken for analysis and comparison with the plaster. During 1990 and 1992 samples of the plaster had been lifted and boxed in groups of related fragments. During the 1991 and 1993 study seasons individual groups were unpacked, test-cleaned, and examined for technological information as well as for joins and details of the decorative scheme(s).

A small number of samples taken in 1991 was analysed during 1992–3 in order to look at the nature of the raw materials and how they related to the function of the plaster or render, and/or to the period of use. Results indicated that a wide range of pigments and pigment-combinations were in use, and this preliminary work formed the basis for the design of a more detailed programme of analysis. Further samples were taken during the 1993 study season and analysed during the period 1994 to 1996 with the aim of discovering more about the ways in which the plaster was prepared, and the ways in which colours were achieved through combination of different pigments. The limited length of the excavation and study seasons, the range of plaster recovered, and the need to select a finite number of samples inevitably imposed limitations on the extent of the study, therefore the results are qualitative rather than quantitative.

Nature of the Wallplaster Deposits

The area of the site in which painted plaster was first found (95, 99, 100; Phase 9) was a deep room (Room 5) whose walls were constructed of mudbrick (detectable only in the form of layers of fine clay) laid on stone and rubble footings. Much of the rubble remained, but some of the stone blocks had been robbed out at some stage. The deposit consisted of sheets of plaster, mingled with disintegrated mud-brick, stones and occasional ceramic sherds. At the western edge of the room some of the plaster fragments were lying almost vertically, where they appeared to have fallen down the face of the wall. Excavation in the south-west sector of the room revealed a section of the wall where the footings were relatively intact and here some plaster appeared to be still attached to the wall. The initial impression, therefore, was of plaster that had collapsed *in situ*. It is possible that this was originally used to decorate the phase 8a or 8b domus (see Chapter 3).

Exploratory excavation indicated that the companion deep room (Room 4) to the west of (100) was also probably full of painted wallplaster. Subsequent excavation revealed large quantities of painted fragments apparently representing a number of different decorative schemes from different rooms or buildings but now scattered in small individual groups over the site. Apart from a few examples of plaster or render still attached to structural features, almost every group consisted of fragments mixed with other debris, and was impossible to relate to a specific wall or building.

Condition of the plaster

The plaster varied in condition. Some of the material in the upper levels of (95), (99) and (100) was in very poor condition.This may have been due to the fact that after collapse or demolition the fragments were further disturbed, then lay exposed to the weather for some time, or it may be because the upper layers of the deposit were not far below the present soil-surface and so had been affected by ploughing and irrigation. The upper layers of the plaster had also been exposed to the sun when first discovered in 1989, resulting in drying and hardening of the superficial clay deposits covering the plaster fragments. This combination of factors meant that these fragments were difficult to excavate, needed careful cleaning, and the readability of the painted surface was not as good as on the plaster found at greater depths.

Reconstruction of Decorative Schemes

Almost all the wallplaster fragments appeared to have been removed from their original position and mixed with demolition debris. It was also apparent that much of the plaster had been totally destroyed (through normal deterioration processes, or deliberate clearance, or recent ploughing). This meant that no decorative scheme was present in its entirety and some were represented by tantalisingly few fragments. There were very large quantities of mixed plain coloured fragments, or of fragments consisting of two colours juxtaposed in the manner normally found in plain fields and borders, but there were few other recognisable motifs. This made it difficult to reconstruct more than a few groups of fragments and it was impossible to establish exactly how any one of the schemes functioned.

Work focused on groups that seemed potentially the most productive and informative. Fragments were cleaned, and rejoined wherever possible (details of methods are given in Appendix 9). The following schemes were identified, though only partially reconstructed:

Grey/ blue field with orange borders

In the upper layers of the western side of the deep room were a number of smooth, hard, fine-quality fragments with a sparkling almost translucent surface, which were apparently decorated in grey and pale orange. Microscopic examination indicated that the grey had originally been blue but weathering had removed much of the original bright

Egyptian blue exposing a blue-grey underlayer. The scheme consisted of a plain blue field possibly about 500 mm wide with a few fragments of orange border remaining on either side (Figs. 7.1 and 7.2). Because of the way the fragments had fallen (or been shovelled) into the room they were scattered and dissociated, and as some of the joins were fairly tenuous it was difficult to be certain about the dimensions of the panel.

Marble panels

Partially mixed with these blue and orange fragments but largely lying beneath them in 100 were fragments of imitation marble which were different in quality and finish. The design consisted of large areas of a white and yellow marble with purple veining, closely associated with a purple with white flecks, a grey speckled with red and yellow, and a green consisting of distinct green blobs.

The yellow and purple marble predominated and consisted of rounded patches of yellow, approximately 100–150 mm in diameter surrounded by freely drawn dark purple veining – possibly imitating *giallo antico*. The purple was covered with distinct white flecks and was possibly intended to imitate porphyry; the grey was a pale bluish-grey with both white and red flecks giving an approximation of a granite-like appearance. The green consisted of distinct blobs of colour much larger than the flecks on the other 'marbles' (about 10–15 mm in size) possibly intended to imitate rounded green inclusions. Largish translucent inclusions were evident within the plaster itself and may have

Fig. 7.1. Grey/blue field with orange borders: photo of reconstructed fragments
(20 centimetre scale: each division 5cm)

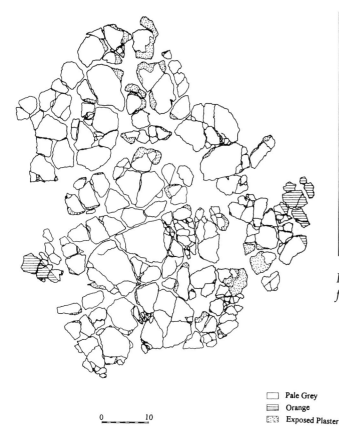

Fig. 7.3. Imitation marble: photograph of some fragments to show "giallo antico" design (20 centimetre scale: each division 5cm)

◻ Pale Grey
▤ Orange
▨ Exposed Plaster

Fig. 7.2. Grey/blue field with orange borders: reconstructed fragments (scale in centimetres)

0 _____ 10

been intended to reinforce the porphyry or granite appearance of the painted surface.

Where it was possible to reconstruct parts of this design, it consisted of bands of marble associated with red ochre borders. Two groups of fragments appeared to show bands of *giallo antico* framing, in one case a panel of porphyry, and in the other a panel of the green marble (Figs. 7.3 and 7.4). The first group of fragments showed a panel of green and a panel of grey lying outside the *giallo antico* frame, and the second group joined onto a plain red border (Fig. 7.5). A further group of fragments appeared to show a roundel of the green surrounded by the *giallo antico*.

Mixed with, and below, the marble scheme, and spread throughout the room were large quantities of red fragments, some associated with blue and white bands or lines (some double white lines) presumed to be from fields and borders, and possibly related to the marble scheme. Five fragments of the marble scheme were found in a dump outside the room (254, Phase 9) associated with about forty red, blue and white field or border fragments (some with double white lines similar to the fragments possibly associated with the marble scheme). Another large group of red fragments

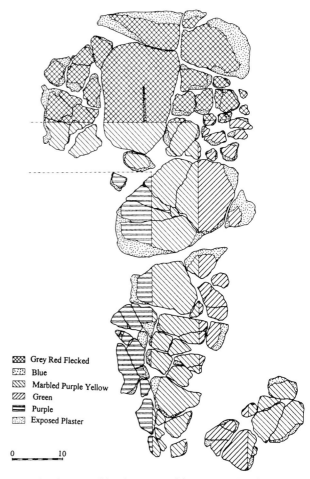

▨ Grey Red Flecked
▦ Blue
▧ Marbled Purple Yellow
▨ Green
▤ Purple
▨ Exposed Plaster

0 _____ 10

Fig. 7.4. Imitation Marble: drawing of fragments (scale in centimetres)

found in (100), but only in the central area, had damaged and worn surfaces revealing an under-layer of yellow, some apparently marbled red on yellow, but some so damaged that the surface was difficult to read. It is possible that the plaster of these marbled fragments was similar to the grey/blue and orange scheme but unfortunately this was not suspected when samples were selected so cannot be confirmed.

Red and black scheme

A number of very fine fragments were found scattered in (306), (345) and (348) (Phases 7b–9, 9, 12) which came from a scheme with black (which may have formed plain fields) combined with vivid red, decorated with green (probably foliage) and white and green bands; these may have formed borders round black areas. This scheme was represented by a large quantity of plain black fragments and a very few of the red and green so

it was impossible to reconstruct the original design. The foliage was very subtly painted, using several shades of green and the overall quality of both plaster and decoration was excellent. Figure 7.6 shows a single decorated fragment and Fig. 7.7 shows several fragments laid out to indicate the type of detail present.

Yellow background with dark red scrolls and animals

Another scheme, from (601), (609) and (641) (Horizon 7a–9), consisted of about 30 fragments of plain mustard yellow, a few fragments of which were over-painted in deep purple-red with a free-flowing curvilinear design and one fragment decorated with the head of an animal (possibly feline) painted in the dark red with white or pink details (Figs. 7.8 and 7.9).

Red-painted column rendering

About thirty red fragments from (796) and (797) (and one from 389) (Phases 8a and b) had a marked curve on them and were interpreted as rendering from columns of approximately 560 mm in diameter (Fig. 7.10). This render would have been used to produce a smooth glossy weather-proof surface finish over columns constructed of stone, brick or tile (Adam 1994).

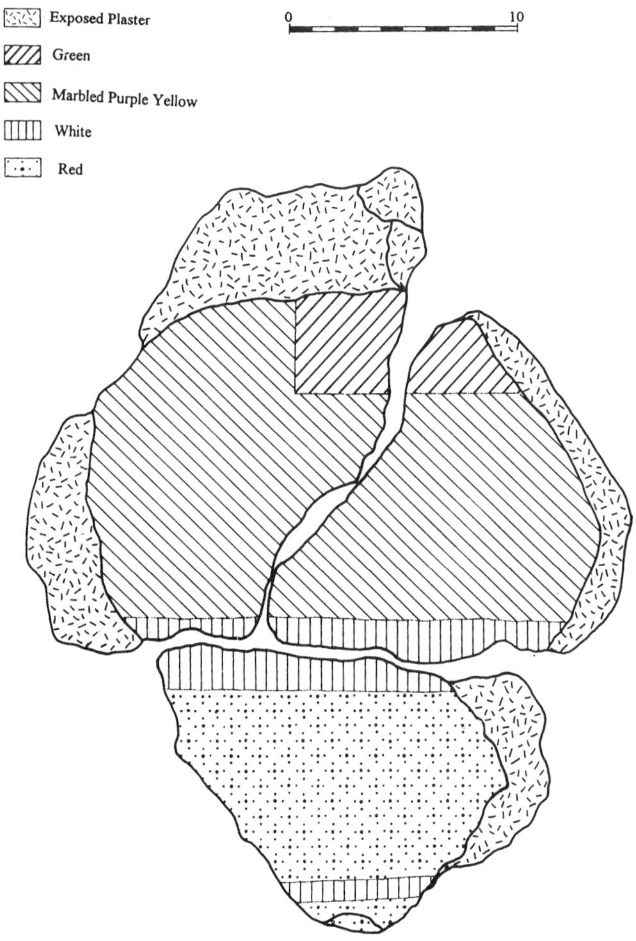

Exposed Plaster

Green

Marbled Purple Yellow

White

Red

0 ———— 10

Fig. 7.5. Imitation Marble: to show junction between marble and red border (scale in centimteres)

Fig. 7.6. Red and Black scheme: photograph of a single fragment showing green foliage on red ground (scale in centimetres)

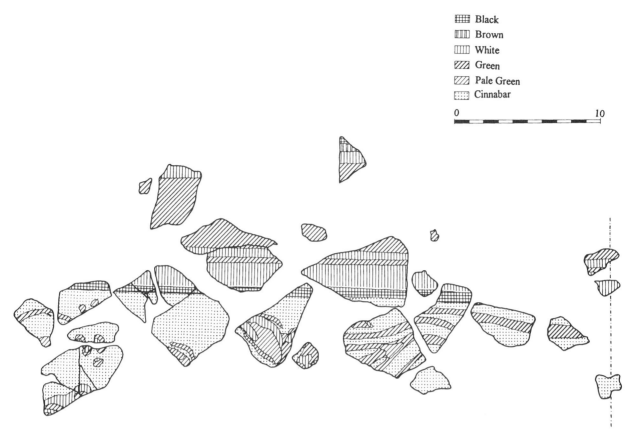

	Black
	Brown
	White
	Green
	Pale Green
	Cinnabar

Fig. 7.7. Red and Black scheme: fragments laid out to show possible design (scale in centimetres)

Analysis of Raw Materials and Manufacturing Techniques

Analysis of plasters

Lime (calcium carbonate) was commonly used in the Roman period to manufacture plasters, low relief *stucco* mouldings, mortars and renderings. A layered structure is normally clearly visible in section (eg the edge of a broken fragment) with the different layers distinguished by colour and texture. The structure normally takes the form described below, and shown in Fig.7.11 (Frizot 1984).

Reading from the finished outer surface:

Layer (a): a very thin final surface layer (prepared for painting) possibly only 1–2 mm thick, sometimes almost pure lime wash; not always present

Layer (b): a thicker preparation layer (5–10 mm) possibly with marble or calcite or other white filler to provide a fine finished surface; possibly more than one layer of this type

Layer (c): a preparation layer beneath (5–10 mm) which is often coarser, darker and richer in sand – obviously the texture and colour does not affect the finished surface; again possibly more than one layer of this type

Fig. 7.8. Photograph of animal on yellow background (scale in centimetres)

Layer (d): a much coarser first preparation layer (not always remaining) which may be different in colour and contain much larger aggregate.

Preliminary examination in the field, using a

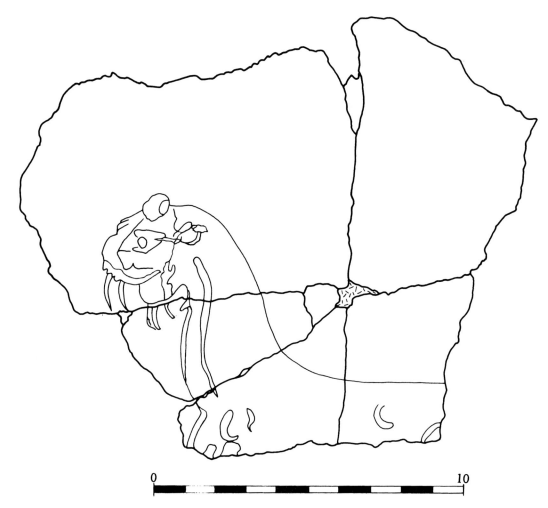

Fig. 7.9. Drawing of animal on yellow background (scale in centimetres)

stereo microscope, revealed a typical layered structure on most of the fragments, as well as the probable presence of several different plaster and render types. A limited range of samples was taken for laboratory examination at UCL, based on both the assumed significance of the contexts and the apparent range of plaster-types.

In the laboratory the chemical composition of the plaster was examined. A sample of the plaster readily dissolved in hydrochloric acid, producing an effervescent gas, probably carbon dioxide, indicating the presence of a carbonate. Microscopic examination showed a typical calcium carbonate structure without fossils such as coccoliths (these would have been destroyed during the manufacture of the lime by calcination – heating – of limestone). Energy dispersive x-ray analysis (SEM-EDS) produced a strong calcium peak. These results indicated that it was indeed lime (calcium carbonate) plaster. The proportion of filler to lime, and the type of filler were also examined. (Further details of laboratory procedure are given in Appendix 9).

Range of plaster and mortars identified

On the basis of both visual examination and an analysis of proportions and types of filler, it was possible to suggest that there were at least 6 types of plaster or render represented amongst the material sampled from the site. These were designated Types A to F:

A *Painted plaster:* Layer (a) was present and appeared to contain fine sparkling particles, possibly marble powder. Layer (b) was a fine, dense white plaster with a few dark sand inclusions giving a greyish appearance; the average proportions in this layer were 34% lime to 66% insoluble filler. Layer (c), where present was coarser, darker and filled with river sand.

B *Painted plaster:* Layer (a) was present, layer (b) contained angular water-rounded pale inclusions, presumably river-sand, with an average of 36% lime to 64% filler. Layer (c) was grey and contained rounded medium to coarse dark river sand, with similar proportions of filler to plaster.

C *Painted plaster:* Layer (a) was absent and layer

Fig. 7.10. Red-painted column rendering: photograph of curved fragments laid out over stone column of appropriate diameter (scale in centimetres)

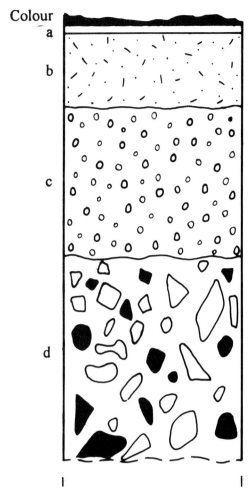

Fig. 7.11. Diagram of the layered structure of a Roman plaster (not to scale)

(b) was of excellent quality – very white with angular translucent inclusions possibly crushed stone, with an average of 38% lime to 62% filler. Layer (c) was dark and contained multicoloured inclusions

D *Possible ceiling plaster* or *stucco*, with a very high lime content in layer (b) which had a chalky texture (75–90% lime to as little as 10–25% filler). Layer (c) varied from one fragment to another and contained a range of filler, often coarse.

E *Rendering* for column and base with a smooth white surface layer (a) and fine river sand in layer (b) in the approximate proportions of 40% lime to 60% filler. The filler in layer (c) was also rounded river sand which was generally fine but with some coarser inclusions.

F *Coarse hard rendering* for water features etc, the filler was large and varied aggregate including ceramic.

PLASTER TYPE A

This plaster was mainly represented by the blue/grey and orange scheme from (100) (Phase 9). It had a marked tendency to fracture easily between

layers (b) and (c) so most of the excavated fragments were comparatively thin, but the density of the plaster of layer (b) had prevented fragmentation. The surface sparkle and the smooth surface finish were very evident and distinguished this from other types.

It was also apparently represented in at least two other contexts (and could well have been present in more but the limitations of the sampling process did not pick it up). Context (537) (Phase 8a) yielded about 30 fragments characterised by decoration in a particularly dark red, with black and blue-grey. There was no discernible design apart from some fragments which were apparently marbled with red, black and white. Context (600) (Phase 12) yielded five fragments of plaster showing red, yellow, black, and pink including one fragment which showed a black border outlined in white dividing two areas of yellow. These had some similarity to the fragments from (651) (Phase 12) and (653) (Phase 9) which were each decorated with yellow and other colours.

PLASTER TYPE B
Most of this type of plaster was found in (99) and (100) (Phase 9) and included the marble scheme and the red and blue borders. The fragments had two and possibly three preparation layers with an average total thickness of 450–500 mm; the final preparation layer (a) was normally 2 to 3 mm thick. There seems to have been a deliberate selection of different qualities of sand for layers (b) and (c). This same plaster was detected in samples from 3 different areas of (100), in two samples from (99), two from (254) and one from (264) (all Phase 9). Context (254) yielded fragments decorated in the same way as the marble in E. 100 and clearly from the same scheme. Context (264) yielded a few very mixed fragments not apparently related in terms of colour or design to the other fragments in this plaster group. Visual examination indicated that many of the other scattered fragments found across the site were probably of this general plaster type, unfortunately the sampling strategy did not help to clarify this.

PLASTER TYPE C
This was represented by fragments of the black and red scheme from (348) (and (306), (342), (343), (345)) which were distributed across Phases 7b–9, 9 and 12, and by the yellow and dark red scheme from (601), (609) and (641) (Phase 7a–9). This was exceptionally well-prepared plaster with very high-quality decoration. Layer (b) had obviously been carefully prepared to provide a smooth and very white surface. Several of the fragments from (641) retained a greenish sandy layer (d) which was unlike any other material on the site.

The thirty fragments of curved rendering interpreted as being the finished outer surface of columns were excavated from (796) (Phase 8a) and (797) (Phase 8b). These were found to have a structure related to Plaster Type C. Layers (b) and (c) of the curved rendering were very similar to other examples of this plaster type, but the layer (d) was specific to these fragments and was filled with coarse aggregate as would be normal for an initial render coat.

PLASTER TYPE D
There were a few fragments, from (95), (354), and (264) (all Phase 9), of what was possibly ceiling plaster or *stucco*, with a very high lime content. The lack of filler would make the plaster lighter but also less durable so it was not surprising that very few fragments of this type were found. One example from (354) had parallel impressions in one surface characteristic of *stucco* or ceiling plaster applied to bundles of reeds, as recommended by Vitruvius (VII, iii, 11).

PLASTER TYPE E
These samples were taken from the rendering still *in situ* on a column and base – Sample 9 from (525) (Phase 8b), and from the rendering on a screen between columns – Sample 14 from (752) (also Phase 8b). The fine filler in layer (b) was clearly chosen to provide a tough, smooth surface which could be shaped to provide architectural detail over a base of stone or tile.

PLASTER TYPE F
Samples of rendering were also taken from the water features. Sample 10 was taken from the coarse rendering on the rectangular pool (300, Phase 8b), sample 15 from a water feature (703), and sample 17 from an area of tumble (723). In each case the surface was relatively smooth and tough but the filler was large and varied aggregate, obviously intended to provide the degree of durability needed in drains, tanks etc.

Analysis of pigments
Preliminary examination in the field was carried out using a stereo microscope. Samples for analysis were selected on the basis of both the features detected during initial examination and the apparent significance of the context. Samples were taken of the main colours, and small fragments were reserved from the main decorative motifs (borders and marble designs), taking care not to select any fragments which might play a key role in the reconstruction.

The methods of analysis are detailed in Appendix 9; the following pigments were identified:

RED
A strong brownish red pigment was common throughout the wallplaster and samples from several contexts were examined microscopically. In each case the particles of the pigment were reddish to yellowish brown, and anisotropic, sometimes some transparent yellowish particles were also present. The samples compared well with the red ochre in the reference collection. Energy dispersive x-ray analysis (SEM-EDS) showed the presence of iron confirming that the pigment was red ochre, an iron-oxide red. A darker shade of red (almost purple) occurred on the marble motif from (100) and from some other contexts. Examination indicated that this too was a red-ochre. Iron oxide deposits can vary widely in hue depending upon the degree of hydration, and this was the probable explanation for the darker shade, though the darkening could also be achieved artificially by heating (Gettens and Stout 1966).

YELLOW

Several samples of yellow were examined, particularly from the marble motif in (100) and from the yellow scheme in (641). Microscopically, yellow to brown particles could be seen and the sample matched the yellow ochre examples in the reference collection. SEM-EDS showed a definite iron peak, thus confirming that this pigment was yellow ochre – a yellow form of hydrated iron oxide (Gettens and Stout 1966).

ORANGE

A clear pale orange occurred on the grey and orange scheme from (100). Microscopic examination supported by the Electron Probe Microanalyser (EPMA) indicated that this also was an iron oxide. It is known that orange can be obtained by heating yellow ochre at a low temperature (Gettens and Stout 1966; Béarat 1997a)

BRIGHT RED

The bright orange red on a small number of fragments of the black and red scheme found in (345) and (348) was particularly interesting The pigment was strong in colour and the painted surface was smooth and glossy. By reflected light the particles seemed to have a waxy lustre, and under transmitted light they were translucent and deep red in colour. The bright colour and high quality suggested that this mineral was cinnabar, a red mercuric sulphide; both SEM-EDS and EPMA confirmed this by indicating the presence of mercury and sulphur (Gettens *et al* 1993).

BLUE

Several samples of blue were examined, each apparently from a border area. The pigment particles tended to be comparatively large, glassy and angular, and usually a pure bright blue in colour. Under transmitted light the crystals varied in colour from blue to faint lavender. SEM-EDS showed the presence of copper, thus indicating that that the pigment was Egyptian blue (cuprovivianite) (Riederer 1997).

BLUE-GREY

A grey to grey-blue occurred on the marble motif in (100). Under the microscope opaque grey to black particles were visible. This was almost certainly a form of carbon, the most commonly used black pigment. Further work would be needed to establish which form of carbon, though it appeared to be very similar to bone black in the reference collection. In some areas, for example in (99) and (100), it appeared to have had Egyptian blue overlying, or mixed with it. The blue-grey colour was achieved by mixing the carbon with a white carbonate (Gettens and Stout 1966).

BLACK

The strong black found on the plaster fragments from the black and red scheme from (345) and (348) was composed of similar opaque black or brownish black particles, again certainly carbon.

GREEN

Although green was not so well represented as the other colours several samples were examined, e.g. from the marble scheme in (100). The pigment commonly had low covering power and consisted of yellow to green granular particles very similar to the green earth sample in the reference collection. SEM-EDS indicated the presence of iron and thus supported its being green earth. This pigment occurs in the form of either glauconite or celadonite, each of which is a clay mineral with a significant iron content. The colour is influenced by the iron and ranges from light yellow-green to pale greenish-blue (Grissom 1986).

BLUE-GREEN

A subtle pale blue-green found on the black and red scheme in (348) was, at first, difficult to interpret. It had good covering power and microscopically it consisted of fine pale blue glassy particles and a few greenish particles. The SEM-EDS spectrum gave an iron peak, and strong peaks for calcium, aluminium and silicon as well as some magnesium. EPMA showed some copper. It is likely that this was a mixture of green earth with a finely ground Egyptian blue – this would have been a pale and not particularly granular blue which would have enhanced the covering power of the green earth and imparted a bluish tinge to the overall colour (Béarat 1997b).

WHITE

Details such as narrow bands delineating the borders, or flecks used to create a mottled marble effect were carried out in white. This pigment readily dissolved in hydrochloric acid, producing an effervescent gas, probably carbon dioxide, indicating the presence of a carbonate. This was obviously a form of calcium carbonate but more detailed identification of type was not carried out.

Modifications and combinations of pigments

Modifications of pigments seen at Peñaflor were similar to those found on other Roman sites (Béarat 1997a). They included the probable heating of ochres to obtain darker shades, for example heating yellow ochre to produce orange (100); and the grinding of

Egyptian frit to produce a smaller particle size and hence a lighter shade (348). Another method of modifying the colour was, of course, to mix more than one pigment. White was regularly mixed with other colours for example with red ochre to produce a pink (641) and with carbon black to produce a blue-grey (100). Green earth mixed with Egyptian blue to produce a bluish green was another known combination (348).

One colour was frequently applied over another probably to strengthen the final colour. Egyptian blue was commonly painted over a grey or black undercoat (Béarat 1997a) and this was found in several contexts at Peñaflor (11, 99 and 100). The Egyptian blue is a coarse granular pigment and the overall colour would be strengthened by the presence of the homogeneous underlayer. The underlayer would also allow the painters to use rather less of the blue – as it was a manufactured pigment it would have been more expensive than the basic earth pigments, and might not have been readily available in sufficient quantities. The coarse blue particles would have stood out on the surface above the finer grey black and would have been more vulnerable to wear and weathering. In some cases (as in the blue/grey and orange scheme found in 100) the blue had been largely eroded leaving a muted grey surface, but particles of the Egyptian blue could still be detected microscopically.

A yellow or cream undercoat beneath cinnabar is also quite common (Béarat 1997a) and yellow ochre was found beneath the cinnabar in the samples examined from (345) and (348). There was also a group of red fragments in (100) where red ochre was painted over yellow ochre.

Wallplaster related to Phases on the Site

Almost all of the painted plaster came from Phase 9 which was the period when the double courtyard house was demolished and robbed; small quantities came from several earlier phases and some came from Phase 12, which consisted of surface material disturbed by recent agriculture.

Phase 6d

This phase marks the last structural alteration prior to the building of the Phase 7a complex but the ten small fragments of wallplaster from (560) and (561) cannot really shed any light on the function of the structures at that time. The fragments were recognisably Roman in character and include red, white and green pigments but no discernable design.

Phase 7a

This phase marks the preparation for the building of the large complex tentatively identified as the forum (see discussion in Chapter 9), but only eight small pieces of red and yellow plaster were found in (262) and (263). Again these were recognisably Roman but do not otherwise provide any information.

Phase 7b

This was the period of the building of the complex. Only one fragment of plaster came from this phase (342) but it represented one of the most interesting of the wallplaster types found on the site – the red and black scheme.

Between Phases 7a and 9

Rather more plaster was found in contexts which are assignable to some time between these two phases. Over eighty small fragments of the red and black scheme came from (348); most of the fragments were plain black but there were some more fragments showing the red with green motif. The remaining forty or so fragments of plaster from this phase were predominantly from the yellow ochre scheme and came from (601), (609) and (641).

Between Phases 7c–8c

Two fragments of white plaster with black and yellow splashes on them (probably in imitation of marble) were found in a single context (276) at some time between these phases. They were not obviously related to any other scheme identified on the site.

Phase 8

Only ten fragments of predominantly red plaster were found in this phase as a whole in (365) and (748). One fragment was black with white splattering on it (probably in imitation of marble) and one appeared to come from a border where red meets green.

Phase 8a

During this phase the double courtyard house was constructed on the site of the Phase 7a complex. About forty-three fragments of dark red plaster or render were found in (537), (636), and (796). Nine fragments of the curved rendering interpreted as having come from columns were found in (796).

The plaster from (537) included fragments decorated with dark red, black and blue-grey, and some marbling. This group of fragments may have been related by plaster-type to the grey/blue and orange scheme found in (100). Although this and the wallplaster with marble decoration was found in a context of Phase 9, it is likely that it was actually established in this or the next phase.

Phase 8b

More of the curved red rendering was found in this phase. Twenty-five curved fragments were found in (797), one of which joined to a large fragment from (389). The remaining sixty fragments from (389) and (728) were all very small, and included a range of colours.

Phase 9

Most of the painted plaster was found in contexts relating to this phase when the double-courtyard house was demolished and cleared, and probably represents the detritus of wallplaster used to decorate the Phase 8a or 8b domus. The two deep rooms (Rooms 4 and 5) were filled with plaster but only one was investigated, and about 750 fragments were excavated from (95), (99) and (100) (the fill of Room 4). Two main schemes were probably represented: the marble scheme and the grey/blue and orange scheme. There were also large numbers of plain red and blue fragments in the fill of the room. At least another five fragments of the marble scheme were found outside the room (254).

Twenty-four more fragments of the red and black scheme were found in (136) and (345), but most of the material from this phase seemed similar in plaster-type and colour-range to the imitation marble scheme from (100). There were large quantities of fragments representing fields or borders of plain colours such as red, blue, yellow, and some orange and green. The quality of the plaster and pigments was good but not as outstanding as the red and black scheme. In all there were about seven hundred fragments of varying sizes from this phase, in addition to the 750 or so fragments removed during the excavation of the deep room.

Phase 12

Small quantities of predominantly ochre red fragments were found in a number of different contexts during this phase, none of which was informative, but it should be noted that 14 more fragments of the red and black scheme were also found in this phase in (306) and (345). The red, blue and white plaster exposed in (11) (the northern end of the companion room to the west of (95), (99) and (100) was allocated to this phase.

Discussion

Plaster provides both a hard-wearing smooth finish over timber, brick or stone, and a surface suitable for decoration, and painted wallplaster was a common feature of Roman buildings. To the archaeologist painted wallplaster provides an insight into the interior decoration of domestic and public buildings and is a potential indicator of the influence, and spread, of techniques and fashions throughout the Empire and provinces. Apart from exceptional preservation on some sites, much of this plaster remains only in the form of fragments which fell from walls when buildings were abandoned or demolished. On some sites there are a few scattered and apparently unrelated fragments, on others there may be large deposits filling the rooms which the plaster once adorned.

There are both practical and ethical problems involved in dealing with large quantities of plaster. To retain the relationship of the individual fragments requires careful recording during excavation, but if the plaster dries during this process the deposits of soil and salts on the fragments harden, sometimes to the point where they are almost impossible to remove without damage. The cleaning and reconstruction process can be very slow, but without reconstruction it is difficult to interpret the decorative scheme. The fragments, either partially or wholly reconstructed, take up a great deal of space in archaeological stores. With the growing conviction that both investigation of sites and conservation of their contents should be undertaken in the least invasive manner possible, it seems increasingly inappropriate to remove large quantities of painted wallplaster from an unthreatened site. A large quantity of plaster remains on the site at Peñaflor which could be investigated at some future date.

Formation of the wallplaster deposit

Interior plasters were not as durable as exterior renders and mortars, and tended to sheer off the wall if exposed to the weather. Once a building was demolished or abandoned, and the roof failed, the plaster separated from the walls, and came off in sheets which "folded" as they collapsed onto the floor below. Wallplaster deposits tend, therefore to consist of broken sheets which lie in concertina-fashion, some face-down and some face-up. Where building construction involved substantial stone footings (which often survive) some plaster may remain attached to this part of the wall, protected by the deposit of fallen fragments. A similar pattern of collapse could be caused by deliberate demolition of walls.

The deposit in the deep room 5 (contexts 95, 99 and 100; Phase 9) was difficult to interpret. At first the room was thought to be full of plaster which had collapsed *in situ*. However the nature and condition of the upper levels indicated that there had been both disturbance, and apparent incursion of material from other parts of the site. It was only when the deposit was cleared down to the lower levels that folded sheets of plaster, typical of material which had collapsed *in situ*, became evident. The deposit seems to have consisted of plain red and blue plaster which had fallen off the walls, overlaid by the marble scheme which may possibly also have come from the room. It was then partly covered in clay and other debris and the grey/blue and orange plaster was pushed in over the top. The plaster in the upper levels of the room was mixed and incomplete as if broken up by digging or shovelling, and the relatively solid mass of fragments petered out into small jumbled piles mixed with stone, mortar and ceramic in the southern end of the room. A possible interpretation is that the mud-brick upper walls collapsed or were deliberately demolished and the plaster fell into the room, then during clearance and robbing of parts of the walls the upper layers of the deposit were disturbed and some plaster was distributed beyond the room, while at the same time material was pushed in from other rooms or buildings. Some of the surface disturbance could also be due to recent ploughing and cultivation.

The grey/blue and orange scheme (plaster type A) which probably came from another room or building was much finer and very different in quality from most of the material in the room (plaster type B).The two plasters were sufficiently dissimilar for it to have been unlikely that they represented different areas of the same general decorative scheme, and there were no signs of superimposed phases of painting. The grey/blue and orange plaster lay in a limited area to the west of the centre of the room, overlying a distinct layer of clay and potsherds, and was probably pushed or shovelled into the deep room during clearance on the site. It also appeared that additional material may have been pushed in from the north as the depth of plaster in the northern end of the room was much greater than at the southern end where the deposit consisted of small piles rather than a mass of fragments. The northern ends

of both this room and of the companion room 4 to the west (11 of Phase 12) were filled with red, blue and white fragments.

The marble scheme may have belonged in the room, but only part of it remained and some had been spread beyond the room. Most of the fragments were found in a band across the central area of the room on or near the surface of the fill, but at least five were found well outside in (254). Plain red and blue fragments occurred at different depths throughout the fill of the room, and included some of the material which appeared to have collapsed *in situ*. Some of the red was linked to the marble scheme (there was one join between the marble and a red border fragment) however, red and blue were so commonly used that it is possible that some of the disturbed fragments were not from the room.

At lower levels the plaster appeared to have collapsed and remained *in situ*, with large sheets lying on top of each other and some fragments apparently still attached to parts of the remaining stone footings. Excavation at the south end of the room exposed a large sheet of plaster lying face-down on what was probably the original floor. All of the fragments excavated at this level were plain red and blue including a few fragments which were reinforced at the back with pieces of tile and probably came from an area of the wall where extra strength was needed possibly near the base of the wall, or round the opening for a door.

In other areas some patches of render were still in their original position, but the isolated deposits of painted plaster found across the site were clearly not *in situ* and it was apparent that during periods of clearance and building any plaster present was disturbed and spread across the site, with the result that material from the same general scheme was found in a number of different contexts and phases. The plaster deposits as a whole appeared – from character, location, and phasing – to be clearance debris. Some may have been the result of deterioration and collapse but much was apparently simply shovelled out of the way during major changes on the site. Consequently, although they could indicate the quality of the decoration it was difficult to link any of the decorative schemes to particular rooms or buildings.

The plasters and renders

One of the aims of the project was to establish whether the plasters and mortars at Peñaflor were manufactured using Roman techniques. The normal Roman process involved mixing slaked-lime (lime and water – calcium hydroxide) with sand or organic material – to prevent shrinkage-cracks and to aid the drying process – and applying it to the wall. Drying and hardening involved the evaporation of the water and a slow reaction with atmospheric carbon dioxide (carbonation), and the final product was a hard lime (calcium carbonate) plaster.

The first rendering coat was coarse, consisting of lime mixed with sand, crushed stone or brick, and was applied relatively thickly to even-up the surface of the wall. Vitruvius then recommended three coats of coarse preparatory plaster or render containing sand but, in practice only one coat was often used. To produce a finished surface, a finer-grained lime plaster, (which Vitruvius suggested should contain crushed marble to impart a fine white surface suitable for painting) was then applied and smoothed down. Three coats of this finer plaster or render were stipulated by Vitruvius, but again, it is common to find only one or two coats (Vitruvius VII, iii, 6).

All the plaster from the site appeared to be lime plaster, which was well-mixed and prepared and typical of Roman painted plaster. Most fragments were between 10 mm and 30 mm in total thickness, and showed a typical layered structure consisting of a very thin final surface preparation layer of 1 to 3 mm, a good quality second layer, and a similar but often slightly darker first preparation layer. Most fragments had lost the remains of the coarser preparatory coat but the full thickness of up to 50 mm could be seen in some fragments. The renders which remained *in situ* were durable and the surfaces well-finished. The fact that the pools have stood above ground for many centuries and are still in remarkably good condition attests to the good quality of the materials and workmanship.

The coarse lime mix would normally have sand added in the proportions of one part of lime to two parts of sand (river sand was preferred to sea-sand because it was free of damaging salts). Marble powder was added either in approximately the same proportion as the sand, or in proportionally smaller quantity thus the ratio varied from one part of lime to two parts of marble, to equal parts of each. The final thin plaster coating often had little or no filler in it, though it might be applied over a layer with marble powder or other pale filler (Ling 1991; Adam 1994). The Peñaflor samples showed that the plaster followed this pattern. The filler, much of it apparently river sand, had been added in the recommended proportions, marble and other pale or sparkling fillers had been used in the finishing layers, and the thin surface layer was often almost pure lime.

Hydraulic plaster, mortars or renders were used in damp conditions, or for making structures, such as pools or drains, which contained water. Durability was achieved by adding filler materials rich in silica and alumina such as volcanic ash (*pozzolana*) or crushed ceramic (which imparted a pink colour). Instead of setting by drying, this mix set in contact with moisture, producing silicates within the fabric which made the resulting material very tough and resistant to water. The structure of the water features at Peñaflor was hard, very durable and whitish in colour, and the hydraulic properties must have been achieved by adding volcanic material (Adam 1994).

The pigments

The pigments usually used on Roman wallpaintings consisted of inert mineral compounds, such as the earth colours (eg the ochres) because they are unaffected by the highly alkaline lime and by the setting process; organic pigments were rarely used, apart from carbon (in the form of charcoal) which was very common. Some semi-precious minerals such as cinnabar were used but were limited to higher-class paintings because they were expensive. A few pigments were prepared artificially such as Egyptian blue which was made by heating and fusing several minerals.

The pigments were mixed with water to form a slurry and brushed onto the final plaster layer while it was still wet. As the plaster dried, the calcium hydroxide of the slaked lime slowly converted to calcium carbonate and effectively held the pigments in position on the surface. No adhesive (medium) was needed to hold the pigments in place and the resulting painted surface was very durable. This method is usually known as the *fresco* technique. If the painter worked quickly further detail could be added to the surface before the plaster started to harden, but once the plaster had set pigments could be applied successfully only if they were mixed with diluted slaked lime (lime-water) or some form of medium such as egg.

The paintings at Peñaflor were undertaken using the *fresco* technique. This was borne out by the use of lime plaster, by the range of pigments employed (those normally associated with the *fresco* technique). The adherence of the paint to the plaster, with none of the crazing and flaking typical of some other forms of painting was also indicative of *fresco* painting. It is not clear how often, if at all, an adhesive organic medium was used, and it was beyond the scope of this project to attempt to look for evidence of media because of the difficulties of identifying them, particularly as they would have deteriorated during burial.

Examination of the samples confirmed that the pigments commonly used by Roman wall painters throughout the Empire were clearly present on the plaster at Peñaflor It also showed that at least one of the inhabitants had been wealthy enough to commission paintings using an expensive pigment, cinnabar.

Combinations of different pigments were used either to achieve a different colour or to provide better covering power, or possibly to extend a pigment which was expensive or difficult to obtain. The combinations seen in the material from Peñaflor are well-known from other sites indicating that there was a technology common to Roman painters (Béarat 1997a).

Sources or raw materials

Lime and sand were such frequently-used building materials that they would almost certainly have been obtained locally, though lime of good enough quality might have been difficult to achieve in some areas. Water features were frequently constructed so suitable additives to produce hydraulic mixes must have been readily available. Some of the sands and other fillers were obviously specially selected for a particular purpose eg pale-coloured sand, translucent crushed stone, or white marble-powder in layer (b) of the plasters. These presumably were brought to the site for the purpose whereas the coarser rounded dark river sand frequently found in layer (c) could well have been dug out of the river near the site. However plaster and renders were so widely used that a range of fillers of different qualities might have been easily obtainable from a good local source. Unfortunately it was not possible to source the raw materials as part of the project.

Since even the commonly-occurring earth colours needed some preparation and refinement, and some pigments were made artificially (for example, Egyptian blue) it has been suggested that there were pigment manufacturing centres (Bachmann 1977). Presumably such centres would be in mineral-rich areas where the raw materials would be readily available, and the pigments would have been distributed from these centres in ready-to-use form. Certainly pigments which were apparently ready to use are frequently found in containers on archaeological sites (Barbet *et al* 1997) and Pliny indicates that painters kept a stock of the basic cheap pigments, and charged extra for the more expensive ones such as cinnabar (Pliny, *NH* 35, 13). While travelling painters probably carried some basic pigments with them as their stock in trade, cinnabar was highly-prized and expensive and they might not routinely carry a supply because of its cost.

Many of the pigments could have been obtained in mineral-rich Spain, and were possibly processed and exported from there. According to Pliny,

almost the entire Roman supply of cinnabar came from Sisapo in Baetica (Spain). The source is probably the Almadén mines which are still an important source of mercury (Pliny *NH*, 33, 118; Gettens *et al* 1993), and are located in the Sierra Morena to the north of Sevilla. Further research would be needed to trace the Peñaflor pigments to their source.

Decorative schemes, and dating

Certain design conventions occurred fairly regularly on provincial Roman wall paintings. The walls were frequently divided into three horizontal zones: the lowest – the dado – varied in height between 300 and 900 mm; the main zone was approximately three times the height of the dado; and the upper zone varied in size and was not always present. Low-relief *stucco* mouldings were often used at junction points, such as where walls met ceilings.

The main zone was the area most clearly visible when the room was in use, and tended to contain the most striking colour or the most detailed design. A common theme in the main zone was fields or panels of colour separated by bands of another colour, the panels might be plain or might contain figurative or other detail.

Decorative schemes are normally described in terms of the type-styles identified at Pompeii however styles of wall painting took some time to become established in the provinces, and were often modified in the process. It might be possible to assign the red and black scheme (Plaster Type C; Phases 7b–9, 9 and 12) to the Pompeian third style which occurred in the second half of the first century BC and was characterised by red and black schemes sometimes including plant motifs (Ling 1991, Barbet 1980a). Red and black schemes were also found in the fourth style but the fact that the fragments from Peñaflor were conspicuously better in quality than other material on the site might indicate that they were third style since, according to Ling (1991), the quality of wallpaintings declined during the fourth style because of greatly increased consumption.

The imitation marble and large areas of plain colour found in context 100 (Phase 9) possibly represent a scheme consisting of marble decoration in the lower, dado, zone of the walls, and fields of red with blue borders (or *vice-versa*) above. This is typical of many provincial schemes based on the Pompeian fourth style. In Italy this style first began to appear during the first century AD, and introduced much greater variety of decoration and colour than had been present in earlier styles. The plaster (Type B) was good but not excellent in quality.

The blue/grey and orange scheme (100, Phase 9) might be either third or fourth style since large areas of plain colour were typical of each style. It is tempting to assign this to the late third style, because it is of high quality, and because towards the end of the third style other colours, including blue and green, were added to the normal red and black. Apparently linked to the blue/grey and orange scheme were fragments from (537) (Phase 8a) which were decorated with dark red, black and bluish grey. Both were painted on the same better quality plaster (Type A) and exhibited a rather different range of pigments to the mass of material from the site, and it is possible that they came from the same, or a similar scheme. The fragments decorated in red marbled over yellow, from (100), might have been related to the blue/grey and orange scheme since the plaster had similar characteristics, but unfortunately this possibility was not realised when samples for further analysis were selected.

Yellow backgrounds and use of all-over patterns of foliage and animals (such as seen in context 641, Phase 7a–9) are normally considered typical of the fourth style but the plaster of this scheme (Type C) was of excellent quality and the same as that used for the red and black scheme (most of which was found in Phase 7b–9) as well as the column-rendering (found in Phases 8a and b). The coincidence of plaster type shows that these decorative schemes were almost certainly contemporary, and the presence of the yellow scheme in this group probably, in fact, places all of them firmly in the fourth style (Ling 1991, Barbet 1980b).

Although it is difficult to assign a date to provincial paintings purely on a stylistic basis since the styles took time to reach the provinces, the flourishing trade in oil and other commodities between Baetica and the centre of the Empire during this period (Keay 1988; see also Chapter 10), meant that communications were very good, and that new styles might have arrived at Celti relatively quickly. Possibly, therefore, the red and black scheme, and the yellow schemes, plus the red columns can be assigned to the early fourth style. It is not, however, clear whether they derived from the building in which they were found or whether they were simply rubbish from another part of the site. It is also possible that rather than being strictly contemporary with early fourth style decoration in Italy, they might represent the choice of a deliberately "old" style chosen by the owners of the Phase 8a/b house in the later 2nd/early 3rd centuries AD.

The marble design represents a rather later stage in the development of wall decoration at Celti. It appears to be very similar to the panels of painted marble found on wallplaster from the Casa del Anfiteatro at Emerita Augusta (Mérida), where rectangles and roundels (as well as lozenge shapes) of imitation marble were used to decorate the base of the wall (Abad Casal 1982a, Figs. 88, 90, 92). This scheme is difficult to date, largely because of uncertainties over the date of the construction of the Casa del Anfiteatro itself. Recent estimates vary between the 1st (García Sandoval 1966) and 3rd centuries AD (Balil 1976). However, a later, rather than earlier date seems likely. This would suggest that this decorative scheme at least may have derived from the Phase 8a/b houses. Given the close similarity between the Emerita and Celti wallpaintings, it is not impossible to suggest that the same painter(s) could have been responsible for both sets of paintings and even that a local school had become established in the area which then developed some local stylistic characteristics (Ling 1991). Further work comparing the materials and techniques of the two groups of plaster, however, would be needed to test this hypothesis.

Conclusion

The composition of the plaster, and the nature and application of the pigments are all typically Roman and more sophisticated than some provincial material. The overall picture provided by the painted wallplaster at Peñaflor is of a community which was flourishing by the late first century BC and through the first century AD, and was certainly not a provincial backwater. The fact that some of the painted plaster was of the very highest quality is indicative of considerable wealth and of a desire to decorate rooms, or whole buildings, in contemporary Roman style. The character of the decorative schemes indicates that skilled and experienced plasterers and painters, who were familiar with current Italian designs, worked at Celti, and possibly that a local school of painters also developed in the area.

Acknowledgements

I am very grateful indeed to all who participated in, or funded the work on the wallplaster. The following conservation students from UCL Institute of Archaeology were involved during the excavation and study seasons: Holly Ferguson and Joanna Girling (1990); Dean Sully (1991); Maria Mertzani, Irit Narkiss and Andrew Wilson (1992); David Goldstein, Irit Narkiss, Asaf Oron (1993). Madelaine Abey-Koch (by then a former student of the Institute) joined the team during the season of 1991. The project was funded by the British Academy, the Gordon Childe Fund of the Institute of Archaeology, the Conservation Unit of the Museums and Galleries Commission, and the Irwin Fund (the University of London Central Research Fund). The 1993 study season was based at the Roman site of Italica where working facilities were very generously made available by the then Director, Jose-Manuel Rodriguez Hidalgo. The analytical work was undertaken by Maria Mertzani and funded by a generous grant from the British Academy. The illustrations were drawn by Dorella Romanou, and Nick Balaam read and criticised the text.

Chapter 8
The Topography and Epigraphy of Celti

José Remesal Rodríguez

Abstract

This chapter begins with an analysis of the available historical and epigraphic evidence for the identification of ancient Celti with Peñaflor. It then goes on to provide a catalogue of all known inscriptions from the site. This work builds upon earlier catalogues and commentaries to present a fairly large number of inscriptions, 65, quite a few of which are previously unpublished. This is the first time that all the inscriptions from a Baetican municipality are published together with a detailed excavation and survey, and enables a fairly full discussion of the mid to late 1st century AD town to be presented in Chapter 10. A detailed discussion of the material points out a number of idiosincracies in the epigraphic repertoire from the town, not least that the inscriptions are virtually devoid of any reference to external activities, such as imperial or municipal administration or military service. However, they do allow us to identify some of the key families at Celti, their relationships to each other and to the province of Baetica as a whole.

Introduction

Uncertainty over the location of ancient Celti has been the subject of discussions that continue to the present-day. This is largely due to the rarity of inscriptions that might have allowed its location to have been established with certainty. There are two main sources of information. Firstly, Pliny the Elder, who names Roman towns between Corduba (Córdoba) and Hispalis (Sevilla), and secondly, the Antonine Itinerary. Those towns mentioned by Pliny, which include Celti, were located on the banks of the river Guadalquivir and analysis of their inscriptions demonstrates that they were granted municipal status during the Flavian period. The Antonine Itinerary, however, suggests that Celti lay further inland. This chapter begins with an attempt to look at the problem again, and is followed by a new analysis of all known inscriptions from Peñaflor and its immediate region. It thus complements and develops some of the comments made in Chapter 1 of this volume.

The History of a Name

Pliny's text (*NH* 3, 11) allows the towns of Celti, Axati, Arva, Canama, Naeva and Ilipa to be placed in the conventus hispalensis. Moreover, the discovery of inscriptions has meant that the location of Axati (Lora del Río)[1], Arva (El Castillejo, Alcolea del Río)[2], Canama (Alcolea del Río)[3] and Naeva (Cantillana)[4] have been known for a long time. The greatest difficulty has been trying to establish the exact location of Celti and Ilipa – both of which have been discussed for many years. Ambrosio de Morales, who visited Peñaflor during the 16th century,[5] considered it to have been the site of Ilipa (Ambrosio de Morales 1575). Strabo (3; 5; 9) mentions that the Guadalquivir was navigable by large ships as far as Ilipa, and Morales noticed that Peñaflor was the point where the volume of the river increased, on account of the inflow from the Genil. Further weight to his argument was added by the fact that he thought that the remains of El Higuerón could be interpreted as part of the remains of an ancient port that could have sheltered ships when the river flooded. I have demonstrated elsewhere[6] that this impressive structure has little to do with port installations and that it is best interpreted as having formed part of the defences of the pre-Roman settlement of Peñaflor. Thus, Ambrosio de Morales' arguments are merely conjectures based upon the oft cited text of Strabo and a reading of the archaeological remains visible during his day.

The correct identification of Celti with Peñaflor and Ilipa with Alcalá del Río was first proposed by Maldonado de Saavedra in the later 17th century.[7] He recognised that the influence of the Atlantic tides upon the current of the Guadalquivir extended no further north than Alcalá del Río and that this coincided with Strabo's observation about the limits of the river's navigability. He also drew upon the evidence from the Antonine Itinerary and the known location of the other towns cited by Pliny. Furthermore, he suggested that the name of Celti was derived from a Celtic population and that the town functioned in part as a port for the export of metals mined in the Sierra Morena. Thus he followed Jerónimo de Zurita in suggesting that Celti be identified with Peñaflor, and rejected other names that had been attributed to the site. Maldonado de Saavedra's ideas reveal a sound understanding of the classical sources and contemporary literature, given that he remarks that the authority of Ambrosio de Morales had led many – whose names he lists – to identify Peñaflor with Ilipa. In particular, he highlights Rodrigo Caro's change of opinion. He had followed Morales in principle, but later believed that Alcalá del Río should be identified with Ilipa, without returning to the matter of the location of Celti, which Rodrigo Caro had placed in the vicinity of Regina. He also collected together the known inscriptions of Peñaflor.[8]

This debate contined for almost a century and, in May 1743, Alonso Carrillo wrote a work entitled "Discurso Geográfico" in which he argues that the ancient Ilipa Magna on the Baetis was not located at the village of Peñaflor, as was generally believed, but at Alcalá de Río instead.[9] A little later, Padre Enrique Flórez was inclined to locate Celti near Puebla de los Infantes, not far from Peñaflor.[10] Polemic on the location continues down to the present day, owing to the fact that it is difficult to reconcile the locational information provided by the Antonine Itinerary (It.414, 5) and the Ravenna Cosmography (Rav.IV.44, 315, 2) and the fact that the town was located on the banks of the Guadalquivir. Some scholars have located the town in the hinterland of Peñaflor, more or less within the Sierra Morena: thus Hübner, followed by Blanco and Luzón, sited it near Mellaria in the

vicinity of Fuenteovejuna (Córdoba).[11] Others, whose ideas were closer to those of Flórez, sited Celti somewhere between Constantina and Peñaflor. Antonio Blázquez, for example, located it near Constantina, while Saavedra sought it in Las Navas de la Concepción. Corzo and Jiménez doubted between Peñaflor and Puebla de los Infantes, while Tovar prevaricated and Roldán did not commit himself.[12] Others, however, have followed the identification of Celti with Peñaflor.[13]

The Epigraphy

The aim of this section is to provide a catalogue of all known Roman inscriptions on stone from Celti. It includes texts recently published in CILA 2.1, with commentary and, where necessary, corrections. It also contains a substantial number of new texts that have come to light at Peñaflor in various circumstances in recent years. The chapter concludes with a series of general reflections on the overall epigraphic assemblage from the town and the light that it sheds upon the society of ancient Celti.

The first epigraphic records from Celti were collected together by Florián de Ocampo and annotated in the Codex Valentinus,[14] which is dated to between 1525 and 1544.[15] Some inscriptions from the site were also collected together by Zurita in his Baetican series, which suggests that he may well have visited Peñaflor.[16] The same is probably true of Ambrosio de Morales. Known inscriptions from the site were also collected together by Maldonado de Saavedra in his book, while Pedro Leonardo de Villacevallos kept several inscribed stones in his museum.[17] F. Fita, A. Blázquez and F. Pérez Minguez made known some texts through publication in the Boletín de la Real Academia de la Historia. More recently, A. Blanco Freijeiro, G. Chic García, M. Ponsich and J. González have all published new texts.

The Catalogue

INSCRIPTIONS FROM THE 1988 SYSTEMATIC SURFACE SURVEY
These are discussed and illustrated (Figs 5.43, 5.44 and 5.45) in Chapter 5.

OTHER INSCRIPTIONS
Most of the texts already published in CILA 2.1 are not illustrated here. New texts, however, have been illustrated with photographs wherever possible. All of these are in private ownership, which has made the task of photography difficult. Consequently, therefore, the quality of photographs is not ideal.

1. Unpublished (Fig. 8.1 and 8.38)

This text was unusual in being inscribed on a plaque of pink marble with moulding on both sides and a groove along the upper edge. It is not known whether this grooving was contemporary to the primary function of this piece or whether it was created at a later date. It is possible that the piece derived from a balustrade, possibly of a tribunal, upon which the inscription was cut. The first line is inscribed on a plinth below the mouldings.

Measurements: 44cm wide by 16cm high; thickness 14.5cm. The letters are *scriptura actuaria*. Height of the letters: 5cm in the first line. Triangular stop. It was discovered in La Viña and is now in the possession of D. José Higueras Muñoz.

> ----]pro honore[---
> ...(c.15 letters)...

The second line is illegible although it must belong to an imperial title. The first letter on the left hand side could be an L, the second a C or an S, the third an E and the fourth either a P or an R, after which there is a gap corresponding to some 7 or 8 letters. The last three letters could have been either S or C, the head of an E or I and the upper part of the left arm of a V. It is impossible to propose a full reading of this, although it might possibly be interpreted as: *pro honore.../...L(uci). Sep([timi]) Sev([iri])*, a reading which would be consistent with the dating suggested by the form of the letters. If this reading is correct, then this may well be an important document recording a dedication to an Emperor who, after the defeat of Clodius Albinus, intervened directly in the economic reorganization of the region.[18]

2. Unpublished (Fig. 8.2)

A pedestal made from grey marble with black veins, with the upper and lower sections missing. The maximum conserved height was 70cm, the width was 59cm and the thickness 50cm. The epigraphic field is defined by a border. It was discovered in La Viña although its exact findspot is unknown. The height of the surviving epigraphic field is 40cm. Width is 36cm. The height of the letters: line 1 and 2: 5cm; lines 3 and 4: 4.5cm; line 5: 4cm. Width of the interlineal space: 3; 2; 5; 2; and 3cm respectively.

Triangular stops. Apice on the first E of Aeliae. The 4th line shows a clear tendency towards the cursive script on Dressel 20 amphorae. The inscription is in the possession of D. José Fernández Rosa.

> Aéliae . Q(uinti)
> F(ilia). Flaccinae
> Post . mortem
> Aelia. M(arci) . F(ilia). Marcellina . f(ilia)
> 5. D(onum) D(at)

"To Aelia Flaccina, daughter of Quintus, this pedestal and statue is dedicated afer her death by Aelia Marcellina, daughter of Marcus (Aelius) and of (?Aelia) Marcellina."

Fig. 8.1. Photograph of inscription no. 1

Fig. 8.2. Photograph of inscription no. 2

The type of lettering allows this inscription to be dated to the second half of the 2nd century AD. This text is interesting in that it is a dedication to one woman by another in the same family. Since the dedicant is the daughter of Marcus Aelius and the person to whom it is dedicated is named as the daughter of Quintus Aelius, it is possible she may be her cousin, aunt or paternal grandmother. It is interesting to note that feminine filiation of the dedicant is recorded. Given that only the *cognomen* of the mother is recorded, the proposed restoration of the name of the mother of the dedicant is given as Aelia.

3. (Fig. 8.3)

This belongs to a pedestal of white marble with orange veins, the top of which was prepared to receive a bronze sculpture.[19] Prior to this study it had not been noticed that it was never finished, since the upper part had yet to be properly cut (Fig. 8.32). Measurements: height: 1.48m; width: 75cm; width: 50cm. The epigraphic field is defined by a listel and cyma recta measuring 81 × 53cm. The letters take the form of capitals in *scriptura actuaria*. The height of the letters is 5cm. The stops are triangular. The inscription is to be found at the corner of the building which used to be the Ayuntamiento and which is now the Biblioteca Pública of Peñaflor, in the Plaza de España No. 1.

> Q(uinto) Aelio Q(uinti) F(ilio) Optato
> Aelia Q(uinti) F(ilia) Optata
> testamento
> poni iussit
> G(aius) Appius Superstes
> Canninius Montanus
> H(eres) P(onendum) C(uravit)

"In her will, Aelia Optata ordered that this monument was put up in honour of her father Quintus Aelius Optatus, son of Quintus. Caius Appius Superstes Canninius Montanus, her heir, ensured that this should be done."

I have transcribed this text according to the text published in CIL. II 2329; Thévenot 1952; Caamaño Gesto 1972; Ponsich 1979; 102 no. 82 Lám. XXXII; Blázquez Martínez 1980, 28; Bonneville 1984, 72–3; CILA 2.1, 143 no. 168; There is a copy of this text signed by Zurita although it is probable that he received it from Ginés de Sepulveda (Gimeno Pascual 1997, 130 no. 191). Today, only the first two lines of the text are legible.

The person commemorated in this inscription has been related to the Quintus Aelius Optatus known from Dressel 20 amphora stamps. [20] The stamps which bear the name of this individual have appeared at the nearby Dressel 20 kiln sites of El Castillejo[21] and La Catria,[22] both of which are near to Lora del Río (Axati). However, it is probable that at least the latter – and possibly both – were located in the territory of the town named "Mesa de Lora" or "Lora La Vieja". [23] This should not create any conflict, since there is no reason why a distinguished individual from one town should not possess property in the territory of a neighbouring community. Indeed it is emblematic of the links and mobility that existed between the municipal elites in the region.

A surprising feature of this text is that the person responsible for erecting this monument is considered as an heir without having adopted the family *nomen*. This, of course, assumes that we consider Appius Superstes to have been the surviving husband of Aelia Optata. If this were the case, the normal practice would have been that he would have appeared in the text explicitly in this role. It is also curious that this individual, whose name is rare in Baetica, was also considered to have been the heir of Calpurnia Sabina, and dedicated a similar pedestal and statue *ex testamento* to her son Fulvius Lupus (No. 17 below), even though there was no formal familial relationship between them.

4. (Fig. 8.4)

Funerary altar in white marble. This is decorated with a pediment with loculus, at the edges of which are sheaves while the front is decorated by two rosettes. [24] The piece is well conserved and is to be found in Peñaflor. Measurements: height: 92cm; width: 49cm; thickness: 32cm. The epigraphic field is defined by a

Fig. 8.3. Photograph of inscription no. 3

Fig. 8.4. Photograph of inscription no. 4

moulding and stands 30cm high and 36cm wide. The capital letters are squared. Height of the letters: 1st line 7cm; 2nd line 6cm. Triangular stop. This is no longer in the Ermita de Villadiego where it was seen by González (CILA 2.1 no. 172) or in the Biblioteca Pública where this writer saw it.

> Q(uinti). Aelii
> Zenonis

"(The monument) of Quintus Aelius Zeno".

CIL. II 2331; ILER 2176; Chic Garcia 1975, 358–9; Ponsich 1979, 98 n° 72, Lám. XXIV; CILA 2.1 no. 172; Gimeno Pascual 1997 191, 1.

This inscription has been dated by González to the first half of the 2nd century AD (CILA 2.1, 146–7). However it is probable that this dedication, in the genitive, is earlier and possibly dates to the Flavian period. The Aelii seem to have been an important group within the society of Celti. If Quintus Aelius Optatus can be identified with the person identified on the Dressel 20 amphora stamps (supra pp.144), it is surprising that he did not achieve any public office in the town. In their filiation, our Aelii only indicate their father and do not invoke the names of earlier generations. This would suggest that they were second generation and that their ancestors only gained Roman Citizenship in the immediately preceding generation. All of our Aelii bear the *praenomen* Quintus, with the exception of the father of the dedicator of the inscription to Aelia Flaccina, who was called Marcus.

5. (No Surviving Illustration)

Plaque or pedestal, whose current whereabouts is not known.

> Venerem. Aug(ustam). cum parerg(o). item phialam
> argent(eam). Aemili Rustici
> item trullam argenteam. M(arcus). Annius Celti
> tan(us). Testamento
> suo post mortem Aemiliae Arthemisae uxoris et
> Heredis suae poni iussit. Aemilia
> 5. Arthemisa filia posuit eademq(ue). de suo
> annullum aureum gemma meliore

"In his will, Marcus Annius Celtitanus stipulated that upon the death of his wife and heir, Aemilia Artemisia, a statue in the form of Venus with her attributes would be erected to her. Aemilia Artemisia, his daughter, erected this monument and, for her part, added a ring of gold with precious stones of the best quality. Aemilius Rusticus, for his, gave a cup and a tray of silver".

CIL. II 2326; ILER 418; Thouvenot 1940, 286; Remesal Rodríguez 1986–87, 140–1; Larrey Hoyuelos 1987, 530; CILA 2.1, 140, n° 165; Gallego Franco 1993, 123 n° 4; Melchor Gil 1993–1994, 340; del Hoyo 1994, 428 n° 3; Gimeno Pascual & Stylow 1999.

Here I have followed the new version of the text put forward by Gimeno Pascual and Stylow (1999)[25], which adheres to the text recorded by Fernández Franco (Biblioteca Nacional: Ms 577). I also follow their view when they suggest that this was a *consecratio in forma deorum* to the deceased, rather than a dedication to the goddess Venus. The new reading of the inscription proposed above, allows us to distinguish the names of the people who were involved in the creation of this monument: Annius Celtitanus, his wife Aemilia Artemisia and their daughter who has chosen to take her mother's name; Aemilius Rusticus, who supplemented the gift, was, in my opinion, brother of Aemilia Artemisia (the mother). This is not the only case at Celti where the daughter retains the *nomen* of the mother (infra no. 35).

6. (Fig. 8.5)

Plaque of pink marble, whose upper left-hand corner is missing. In CILA 2.1 no. 173, it is recorded as measuring 27.5cm in height; 4.17cm in width and 2.5cm thick. The letters are in *scriptura actuaria*. The height of the letters oscillates between 5.3 and 3.8cm. Triangular stops on the 3rd line, hederae in the 2nd and 4th lines. The final letters *us* of the second line are ligatured. The P of pius is raised. The I in *suis* is long.

The inscription is conserved in the Museo Arqueológico Provincial de Sevilla.

> [M(arcus) A]emilius.
> M(arci) (hed.) F(ilius) (hed.) Marcianus
> ann(orum) . XXXXIII . pius
> in (hed.) suìs (hed.) H(ic) (hed.) S(itus)/(hed.) E(st)
> (hed.) S(it) (hed.) T(ibi).(hed) T(erra) (hed.) L(evis)
> (hed.)

"(Marcus) Aemilius Marcianus, son of Marcus, of 45 years. Here he lies. May the earth rest light upon you!"

CIL. II 5539; ILER 3020; Fernández Chicarro 1946, 120 n° 18; Fernández Chicarro & Fernández Gómez 1980, 129 n° 4; CILA 2.1 no. 173.

González (CILA 2.1, 147–8) dates this inscription to the middle of the 2nd century AD on the basis of letter shape. However, it should be noted that the inscription lacks any invocation to the Dii Manes, which suggests that it might date to the end of the 1st century AD.

7. (Fig. 8.6)

A grey marble plaque. Measurements: height: 27cm; width: 31.5cm; visible thickness: 1.5cm. The stonecutter has attempted to use squared capital letters which, in the end, have been mixed with letters in *scriptura actuaria*. The height of the letters: 3.5cm. Triangular stops. The final S of the first line is of a lesser size. This inscription was discovered in Peñaflor, although the exact findspot is not known. It is currently embedded in the wall to the left of the main door of the Ermita de Nuestra Señora de Villadiego.

> Apollonius
> ann(orum) XXXIII. piu[s]
> in (hed.) suis (hed.) H(ic) (hed.) S(itus) E(st) (hed.) S(it)
> (hed.) T(ibi) (hed) T(erra) (hed,) L(evis) (hed.)

"Apollonius, 33 years and devoted to his own. Here he lies. May the earth rest light upon you !"

CILA 2.1 no. 174; HEp 4, 1994, no. 777. González (CILA 2.1, 148–9) did not point out that the inscription was cut onto a piece of reused marble with coarsely re-cut

Fig. 8.5. Photograph of inscription no. 6

edges. The smaller sized S in the first line was not due
to the stonecutter's strain, as the compiler suggests,
but was requested by whoever composed the text. It is
sufficient to compare this with the space taken up by
the second line where, although the González does not
point it out, the final S of *pius* is missing on account of
being broken.

8. (CILA 2.1. Fig. 91)
Small (12 × 16cm) plaque of yellowish marble, the upper
part of which is decorated by two doves supporting a
garland held between their beaks, at the centre of which
there is a crown. Letters are in *scriptura actuaria* with
triangular stops. There is a ligature XV in the age of
the deceased. The inscription was discovered in 1916,
owing to flooding of the Guadalquivir in the vicinity
of Peñaflor. H. Sandars sent a pencil tracing of the
inscription to F. Fita.[26] The stone is conserved in the
Museo Arqueológico Provincial de Córdoba (Inv.2638).[27]

> (dove) (crown) (dove)
> D(is) M(anibus) S(acrum)
> Bruttia Victorina
> Celtitana . A<n>nor(um) . XXXV
> Pia . in . suis
> H(ic) . S(ita) . E(st) . S(it) . T(ibi) . T(erra) . L(evis)

"Dedicated to the Dii Manes. Bruttia Victorina, from
Celti, of 35 years and devoted to her own. Here she lies
! May the earth rest light upon you !"
Fita 1916, 120–3; Larrey Hoyuelos 1987, 530; CILA 2.1
no. 177, where *annor(um)* is transcribed when the
manuscript actually reads *a<n>norum*. Here, the name
Celtitana must be an indication of the *origo* of the
deceased although, as we have seen in the case of the
Fabii, it is also possible that it may have been a second
cognomen (see infra no. 14).

Fig. 8.6. Photograph of inscription no. 7

9. Unpublished (Fig. 8.7)
Fragment of a plaque of white marble which lacks
the upper right-hand corner as well as the lower part
of the inscription. Measurements: maximum height:
24 cm; minimum width: 40.5cm; thickness: 4.5cm. The
epigraphic field measures 26.5cm wide by a minimum
of 17cm high and is defined by a moulding. The
inscription was discovered in gravel works to the east
of Peñaflor "a bit beyond the roof". The letters are
scriptura actuaria capitals and measure: line 1: 5.5cm;
line 2: 5cm; line 3: 4cm. The interlineal spaces measure
2 and 1.5cm. The first two stops are hederae, the third
is triangular. The I and V of Bruttius are of a smaller

size to enable the *nomen* to fit onto the first line. The lower part of the G of Primigenius is rounded, while the stonecutter has omitted the E of the *cognomen*. The inscription is in the posession of D. José Carranza Cruz.

> Sex (hed.) Bruttius
> Primig<e>ni-
> us (hed.) ann . XXXX
> [--------]

"Sextus Bruttius Primigenius. 40 years of age......"

Two or three lines with the usual formulae found on Peñaflor inscriptions are missing (such as *pius in suis, H.S.E. S.T.T.L*). It is possible that the deceased was more than 40 years old at the time of death.

10. Unpublished (Fig. 8.8)
Fragment of a plaque, of which only a small part of its upper margin remains, and which exhibits a hole for a nail. Measurements: minimum height is 16.5cm; maximum width: 10cm. Regularly executed letters in *scriptura actuaria* style. Height of the letters on the first line: 6cm. Triangular stop. This inscription is recut onto the back of an earlier text, given that there are traces of a large upright letter on the reverse side. It was probably found at the farm of El Tesoro.

> --- B]ruttius [---
> --- i]n suos . H[---
> [----]

Since the upper edge of this inscription survives, it is certain that it lacked the formula *D(is) M(anibus) S(acrum)*. It is not possible to posit relationships between people bearing the name Bruttium, a family well represented at Celti. It is worth pointing out that two of the three inscriptions mentioning this family, lack the formula *D.M.S.* (It is probable that the order of the funerary formulae is altered and that here *Pius in suis* appears before the mention of age).

11. (CILA 2.1. Fig. 92)
Plaque of pink marble. Measurements (according to CILA 2.1.no. 178): height: 34 cm; width: 32cm; thickness: 2cm. Capital letters are used on the first line, with letters in *scriptura actuaria* in the remaining lines. Height of the letters is between 2.8 and 5cm. Triangular stops except on the first line where all the stops are hederae with an upright stalk inclined to the right. Some letters are raised: all the Ls, the C of Caesia, the G of Gallus, the I of in, the S of suis and the H in the formulario of Caesia, the P of pius of Gallus.

> D(is) (hed.) M(anibus) (hed.) S(acrum)
> Caesia . Annula . ann(orum) XXV
> pia . in . suis . H(ic) . S(ita) . E(st). S(it) . T(ibi)
>   T(erra). L(evis)
> L(ucius) . Licinius . Gallus . ann(orum)
> 5. LXV . P(ius) . in . s(uis) . H(ic) . S(itus) . E(st). S(it)
>   . T(ibi) T(erra). L(evis)

"Consecrated to the Dii Manes. Caesia Annula, 25 years of age, devoted to her own. Here she lies. May the

Fig. 8.7. Photograph of inscription no. 9

Fig. 8.8. Photograph of inscription no. 10

earth rest light upon you ! Lucius Licinius Gallus, 65 years of age, devoted to his own. May the earth rest light upon you !"

García y Bellido 1960, 192; HAE 1964; ILER 3144; CILA 2.1 no. 178.

González (CILA 2.1, 152) considers that in this inscription, "the pagination (arrangement of the text) is careless". I do not believe this to be the case. Two lines have been dedicated to each of the deceased, emphasizing the line from the beginning of the name of each of the deceased (1st and 3rd). The inscription provides no clue about the relationship between them. They may have been husband and wife, or father and daughter. Despite their age difference, the inscription was cut at one moment in time which may point to them being a married couple who died together for unknown reasons. [28] Annula is a rare *cognomen*.[29]

12. (CILA 2.1. Fig. 94)

Fragment of a white marble plaque, chipped on all edges. Measurements: height: 19,5cm; width: 25cm; thickness: 15cm. Capital letters with elements of *scriptura actuaria*, and the I of libertus raised. Height of the letters: 3.5cm. Triangular stops. The precise place of discovery in Peñaflor is not known. The inscription is conserved in the Museo Arqueológico Provincial de Sevilla (CILA 2.1, 154).

        C]orneli[us ---
    ---]mani . lib[---
    ---] annor(um) . X[---
         [--------]

"----Cornelius---, libertus of (Cornelius) ----- hand of ? years."

CILA 2.1 no. 180; HEp 4, no. 799. I understand the second line as referring to the *cognomen* of the patron. This is the thickest funerary plaque from Celti.

13. (Fig. 8.9)

Small plaque in pink marble, according to one scholar, and yellow, according to another. The upper part of the inscription is missing. The lower part is decorated with a palm, an animal variously identified as a rabbit, boar or dog, and a bull. Measurements: minimum height: 16.5cm; width: 16.5; thickness: 2cm. The script is in the form of squared capitals, although it tends towards *scriptura actuaria*. Height of the letters: between 1 and 1.5cm. Triangular stops. It is conserved in the Museo Arqueológico Provincial de Sevilla.

         -----
    us Chres[---
    os . mensi<u>m
    VI . pius in sui-
    s.Hic.S(itus).E(st).S(it).T(ibi).T(erra).L(evis)
    (palm) (bull)

"...us Chres...os, 6 months old, devoted to his own. Here he lies. May the earth rest light upon you !"

CIL.II 5542; ILER 3021; Fernández-Chicarro 1951, 50;

Fernández-Chicarro & Fernández Gómez 1980, 89 n° 2; CILA 2.1 no. 179; HEp. 4, 1994, no. 778.

There is no agreement about how the *cognomen* should be expanded: Hübner preferred *Chres[ti]cus*; Fernández Chicarro and Fernández Gómez chose *Chrisos*; González (CILA 2.1, 153) inclined for *Chres[t]os*, while *Chris[tin]os* and *Chrys[er]os* were proposed in Hep 4, 1994.

14. Unpublished (Fig. 8.10)

Block of grey marble belonging to a funerary monument. It measures 37cm in height and 1.70m long, although part of its left-hand side is missing, and is 29cm thick.[30] The epigraphic field, 16cm ´ 1.17m is defined by a cyma. Letters in *scriptura actuaria* style. Height of the letters: 1st line: 5cm; 2nd line: 4cm. The stops are hederae. The F of Fabia and the C of Celtitana are raised. The crossbars of the letter A are sometimes horizontal and sometimes inclined. The text is displaced towards the left-hand side of the epigraphic field, both in the first and the second line. The inscription was discovered in El Camello and is currently to be found

Fig. 8.9. Photograph of inscription no. 13

Fig. 8.10. Photograph of inscription no. 14

as the architrave of the chimney in the Huerta de Corbacho, the property of D. Fernando Mallén Cabrera.

Fabia (hed.) M(arci) (hed.) F(ilia) (hed) Sempronia (hed.) Aciliana (hed.) Celtitana Ann(orum) (hed.) XV (hed.) mens(ium) (hed.) VIII (hed.) dier(um) (hed.) XIII

"Fabia Sempronia Aciliana Celtitana, daughter of Marcus, 15 years, 8 months and 13 days."

The inscription was reported by Larrey Hoyuelos (1987), and referred to in HEp 4 (1994, no. 773) although no commentary was provided. There is little doubt that the young lady commemorated on this inscription came from one of the most distinguished families in Celti, as her *nomen* and *cognomen* indicate. The type of inscription suggests that it formed part of a monument of notable proportions, perhaps a tower-shaped mausoleum. An inscription from Corduba provides us with more information about the young lady's family. In effect, a certain Fabius, whose *cognomen* remains unknown, was *flamen divorum augustorum provinciae Baeticae* between July/August of AD 215 and July/August of AD 216. The inscription and statue dedicated to him was paid for by his father, Marcus Fabius Basileus Celtitanus. The father of the young lady commemorated on the inscription from Celti was also Marcus Fabius, probably with the *cognomen* Celtitanus.[31] I therefore believe that both inscriptions refer to people from the same family. In our current state of knowledge it is not possible to be specific about the degree of the relationship between them, even though the chronological similarity between the two suggests that it may have been close. The *nomen* and one of the *cognomina*, however, lead us to raise another question. It has been supposed that the twice Consul Lucius Fabius Cilo had a Baetican origin.[32] The study of Dressel 20 amphora stamps from the Cerro de los Pesebres[33] suggests to me that the initials of the stamp LFCCVFS and other variants may be an abbreviation of the name Lucius Fabius Cilo: *L(ucius) F(abius) C(ilo) C(larissimus) V(ir) F(iglina) S(calensia)*.[34] To accept this reconstruction would be to reinforce the idea that Fabius Cilo was Baetican in origin (see also Chapter 10). Amongst the *cognomina* of Fabius Cilo is to be found that of Acilianus,[35] a name which was also shared by the young lady commemorated on this inscription, and which may help us define the origin of this Consul even more precisely than has hitherto been possible.

15. (No Surviving Illustration)
An inscription which has disappeared and which, according to old records, served as the support for the holy-water stand in the Peñaflor parish church.

Victoriae Aug(ustae)
At<t>icus . G(ai) . Fabi . Nigri . L(ibertus)
Firmo . Bit(h)y nitis . L(ibertae) . L(ibertus)
augustales . D(onum) . D(ederunt)

"Dedicated to Victoria Augusta. This offering was made by (Fabius) Atticus libertus of Caius Fabius Niger and (Fabius) Firmus libertus of the liberta (Fabia) Bithynis, augustales".

CIL. II 2327; ILER 499; CILA 2.1 no. 166. Gimeno Pascual 1997, 488.

This inscription informs us about the existence of the free-born Fabius, G. Fabius Niger, and three liberti. It also underlines the importance of the gens Fabia in Celti.

16. (Fig. 8.11)
Plaque of white marble. The lower part of the stone is decorated. A bunch of grapes marked with two ivy leaves is at the top end and lower are two flanking doves resting upon branches – possibly olives – who are pecking the grapes. The inscription is currently embedded into a wall inside the Ermita de Villadiego. Measurements: height: 70cm; width: 30cm; thickness: over 3cm. Letters are in *scriptura actuaria*. Lines 1–7 are 5cm high; lines 8–11 are 2.3cm high; line 12 is 1.8cm.[36] The stops are hederae with zigzagging stalks. If my information is correct, this inscription was discovered midway along the Calle Nueva in Peñaflor.

D(is) (hed.) M(anibus) (hed.) S(acrum) (hed.)
Atimeti (hed.) lib(erta) (hed.)
Fabia (hed.) Mer–
ope (hed.) anno–
5. rum (hed.) LXXV (hed.)
pia (hed.) in suis (hed.)
H(ic) (hed.) S(ita) (hed.) E(st) (hed.) S(it) (hed.)
T(ibi) (hed) T(erra) (hed.) L(evis) (hed.)
Si quantum pietas potu-
it tantum fortuna

Fig. 8.11. Photograph of inscription no. 16

10.   dedisset litteris au-
      ratis scribere(m) hunc
      titulum
    (Hed) (Hed)
        (grapes)
    (dove) (dove)

"Dedicated to the Dii Manes. Fabia Merope, liberta of (Fabius) Atimetius. 75 years. Devoted to her own. Here she lies. May the earth rest light upon you ! If my luck was as great as my love for you[37] I would write this in letters of gold".

Chic 1975, 359–66; Correa 1976, 367–9; Ponsich 1979, 95; CILA 2.1 no. 175.

Chic did not point out that the last five lines of the inscription were written in the form of a poetic rythm (Correa 1976). None of the scholars who have studied this text have noticed that it is cut on a re-used plaque, as can be deducted from the irregular profile of its right hand margin. This fact adds emphasis to the verse. The dedicant knew that the elegy to the much-loved person was inscribed upon a slab re-used from an earlier monument. The name of the dedicant is not known to us, although given that the term *Pietas* used in the verse is associated with family love, it is possible that he or she may have been the deceased's husband or, given the age of the deceased (see below), her son or daughter.

17. (Fig. 8.12 & 8.14b)
Pedestal in greyish marble. This probably supported a bronze figure, given the form of the upper plinth and the impressions on its upper surface of the pedestal (Fig. 8.14b). Measurements: height: 144cm; width: 86cm; thickness: 57cm. The epigraphic field was 78.5cm high and 62.5cm wide. Capital letters are in *scriptura actuaria*. Height of the letters: 6.5cm in the 1st line; 6cm in the remaining lines. The text was very eroded and difficult to read. It is conserved in the patio of the Ermita de Villadiego.

> Q(uinto) . Fulvio . Q(uinti) . F(ilio) . Lupo
> Calpurnia . L(uci) . F(ilia) . Sabina . Mater
> testamento . poni . iussit
> C(aius) . Appius . Superstes . Cani-
> nius . Montanus
> H(eres) . P(onendum) . C(uravit)

"To Quintus Fulvius Lupus, son of Quintus. In her will, his mother, Calpurnia Sabina, daughter of Lucius, ordered that this monument be erected. Her heir Caius Appius Superstes Canninius Montanus ensured that it was done".

CIL. II 2330; ILER 5118; Chic 1975, 357–8; Ponsich 1979, 97; CILA 2.1 no. 169; Gimeno Pascual 1997, nos. 96, 188 and 875. Chic suggests that there were two dedicants: C. Appius Superstes and C. Aninius Montanus.

18. (Fig. 8.13)
Plaque of pinkish marble, part of whose right margin is broken. The exact place of discovery in Peñaflor is not known. Measurements: height: 29.5cm; wisth: 17.5cm; thickness: 3cm. Letters are in *scriptura actuaria* although

Fig. 8.12. Photograph of inscription no. 17

Fig. 8.13. Photograph of inscription no. 18

the rendering of the D.M.S in the first line tends towards squared capitals. Height of the letters: 1st line: 3cm; 2nd to 6th lines: 2.5cm. Triangular stops: in the 6th line the stops are hederae. The inscription is conserved in the Museo Arqueológico Provincial de Sevilla[38].

> D(is). M(anibus) . S(acrum)
> Q(uintus) . Fulvius
> Musicus
> annor(um) . XXXXV
> Hic . situs . est
> S(it) (hed.) T(ibi) (hed.) T(erra) (hed.) L(evis) (hed.)

"To the Dii Manes. Quintus Fulvius Musicus, 45 years. Here he lies. May the earth rest light upon you !"

González 1982, 159–60; CILA 2.1 no. 181.

González dates this inscription to the late 2nd or early 3rd century AD on the basis of the letter typology (CILA 2.1, 155). The relationship between this individual and Quintus Fulvius Lupus is difficult to establish (supra no. 17). If the *cognomen* Musicus gives an idea of his professional occupation, then it is possible that this individual may have been a slave of the Fulvii of Celti. The lack of any filiation might be taken as evidence to support this although this cannot be conclusive. The shared *praenomen* might possibly be an index of a certain family relationship between these two people.

19. Unpublished (Unillustrated)

Plaque of coarse-grained white marble. The upper and left-hand margins are straight, while the right-hand and lower margins indicate that the piece had been recut. There is a hole in the upper margin for the fastening of the inscription. Measurements: height: 31cm; width: 21.7cm; thickness: 2.2cm. Height of the letters: 1st line: 3.5cm; 2nd to 4th line: 3cm. The stops are triangular and, in the first three lines, the sharpest angle points upwards: in the last line, however, they point downwards. The former are almost certainly hederae. The cross-bar of the H is inclined; the P is not closed. The inscription was found at the Fuente del Pez.

> D(is) (hed.) M(anibus) (hed.) S(acrum)
> Iul(ius) . Siriacus
> annor(um) . LXVII
> (ius).i(n).s(uis).h(ic).s(itus).e(st).S(it).T(ibi).T(erra).
>   L(evis)

"To the Dii Manes. Iulius Siriacus, 67 years, devoted to his own, lies here. May the earth rest light upon you!".

The use of *duonomina* and the *cognomen* Siriacus suggest that this individual was probably a libertus.

20. (No Surviving Illustration)

White marble stela whose epigraphic field is defined by two horizontal mouldings. The inscription was cut at two separate times. The name of the deceased was inscribed adjacent to the moulding that defined the lower part of the epigraphic field. The formula that follows was written outside the epigraphic field. The inscription is conserved in the Castillo of the Marqueses

Fig. 8.14a. Photograph of inscription no. 21

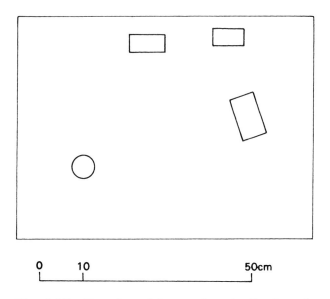

Fig. 8.14b. Drawing of impressions in the top of inscription no. 17

de las Casas in Navas del Marqués. We only have an indication of its height: 50cm. [39] The letters are *scripta libraria*. In the first line the stops are hederae, while in the rest of the text they are triangular stops.

> D(is) (hed.) M(anibus) (hed.) S(acrum)
> Barbatus
> ser(vus) . ann(orum) LI
> pius . in . suis
> H(ic) . S(itus) . E(st) . S(it) . T(ibi) . T(erra) . L(evis)
> et . Iunia . Optatina
> annor(um) . LXXV . pia in suis

"Consecrated to the Dii Manes. Barbatus, slave, of 51 years. Devoted to his own. Here he lies. May the earth rest light upon you ! And Iulia Optatina of 75 years. Devoted to her own".

CIL. II 2332 (follows Ocampo and only publishes the text relative to Barbatus); Blázquez 1920, 539 (who published the complete text for the first time); Pérez Mínguez 1930, 788; Rodríguez Moñino 1940, 44; ILER 3141 (publishes the text as it appears in CIL) and 3147 (reproduces the complete text as published by Rodríguez Moñino); CILA 2.1 no. 176.

This and the following inscription refer to individuals bearing the *nomen* Iunius, since I suggest that Barbatus was a slave belonging to a member of this family. Given the age of both of the deceased, I would suggest that Optatina was the *contubernalis* of Barbatus, who died before gaining his freedom, while Optatina died subsequently. It is particularly interesting to note that the script of the two texts are different: the letters A in the text referring to Barbatus has a horizontal cross-bar while the same letter in that which refers to Optatina has an oblique one in the archaic style – or even lacks it altogether. If we consider that a maximum of 24 years elapsed between the execution of the first and second texts on this inscription, and that both of the deceased had been born the same year, this inscription as a whole sheds light on the evolution of epigraphic style at Celti and helps provide relative dating for inscriptions from the town.

21. (Fig. 8.14a)
Reused plaque of white marble from Almadén, to the north of Seville. The lower part of the inscription is missing. Measurements: minimum height: 22cm; width: 17cm; thickness: between 2.5 and 1cm. Rustic capital letters. There is a nexus in PH. Height of the letters: between 4.6 and 2.9cm. The inscription is conserved in a private collection at Sitges.

> D(is) M(anibus) S(acrum)
> L(ucius) . Iunius . O-
> nesiph-
> orus . An(norum)
> 5.   [LX P(ius) I(n) S(uis)]
> [------]

"Consecrated to the Dii Manes. Lucius Iunius Onesiphorus of 60 years. Devoted to his own......".

Fabre, Mayer & Rodà 1982, 234 no. 41; CILA 2.1 no. 182.

The scholars who originally published the inscription reconstructed, undoubtedly correctly, the 5th line, although the abbreviation P.I.S. is rare at Celti. The *cognomen* of this individual makes one think that this was an individual of libertine status.

22. (CILA 2.1, Fig. 102)
Plaque of white marble with pink veins.[40] In the centre of the lower part of the inscription there is a palm and, to the left, a dove. Measurements: height: 42cm; width: 30cm; thickness: 2cm. Letters are in *scriptura actuaria* style. Their height oscillates between 2.5 and 3.5cm. Triangular stops, except in the 1st and 3rd line where they are hederae. The horizontal bar of the A is inclined in the archaic style. The inscription was found in the olive-grove of D. Alejandro Pinto to the south of Peñaflor and is preserved in the Museo Arqueológico Provincial de Sevilla.

> D(is) (hed.) M(anibus) (hed.) S(acrum)
> Optatinus . Ser(vus)
> annor(rum) (hed.) XVIII
> pius in suis
> 5.   H(ic) . S(itus) . E(st) . S(it) . T(ibi) . T(erra) . Levis
>   (dove) (palm)

"Consecrated to the Dii Manes. Optatinus, a slave, 18 years, devoted to his own. Here he lies. May the earth rest light upon you !"

Fita 1916, 118–20; Fernández-Chicarro & Fernández Gómez 1980, 127 n° 32; CILA 2.1 no. 190.

Previous studies of this inscription have not pointed out that it was cut into a re-used plaque, as is implicit in the good symmetry of the text and the irregular right-hand margin. This also explains why the palm is not flanked by two doves, because once the branch was centred with respect to the text, there was not enough space for another dove on the right. González (CILA 2.1, 190) transcribes the final formula as L(evis) although his published photo shows that it should read *Levis*. As I have suggested, Optatinus must be related to his co-slave Iunia Optatina (supra no. 20). Alternatively, it is possible that he was her son and that he was born before she gained her freedom.

23. (Fig. 8.15)
Plaque of grey marble split vertically into two. Measurements: length: 1.91m; height: 70cm; thickness: 12cm. Squared capital letters are engraved in the marble and have nail holes to allow the bronze letters to be attached. Measurements: height of the letters: 11.5cm. Given the character of the letters, it is impossible to know the nature of the stops.[41] The inscription was discovered at Peñaflor although its exact findspot is not known. Local sources suggest that it may have been found at the angle of the Calle Nueva and the Calle Blancaflor. Today it can be found on the wall of the patio of the Ermita de Villadiego, to the left of the main entrance.

> Licinia. C(ai). F(ilia). Mancina
> ann(orum). XV. H(ic). S(ita). E(st). S(it). T(ibi).
>   T(erra). L(evis)
> C(aius). Licinius. Gal(eria tribu). Lupus
> .H(ic). S(itus). E(st). S(it). T(ibi). T(erra). L(evis).

"To Licinia Mancina, daughter of Caius, 15 years of age. Here she lies. Caius Licinius Lupus, Galeria tribu. Here he lies. May the earth rest light upon you !"

Fig. 8.15. Photograph of inscription no. 23

Blanco Freijeiro 1977, 140–1; Ponsich 1979, 98 n°72; AE 1980, 558; CILA 2.1 no. 183.

If the information about the findspot is correct and my proposal to link this inscription with the Roman tomb known as the Ermita de los Mártires is accepted, then this is the only inscription from Celti whose original location is known. It is also the only inscription that mentions a Roman voting-tribe. Moreover, the inscription lacks reference to the usual formula *Pius/a in suis/os*. The age of the father has also been omitted, possibly voluntarily, so as to avoid giving undue emphasis to the "unnatural" fact that a father had outlived his daughter.

24. (No Surviving Illustration)

A lost inscription which, according to Morales, served as the pillar supporting the holy-water stand in the Parish Church. According to Morales' description it was an altar, which was decorated on its sides by a *simpulum* and a *patera* (Morales 1575, f.88.v).

D(is) M(anibus) S(acrum)
Lurius. Fortunio
vixit an(nis). LXI
P(ius). I(n). S(uis). S(it). T(ibi). T(erra), L(evis)

"Consecrated to the Dii Manes. Lurius Fortunius, who lived 61 years. Devoted to his own. May the earth rest light upon you".

CIL. II 2333; ILER 3431; CILA 2.1 no. 185. Gimeno Pascual 1997, no. 489 mentions the earliest record of this inscription by Zurita, in which the *nomen* appears as Urius and the *cognomen* as Fortunatus, a more common form than Fortunius.

25. (CILA 2.1, Fig. 98)

A white marble altar with a lightly conical shape. It is decorated with a triangular pediment and focus, and adorned on the front by two rolls decorated with flowers, on the right side by a *patera*, and a *simpulum* on the left. Measurements: height: 61cm; width: 31cm; thickness: 17cm. The epigraphic field is delimited by two mouldings in the upper and lower areas. The script tends towards *scriptura actuaria* capitals, although it is quite irregular. Height of the letters is between 1.5 and 3.5cm. Triangular stops.

D(is). M(anibus). S(acrum)
L(urius) Valer-
ianus. v-
icsit. an-
5. nis. XXXI. P(ius)
I(n). S(uis). H(ic). S(itus). est

"Consecrated to the Dii Manes. Lur(ius) Valerianus, lived 31 years, devoted to his own. Here he lies".

CIL. II 5540; Fernández Chicarro 1946, 123; CILA 2.1 no. 184.

I have followed CILA 2.1 no. 184 in transcribing the text since I have not seen the inscription. I would venture to suggest the following interpretation of the

6th line: I(n). S(uis). H(ic). S(itus). E(st). S(it). T(ibi) [(T(erra). L(evis)].

I propose the reading L(urius) for the *nomen* because this and the previous inscription have two elements in common. Both are altars which are rare in the epigraphic repertoire of Celti. Moreover, both are unique in sharing the same the formula *vixit annis* and are two of the three inscriptions with the abbreviation *P(ius/a) I(n) S(uis)*.

26. (CILA 2.1, Fig. 99)

Pink marble plaque. Measurements: height: 37cm; width: 27cm; thickness: 3.5cm. The letters of the first line tend towards squared capitals, while the rest are in *scriptura actuaria* style. Height of the letters: line 1: 4cm; 3.5cm in the remaining lines. In the 4th line the initials are raised, as is the I of Antiocis in line 2, the L of the numeral and the L of the 5th line. In the first two lines the stops are hederae, while in the rest they are triangular stops. The first stop of the 5th line was indicated as a hedera, although the stalk has not been added. The inscription was found in a place named Moncludas and then passed into the ownership of Villacevallos[42]: "The present manuscript, as with the previous one, I obtained from the most reverend Hinestrosa brother of the Marquis of Peñaflor. It comes from a site next to the river, called Las Moncludas, the house of D. Diego Gomez". Today the inscription is to be found in the Museo Arqueológico de Málaga.

D(is). M(anibus). S(acrum)
Marcia. Antio
cis. ann(orum)LXX
Pia. In. Suis
H(ic). S(ita). E(st). S(it). T(ibi). T(erra). L(evis)

"Consecrated to the Dii Manes. Marcia Antiocis of 70 years. Devoted to her own. Here she lies. May the earth rest light upon you !"

Villa y Zevallos 1740, f. 54 v. Antigualla 41; 310–313 n° 51 (Ms. Biblioteca Nacional. 20275); CIL. II 2292 and 2334 (they differ in the age assigned to the deceased: XX or LXX years, depending on how the scraped surface of the stone is interpreted: in my opinion LXX is the correct reading); ILER. 3142; Serrano and Atienza 1981, 45–7 n° 45; CILA 2.1 no. 187.

27. (No Surviving Illustration)

Lost inscription. Fragment of a white marble plaque. Morales, who first published it, suggests that it measured two palms long and a little more than 1 palm high: in other words, ± 43cm × 22cm.[43] It was discovered in Peñaflor at the house of Pedro Ponce, near the Plaza, who gave it to Morales. It was in Morales' ownership and, later, that of his brother Agustín de Oliva in Córdoba. In 1672, the inscription was to be found in the house of the Licenciado Bernardo de Cabrera. Works in his house in 1729 uncovered part of the inscription which was collected by Pedro Leonardo de Villacevallos (Real Academia de la Historia. 9–5770 no. 2, fol. 51 v.–53 v.Antigualla 39). By this stage the inscription had already lost the first line and its invocation of the Dii Manes.

[D(is) M(anibus) S(acrum)]
Q. Marius. Optatus [---
Heu. iuvenis. tumulo. qualis. iacet. a[----
qui. pisces. iaculo. capiebat. missile. dextra [---
aucupium. calamo. praeter. studiosus. agebat [---

CIL. II 2335; CLE 412; Fita 1916, 116ff; García y Bellido 1967, 199ff; Piernavieja 1977, 32–4; CILA 2.1 no. 186. The metric style of this inscription has attracted the attention of various authors and Fita, in connecting this fragment with CIL. II 2314, attempted to reconstruct a graceful text. Sadly, however, that which remains today only allows one to confirm that the young Marius Optatus was fond of fishing and hunting, appropriate activities for a young man of good social standing who, by virtue of hunting, prepared himself for military tasks.

28. (CILA 2.1, Fig. 100)
Grey marble plaque. Measurements: height: 22cm; width: 24cm; thickness: 6cm. The letters of the first two lines tend to be squared capitals, while those of the other lines are in *scriptura actuaria*. The height of the letters is between 1.8 and 2 cm. It was found in the El Camello field and is now in the possession of D. José Mª Parias.

> D(is). M(anibus). S(acrum)
> Maurula
> ser(va) ann(orum) XXXXIII
> Pia. in. suis. Hic. S(ita). E(st)

"Consecrated to the Dii Manes. Maurula, slave of 43 years. Devoted to her own. Here she lies".

García y Bellido 1960, 191 n° 30; CILA 2.1 no. 188. García y Bellido read the last line in the following way ...*hic si(ta)*. I prefer the reading published in CILA 2.1, since there is no evidence for the formula ending with STTL.[44]

29. Unpublished (Fig. 8.16)
Plaque of pink marble with a small fracture on the left edge, which only affects the final S of the third line. The inscription reuses an earlier stone, whose inscribed face is gently curved and of which only the right edge is original: the reverse has been worked. Measurements: height: 35cm; width: 29cm; thickness: between 3 and 5cm. Letters are in *scriptura actuaria*. The height of the letters is the same on all three lines: 3cm. The interlinear spaces, however, are different: 3.7cm for the first, 2.2 for the second and 2 cm for the remainder. The L of Laeta and the I of Pia are raised. The crossbar of the letter A and H of *H(ic)* is a little inclined. The stops are triangular with the stop pointing downwards. The inscription was discovered in El Camello. It is in the possession of D. Manuel Carranza Naranjo.

> D(is) . M(anibus) . S(acrum) .
> Messia . Laeta
> Patriciensis
> An(norum) . XXXXV . Pia .
> in . suis . H(ic) . S(ita) .
> E(st) . S(it) . T(ibi) . T(erra) . L(evis)

Fig. 8.16. Photograph of inscription no. 29

"Consecrated to the Dii Manes. Messia Laeta, from Corduba, of 45 years. Here she lies. May the earth rest light upon you".

Normally, the size of the letters on inscriptions from Peñaflor graduate from larger to smaller, as is common in Latin epigraphy. Here, however, all the letters are of the same height. Attention to certain lines was drawn by creating different interlineal spaces. It is interesting to note the presence at Celti of someone from Corduba, the provincial capital.

30. (CILA 2.1, Fig. 101, Fig. 8.17)
Black marble plaque. Measurements: height: 34cm; width: 56cm; thickness: 2cm+. Quite elegant letters in *scriptura actuaria*. Height of the letters: 1st line: 5cm; 2nd and 3rd line: 4cm. Triangular stops. The place of discovery is not known and the inscription is now to be found inside the Ermita de Villadiego, to the left of the main door.

> Myris Rus-   Cinismus
> ticae . l(ibertus). an(norum)   Rusticae. l(ibertus)
> LII. H(ic) S(itus). E(st). S(it) H(ic). S(itus). E(st). S(it) T(ibi).
>   T(ibi)T(erra). L(evis)   T(erra). L(evis)

"Myris, libertus of Rustica, of 52 years. Here he lies. May the earth rest light upon you ! Cinismus, libertus of Rustica, Here he lies. May the earth rest light upon you !"

CILA 2.1 no. 189; HEp. 1994, no. 780. González (CILA 2.1, 161) considered that Myris was three years old. However, the inscription is broken at the base of the two letter uprights which indicate Myris' age, while the top of the first stroke resembles that of the letter L of *l(ibertus)* and *l(evis)*.

31. (Fig. 8.18)
White marble plaque. The text is framed within a decorative border: in its upper angles, there are two

Fig. 8.17. Photograph of inscription no. 30

Fig. 8.18. Photograph of inscription no. 31

doves whose beaks share a stalk of ivy and which they unite to form a crown at the centre. A stem of ivy trails from the feet of the doves to the lower part of the inscription, finishing in a large leaf; in the centre of the lower part there is a crater from whose handles spring vine tendrils with bunches of grapes, which join up with the ivy leaves adjacent to the border of the inscription. Above the bunches of grapes to the right, there is a dove which pecks at the grapes and, to the left, an animal, almost certainly a dog, which is walking to the left. Measurements: height: 54cm; width: 30cm; thickness: more than 2.5cm. The dedication to the Manes is in squared capital letters, while the rest is in actuary

style. The height of the letters: 1st line: 4.6cm; the remaining lines: 2cm. Some letters are raised: P (in *Pietati*), A (in *Annorum*), I (in *In*), S (in *Sit*), L (in *Levis*), C (in *Coniugi*) and I (in *Indulgentissimae*). The stops are triangular, those at the end of the line are hederae with a zigzagging stalk.

> D(is). M(anibus). S(acrum).
> Pie[tati .] Baeticae.
> annorum. XXI. pia
> in suis. hic. sita. est.
> 5. te rogo praeteries dicas
> sit tibi. terra. levis.
> Barathes. coniugi
> indulgentissumae
> posuit

"Consecrated to the Dii Manes. In memory of Baetica, of 21 years, devoted to her own. Here she lies. I ask that you say when passing, May the earth rest light upon you ! Barathes put up (this dedication) to his most indulgent wife".

Chic García 1975, 360; CILA 2.1 no. 191.

Although Pietas has been attested as a *cognomen* (Kajanto 1965, 168), it is probable that it has another meaning in this case, otherwise this person would have two *cognomina* and no *nomina*. In this case, therefore, Pietas has been taken to signify *memoria*.

32. (CILA 2.1, Fig. 104)
Yellowish marble plaque. Measurements: height: 30cm; width: 22cm; thickness: 2cm. Capital letters in *sciptura actuaria*. Height of the letters: between 2.3 and 3cm. Triangular stops. Discovered in Peñaflor and now to be found in the Museo Arqueológico Nacional de Madrid.

> D(is). M(anibus). S(acrum)
> Pyramis ser(va)
> ann(orum). XXXXV. P(ia). I(n). S(uis)
> H(ic). S(ita). E(st). S(it). T(ibi).T(erra). L(evis)

"Consecrated to the Dii Manes. Pyramis, slave, of 45 years. Devoted to his own. Here he lies. May the earth rest light upon you."

CIL.II 1236; del Rivero 1933, 44 nº 141; ILER 3058; CILA 2.1 no. 192.

33. (No Surviving Illustration)
Plaque which was discovered in "Las Moncruas" and is now housed in the house of Antonio Parias in Peñaflor.

> Romula. an(norum). XVI
> pia in suis
> H(ic). S(ita). E(st). S(it). T(ibi). T(erra). L(evis). D(is).
> M(anibus).S(acrum)

"Romula, 16 years of age, devoted to her own. Here she lies. May the earth rest light upon you ! Consecrated to the Dii Manes".

Clark Maxwell 1899, 298; Bonsor 1931, 20; CILA 2.1 no. 193.

Bonsor was mistaken in the place of discovery. As González notes in CILA 2.1, the placement of the formula DMS at the end of the inscription is unusual.

34. (No Surviving Illustration)

Fragment of a marble plaque found at Peñaflor and obtained by Pedro Leonardo de Villacevallos in 1739: "Finding myself in Écija in the year 1739, I owed to M. R. P. Mro. Hinestrosa of the Order of the Merced, the present fragment of stone, and the next two pieces which will be revealed, and which he brought from the village of Peñaflor." The measurements reported by Villacevallos are: "Considered to be a third in height (approximately 30cm). Approximately a quarter in width (approximately 22cm) and a finger in thickness." Berlanga (1903) sent a tracing to Hübner who affirmed: "Litterae sunt optimae saec. II, pictis simile" (CIL. II 2304).[45]

> Sempronia
> Prixsilla
> a]nnoru[m ---

"Sempronia Prixsilla, ...years......."

Villacavallos 1740, f.54 antigualla 40; CIL. II 2304; Berlanga 1903, 81; CILA 2.1 no. 194.

In CIL. II 2304, the third line is reproduced as *annor(..)*, whereas in fact Villacevallos' own drawing suggests *a<n>no(rum)*, although from the tracing which Berlanga sent to Hübner, it can be established that the formula in fact read *a]nnorum*. The *xs* in the name Prixsilla is probably due to the difficulty that the inhabitants of the region still have in recognizing the sound sc and, thus, in expressing it graphically.

35. (Fig. 8.19)

Plaque of pink marble with dark veins. Measurements: height: 18cm; width: 41cm; thickness is not known since the inscription is embedded in a wall. The letters are squared capitals, although the last line is written in such a way as to suggest that it was written at some time after the main body of the text. Height of the letters: 2.6cm in the first three lines; 2.2cm in the fourth line. Triangular stops. The inscription was discovered in the Cortijo de Malapié. It is now in the possession of D. José Parias.

> Sempronia. Superata
> C. Licini. Capitonis. Filia
> annor(um) XXI. Hic. S(ita). E(st). S(it). T(ibi). T(erra). L(evis)
> et. Sempronia. Peregrina

"Sempronia Superata, daughter of Caius Licinius Capito, 21 years. Here she lies. May the earth rest light upon you ! And Sempronia Peregrina."

García y Bellido 1960, 191 n° 29; M. Ponsich 1979, 107 n° 92; CILA 2.1 no. 195.

García y Bellido considered that Superata "is the natural daughter or of a second marriage". González (CILA 2.1, 165–6), suggests that she was adopted because the father's name was not mentioned. I think that both possibilities are wrong. In the first place, one needs to explain why it is that Sempronia Peregrina appears in the text at all. There are two alternative explanations. The first is that Sempronia Peregrina is the mother of Sempronia Superata and the appearance of her name in the text is to be explained by the wish to mention the names of both the father and the mother. The second is that Sempronia Peregrina could be equally the mother or the sister of Superata who were buried in the same tomb at a later date. The second hypothesis is preferred, given that the form of the letters may indicate a later date: the letters T, E and As of the fourth line tend to be in the *scriptura actuaria*, even though there are some letters in this style in the main body of the text, such as the top of the Ts and the curved foot of some of the Rs. Against this second hypothesis, it can be argued that there is no formula in honour of Sempronia Peregrina even though there is space for a fifth line at the bottom of the inscription. I am inclined to the view that Sempronia Peregrina is the mother of Superata and that her name was added once the monument had been finished. This would have made it harder for the stonecutter to add the name so that he was not able to cut the name with the same fineness and regularity. The fact that Superata followed her mother's *nomen* could be explained by the fact that at Celti the Sempronii were a more important family than the Licinii.

Fig. 8.19. Photograph of inscription no. 35

36. (Fig. 8.20)
Plaque of white marble from Almadén de la Plata. Measurements: Height: 31cm; width: 22.5cm; thickness: between 1.6 and 3.5cm. The first line tends to be in squared capitals, while the remainder is in *scriptura actuaria* style. Height of the letters: between 2.6 and 3.5cm. Some letters are raised. Triangular stops. Incorrect punctuation in the preposition *in*. The inscription was discovered in Peñaflor, although its exact findspot is not known. It is now to be found in a private collection at Sitges (Barcelona).

> D(is) M(anibus) S(acrum)
> Sergia. Rustica
> ann(orum). LXXXX. P(ia)
> i.n. suos. H(ic). S(ita). E(st)
> S(it). T(ibi). T(erra). L(evis)

"Consecrated to the Dii Manes. Sergia Rustica, 90 years, devoted to her own. Here she lies. May the earth rest light upon you !"

Fabre, Mayer & Rodá 1982, 234; CILA 2.1 no. 196.

37. (No Surviving Illustration)
An inscription which is now lost. It was discovered in the Cortijo de la Vega in the Cerro de El Cucharón, opposite Peñaflor.

> D(is) (hed.) M(anibus) S(acrum)
> Successa (hed.)
> ann(orum) (hed.) XXV (hed.)
> pia (hed.) in suos (hed.)
> H(ic) S(ita) E(st) S(it) T(ibi) T(erra) L(evis)

"Consecrated to the Dii Manes. Successa, 25 years, devoted to her own. Here she lies. May the earth rest light upon you !".

CIL. II 1514; CILA 2.1 no. 197.

38. (CILA 2.1, Fig. 107)
Greyish marble plaque. Measurements: height: 22.5cm; width: 30.5cm; thickness: 4.2cm. The letters tend to be in *scriptura actuaria*. Height of the letters: between 2.7 and 3cm. Triangular stops. Discovered at Peñaflor although the precise find-spot is not known. It is to be found today in the Museo Arqueológico Provincial de Sevilla.

> Successus
> ser(vus) ann(orum). XXX.
> H(ic). S(itus). E(st). S(it). T(ibi). T(erra). L(evis).

"Successus, slave, 30 years. Here he lies. May the earth rest light upon you !"

CIL. II 5541; Fernández-Chicarro 1946, 119; Fernández-Chicarro & Fernández Gómez 1980, 130; CILA 2.1 no. 198.

The fact that the *cognomen* of the person commemorated on this and the previous inscription are the same suggests that they were related in some way. Since the text states that Successus was a slave, it is likely that Successa was his fellow slave.

Fig. 8.20. Photograph of inscription no. 36

39. (CILA 2.1, Fig. 108)
Yellowish-pink marble plaque. Measurements: height: 26cm: width: 19cm: thickness: 2.3cm. The first line of text tends to be squared capitals, while the remainder is *scriptura actuaria*. Height of the letters: 2.5cm. The stops of the first line are hederae and triangular stops in the rest of the text. The shape of the letters suggests that the stonecutter was not very skilled. This inscription belonged to Villacevallos' collection: "This, and the previous one, were sent by D. Diego Gómez, from Peñaflor, saying that they had been found at Moncludas adjacent to the Guadalquivir". Today the inscription is to be found in the Museo Arqueológico de Málaga.

> D(is). M(anibus) (hed.) S(acrum) (hed.)
>   Vibia. ser(va).
>   ann(orum). LXV
> 5. pia in s[uis]
>   H(ic). S(ita). E(st). S(it). T(ibi). [T(erra). L(evis)]

"Dedicated to the Dii Manes. Vibia, slave, of 65 years. Devoted to her own. Here she lies. May the earth rest light upon you !"

Villacavallos 1740, f. 55 antigüalla 42; CIL. II 2336; Berlanga 1903, 72, XLII; Atienza Páez 1971, 35 n° 6; Serrano and Atienza 1981, n° 46; CILA 2.1 no. 199.

40. Unpublished (Fig. 8.21)
White marble plaque, none of whose edges survive. Measurements: minumum height: 10cm; minimum width: 11.5cm; thickness: 4.2cm. The inscription retains traces of *ordinatio* on the first surviving line. Height of the letters: 3cm. Triangular stops. At the bottom of the fragment are traces of a final line which probably read *H.S.E.S.T.T.L.*

[----]
---]detumonen[---
---]lxx . pia . [---

The calligraphy is quite cursive in style, similar to that of the tituli picti on Dressel 20 amphorae. Worthy of particular note is the L in the expression of age, the raised P of *pia* and the A without cross-bar. These characteristics permit the inscription to be dated to the first half of the 3rd century AD. The text makes reference to a woman from Detumo who died at 70 years of age. Stylow has recently suggested that this town be identified with neighbouring Palma del Río, 6 km upriver from Peñaflor and the point at which the Guadalquivir intersects with its tributary the Genil. [46]

41. Unpublished (Fig. 8.22)
White marble block of which the upper edge is preserved. Measurements: surviving height: 12cm; surviving width: 15cm; surviving thickness: 5cm. The reverse side of the inscription is polished. The letters are cursive, the F and T a little more raised, and the As without crossbar. The height of the letters oscillates between 3.5 and 2.5cm. In the first line there is a small rectangular stop, in the second there is a triangular stop. The inscription was discovered at the Cortijo de La Laguna. It is in the possession of a potter, Sr. Linares. It is dateable to the first half of the 3rd century AD.

---]a . Faustina[---
---] . pia in [---

Given that it is the upper edge of the inscription that is preserved, it seems likely that that it took the form of an elongated plaque which lacked the formula *D.M.S.*

42. Unpublished (Fig. 8.23)
White marble plaque which is polished on both sides. The upper, lower and right-hand edges of the inscription are conserved. It belongs to an inscription in which there figure at least two names, a feature not noted when it was orginally published (see also no. 30). Measurements: height: 28.5cm; maximum surviving width: 27cm; thickness: 1.8cm. Height of the letters: 1st line: 3.2cm; 2nd line: 2.2.cm; 3rd line: 2.1cm; 4th line: 2.5cm; 5th line: 2cm. The interlineal spaces are also very irregular: 1; 3.5; 3.2; 2.7cm respectively. Triangular stops. Discovered at the crossroads between the Calle Calvario and the Seville to Córdoba road.

[--] ...]S
[---]a A.Hermione
an.XXXV
pia in suis
[---] .S.E.S.T.T.L.]

"(Consecrated to the Dii Manes .... and of (.....) A (....) Hermione, 35 years. Devoted to her own. She lies here. May the earth rest light upon you !"

Larrey Hoyuelos 1987, 530; HEp. 4, 1994, 772.

43.Unpublished (Fig. 8.24)
White marble fragment. Part of the upper edge is preserved. The plaque is decorated above, and towards

Fig. 8.21. Photograph of inscription no. 40

Fig. 8.22. Photograph of inscription no. 41

Fig. 8.23. Photograph of inscription no. 42

the centre of, the epigraphic field by a crown. Two undulating sashes run out towards the edges of the plaque (in reality only the right-hand one survives). Measurements: maximum surviving height: 10cm; maximum surviving width: 8.5cm; thickness: 2.5cm. The letters are *scriptura actuaria*. The inscription was discovered in La Viña. [47] The inscription is now in the possession of D. José Fernández Rosa.

(crown)
---] Rustic[---
[------]

Given the position of the first line of the inscription immediately below the crown, it clearly lacked the invocation of the *Dii Manes*.

Fig. 8.24. Photograph of inscription no. 43

44. Unpublished (Fig. 8.25)

Fragment of a plaque of grey marble with reddish veins. The upper edge of the inscription survives. Measurements: maximum surviving width: 22cm; thickness: 8cm. The edge is polished 1.5cm from the inscribed face. The rear of the inscription is polished. The way in which the edge has been polished suggests that the inscription stood 1.5cm above the wall which supported it. The capitals are quite elegant and in *scriptura actuaria*. Height of the letters: line 1: 8cm; line 2: 6cm; interlineal space: 3.3cm. Very small triangular stops. Discovered in El Camello. The inscription is now in the possession of D. Rafael Castellano (Lora del Río).

---]ius . C(ai) . L(ibertus) . Pis[---
---]XXV . P(ius) . in su[is] . [---

"....ius, libertus of Caius, Pis...., 25 (or more) years. Devoted to his own........".

It is probable that this inscription lacks the formula *D.M.S.*

Fig. 8.25. Photograph of inscription no. 44

45. (Fig. 8.26)

Unpublished. Fragment of a pink veined marble. Only the lower part of the inscription survives. The right and left margins are not regular. Below the text there is an ivy leaf, which is not centred in respect to the text. Measurements: minimum height: 21.5cm; width: 20cm; thickness: 2cm. Letters are in *scriptura actuaria*. Triangular stops. Discovered in El Camello and now in the possession of D. José Carranza Cruz.

[----]
---]ser(us/a)
---]ascutta . ser(va) .
(hedera)

Before the A of the second preserved line, there appears to be another letter which may be a C. The structure of the text and the fact that the hedera is not centred suggests that the inscription has been broken on its left and right hand sides. It is possible that the last surviving line may read as follows:

...]as cutia.ser(va) or ...]ascula.ser(va)

Fig. 8.26. Photograph of inscription no. 45

46. (Fig. 8.27)
White marble plaque, of which only the right-hand
side survives. Measurements: height: 28.5cm; minimum
width: 28cm; thickness: not known. Letters are in
scriptura actuaria. Height of the letters: 4.5cm. The crossbars of the As are inclined. Triangular stops, some of
which tend towards a hedera leaf. The inscription is
embedded in the façade of No. 15 of the Calle Concepción Ruiz in Peñaflor and was discovered during
the digging of a drain.

> ---]cus . ann(orum) . IX
> --- an]nor . XXXI
> ---]us . annor(um) . XXX
> ---]XX . H(ic) . S(itus) . E(st) . S(it) . T(ibi) . T(erra) .
> L(evis)

CILA 2.1 no. 201; HEp. 1994, no. 783.

There is no doubt that this inscription was cut at a
single moment in time, given the regularity and con-
sistency of the letters. Consequently, it seems clear that
the final formula conformed to the common stereotype,
instead of having written: *H(ic) S(iti) S(unt) S(it) V(obis)
T(erra) L(evis)*. The ages of the deceased, of which the
first and the third were male, and the characteristics of
the inscription, suggest that all three died at the same
time. Another interpretation would be that the inscription was only cut after the death of the last person.

47. Unpublished (Fig. 8.28 top left)
Fragment of a white marble plaque. It seems that the
left-hand edge is the original. Measurements: minimum
height: 11cm; minimum width: 7cm. The thickness is
impossible to gauge since the inscription currently
adheres to a block of cement. The findspot is unknown.
The inscription is in the possession of D. José Carranza
Cruz.

> [------]
> Se[---
> vern[---
> [-----]

In the second surviving line, the word verna can be
read, suggesting, therefore, that this inscription com-
memorates a slave born in the home.

48. Unpublished (Fig. 8.28 bottom left)
Fragment of a white marble block. It is impossible to
establish whether or not its upper edge is original, since
the inscription is embedded in a block of cement.
Measurements: minimum height: 10cm; width: 12cm;
thickness: indeterminate. The text is comprised of fairly
elegant capitals in *scriptura actuaria*. Original findspot
is unknown. It is in the possession of D. Jose Carranza
Cruz.

> ?-----?
> --- Cal]purn[---
> [-----]

I believe that the *nomen* Calpurnium can be distinguished here, making it the first time that it has been
attested in Celti.

Fig. 8.27. Photograph of inscription no. 46

Fig. 8.28. Photograph of inscription nos. 47, 48 and 49

49. Unpublished (Fig. 8.28 bottom right)
Fragment of a white marble plaque, none of whose
original edges survive. Measurements: maximum height:
10cm; maximum width: 5cm; thickness: impossible to
gauge owing to the fragment being embedded in a plaque
of cement. *Litterae libraria*. The original findspot is
unknown. It is in the possession of D. José Carranza
Cruz at Peñaflor.

> ------
> ---]uin[---
> ---]TT[---

The first surviving line could also be read as ----]nin[-
--- . I believe that the second line retains part of the

formula *S(it)] T(ibi) T(erra) [L(evis)*, which suggests that the first line should be read as: *pi]u<s> in [suis ----*. Alternatively, the first of the surviving lines could be read in this way: *---]VI M[---* which could be expanded to read: *annorum..]VI M[ensium...* .

50. Unpublished (Fig. 8.29)
Plaque of a yellowy limestone. The back of the piece has been polished and the original lower edge has survived. Measurements: minimum height: 14.5cm; width: 31.5cm; thickness: 4cm. It was discovered at La Cruz de los Guardias (next to the mine on the road to La Puebla de los Infantes). It is now in the possession of D. Juan Bocero Viñuela.

> [---]
> an(norum) . IIII hic
> S(itus/a) . E(st) . S(it) . T(ibi) . T(erra). L(evis)

This is one of the earliest inscriptions from Celti, since it can be dated to the middle of the 1st century AD on palaeographic criteria. It is interesting to note that the inscription is cut into soft limestone and not a harder stone.

51. Unpublished (Not Illustrated)
Fragment of a white marble plaque. Only part of the left side remains. Measurements: minimum height: 13cm; minimum width: 10.5cm; Squared capitals. Height of the letters: 3.3cm. Interlineal space: 2cm. Triangular stops. Discovered at Peñaflor although its precise findspot is not known.

> [----]
> an[---
> P(ius/a) . I(n) . S(uis) .H[---

52. Unpublished (Fig. 8.30)
White marble plaque with grey veins. Only the lower left-hand margin of the plaque survives. Minimum height: 29cm; minimum width: 29cm; thickness: 1.3cm. Traces of the *ordinatio* survive in both lines. The letters, which are markedly cursive in character, are 4cm high in the first surviving line and 3.15cm in the second. Triangular stops in the final line, it is not possible to be certain if there were stops in the previous line. The inscription was discovered at the Huerta de los Velos. A small rectangular terracotta urn covered by two tegulae "a doble vertiente"was discovered adjacent to the inscription. It is now in the possession of D. Pedro Meléndez León.

> ---]US IA[---
> ---]us in [---
> H . S . E . S . T . T . L

The inscription is the tombstone of a youth, of which only part of the final formula remains: *[pi]us in suis (or in suos)/H(ic) S(itus) E(st) S(it) T(ibi) T(erra) L(evis)*. Given that the original border of the right-hand side does not survive, the inscription is off-centre with respect to the rest of the stone. This suggests that this plaque may have had two inscribed texts, an established practice at Celti (see also no. 30).

Fig. 8.29. Photograph of inscription no. 50

Fig. 8.30. Photograph of inscription no. 52

53. Unpublished (Not Illustrated)
Plaque of a schist-like rock. Only the upper and right-hand edge survives. Measurements: minimum height: 12.5cm; width: 18.5cm; thickness: 2.5cm. *Litterae libraria.* Height of the letters: 5cm. Discovered in the Pared Blanca. In the possession of D. Juan Montoro.

> [D(is)] M(anibus) S(acrum)
> [-----]

54. Unpublished (Not Illustrated)
Fragment of a reddish marble plaque with darker veins. The rear-side has been badly damaged. Measurements: minimum height: 12cm; maximum width: 12cm; thickness: 6.5cm. *Litterae libraria.* The A has no cross-bar. Height of the letters: 1st surviving line: 4cm; 2nd line: 3.3cm. Interlineal space: 0.5cm. Triangular stops. Discovered at the Haza de Copete.

> [----]
> ---]fau[---
> ---S.T.T.] L(evis) .

Traces of the bases of the letters of the preceding line are visible; given their angle, it is possible that they are the remains of an A, M or X. After *---]fau* there is an oblique stroke of an A or M.

55. Unpublished (Not Illustrated)
Fragment of a limestone plaque, of which the right-hand and lower margins survive. The rear of the inscription is damaged. Measurements: minimum height: 14.5cm; maximum width: 10.7cm; thickness: 5cm. It was discovered near the Fuente del Pez, on the

path which heads right towards La Puebla de los Infantes. Height of the letters of the first two surviving lines: 1.8cm; line 3: 2.7cm. Interlineal spaces of 1.8cm. It is in the ownership of D. José Carranza.

>   [-----]
> --- anno]r (um) CXV
> ---]s pi[---
> --- ST]T(erra) L(evis)

In the second surviving line the letters PI should be read as corresponding to the formula *pi[us/a in suis]* or *P(ius) I(n) S(uis)*. The person commemorated here is, without doubt, the longest living person attested at Celti.

56. Unpublished (Not Illustrated)

Fragment of a white marble plaque, with a fine moulding in its lower part. There seems to have been a border in the upper part of the inscription, while the back of it seems to have been worked. Measurements: height: 16.5cm; minimum width: 8.5cm; thickness: 2.5cm. Height of the letters: 3.7cm. Interlineal space: 1cm. Triangular stops. The inscription was discovered in front of the Guardia Civíl building at Peñaflor. It is currently owned by D. Miguel Rios at Lora del Río.

>   ---]s.S[---
>   a]n.XX[--
>   --]S.H.S.[--

It seems that there is a stop before the S and, if the surviving upper edge is original, it could be perhaps be interpreted as being the first S in the formula *D(iis) M(anibus)]S)acrum)*. If this is not the case, then the S must belong to the final letter of the *nomen* of a youth in the nominative. The third line could be expanded with the formula *P(ius) I(n)]S(uis). H(ic) S(itus/a) [E(st)*.

57. Unpublished (Fig. 8.31 second from right)

Fragment of a plaque of white marble, which does not retain any of its original margins. Measurements: minimum height: 13cm; minimum width: 15cm. Letters are capitals in *scriptura actuaria*. Height of the letters: 3ms. Interlineal space: 1cm. Triangular stops. The inscription was discovered at the Ermita de Nuestra Señora de Villadiego.

>   [---]
> ---]]erius.[---
> ---]tto.anno[---
> ---]in [suis] H[---

The *nomen* of this individual is surely Valerius. His age was probably written *as annor(um)* or *annorum*. In the third line, the formula *Pius in suis* is clear, followed by *H(ic) S(itus) E(st)*...

58. Unpublished (Fig. 8.31 second from left)

Fragment of a plaque of white marble with red veins, none of whose margins are conserved. Measurements: minimum height: 13.5cm; maximum width: 6.4cm; thickness: 2.7cm. The lettering was relatively rough and similar to that of inscription no. 10. Height of the letters: 3.2cm. Interlineal space: 1 and 1.5cm. Triangular stops. Discovered in El Camello (Peñaflor). It is in the possession of D. José Carranza.

>   [-----]
> ----]r ii[---
> ---]viii[---
> ---].S(it).T(ibi)[---

In the first surviving line, there seems to be an R that in this case would belong to an inscription which would be referring to more than one deceased person and could thus be expanded in the following way: --- *annor(um) II[---*. The second line records a number which must surely be relative to the age of a second person. The third line contains part of the formula ---]S(it) T(ibi) T(erra) L(evis).

59. Unpublished (Fig. 8.31 extreme right hand side)

Fragment of a white marble plaque broken with all its edges broken. Measurements: minimum height: 7cm; minimum width: 11cm. Triangular stops. Discovered at Peñaflor. It is in the possession of D. José Carranza.

>   [---]
> ---]XXVII.[---

60. Unpublished (Fig. 8.31 extreme left hand side)

Fragment of a plaque, of which only part of the left margin is conserved. It probably belongs to a monumental inscription. Measurements: minimum height:

Fig. 8.31. Photograph of inscription nos. 57, 58, 59, and 60

12cm; minimum width: 7cm. Letter height: 4cm. This inscription was discovered in Peñaflor and is in the possession of D. José Carranza at Peñaflor.

> [----]
> IM[---
> [----]

The reading of the second letter as M is dubious.

61. Unpublished (Not illustrated)
Fragment of the upper right hand angle of a plaque of darkish limestone. Measurements: minimum height: 12.5cm; minimum width: 18.5cm; thickness: 2.4cm. Height of the letters: 5cm. This came from the Pared Blanca (Peñaflor). It is in the possession of D. Juan Montoro.

> D(ii)] M(anibus) S(acrum)
> [-----]

62. Unpublished (Fig. 8.32)
Fragment of a plaque of violet-veined marble. Only the upper left-hand margin survives, worked with a hand pick, and with the back of the stone left rough. Measurements: minimum height: 14cm; minimum width: 21cm; thickness: 9cm. The script is quite irregular, tending towards squared capitals. Height of the letters: 3.5cm; spaces between lines 1 to 1.5cm. Triangular stops. Discovered in the Calle Aviador Carmona at Peñaflor.

> [-----]
> cit.s[---
> sepul[---
> nim[---

The reading of the last line is not certain. This may not be Roman.

63. Unpublished (Fig. 8.33)
Fragment of a white marble plaque, lacking its original borders. Measurements: minimum height: 59cm; width: 34cm; minimum thickness: 7cm. Squared capital script. Height of the letters: 14cm. The inscription is built into the western wall of the garden of Don José Parias at Peñaflor.

> [---]
> ---]VIR[---
> [---]

In CILA 2.1 no. 171 this inscription is recorded as unpublished and as still retaining the lower and upper margins. It is probable that this fragment formed part of an inscription published by Clark-Maxwell (1899, 267–98 = EE IX 250) and which has been published by González (CILA 2.1, 167) in the following way and recorded as lost:

> [---]
> ---]VIR (hed.) AV[---
> ---]CVM GRA[---
> [---]

If this background to the inscription was not known, one could be misled into thinking that there were two separate inscriptions instead of one.

Fig. 8.32. Photograph of inscription no. 62

Fig. 8.33. Photograph of inscription no. 63

64. (Fig. 8.34)
Fragment of white marble which, in the opinion of the writer, formed part of a plinth upon which a single line of text was inscribed. González (CILA 2.1, 170) suggests that it had been cut from a pedestal to form a step: "..had been cut on both sides of the text and its faces polished to give it a rectangular form". This analysis is incorrect, since close inspection of the piece shows that the upper and lower faces of the inscription had not been cut in the way that he suggested. Instead, the treatment of the inscription is what one would expect for a stone which had been sandwiched between two other blocks. Measurements: height: 14cm; width: 65cm; thickness: 29cm. Squared capital letters. Height of the letters: 7.5cm. Triangular stops. The P is not closed. This was discovered in Peñaflor and is in the possession of D. José Parias.

> ---]D(e) . S(ua) . P(ecunia) . D(onum) . D(edit)

Ponsich 1979, 103, Pl.XXXI; CILA 2.1 no. 170. This is dateable to the end of the 1st and the beginning of the

Fig. 8.34. Photograph of inscription no. 64

2nd centuries AD. If the interpretation put forward here is acceptable, this fragment is quite important since rather than being cut from an honorary dedication to an individual, it would instead be part of an inscription from a public building.

65. (Fig. 8.35)

Fragment of a white marble plaque, of which only the lower margin survives, while on the left hand side, the surface of the epigraphic field has been lowered. Measurements: minimum height: 27cm; minimum width: 16cm; minimum thickness: 6cm. Squared capital letters. Height of the letters: 1st line: 10cm; second line: 6.5cm. Interlineal space: 2.5cm. Triangular stop. Discovered at Peñaflor and in the possession of D. José Parias at Peñaflor.

[-----]
---]S. A[---
---]DE[---

CILA 2.1 no. 200. González (CILA 2.1, 169) dates this inscription to approximately the 1st century AD. The head of the A suggests that this is doubtful and that it should probably be later.

Characteristics of the Epigraphy of Celti

The Archaeological Context

The archaeological context is of key importance in assessing the value of these inscriptions as a source of information for understanding the Hispano-Roman society at Celti. We are fortunate in having a substantial number of texts as well as knowing a reasonable amount about where they were found. Only a very small number are known to have derived from within the ancient town itself, with many more coming from the surrounding cemeteries and sites elsewhere in the region around the town. The information can be summarised in the following way:

Fig. 8.35. Photograph of inscription no. 65

Approximate Location	Catalogue Number	Total Number
Area of West Cemetery (El Camello)	14, 28, 29, 44, 45, 56 and 58	7
Area of North Cemetery	42 and 50	2
Area of East Cemetery (Peñaflor)	3, 9, 15, 16, 23, 24, 27, 46 and 62	9
Somewhere in Peñaflor	12, 32, 34, 36, 38, 51, 59, 60, 64 and 65	10
Sites in Surrounding Country	4, 7, 8, 10, 17, 19, 22, 26, 33, 35, 37, 39, 41, 52, 54, 55 and 57	17
Unknown Location	5, 6, 11, 13, 18, 20, 21, 25, 30, 31, 40, 47, 48, 49 and 63	15
Total		65

The value of these figures in shedding light upon different parts of the town or its surrounding country should not be over-estimated. Inscriptions, and particularly the larger ones, are prone to be moved from one place to another for re-use in buildings or out of antiquarian curiosity. It is quite possible, therefore, that the eventual findspot of many inscriptions is due to Medieval and later building work in and around Peñaflor. This may well be particularly true of texts from the built-up area of the eastern cemetery in the modern village,

Approximate Location	Catalogue Number	Total Number
Ancient Town (La Viña)	Ch.5 (nos 1 and 2), 1, 2 and 43	5
Ancient Town (Pared Blanca)	53 and 61	2

even though two ancient mausolea are known from here (Chapter 1). By contrast, those from the area of the western cemetery (El Camello) have derived from a green-field area where other archaeological discoveries suggest that an ancient cemetery still lies buried (Chapter 1). Some of the inscriptions from sites in the surrounding country may derive from ancient rural sites while others may have been found at Peñaflor itself in the Medieval, post-Medieval and contemporary periods. Of those inscriptions known to have come from within the area of the ancient town, it is interesting to note that two fragments may have derived from public commemorative inscriptions, as one might expect; the original findspot of other commemorate inscriptions (such as 65), however, is not known. Most of the remainder, however, are clearly funerary, which is curious. Given that early imperial cemeteries were located outside Roman towns, this suggests that the inscriptions were not moved in the post-Roman period or later.

The Epigraphic Mountings

The surviving inscriptions of Celti are almost all funerary stelae. Most were cut onto marble blocks, of which a considerable number had been reused. Most of the marble seems to have been quarried in Baetica. Only three pedestals have come to light and their form and size suggest that they should be identified as statue bases.[48] They were all private dedications and two of them belonged to the family of the Aelii. Only four funerary altars are known. Two were dedicated to the family of the Lurii, one to Barbatus, a slave – possibly of the Iunii –, and one to an Aelius; the latter stands as a clear contrast between the richer and more poorly executed monuments. Most of the other inscriptions were plaques, which derived from funerary monuments, whose character is unknown. The inscriptions themselves, however, can be sub-divided into three groups on the basis of size:

a) The smaller plaques – which account for the majority
b) A few slightly larger plaques, which are taller than they are wide
c) A group of larger plaques or blocks, which are wider than they are tall

It is difficult to assign the groups to types of funerary monument, given that none has been excavated at Celti. Nevertheless, information about occasional finds suggests that inscriptions from group a) may have derived from small funerary monuments, possibly *cupae*, pyramidal tombs built from brick or small tower-shaped tombs. In each case the inscription would have been embedded on

one side of the monument. The two inscriptions that comprise group b) were found in the same spot. Their chronology and typology suggest that they date to the same period and that they may mark inhumation burials. The inscriptions of group c) are of two types: some were smaller with one coming from a collective tomb (no. 46) and others were bigger, and associated with larger monuments. One of these, the inscription to Fabia Celtitana (no. 14) must have been embedded in, and formed part of, a wall – perhaps as the architrave over the entrance. The other, the inscription to Licinia Mancina (no. 23), is a plaque which must have been adjacent to (held by clamps), or part of, a wall. The inscriptions of Aemilia Artemisia (no. 5) and Q. Marius Optatus (no. 27) belong to this same group.

The east cemetery, which lies below the present village of Peñaflor, still retains two of these susbstantial funerary monuments. One of them consists of a vaulted chamber with small niches let into its walls; until recently this was used as a bedroom. This tomb has been long known in that part of the town called "Cortinal de las Cruces".[49] Its characteristics are similar to the tombs at Carmona (Bendala 1976) although instead of being cut into bedrock it was built from concrete. The other monument, however, was unknown until very recently and is embedded within the Ermita de los Santos Mártires. This is a small chapel, which consists of two rooms (Fig. 8.36), and which is entered from No. 15 in the Calle Blancaflor. The first of these through which one enters the tomb has a small barrel vault, the decoration of which dates to the 18th century. The second room, in which the altar is to be found (Fig. 8.36: left), is rock cut. In my opinion, this probably originated as a tower-shaped Roman funerary monument and would have been cut from the bedrock in-situ. The bullrush that crowns the monument rests upon

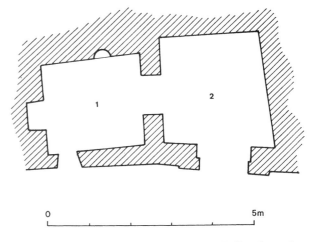

Fig. 8.36. Plan of the tomb at No. 15 Calle Blancaflor in Peñaflor

a small terrace that probably marks the maximum height of the building during the Roman period. The contemporary ground-level would seem to be raised in relation to that of the Roman period. The doorway connecting both rooms in the Ermita was probably created at the time that the monument was built. In the south wall of the ancient burial chamber is a niche, possibly of ancient date. In the north wall there is a window which illuminates the room today. In my opinion, the original entrance corresponds to the gap that is currently visible in the eastern wall below the altar. The interior of the chamber measures 2.10m × 2.33m

by a minimum of 2m. Little more can be said about this monument. Local sources in the village suggest that the inscription to Licinia Mancina (no. 23) was discovered in its vicinity, at the angle of the Calle Nueva and the Calle Blancaflor. Given the characteristics of the inscription, it is thus possible that it may have originally derived from the mausoleum.

Profiles of the monuments to Aelius Zeno, Aelius Optatus and Fulvius Lupus can be seen in Fig. 8.37, and the similarities between them suggest that the pedestals of Optatus and Lupus followed the same design. The profiles of the plaques of

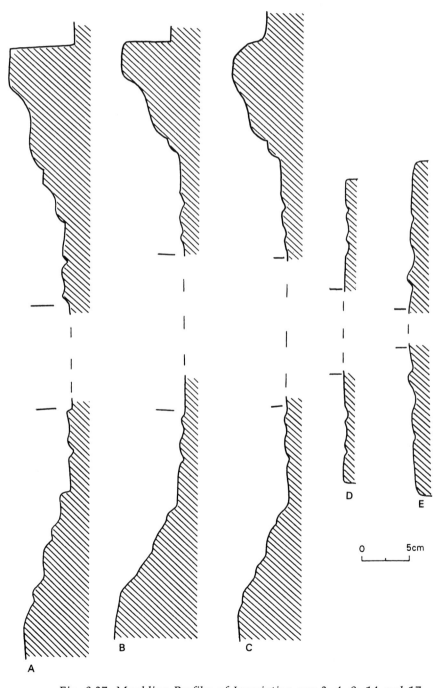

Fig. 8.37. Moulding Profiles of Inscription nos 3, 4, 9, 14 and 17

Bruttius Primigenius and Sempronia Aciliana Celtitana also resembled each other (Fig. 8.37). A section of the inscription -----]*pro honore*[---- and the impressions on the upper surface of the pedestal of Fulvius Lupus can be seen in Figs. 8.14b and 8.38. The surviving drawings of the inscription of Marcus Optatus lack decoration, while the copy of the same text recorded on Manuscript no. 577 in the Biblioteca Nacional de Madrid seems to suggest that it was carved on a plaque with mouldings. The other inscriptions from Celti lack any kind of geometric framing.

The Epigraphic Formulae

The inscriptions from Celti are distinctive, and so allow possible inter-relationships to be proposed and chronological and typological groupings to be suggested. Only small fragments of public inscriptions survive, while none mentions any member of the local governing elite. Only one voting tribe, the *galeria*, is mentioned. This, like the *quirina tribu*, is common amongst towns in those regions which were granted the title of *municipium latinum* in the Flavian period.

The nomenclature of known people allows us to suggest that filiation was rare amongst young men: in only three cases are the names of fathers mentioned (nos. 3, 6 and 7). However, it is more common amongst young women with the names of at least seven fathers being attested (nos. 2, 3, 5, 14, 17, 23 and 25). In three cases we also know the name of the mother of young women, two of whom also took the *nomen* of their maternal family, Aemilia Artemisia (no. 5) and Sempronia Superata (no. 35). The reason for this must be sought in the relative prestige of the maternal name.

Young free men always use tria *nomina* in their nomenclature.[50] The liberti use *duo nomina*. Three males whose social background is uncertain (since the inscription provides no indication) use the *duo nomina* Iulius Siriacus (no. 19) and the two Lurii – Fortunius and Valerianus (nos. 24 and 25). The *cognomen* of the first of these suggests that he was a *libertus*. In the latter two, however, the use of *duo nomina* is more likely to have been an indication of the period when the inscription was cut rather than an index of their personal status, since these are amongst the latest inscriptions from the town. Thus, those individuals who are only referred to by their *cognomen* are likely to have been slaves – even if there was no formal indication as such. Amongst those women who appear to be freeborn and those freedwomen who use *duo nomina*, filiation is used to indicate a better social position. This is why it is more frequently used than amongst young men. Fabia Merope and

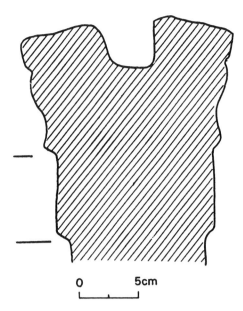

Fig. 8.38. Section through inscription no. 1

Bithynis are both explicitly mentioned as a liberta, while Fabia Bithynis, Marcia Antiocis and Iunia Optatina must have had the same status.

The presence or absence of the formula *D(is) M(anibus) S(acrum)* has become a key element in dating inscriptions, with those bearing the formula *D.M.S* generally dating from the end of the 1st century AD.[51] At Celti the majority of inscriptions which lack this formula also lack the formula *pius/a in suis*. Most of these belong to that group which I have defined as c) that is, inscriptions that are wider than they are tall, as well as the two largest inscriptions known from the site. It is almost as if the elite of Celti were less interested in this kind of advocation or, simply that it was strictly associated with altars and small monuments. It should be remembered, however, that the formula was also absent from the epitaphs of a slave, Successus (no. 38) and the liberti Myris and Cinismus (no. 30). On the other hand, the formula *pius/a in suis* also appears on all those inscriptions which bear *D.M.S*,[52] with the exception of the epitaph of Q. Fulvius Musicus (no. 18). All of these inscriptions are cut onto plaques that belong to our group a). The formula *pius/a in suis* is common in Celti and is usually written in full and not abbreviated. On the epitaph of Caesia Annula and L. Licinius Gallus (no. 11) was inscribed: *P(ius) in S(uis)*, a formula which is repeated on another fragment. The formula *pius/a in suos* only appears in three cases: the fragment referring to Bruttius, and the inscriptions to Sergia Rustica (no. 36) and Successa (no. 37). The formula *P(ius/a) I(n) S(uis)* is equally rare and only attested on the epitaphs of the Lurii,

Pyramis and Iulius Siriacus (nos. 19, 24, 25 and 32). The formula *hic situs/a est* is normally abbreviated to *H(ic) S(itus/a) E(st)*. In its unabbreviated form it only appears on the epitaph to Baetica and Q. Fulvius Musicus (nos. 31 and 18). Only three epitaphs lack this formula (nos. 14, 20 and 25). The indication of age under the formula *vixit annis* is only attested in the inscriptions of Lurius Fortunatus and L(urius) Valerianus (nos. 24 nd 25), texts in which the rare abbreviation *P(ius) I(n) S(uis)* also appears. The formula *Sit tibi terra levis* is always abbreviated as *S(it) T(ibi) T(erra) L(evis)* – except for the epitaph of Baetica (no. 31). Although the lettering in most inscriptions tend to be in *scriptura actuaria*, the formula *D.M.S.* almost always appears in the form of squared capitals and in a larger size than the rest of the text. With the exception of the formula *D.M.S.* the remainder of the lines are approximately of the same height and, where this was not possible, the same optical effect was created by varying the height of the interlineal space.

Calligraphy and Chronology

We lack the absolute dates necessary for establishing a chronological seriation of the inscriptions from Celti. However, the table in Fig. 8.39 lists the characteristics that have helped to define the evolution and chronological grouping of some of the funerary inscriptions. Our current understanding of inscriptions in the region suggests that although there are common threads in their development, the epigraphic traditon of each urban centre is distinctive.[53] On the other hand, it should be admitted that writing was quite a common practice in this part of Baetica. After all, it was a region from which thousands of olive oil amphorae were exported, each one bearing an extensive handwritten "label" (*titulus pictus*), as well as frequent *ante-cocturam* graffiti.[54]

The study of the inscriptions from Celti makes it clear that, apart from the large workshops which were capable of importing marble from distant quarries and undertaking large monuments like pedestals and statues, there must have been a multitude of smaller workshops. These would have satisfied the normal demands of the town and, in doing so, would have quite frequently reused marbles from earlier monuments. Consequently, it is important to distinguish two large groups of inscriptions at Celti and, indeed, many other towns in the region. Firstly, there were monumental inscriptions –both public and private- most of which would have been created away from Celti. Secondly, there were what one might term

"ordinary inscriptions" and were fundamentally funerary texts from small monuments that were actually cut at a local workshop in Celti, sometimes by inexperienced individuals, as may have been the case of the inscription to the slave Vibia (no. 39).

The two most accomplished funerary inscriptions from Celti were dedicated to two young 15 year old girls, Fabia Sempronia Aciliana Celtitana and Licinia Mancina (nos. 14 and 23). Both belonged to distinguished families and their epitaphs lacked the formula *D(is) M(anibus) S(acrum)*. The latter feature suggests that they dated to the late 1st or early 2nd centuries AD. However, the calligraphy of the former inscription indicates a date somewhat later, around the second half of the 2nd and the beginning of the 3rd century AD. Although the inscription dedicated by Fabius Basileus Celtitanus at Corduba is now lost, the manuscript copies of it which have survived suggest that both inscriptions were stylistically related.[55] This fact supports three of our suggestions:

a) that both these people were related
b) that both inscriptions came from the same workshop, perhaps at Corduba
c) that the styles and epigraphic formulae were conditioned by the monument for which they were destined and, equally, that the calligraphy and textual formulae were largely dictated by the character of the monument they were destined to decorate

Consequently, even though it was very common to record the formula DMS during this period, it is absent in this inscription.

Another interesting fact about the inscriptions from Celti is that nearly all the decorated examples were dedicated to women.[56] Similarly, those inscriptions with *litterae lungae*,[57] decorated with hederae[58] or where stops and hederae appear in a single text,[59] were nearly all dedicated to women.

Other details are of assistance in grouping inscriptions together, such as the presence of hederae with a zigzagging stalk on the texts of Aemilius Marcianus, Fabia Merope and Baetica (nos. 6, 16 and 31). These examples share a further characteristic: the formula *annorum* is used to indicate the age of the deceased. Otherwise, the distinctiveness of the letter G allows the inscriptions of Caesia Annula and Licinius Gallus, Baetica and Sergia Rustica to be grouped together (nos. 11, 31 and 36). The letter L with the arm inclined downwards allows the epitaphs of Caesia Annula, Licinius Gallus, Baetica and Vibia to be grouped together (nos. 11, 31 and 39). The letter x with the upper right-hand arm over-raised, and the letter A in cursive style are two other concomitant

Núm.	Inscription	DMS	Annorum	Pius In Suis	Decoracion	Hederae	G	Litterae Lungae	L	X	A	Stops and Hederae	Ligatures
4	Q. Aelius Zeno												
6	M. Aemilius Marcianus		+++ (43)	++				+++		+		+++	++
7	Apollonius		ann.(33)	++									++
8	Bruttia Victorina	+++	annor. (35)	++	++					++	+	+++	
9	S. Bruttius Primigenius		ann. (40?)							++		+++	++
10	---]Bruttius[---			Suos									
11	Caesia Annula	+++	ann. (25)	++			+		+	++	+	+++	
11	L.Licinius Gallus		ann. (65)	++						++			
12	---]Cornel[ius---	?	annor(10+)										
13	---]us Chres[--]tos	?	mensium		++++								
14	Fabia Sempronia Aciliana Celtitana		ann. (15)			+++					+		
16	Fabia Merope	+++	+++(75)	++	++++	+++					+	+++	
18	Q. Fulvius Musicus	+++	annor.(45)							++	+	+++	
19	Iulius Siriacus	+++	annor.(67)	P.I.S.						++			
20	Barbatus	+++	ann.(51)	++								+++	
20	Iunia Optatina	+++	annor.(75)	++								+++	
21	L.Iunius Onesiphorus	+++	an.(60?)	++									
22	Optatinus	+++	annor (18)	++	++++							+++	
23	Licinia Mancina	+++	ann (15)										
23	C. Licinius Lupus	+++	vixit (61)	P.I.S.									
24	Lurius Fortunius	+++	vixit (61)	P.I.S.					+				
25	Lurius Valerianus	+++	vicsit (31)	P.I.S.									
26	Marcia Antiocis	+++	ann (70)	++			+	+++		++	+	+++	
27	Q. Marius Optatus	+++											
28	Maurula	+++	ann. (43)					+++		++			
29	Messia Laeta	+++	an. (45)	++				+++		++			
30	Myris		an (52)								+		
30	Cinismus										+		
31	Baetica	+++	+++ (21)	++	++++	+++	+	+++	+	++	+	+++	
32	Pyramis	+++	ann (45)	++?						++			
33	Romula	+++	an. (16)	++									
34	Sempronia Prixsila	?	+++ (?)										
35	Sempronia Superata		Annor (21)										
35	Sempronia Peregrina												
36	Sergia Rustica	+++	ann.(90)	suos			+	+++		++	+		
37	Successa	+++	ann. (25)	suos		+++							
38	Successus		ann. (30)								+		
39	Vibia	+++	ann.(65)	++					+	++	+	+++	
40	Detumonen(sis)	?	? (70)	++?						++	+		
42	---]a Hermione	+++	an. (35)	++									
43	---]Rustic[---		?	?	++++								
44	---]nius C.L. Pis[---		? (25+)	++						++			
46	Fragment of the four individuals	?	ann. (9) annor. (31) annor.(30)										

Fig. 8.39. Synoptic Table for Inscriptions from Celti

elements. However, given the frequency of both these letters A and x in epitaphs, they are of a broader relevance than some of the other letter characteristics discussed here. Inscriptions with the formula *pius/a in suos* (nos. 10, 36 and 37) also form part of this group because the inscription of Sergia Rustica (no. 36) also belongs to it. On the basis of its calligraphy, the fragment of .....] *Bruttius*[.. (no. 10) could certainly be included within this group, while only the Successa text differs from it even though use of the formula *pia in suos* and the manner of indicating age by use of the formula *ann[orum]*) is similar to the Sergia Rustica inscription.

All these characteristics allow us to define a group of inscriptions, which could date to the end of the 2nd and the first half of the 3rd centuries AD (Fig. 8.39). The lack of the formulae *D(is) M(anibus) S(acrum)* and *pius/a in suis* allow us to date these inscriptions in general terms to the first half of the 2nd century AD, with the exception of the epitaph of Fabia Sempronia Aciliana Celtitana which, as was mentioned earlier, must date to between the end of the 2nd and the beginning of the 3rd centuries AD. Between both of these groups should be those with the formulae *DMS* and *pius/a in suis*, and whose letters tend towards capitals in *scriptura actuaria*, a group dating towards the middle of the 2nd century AD.

Non-funerary monumental inscriptions are not difficult to date, although the site has only produced fragments.[60] Private monumental inscriptions, or monuments dedicated by individuals to people without public involvement or not involved in public life, are represented by the pedestals dedicated to Aelius Optatus, Fulvius Lupus and Aelia Flaccina (nos. 2, 3 and 17). The pedestals of Aelius Optatus and Fulvius Lupus must have been created within a short space of each other, some time towards the middle of the 2nd century AD. The typology of the letters on Aelia Flaccina's pedestal suggests a somewhat later date.

Epigraphic Evidence for the Society of Celti

Despite the relative abundance of inscriptions from Celti, it is not possible to discuss the elites from the town, since we lack the epigraphic records of those who exercised administrative and political posts at the town, in imperial service or in the army. This stands in contrast to the epigraphic record from a range of neighbouring river towns in region, such as Axati (Lora del Río), Arva (El Castillejo) and Canama (Alcolea del Río), despite the relatively high number of inscriptions from the town.

In any event, the use of filiation, which is quite rare at Celti, does provide us with one way of learning about the more distinguished families at the town. Those individuals who did record their filiation were indicating that they were descendants of people who possessed Roman Citizenship, which had probably been acquired by virtue of having exercised a political post in the town after it had been granted the Latin Right under the Flavians (see Chapter 10). Of course, some individuals at Celti could well have enjoyed Roman Citizenship before this date. The majority of people commemorated on these inscriptions, however, would have gained it from the Flavian period onwards.

In this context, the epitaph of Licinia Mancina (no. 23) is interesting. It states that she is the daughter of Caius and, moreover, born to an individual who was a Roman Citizen. Her father, Caius Licinius Lupus, is mentioned on the same inscription and, although he belonged to the Galeria voting tribe, does not mention his filiation. One must conclude, therefore, that Licinius Lupus was the first in his family to gain Roman Citizenship. This would explain why he did not advertise his filiation but did mention his membership of the municipal elite by explicitly stating his voting tribe – which was a characteristic feature of Roman Citizenship.

Of particular note are those individuals to whom reference is made, but who belonged to generations preceding people dedicating, or being commemorated by, inscriptions at Celti. Thus, we know of four previous generations of the Aelii: Quintus Aelius, father of Aelius Optatus (no. 3); Quintus Aelius, father of Aelia Flaccina (no. 2)[61]; Marcus Aelius, father of Aelia Marcellina (no. 2) and Aelia ?Marcellina, mother of Aelia Marcellina (no. 2). For the Aemilii, we know of a Marcus Aemilius, father of Aemilius Marcianus (no. 6). For the Fabii, we know of a Marcus Fabius, father of Fabia Semproniana Aciliana Celtitana (no. 14). For the Fulvii, we know of a Quintus Fulvius, father of Fulvius Lupus (no. 17) and the maternal grandfather of Fulvius Lupus, Lucius Calpurnius (no. 17). Finally, amongst the Licinii, it is recorded that Caius Licinius Capito was the father of Semproniana Superata (no. 35).

Personal relationships are not expressed on funerary inscriptions from Celti, apart from the inscription to Baetica by Barathes, in which the latter states that she was a *coniux indulgentissima*. Instead, only the names of the deceased are mentioned. I have assumed that when the names of a man and a woman appear on an inscription, they were a married couple. In this sense, Caesia Anula would be the wife of Licinius Gallus (no. 11); Barbatus must have been the *contubernalis* of

Iunia Optatina (no. 20) and, perhaps, Optatinus servus might have been the offspring of this union (no. 22).

Monumental inscriptions have left further traces of the connections between different families. In this way we know that one Calpurnia married Fulvius (no. 17), that one Licinius married a Sempronia (no. 35), and that an Annius married an Aemilia (no. 5). The double *nomen* of the young Fabia Semproniana (no. 14) permits us to suppose that there was a marriage between a Fabius, Marcus Fabius, her father, and a Sempronia – who may or may not have been related to Sempronia, the wife of Licinius Capito (no. 35). If we accept this reconstruction, it would suggest that the Sempronii were an important gens at Celti, as also seems to be inferred from the fact that the daughter of Lucius Capito chose to use the name of her mother, Sempronia (no. 35), and not her father. This is not the only case attested at Celti. Aemilia Arthemisia (no. 5) is another case, where a woman chose the name of her mother rather than her father. Other women took an active part in the social life of Celti, particularly those belonging to the Aelii, dedicating inscriptions to both young men and women. Moreover, as has already been pointed out, the more attractive inscriptions in terms of their form and content were dedicated to women.

The most disconcerting case at Celti is Caius Appius Superstes Caninius Montanus (nos. 3 and 17). The two inscriptions that refer to him suggest that he was simultaneously the heir to the fortunes of two separate families, the Aelii and the Fulvii. Furthermore, it is even more curious that even though he bore several names, he had not adopted the *nomina* of either of the families from which he had received bequests. As both inscriptions are in a poor state of preservation, it is not possible to read this man's name clearly. It is probable that the inscriptions have long been this way and that, therefore, this reading of his name cannot be confirmed.[62] It is probable that, either by error or through difficulty in reading the inscription, the same name has been recorded for both inscriptions. Moreover, it is possible that, in reality, this polynym represents two different people and that each one of them would have been commemorated on a different inscription. We could also suggest that the *nomen* APPIUS is really a misreading of the *nomen* AELIUS. For example, if the E was read as a P – an easy mistake – the reader of the inscription would follow the logic of a name which he thought began with AP and interpret the L as a second P, suggesting APPIUS instead of AELIUS. After all, the number of letters was the same and they followed the same order. If we accept this reconstruction, the descendant of Quintus Aelius Optatus would be the son of his daughter and would have borne the *nomen* of his mother and not his father. In this way, we avoid the social problems that would be implied by one individual being the heir of two families without bearing the name of either.

If, however, we retain the traditonal reading of the inscriptions, we could suggest the following sequence of events. Appius Superstes was the husband of Aelia Optata and that when she died without an heir, he carried out her testamentary wish to erect a monument to her father. Subsequently he married Calpurnia Sabina, widow of Quintus Fulvius, and again carried out her will and erected a statue to her predeceased daughter. Alternatively, it could equally be suggested that he married Calpurnia Sabina first and Aelia Optata second. As I have suggested above, the monument to Aelius Optatus was never finished, or at least it never bore its statue. In one way or another, this man inherited the wealth of two of the notable families of Celti.

There now follows an attempt to synthesize our current state of knowledge of some of the families of Roman Celti.

The Aelii: This is the best represented family in the epigraphic repertoire from Celti. The earliest known individual was Quintus Aelius Zeno (no. 4). Given that his *cognomen* is Greek and that he makes no reference to his antecedents suggests that he was a libertus. Aelius Zeno must have lived in the second half of the 1st century AD. Quintus Aelius Optatus (no. 3) only mentions one ancestor, his father, who also bore the *praenomen* Quintus. Given that the inscription of Quintus Aelius Optatus can be dated to the 2nd century AD, it is possible that his father was a descendant of the same Quintus Aelius Zeno. Quintus Aelius, father of Flaccina (no. 2), and Marcus Aelius, father of Marcellina (no. 2), must have belonged to the same generation as Quintus Aelius Optatus. This points to the existence of two branches of the family, one with the *praenomen* Quintus and the other with the *praenomen* Lucius. It could also be suggested that the father of Optata and Flaccina were one and the same person and that Quintus Aelius Optatus and Marcus Aelius were brothers. The epigraphy suggests that the last generation of these Aelii was composed of women: Aelia Optata (no. 3), Aelia Flaccina and Aelia Marcellina (no. 2).

The Aemilii: We have little information about this family (nos. 5 and 6). However, they are sufficient to suggest that one Aemilia Artemisia was married to a rich man called Annius Celtitanus, who wished to see her in the guise of the goddess Venus. This wish was carried out generously by his daughter, who bore the same name as her mother, and by Aemilius Rusticus, a young man of the Aemilii, who may well have been her brother.

The Bruttii: Although this family is attested by three inscriptions (nos. 8, 9 and 10) we do not know if they came to play an important role in Celti.

The Fabii: Available information suggests that this was most significant family at Celti. Whether or not one accepts the link between the Fabii of Celti and the Senator Fabius Cilo, there is evidence to do so. Apart from the fact that the funerary monument to Fabia Sempronia Aciliana Celtitana (no. 14) must have been of large proportions and that her inscription was created in Corduba, as I believe that I have shown, there is other evidence which attests the wealth of this family. Our inscription no. 15 is a dedication to Victoria Augusta by Fabius Atticus and Fabius Firmus, freedmen of one Fabius Niger, and by Fabia Bithynis a freedwoman of the Fabii. Atticus and Firmus were Augustales, which implies that they belonged to the group of rich liberti of Celti. This inscription can be dated to the 1st century AD. This means that we have information about the Fabii for over a century, since the inscription dedicated to Fabia Sempronia Aciliana Celtitana (no. 14) and to the liberta Fabia Merope (no. 16) are dated to the end of the 2nd or the beginning of the 3rd centuries AD. Moreover, the inscription to Fabia Merope, a deceased old lady, that bore some doleful sentiments, was inscribed upon a reused stone.

The Fulvii: This family is only attested once, but the nature of the inscription (no. 17) – which mentions that Calpurnia Sabina honoured her son Quintus Fulvius Lupus with a bronze statue – gives us some idea of their social standing in the town. It is difficult to posit a link between this and the inscription to Quintus Fulvius Musicus (no. 18) with certainty, although Musicus probably belonged to a later generation and may have been a libertus of the family.

The Licinii: The inscriptions inform us about various members of this family, which must have enjoyed a certain degree of importance during the 1st century AD, the period to which date the inscriptions of Caius Licinius Lupus (no. 23) and the daughter of Caius Licinius Capito (no. 35). The inscription of Lucius Licinius Gallus (no. 11) dates to the 2nd century AD. Two members of this family bore names that referred to totemic animals: Lupus and Gallus. The inscription that

Caius Licinius Capito dedicated to his daughter, Sempronia Superata (no. 35), and which Caius Licinius Lupus dedicated to his, Licinia Mancina (no. 23), correspond to two funerary monuments of some importance. In particular, the latter of the two may have derived from the tower-shaped mausoleum known today as the Ermita de los Santos Mártires. It is probable that Caius Licinius Capito and Caius Licinius Lupus belonged to the same generation and may have been brothers who suffered the same destiny: to see both their daughters die young. Lucius Licinius Gallus belongs to a later generation.

***

Little can be said about other families, amongst whose number one should count the Marii, one of whose deceased was a young man and to whom was dedicated a metric inscription and, almost certainly, a funerary monument of some pretension.

Even less can be said about the lower social classes, since inscriptions that commemorate slaves and liberti do not usually say to whom the people commemorated belong. Consequently, although we know the names of one or two, we do not know which family they belonged. Apart from the liberti of the Fabii, to whom reference has already been made, it has only been possible to identify Iunia Optatina and Barbatus (no. 20). As has been noted, Optatinus servus (no. 22), was perhaps the offspring of this union, and born before his mother had gained her liberty. The relationship between these individuals and L. Iunius Onesiphorus (no. 21), is not known, although the latter bore a Greek *cognomen* which suggests that he was a libertus or son of a libertus. The chronology of these inscriptions, second half of the 2nd and beginning of the 3rd centuries AD, suggests that all these individuals were contemporary.

The double inscription of Myris and Cinismus (no. 30) only gives us the *cognomen* of their patron, Rustica, which suggests that she belonged to a well-known family in the town. Rusticus is a *cognomen* attested amongst the Aemilii at Celti. However, it is not possible to directly link her with this family, since Rusticus/a is a common *cognomen* in Baetica. Barathes (no. 31) praises his partner, Baetica, as *coniux indulgentissima*. Legally, however, Barathes could not call his contubernalis *coniux*. Devotion, however, seems to have permitted such licence.

Known inscriptions from Celti inform us that there were women not native to the town. One, Messia Laeta (no. 29), came from the provincial capital Corduba, while the other, whose name is unknown, came from the nearby municipality of

Detumo (Posadas). It is interesting to note in this context that both came from the conventus cordubensis even though Celti itself lay within the conventus hispalensis. Other sources of evidence suggest that relations with Corduba were probably more frequent than with Hispalis, given that even though Celti lay at the junction of both conventus, it was geographically closer to Corduba. For example, several *nomina* attested at Corduba, such as Lurius (CIL. II 2248a) or Caninius (CIL. II 2211 and 2266), are only otherwise attested at Celti in Baetica.

Conventional analysis of the age pyramid from the Celti inscriptions might suggest that women died more frequently between 20 and 30 years of age (Fig. 8.40). This could perhaps be related to post-natal illnesses – a source of female mortality down to comparatively recently. Those who survived this age may have lived longer than their male counterparts. The greatest attested age was 115 years, although it is not known whether the person was male or female (no. 55).

The economy of Celti depended upon both agriculture and mining. If the Quintus Aelius Optatus attested on the pedestal from the town is to be identified with his namesake known on Dressel 20 stamps (see Chapter 10), then we have good evidence for the source of his family's wealth. We lack direct epigraphic evidence for the mineral wealth of Celti (see Chapter 10). Perhaps, however, the young Quintus Marius Optatus (no. 27) was related to the famous Sextus Marius. This man,

who possessed many of the mines in the region of Corduba during the reign of Tiberius, was accused of incest by the Emperor as a pretext for laying hands on his wealth (Tacitus *Annals* 6, 19; Pliny, 34, 4)

In sum, therefore, as the reflection of a profoundly romanized environment, the epigraphy from Celti exhibits the normal characteristics of Latin inscriptions, with a range of names which follow normal Roman rules. Although there is no direct evidence as to who exercised municipal posts, it has been possible to identify some of the principal families in the town, some of whose members would almost certainly have held public office. Nor is there direct evidence as to which, if any, members of the local elite achieved promotion into the upper governing classes of the Empire – the *ordo senatorius* and the *ordo equester*. If, however, one accepts the interpretation proposed for the inscription of Fabia Sempronia Aciliana Celtitana (see also Chapter 10), there is evidence of at least one member of a family from Celti being elected to the provincial flaminate and, perhaps, being related to the twice-Consul Lucius Fabius Cilo.

Index of Latin Names from Celti

C. Appius Superstes Canninius Montanus: no. 3, 17
Aelia Q. F. Flaccina: no. 2
Aelia M. F.Marcellina: no. 2
Aelia Q. F. Optata: no. 3
Q. Aelius Q. F. Optatus: no. 3

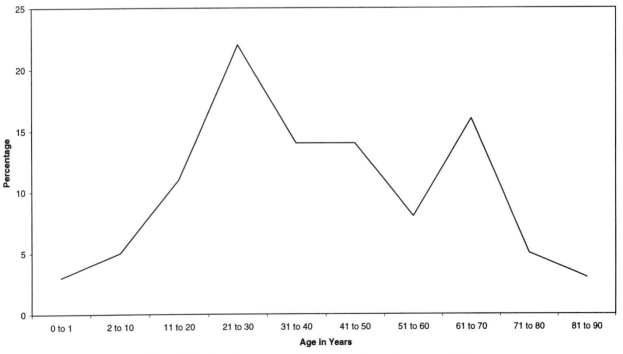

Fig. 8.40. Graph representing ages on inscriptions at Celti

Q. Aelius Zeno: no. 4
Aemilia Artemisia (mater): no. 5
Aemilia Artemisia (filia): no. 5
M. Aemilius M. F. Marcianus: no. 6
Aemilius Rusticus: no. 5
M. Annius Celtitanus: no. 5
Bruttia Victorina Celtitana: no. 8
Sex. Bruttius Primigenius: no. 9
...... Bruttius.....: no. 10
Caesia Annula: no. 11
Calpurnia L. F. Sabina: no. 17
Cal]purn[ius/ia: no. 48
.... C]orneli[us/a ...: no. 12
Fabia Bithynis.F.L(iberta): no. 15
Fabia Merope: no. 16
Fabia M.F. Sempronia Aciliana Celtitana: no. 14
Fabius Atimetus: no. 16
Fabius Atticus: no. 15
Fabius Firmus: no. 15
G. Fabius Niger: no. 15
Q. Fulvius Q. F. Lupus: no. 17
Q. Fulvius Musicus: no. 18
Iulius Siriacus: no. 19
Iunia Optatina: no. 20
L. Iunius Onesiphorus: no. 21
Licinia C. F. Mancina: no. 23
C. Licinius Capito: no. 35
L. Licinius Gallus: no. 11
Licinius Galeria (tribu) Lupus: no. 23
Lurius Fortunius: no. 24
Lurius Valerianus: no. 25
Marcia Antiocis: no. 27
Q. Marius Optatus: no. 26
Messia Laeta patriciensis: no. 29
Sempronia Prixsilla: no. 34
Sempronia Peregrina: no. 35
Sempronia C. Licini Capitonis F. Superata: no. 35
Sergia Rustica: no. 36
...]a Faustina: no. 41
...]A Hermione: no. 42
...] Rustic[us / a: no. 43
....]ius C. L. Pis[...:no. 44
...]ascutta: no. 45
...]cus[...: no. 46
...]us [...: no. 46
...]us Chres[...: no. 13

Individuals of servile origin
Apollonius: no. 7
Baetica: no. 31
Barathes: no. 31
Barbatus: no. 20
Cinismus: no. 30.
Maurula: no. 28
Myris: no. 30
Optatinus: no. 22
Pyramis: no. 32
Romula: no. 33
Rustic(us/a): no. 43
Successa: no. 37
Successus: no. 38
Vibia: no. 39

Notes

1. CIL. II 137ff
2. The first to identify the location of Arva was Tomás Andrés Gusseme (de Gusseme 1773, 237; see also Remesal (ed.) 1981, 46ff). Hübner, in CIL. II, 138ff erred in his location of the town.
3. CIL. II 140ff
4. CIL. II 140ff
5. A. de Morales 1575, fol.88 (Madrid 1792, 319ff).
6. Remesal Rodríguez 1991, 281–95
7. Maldonado de Saavedra 1673
8. Maldonado de Saavedra was a Sevillan erudite in the 17th century, whose work has not been studied until the present day. His manuscripts are collected together in a tome in the Biblioteca Colombina (Biblioteca Colombina Ms. 59-2-36), amongst which is to be found a printed copy of his discourse on Peñaflor, other notes on this text and observations on the work by Diego Ortiz de Zúñiga and the Carmelite Padre Fray Juan Felix Jirón and some sonnets in praise of the work. He wrote another dissertation on the various towns which bore the name Ilipa and other Baetican towns.
9. Manuscript in the Real Academia de Historia 9–5996, in which Saavedra's ideas were taken up again and he insisted upon the distance of Ilipa from the Ocean. He also collected together the inscriptions from Alcalá del Río, amongst which he informs us about CIL. II 1091 for the first time. This carried the place-name Ilipensis. He also mentions the discovery of many coins bearing the name Ilipa. E. Hübner in CIL. II did not cite Carrillo's work, only that of Merchante, a contemporary of Carrillo's, and who wrote few years later.
10. Flórez 1754 (Tome IX), 24–5.
11. CIL. II 321; Blanco and Luzón 1966, 87.
12. Blázquez 1892, 73; Saavedra 1914, 862; Corzo & Jiménez 1980, 41; Tovar 1974, 158; Roldán Hervás 1975, 230–1.
13. Ceán Bermúdez, 1832, 275–7; Clark-Maxwell, 1899, 262; Bonsor 1931, 19–21; Thouvenot 1940 (2nd edtion 1973); García y Bellido 1960, 191–2; Ponsich 1979, 101 no. 82; Sillières 1990, 467–8; González in CILA 2.1, 139–40 (=CILA 2.1).
14. Inscripciones de memorias Romanas y Españolas antiguas y modernas, recogidas por D. Gaspar Galceran de Pinos y Castro. This manuscript is discussed by H. Gimeno Pascual 1997.
15. Gimeno Pascual 1997, 35.
16. Ead. Op. cit. 31, 33, 230; Remesal 1998a.
17. Pedro Leonardo de Villacevallos, a gentleman from Córdoba, formed a museum at his home in which he placed numerous inscriptions from Córdoba, together with other places in Andalucía including Peñaflor.
18. Remesal Rodríguez 1996, 195–221. For the third century AD in Hispania see Cepas Palanca 1997 and bibliography.
19. J. González in CILA 2.1 no. 168 Fig. 83. The inscription has not lost its left side as González suggests, rather that this had partly deteriorated and had been obscured by a modern construction. Nor is the upper moulding absent, as the same author suggests, since this inscription served as a base for supporting a bronze sculpture whose plinth covered the upper part of the marble base.
20. Thévenot 1952; Caamaño Gesto 1972; Ponsich 1979, 101 no. 82 and Pl.XXXII; Blázquez Martínez 1980, 28; Bonneville 1984, 72–3; Gallego Franco 1993, 124 no. 6; most recently, Chic 1992 with bibliography.
21. Bonsor 1931; Ponsich 1974, 193 no. 145–6.
22. Remesal Rodríguez 1977–1978.
23. Remesal Rodríguez 1997.

24 Gamer 1989, 266, No. SE 37.

25 I would like to thank both authors for kindly allowing me to see their manucsript on this inscription and who put at my disposition all the information collected together at the "Centro CIL" at Alcalá de Henares (Madrid).

26 Fita 1916, 118.

27 A. Stylow (personal communication: CIL. II archive).

28 These hypotheses need to be treated with caution. It is possible that upon the death of the second of these two people, the inscription was created in honour of both even though one had already been dead for one year.

29 Albertos Firmat 1964, 221; Francia Somalo 1988, 20.

30 If the epigraphic field was centred is length would have been 1.79m.

31 I understand that in these cases the name Celtitanus/a is functioning more as a *cognomen* than as an indication of origo. In any event, however one understands it, the name is valid to relate both inscriptions.

32 For this individual see Caballos 1990, 132–135.

33 Ponsich 1979, 139 no. 152.

34 Remesal Rodríguez 1989

35 His full name was: L. Fabius, M.f., Gal.,Cilo Septiminus Catinius Acilianus Lepidus Fulcinianus.

36 Both Chic 1975, 360 and González in CILA 2.1 no. 175 err in measuring the letters and only count 11 of the inscription's 12 lines.

37 I have translated the verse with a certain degree of freedom.

38 Correa 1976

39 A copy of this inscription is embedded in the inner wall of the ermita de Villadiego, to the left of the door.

40 This is the way that it is defined by González in CILA 2.1 no. 190. According to H. Sandars, who informed Fita (1916, 118) of its existence, it was a plaque of "white-yellow marble". Moreover the measurements given by González and Fita do not coincide: the first saw and photographed the text while the second only saw a tracing.

41 In CILA 2.1, 183 it is affirmed freely that they were circular.

42 A piece of information gleaned from Pedro Leonardo de Villa y Zevallos, an erudite Córdoban of the 18th century, who created a lapidary museum in his house. Many copies of his handwritten catalogue are known. These have been added to over the years and there are copies of it in the Biblioteca Nacional de Madrid and the Biblioteca Colombina in Sevilla. Recently a copy was discovered in the Real Academia de Madrid, and it is this copy which I have used as a source.

43 There is an error in the measurements published in CILA 2.1.

44 I attempted to establish whether this was possible. However, the stone could no longer be found in the garden of its owner.

45 In this respect, González (CILA 2.1) translates Hübner badly, "the letters were painted, excellent and of the 2nd century".

46 Stylow 1988.

47 It is surprising that this funerary inscription should come from La Viña, the site of the urban centre of Celti (Chapter 2). However, given the fact this is a small fragment, it could have arrived at the site in a number of different ways. Alternatively, there could be some mistake about its find-spot.

48 It seems that one of these, that of Aelius Optatus, was not completed.

49 See Chapter 1.

50 Only Aemilius Rusticus (no. 5) used two *cognomina*, probably for reasons of space, as the new copy of the inscription suggests.

51 Stylow 1988.

52 The root of the problem lies in determining whether the funerary inscription was cut over a period of time, adding the name of a deceased after each passing, or if all the names were inscribed at the same time, or whether it was solely a matter of space. The indication of the age of the deceased appears in the formula *Ann(norum)*, *An(norum)*, *Annor(um)* and *annorum*. The formula *Ann(orum)* is chronologically earlier than the formula *Annor(um)* in the inscription of Barbates and Iunia Optatina and, perhaps, may be in no. 46.

53 As an example, I could cite the formula *C(arus/a) S(uis)* which is characteristic of Gades (Cádiz), or the *formula memoria* aeterna which is typical to Corduba.

54 For the amphora epigraphy of the region there is an ample bibliography. See, for example, the recent volume J. M. Blázquez Martínez and J. Remesal Rodríguez (eds.) 1999, *Estudios sobre el monte Testaccio (Roma) I. Instrumenta* (Barcelona).

55 The manuscript copies are collected together in CIL. II ^{2}/7, 295 and reproduced in the microfiche. The similarities were clear in individual letter forms. For example, the letter F, with its raised upper arm was very similar in both inscriptions. The same is true of the B, whose upper and lower sections differs, and particularly the C, whose upper arm was raised.

56 Although two inscriptions dedicated to young males, the child Chres[..]tos and the youth Optatinus, were decorated, they cannot be readily compared to the decorative scheme on inscriptions dedicated to young women.

57 The epitaph of Aemilius Marcianus (no. 6) is the exception.

58 The epitaph of Bruttius Primigenius (no. 9) is the exception.

59 In this case the one exception is the epitaph of Bruttius Primigenius (no. 9).

60 In this context I take as "public" those inscriptions financed by the municipality or dedicated by individuals for a public function.

61 It is possible that the father of Optatus and Flaccina were the same person.

62 In fact, in Manuscript 5973 of the Biblioteca Nacional de Madrid which is attributed to Fernández Franco and which records both inscriptions, this man is named only as C. Appius Superstes. The inscription of Aelius Optatus (f.110) is copied with many deficiencies, but is still better than that of Fulvius Lupus (f.110).

Chapter 9
Reconstruction of the Site

Simon Keay with Sheila Gibson and Kate Wilson

Abstract

This Chapter explores the character and function of the Phase 7 and 8 buildings at Celti by attempting to reconstruct them. It recognizes, however, that given the fragmentary state of the archaeological evidence this is an even more hazardous undertaking than normal. It begins with a summary description of the structures for each phase, suggesting that that in Phase 7 was clearly a public building of some kind, possibly the forum, while that in Phase 8 was either two houses or a single house divided into two. The Chapter then continues with attempted reconstructions of each building. Two archaeologists attempt two separate intrepretations of the Phase 7 buildings, both agreeing that the building should be interpreted as a forum, but differing in details. One archaeologist then attempts to reconstruct the Phase 8 house. If the identification of the Phase 7 building as a forum is correct, then it raises some important legal issues since, in theory at least, it was forbidden to demolish a sacred building (as would be implicit in the fora plans proposed) and replace it with a secular structure.

Introduction

One of the key objectives of this project was to make a contribution to our understanding of the development of urbanism in the lower Guadalquivir valley. To this end it is clearly important to have the clearest possible understanding of the structures excavated at the Peñaflor. However, the fragmentary record of the buildings uncovered make it clear that only those of Phases 7a and 8a/b are complete enough to merit any kind of architectural reconstruction. Attempted reconstructions of any Roman buildings, let alone examples as poorly preserved as these, are difficult enough and it is important to be as explicit as possible about the reasoning behind them. Consequently, two archaeologists with architectural training and with experience in the reconstruction of Roman buildings were each commissioned to produce their own version of the buildings of each phase. They had all the necessary plans, sections and photographs at their disposal, as well as the broader contextual information provided by the geophysics and systematic surface survey of La Viña (Chapter 2). In addition they were also given comparative plans from other sites in the Iberian peninsula.

The Archaeological Evidence

Prior to attempting the reconstructions, an interpretative plan of the archaeological evidence for each of the two phases was produced. These were the basis of an initial interpretation of the nature of the building in each phase. For the Phase 7a/b building, the palaestra of a bath complex, an "axial peristyle" house, or the southern part of the forum of the town were all suggested as possible interpretations. In the final instance, however, the forum was the preferred interpretation. The Phase 8a/b structure was identified as the southern part of two adjacent *domus*.

Phase 7a/b: The excavated structure (Fig. 9.1)

The interpretative plan shows quite clearly that this was the southern sector of a large plaza or garden, surrounded on at least three sides by a portico. The

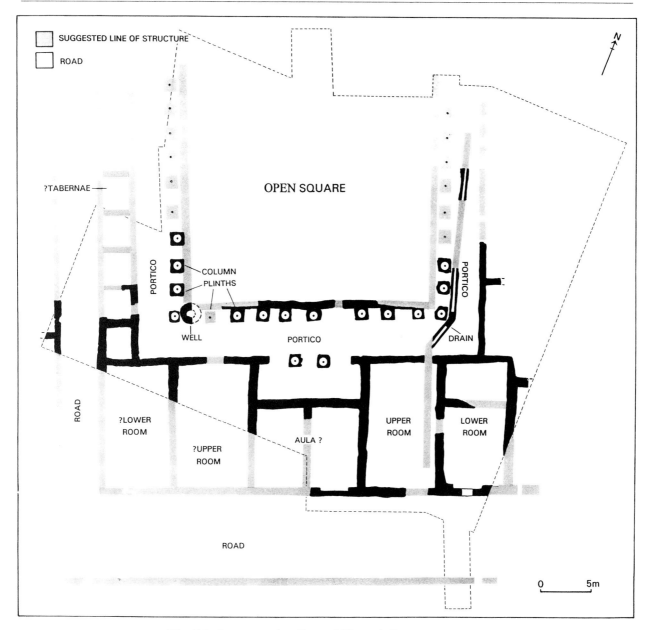

Fig. 9.1. Interpretative Ground Plan of Phase 7a structure

complex was terraced into the south-facing slope of the western hill of La Viña so as to afford the site a magnificent view over the Guadalquivir.

Its interpretation is difficult, since none of the building survives above foundation level. The enclosed space measures 24m from east to west: its north–south length is not known since the building is incomplete. The width of the enclosed space and portico is c. 28.50m. The complex is symmetrical about a central axis, which runs north–south through a large room (the 'aula': c.12.5 × 13.0m) which is partially shut off from the portico by two columns. On the eastern side there is one shallow, or 'upper' room and another deeper one at a 'lower' level: one assumes that the same arrangement existed on the western side. No architectural

fragments survive except for one white marble column base which was found removed from its original context (Chapter 5: Fig. 5.39), but which probably belonged to some part of this building. The width of the base was 0.75m and is well within the range of those often employed on public buildings (for temples, for example, see Gros 1996, 122–206). It could also have fitted well within the c.1.00m square column foundations that help define the south, west and east sides of the enclosed space. Moreover, the closest parallel for the column base, from the basilica at Baelo, is almost exactly contemporary with the Phase 7a/b complex (see Chapter 5). This evidence strongly suggests that the complex be identified with a public building of some kind.

Even less can be said about the function of any of these rooms. In the first instance all the floor surfaces had been robbed out. However, fragments of *opus signinum* and *opus spicatum* fragments together with some mosaic tesserae from contexts in this phase (Appendix 5) suggest that they ranged from the luxurious to the workaday. Even less can be deduced from an analysis of the distribution of the ceramics and other finds. This is because no occupation surfaces have survived. Consequently, the ceramics, construction material, butchered bones and metalwork largely derive from the levelling dumps which preceded the laying of floors, only exposed towards the middle and at the eastern end of the southern portico, and the area immediately to the south (generally see W/Chapter 3). Moreover, the distribution of metalwork was badly compromised by the work of metal-detectors (Chapter 5). Little is known about the internal decoration of the building, and although a few fragments of plain coloured wall-paster and fragments of marble were discovered, these were not in-situ (Appendices 5 and 7). Nothing is known about the surface of the enclosed square or garden on account of later demolition, rebuilding and ploughing.

The geophysics and the survey of Platforms 2 and 3 in the western part of La Viña

The plan presented in Chapter 2 (Fig. 2.38) shows the excavated area of the site set within the features identified from the geophysical survey and partially overlaid by the results of the intensive survey in this part of La Viña. This suggests that the Phase 7a/b complex was set within an *insula* block or *area* defined by roads on its south and eastern sides: the module implied is just under 70m × at least c.60m. Along the northern side of the area lies a range of rooms which seems to have been built from brick and to have had tessellated floors; immediately to the south of this was another narrower range of rooms with *opus spicatum* flooring. Otherwise, there were small concentrations of brick and *opus signinum* close to the north-western corner of the area and of brick and tile on its eastern side. To the north of the area, the northern road is approached by a number of narrower roads that define spaces characterized by different kinds of building rubble. Little sense can be made of these without further excavation.

None of this is chronologically specific, although it is more likely to reflect later structures, in other words of Phase 8a/b, than 7a. If it is assumed that the small excavated portion of the western road was maintained throughout antiquity, it seems likely that the same was true of that running along

the northern side of the *insula*. If that was the case, it seems legitimate to suggest that the northern road defined and was probably contemporary to the Phase 7a/b complex.

Phase 7a/b: Interpretation of the Structure

Interpretation of the Phase 7a/b building is difficult, given the advanced state of destruction and the disappearance of any floors or walls above floor level. Consequently, any interpretation has to be derived from an analysis of the plan alone.

The first possibility is that the porticoed square represents the *palaestra* of some public baths. Similar porticoed enclosures, for example, have been found at the Central Baths in Pompeii (Ward Perkins 1981: Fig. 93). This is unlikely to have been the case at Celti on two counts. Firstly, the complex is situated just below the highest point in the town (75.14m). Such a location as this would present considerable difficulties in ensuring the regular and large-scale supply of water necessary for a bath complex. Secondly, there are few examples of bath buildings with *palaestra* prior to the late 1st century AD in Hispania. One of the earliest is the baths-palaestra complex at the Colonia Latina of Carteia (San Roque, Cádiz), traditionally dated to the late 1st century AD (Roldán Gómez 1992, 106–29 and Fig. 31), while another example at Conimbriga was begun in the Flavian period but was not completed until the reign of Trajan (Alarcão & Etienne 1977). In its most developed form in Iberia, the baths-palaestra appears at the *nova urbs* at Italica (Santiponce) in the Hadrianic period (Rodríguez Hidalgo *et alii* 1999) – although the architectural inspiration is exceptional for the region and probably derives from Asia Minor.

A second possibility is that the Phase 7a/b colonnade be identified with the peristyle of a large private house. The argument here would run as follows. The arrangement of rooms along the south side of the square could be taken to resemble large peristyle houses in Italy, such as the Casa del Fauno (Richardson 1988, 115–117), with a *triclinium* at its middle point and small *cubiculi* running along its western side. In general terms, there are dangers in directly invoking parallels from outside the region. However, the Casa nr.1 at Emporiae, dated to the second half of the 1st century BC, and the early imperial 'Casa nr.2' at Emporiae (Santos Retolaza 1991, 25–57), remind us that Italian style houses with peristyles similar to that at Celti can be expected in certain situations. After all, Emporiae had been a major centre of Roman power since the late 3rd century BC and had developed a major urban complex in the Roman style as early as 100 BC. By contrast, Celti seems to have been a largely native centre that only began to assume Roman cultural characteristics in the course of the early imperial period (see Chapter 10).

It is perhaps more appropriate to draw comparisons with house-types which are quite frequent in the region. A recent study of peristyle houses suggests that a particular type, the "axial peristyle", made its appearance in Hispania and other parts of the Roman Empire during the late 1st century AD (Meyer 1999). Examples have been discovered at Munigua (Castillo de Mulva), Baelo (Bolonia) and Italica and, further afield, at Emerita Augusta (Mérida). Analysis of some of the plans of some of these does provide some grounds for suggesting that the Phase 7a/b complex represents the peristyle and centrally-placed *triclinium* of a large private house. However, objections can be made on the basis of size and chronology. These will be discussed below in the context of the reconstruction drawings. There is also a very practical consideration. The large porticoed courtyard was south-facing and in summers where the temperature frequently rises above 40 degrees, this open space would have been an intolerably hot 'desert' for the inhabitants of the house. Indeed, Vitruvius recommends that summer dining rooms (*triclinia*) ought to face north to avoid unneccessary exposure to the sun and to keep the room cool (6.4.2).

The above arguments suggest that the Phase 7a/b structure does not readily lend itself to being identified as part of a bath building or the peristyle of an "axial-peristyle" house. It is simply too large. It seems probable, therefore, that it should be identified with some kind of public building. Consequently, a third possible identification is that it should be identified with a market building, or *macellum*. There is quite a wide range of variation in the known plans of these (De Ruyt 1983), although the common features include a rectangular plan with shops opening onto flanking streets and some kind of central building enclosed within a square or rectangular plan. For example, the mid 2nd century AD *macellum* at Djemila (De Ruyt 1983, Fig. 24) provides quite a close parallel to the Phase 7a/b complex – even though it is very much later in date. However, the location of this kind of building close to the highest point of the town would not seem to have been ideal. It would have been away from the forum – which in this scenario one would assume could only have been located in a lower part of the town to the west – and would have presented logistical difficulties in the uphill transportation of bulky market commodities.

A fourth interpretation might be that the Phase 7a/b complex be identified with a meeting house (*schola*) for a *collegium*. This is not exactly a canonical class of public building and there is quite a range of variation in the plans (Gros 1996, 376–85). There are, however, some common features, such as a portico enclosing a central space with small meeting rooms opening off it. There are, however, few contemporary parallels in the region – apart from the possible Hadrianic schola at the Casa de la Exedra at Italica (Rodríguez Hidalgo 1991, 299).

A fifth and final interpretation would be that the building be interpreted as the southern part of the forum of the town. In this scenario, the area enclosed by the colonnade would be identified as the forum square. This would have been flanked by *tabernae* along its western side while along the southern side would have been a range of rooms arranged on either side of a room central to the north–south axis of the complex. This room was fronted by two columns set back from the colonnade. The structural evidence for the organization of the area to the east and the north of the square has not survived.

The justification for this interpretation is as follows. In the first instance, the construction of the building in such a dominating position at this time was a major architectural undertaking with no apparent precedent. At the very least, it involved the levelling of earlier structures and the construction of a major terraced platform. Secondly, the size of the column foundations and white marble column base from the site are sufficiently large to have supported a public building of some kind. Thirdly, if one assumes the forum square (with porticoes) was a true square (28.50 × 28.50m) – although it could have been rectangular with a longer north–south axis – it was clearly small. However, comparative figures from broadly contemporary fora elsewhere in the Hispaniae suggest that it would not have been excessively small. Relatively few fora are known from Baetica. Nevertheless, the size of the forum square proposed for Celti would have compared favourably with the Flavian example at Munigua (c.20 × 21m: Hauschild 1991, Fig. 2), although it is smaller than the Claudian example at Baelo (37 × 30m: Sillières 1995, 103). Elsewhere there is a close parallel at Conimbriga (c.22m × 33.5), where the first forum complex is conventionally dated to Augustus (Alarcão & Etienne 1977), but which has recently been re-dated to the Julio-Claudian period (Alarcão, Étienne & Colvin 1997). There is another complex of similar size at Ruscino in south-eastern France (33.60 × 22.45m: Barruol & Marichal 1987), which is conventionally dated to the Augustan period. The layout of the 'aula' provides few clues as to identifying the cult to which it might have been dedicated. However, its central position hints at a small temple or that it was even an *aedes augusti*. At the very least, the now lost dedication by the *augustales* Fabius Atticus and (Fabius) Firmus (Chapter 8: no. 15) suggests that there was probably a shrine to a cult of the Emperor somewhere in Celti during the early imperial period.

It might be argued that the Phase 7a/b complex could not possibly be the forum since there is no evidence for the monumental paving and archi-tectural details which are commonly attested at many fora. However, this part of the site was heavily transformed in the early 3rd century AD, demol-ished at some time in the early 5th century AD, subsequently robbed and has been systematically despoiled and ploughed down to the present day. Indeed, it is possible that the many pieces of architectural sculpture in private collections in the village and built into later buildings in the village might have originated here and have adorned the forum. It might also be suggested that the well adjacent to the south-eastern corner column is more typical of a private house than a public building.

A final objection that might be laid against identifying the Phase 7a/b complex with the forum is that it lies away from the centre of the town, and not at the centre of the town – the usual position for many fora. In Baetica, this is certainly the case at Baelo (Sillières 1995, fold out plan), Munigua (Hauschild 1991), Corduba (Ventura *et alii* 1998, Fig. 2), and probably Italica (Rodríguez Hidalgo & Keay 1995). However, the early fora at Carteia (Roldán Gómez *et alii* 1998, 145, Fig. 153) and Tarraco (Mar & Ruiz de Arbulo 1987, Fig. 1) are both located "off-centre" at the south-western corner of the town.

In conclusion, there seems to be little doubt that the Phase 7a/b structure was a public building of some kind. It is less easy to readily identify it with a given class of building, although the above discussion suggests that the strongest possibility is that it be identified with the forum of the town. Nevertheless, it should be stressed that this is only a tentative suggestion and that one should beware of too readily trying to associate incomplete building plans with canonical building types. Indeed, there are some quite serious legal impli-cations to this identification, as will become apparent below.

The Phase 8b Domus (Fig. 9.2)

The excavated plan clearly reveals that much of the Phase 7a/b structure was demolished in Phase 8, and that the site was divided into two roughly equal spaces; these were occupied by the peristyles of two adjacent houses: House A and House B. The arrangement of walls for both houses in the southern part of the block is unclear since all footings down to the foundations of the earlier Phase 7a/b building had been removed. The organization of the houses at the northern end is unclear since its excavation was not completed. Consequently, our understanding of both houses is only partial.

The area occupied by House A measured c.21.5m × 43m. The main visible feature consisted of a small square peristyle that was defined on at least three sides by a colonnade. Along its western side the columns rested upon foundations that were in-stalled during the Phase 7a/b phase, those to the north and east were innovations for this phase. The small garden enclosed by the peristyle was sur-rounded on three sides by a concrete water channel that was fed from a drain running southwards from further north. At its southern end it defined a small rectangular pool lined with *opus signinum*; this was drained into a street drain by a small outflow at its south-eastern corner. To the north of the peristyle were at least two rooms enclosed by walls built from blocks of stone and Dressel 20 amphora sherds. The layout of the rooms further north is not fully understood.

The area occupied by House B measured 19m by at least 43m. Here the peristyle was rectangular and was defined by columns, which ran along the eastern side and must have reused the foundations of the Phase 7a/b colonnade. The colonnade along the north side was an innovation, while that along the western side had been robbed out in Phase 9 and has been interpolated. From the one base in situ and the fragments found in the Phase 9 rubble, it seems that at least some of these these were of mudbrick coated with a number of layers of plain and red plaster (Chapter 7). At the north end of the garden enclosed by the peristyle was a small square water tank lined with *opus signinum*; at the south end was a semi-circular pool also lined with *opus signinum*. Water from the former flowed clockwise around the north and eastern sides of the peristyle in a purpose built drain, and south-wards until it eventually reached the south east–west road. A small cistern was sited off-centre within the garden area (see Jansen 1991 for similar cistern arrangments). Much of the garden area was floored with *opus signinum*, while the amphora standing at the northern end of the garden may have held a small fruit tree. Little is known about the rooms opening off the north and east porticoes.

Very little is known about the flooring and decoration of the rooms in both houses, because the floors had nearly all been robbed out. How-ever, mosaic tesserae, *opus spicatum* and *opus signinum* fragments from Phase 9 and 12 contexts suggests that some were richly decorated while others were not. This is supported by the evidence

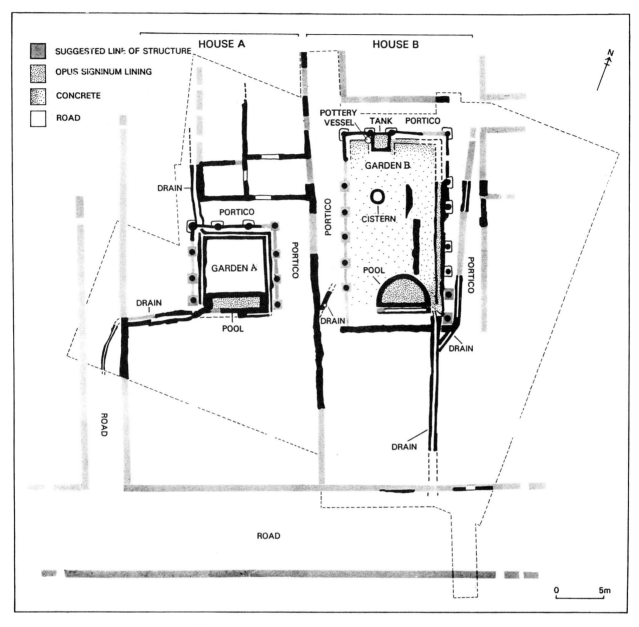

Fig. 9.2. Interpretative Ground Plan of Phase 8 Houses

from the decorated wallplaster, some of which was in-situ and some of which was redeposited during a later phase (100: Chapter 7). The known decorative themes included imitation *giallo antico* marble and porphyry as well as figured representations. It was impossible to attempt any characterisation of room function on the basis of finds patterning because there were virtually no deposits of significant size (see also W/Chapter 3). At the time of the house's demolition in Phase 9, large amounts of animal bone were deposited in the garden cistern and quantities of amphora were dumped in the easternmost lower room, between the well and the semi-circular tank and

the north-western-most corner of the site. This, however, tells us more about processes of final demolition and abandonment in the 5th century than its occupation during the preceding centuries.

The Reconstructions

The reconstructions were produced by archaeologists with architectural training and familiarity with Roman architecture. One, Sheila Gibson, who has long experience in the reconstruction of Roman buildings, did not actually visit the site but was provided with all the plans and sections, together with the results and interpretation of the systematic "platform" survey and geophysical survey of the area (Chapter 2). Her drawings were completed by hand. The other, Kate Wilson, was provided with the same materials but had the advantage of having worked at the site for two seasons. Her drawings were completed in Autocad 14 (with the assistance of Gillian Wilson). Both of them took part in the discussion about the possible interpretation of the Phase 7a/b and 8b buildings.

In undertaking their reconstruction drawings of Phase 7a/b and 9 structures, both archaeologists worked from the following criteria:

1. Is the final reconstruction consistent with the survey, excavated evidence and other associated artifactual and architectural evidence ?
2. Is the final reconstruction consistent with the known technological expertise of the period being considered ?
3. Would the reconstructed buildings have been able to stand in practice ?
4. Is the layout complex proposed consistent with other contemporary complexes in the region and elsewhere in the western Mediterranean?

The Phase 7a/b building as either a baths/palaestra complex or macellum

Neither of these was attempted, since it was felt that they were the least likely interpretation.

The Phase 7a/b building as a domus

As was suggested above, there are grounds for reconstructing the Phase 7a/b building as a *domus* even though, in the end, the forum was considered to have been the most likely interpretation. Consequently, an attempt to do this was undertaken by one of the archaeologists. The resultant image (Fig. 9.3), by Kate Wilson, reveals a building dominated by a very large peristyle. The large room in the centre of the southern side could perhaps be interpreted as a *triclinium* while those on the west side of the peristyle could be seen as *cubiculi*. Nothing can really be said about the arrangement of rooms along the north side of the building. However, it would seem probable that the house would have been entered from the road, providing access to a vestibule of some kind.

As reconstructed, the building could fall within the class of early imperial town-houses known as "axial-peristyle" houses (Meyer 1999). This term includes a range of houses with a number of features in common, including a plan dominated by a major longitudinal axis, along which are the vestibule and peristyle arranged symmetrically

and in a sequence. The latter are built on a grand scale and the size of the house can be considerable. Despite superficial similarities, there are sufficient differences between the Phase 7a/b house and parallels in the region and further afield to suggest that the building is better identified as a small forum complex as discussed above.

There is little doubt that the Phase 7a/b structure bears close resemblance to better preserved examples of axial peristyle houses in the region, such as the Casa de los Pájaros at Italica, the houses in the port area at Baelo, and to a lesser extent the houses at Munigua (Meyer 1999, 102–7 and Fig. 3A). In all of these, symmetry and visibility are paramount. While this appears to be true at Celti, there appears to be one crucial difference which suggests that it stands apart from the rest. The *triclinium* here was provided with a single wide entrance subdivided with two columns, an arrange-

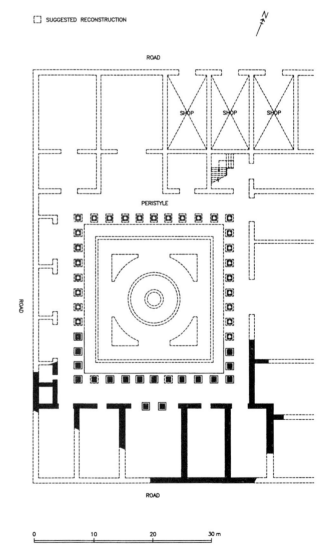

Fig. 9.3. Ground Plan of a Possible Domus on the Site of the Phase 7a structure (KW)

ment which would seems to be exceptional in axial-peristyle houses (Meyer 1999, 114–5). This peculiarity is important because the two columns in the entrance to the large room at Celti block direct visibility from the peristyle and vice versa by being placed behind the intercolumnar spaces of the peristyle. In other words, the room was only designed to be seen diagonally across the peristyle and not axially.

The proportions of different elements in the house are such that if it were classed as an axial peristyle house, it would be exceptionally large. Thus, Meyer (1999, 107–108 and Table) stresses the importance of the relative proportions of the peristyle and *triclinium* in assigning a house to the axial peristyle class. At Celti, the key proportions would be as follows:

Area of House	3405m² (minimum)
Area of Peristyle	812.25m²
Area of *Triclinium*	162.5m²
Area of Vestibule	Not Calculable
Peristyle as % of House	28.62%
Triclinium as % of House	4.77%
Vestibule as % of House	Not Calculable

In comparative terms, the proposed minimum area of the house would be amongst the largest in the Iberian peninsula, being larger than the Casa de los Repuxos at Conimbriga in northern Lusitania (3200m²) and surpassed only by the Maison des Chapiteaux à consoles at Apamea in Syria (Meyer 1999, Table). The same would be true of the area of its peristyle and *triclinium*. The former would be nearly double the size of its nearest parallel, the Casa de los Repuxos (438m²) at Conimbriga and again only surpassed by the Maison des Chapiteaux à Consoles (1250m²) at Apamea (Meyer 1999, Table). Moreover, the *triclinium* would seem to have had few, if any parallels. The closest would be the Maison des Dieux Océans – Phases III/IV (130.5m²). The impression is that if the Phase 7a/b building at Celti was to be identified as an axial peristyle building, it would be one of the largest in the Roman world. On the other hand, the proportion of total house space occupied by the peristyle and *triclinium* can be paralleled at a number of sites in Hispania and elsewhere in the Empire (Meyer 1999, Table).

In terms of the comparative chronology, there are parallels in other parts of Baetica and southern Lusitania for seeing the Phase 7a/b complex at Celti as an axial peristyle house. In view of its large size, however, it does stand out as exceptional. The examples at Italica and Baelo are both later, dating to the second century AD (Rodríguez Hidalgo *et alii* 1999 for Italica; Sillières 1995, 173 for Baelo). The examples at Munigua are contemporary to Celti

but somewhat different in their layout (Meyer 1999, Fig. 6). Further afield, the Casa del Anfiteatro at Emerita Augusta in southern Lusitania is cited as another example (Meyer 1996, Fig. 3D) and, although similar, may well be 2nd century AD or later in date (García Sandoval 1966, 43; Alvarez Sáenz de Buruaga 1974, 184).

The Phase 7a/b building as a Forum

Two reconstructions of the proposed forum are presented in the first instance, each of which is equally possible in the context of the recorded remains. They are not intended as definitive statements but are meant to stimulate discussion and debate. They are by no means the only possible reconstructions from the available evidence, and should be modified once new data becomes available.

The first of the two alternative reconstructions of the forum, by Sheila Gibson, envisaged it as follows (Fig. 9.4–6). The forum square itself was defined on four sides by a colonnade; analysis of the ground plan and the adjacent systematic geophysical and surface survey seemed to provide sufficient grounds for this hypothesis. The range of rooms to the south were flanked by a large central room which lay on the north–south axis of the complex as a whole. This room, named the 'aula', was fronted by two columns, which were positioned in such a way as to impede viewing the inside of the room behind from the forum square. The size and arrangement of these columns was such as to suggest that the 'aula' did not project into the forum square. However, its roof-line would have risen prominently above that of the rest of the southern range, presenting an impressive facade overlooking the Guadalquivir to the south. The function of the rooms to east and west of the 'aula' is not known, although the easternmost room has been interpreted as housing steps to allow communication between the east–west street and the forum colonnade. At the northern end of the site, a range of rooms running east–west has been postulated, with a temple lying at their centre and on an axis with the 'aula' to the south. *Tabernae* are suggested for the western side of the site, while a basilica is postulated for the east. There is no archaeological evidence for the suggested windows. It should be pointed out that throughout, this reconstruction was undertaken without the artist having visited the site. The guiding principles were working from the known to the unknown, while drawing upon an accumulated experience of reconstructing buildings in the Roman Mediterranean and a familiarity of broadly contemporary forum complexes in Hispania. Thus, the proposed arrangement of temple and basilica

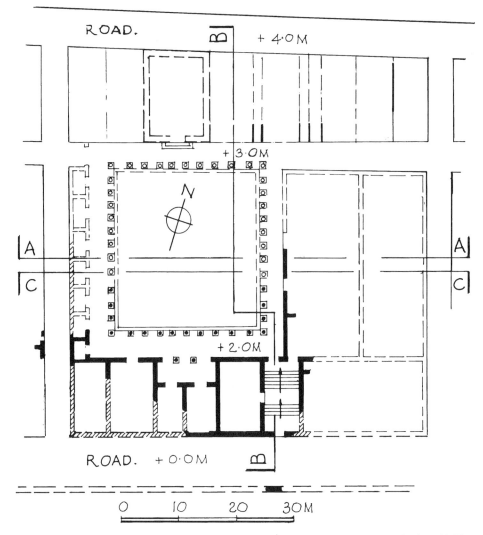

Fig. 9.4. Phase 7a structure. Reconstruction A: Forum Area Ground Plan (SG)

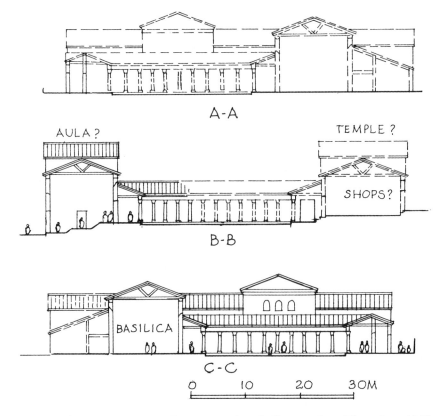

Fig. 9.5. Phase 7a structure. Reconstruction A: Forum Area Elevations (SG)

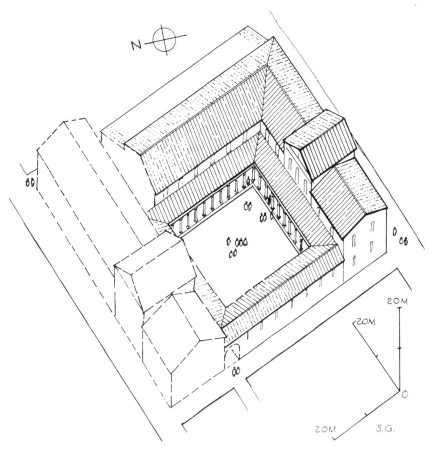

Fig. 9.6. Phase 7a structure. Reconstruction A: Forum Area Axonometric (SG)

can be paralleled by the Julio-Claudian complex at Conimbriga (supra). It is also in some ways similar to that at Munigua (Hauschild 1991, Figs. 2, 3 and 4), with the basilica situated along the south side, the tabularium and curia to the north, but with the temple placed centrally.

The second reconstruction was undertaken out by Kate Wilson. The proposed layout is quite similar to the first (Figs. 9.7–9.9). In the first instance, the geophysics and systematic surface-survey provides grounds for suggesting that the forum piazza would have been square and defined by a colonnade on all four sides. The columns were assumed to be of the Corinthian order, and while no corinthian capital of the appropriate size was actually found on the site, several examples have been discovered in modern buildings in the village of Peñaflor. One of these, together with the diameter of the excavated column base on the wall (177), was used to provide the diameter of the column. The intercolumnation of the forum colonnade was approximately 5½ times the diameter of the column base, while the height of the columns was based upon the Vitruvian principle

that it should be 9½ times the diameter of the column (Vitruvius, 3.3).

This reconstruction also resembled the first in that the 'aula' does not project into the square beyond the forum colonnade, although its roof would have risen above the line of the rooms on either side of it. Where this reconstruction does differ from the earlier one, is in suggesting that the 'aula' be identified as a temple and that the rooms at the south-eastern and the south-western corner would have housed monumental staircases for communication between the east–west road and the east and west forum porticoes. There is, of course, no evidence for the identification of the temple. With the temple lying at the central point of the southern range of rooms, the basilica is placed intuitively on an axis at the northern end of the complex. Such an arrangement of a temple fronting the basilica at opposite ends of the forum square can be paralleled by the mid–1st century AD complex at Baelo (Bolonia: Sillières 1997, 85–129), although here there were three temples side-by-side on a raised platform. Further afield, another parallel of Augustan date can be found at

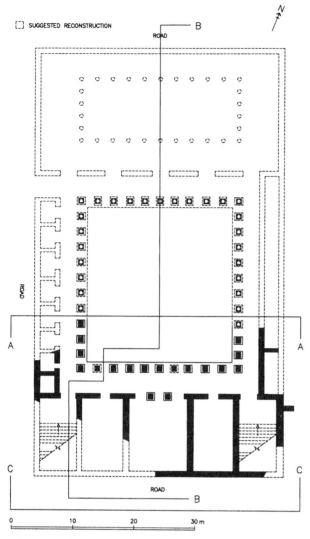

☐ SUGGESTED RECONSTRUCTION

Fig. 9.7. Phase 7a structure. Reconstruction B: Forum Area Ground Plan (KW)

Velleia in northern Italy. Here, the basilica and forum are an integrally planned unit. However, there is no evidence that there was ever a temple within the forum complex (Calvani 1975, 49–52 and fold out plans). The same was true of the Augustan forum at Ruscino (Barruol & Marichal 1987), and the early 1st century AD complex at Glanum (Roth Congès 1992, 49–55 and Fig. 14). The small rooms along the eastern edge of the forum colonnade at Celti are interpreted as *tabernae*, while the organization of space behind the western colonnade is unclear.

In proposing this reconstruction, the topographical situation was seen to have been of key importance (Figs. 9.10 and 9.11). The complex overlooked the Guadalquivir on sloping ground just below the highest point of the site. It is therefore likely that the architects would have designed a complex, which took full advantage of this terrain and enhanced the impression of the town when approached from the river. Consequently, the reconstruction proposes that the southern side of the complex would have been graced by a colonnade.

The Phase 8b Domus

This building was even harder to reconstruct than the Phase 7a/b forum. Even though it is clear that the Phase 8b structures clearly belongs to a residential complex, not enough of them remain to allow us to accurately reconstruct all of its layout – particularly in the northern part of the site. Sheila Gibson felt that there was insufficient evidence to attempt the task. Kate Wilson, however, did feel

☐ SUGGESTED RECONSTRUCTION

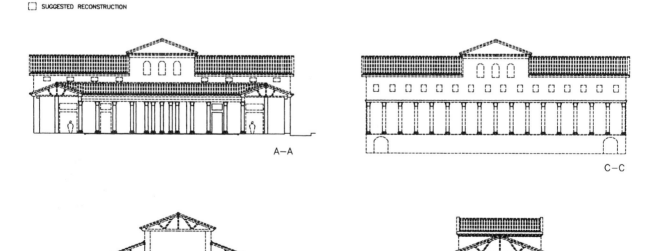

A–A

C–C

B–B

Fig. 9.8. Phase 7a structure. Reconstruction B: Forum Area Elevations (KW)

RECONSTRUCTION OF PHASE 7A

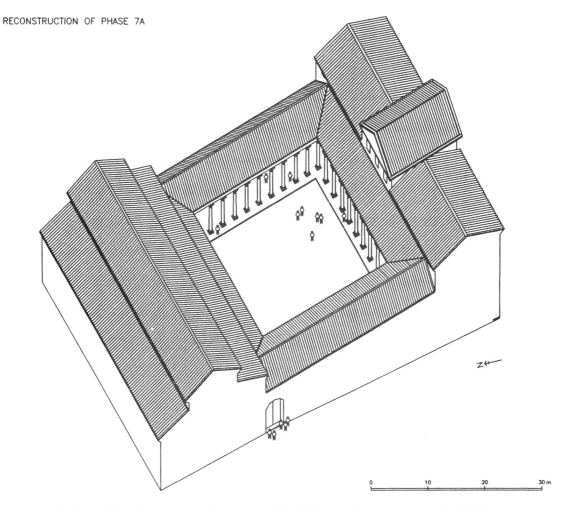

Fig. 9.9. Phase 7a structure. Reconstruction B: Forum Area Axonometric (KW)

Fig. 9.10. Aerial photograph showing the dominant position of the Phase 7a overlooking the Guadalquivir: the excavations lie at the centre of the picture

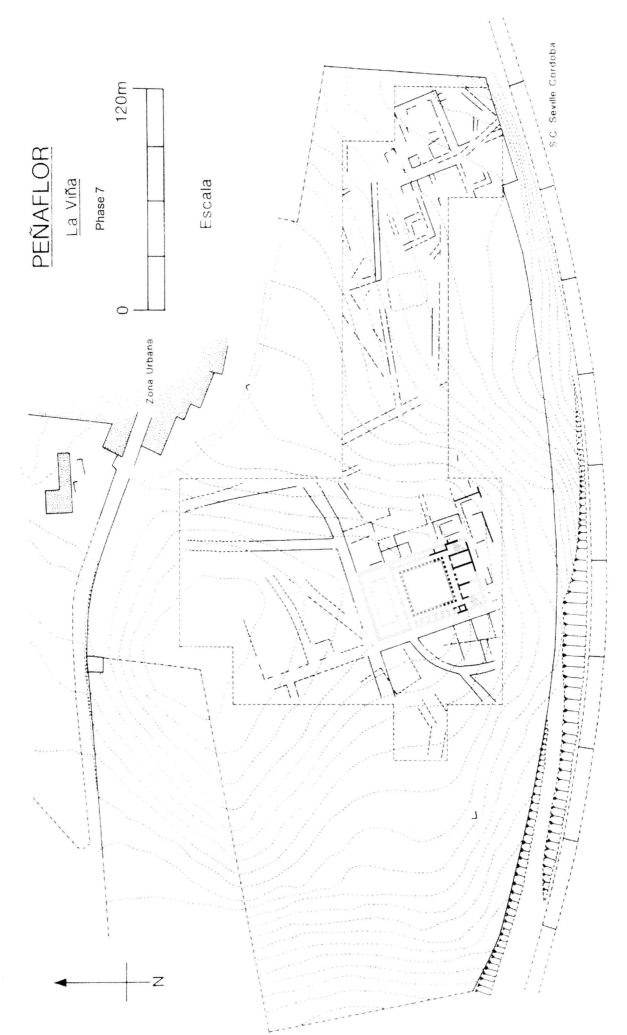

PEÑAFLOR

La Viña

Phase 7

Escala

0   120m

Zona Urbana

N

S.C. Seville Cordoba

Fig. 9.11. Phase 7a structure. Reconstructed Forum within the Celti town plan

that she had enough intuition from accumulated on-site experience to attempt it. The resulting reconstructions (Figs. 9.12–14) work from the available archaeological evidence together with an awareness of contemporary paralells in Baetica, such as Munigua and Italica. It was assumed that the building covered the same ground area that it had occupied in Phase 7a/b, but was subdivided into two contingent properties by a north–south wall. In both properties the southern part of the forum square was occupied by two gardens with peristyles. Surviving column plinths provided the evidence for calculating the height of the colonnades. The block to the south is seen as a unitary construction consisting of one range of rooms opening onto the east–west road and another range of rooms opening onto the peristyles; a corridor separates them. *Cubiculi* are envisaged to have run along the western wall of the western house. In the area lying to the north, a *triclinium* is posited for the northern side of the eastern house with an atrium and adjacent rooms between here and the road. The evidence for the western house is less clear, but an atrium has been assumed here too. Given the evidence for *opus signinum* from an upper storey (supra; Chapter 3), stairs have been placed at different points in both houses.

The Implications

The suggested replacement of the mid to late 1st century AD forum at Celti by two private houses would have involved the demolition of a key public building and represented a change in the title and function of this sector of urban land from public to private. This raises several legal questions, which

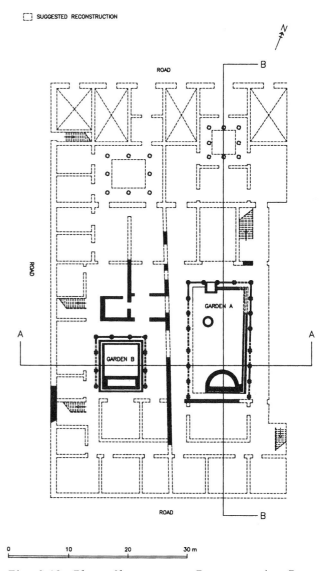

Fig. 9.12. Phase 8b structure. Reconstruction B: House Ground Plans (KW)

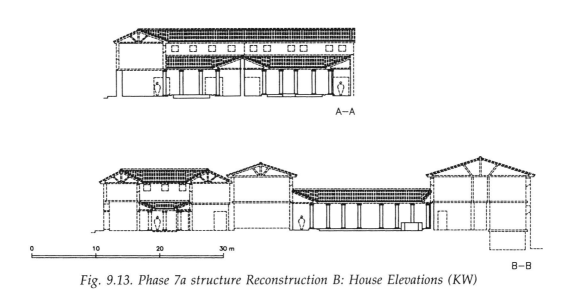

Fig. 9.13. Phase 7a structure Reconstruction B: House Elevations (KW)

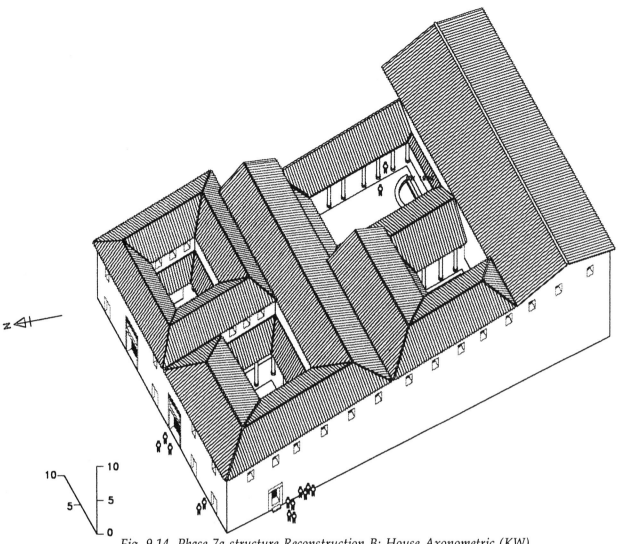

Fig. 9.14. Phase 7a structure Reconstruction B: House Axonometric (KW)

might be taken as arguments against the interpretation of the Phase 7a/b structure as the forum of the town. In essence, was it permissable or possible for a major public building, like the forum, to be demolished and replaced by a residential building?

Since it is likely that Celti was granted municipal status in the Flavian period (Chapter 10), the Flavian municipal law is the first place to look for any explicit prohibition. In the Lex Irnitana, the only relevant clause states that the unroofing, destroying or demolishing of a building was forbidden "except by resolution of the decuriones or conscripti, when the majority of them is present, unless he is going to replace it within the next year" (González 1986, 196: Tab. VIIA.Ch.62). Although it is less relevant, a similar clause can be found in the colonial law of Urso:

"No-one in the town of the colonia Iulia is to demolish or dismantle a building, unless he shall have furnished guarantors, according to the decision of the IIviri, that he is about to rebuild

it, or unless the decurions shall have decreed (that he may)." (Ch.LXXV: Crawford 1996, 424).

This evidence suggests, therefore, that the law does not explicitly prohibit the demolition of the forum or other public buildings in *municipia* like Celti. The municipal law seems more concerned with maintaining the *dignitas* of the town by making sure that any demolition was undertaken with the foreknowledge of the *ordo* and that the building concerned was replaced with another. This view seems to be echoed in Roman law generally (Ulpian D.43.8.2.pr). At the same time, however, it could also be argued that however strictly this law was observed in the late 1st century AD, it cannot be assumed that the community at Celti would have strictly adhered to this law in the later 2nd/earlier 3rd century AD, when it is suggested that the forum was demolished and replaced by the houses. Excavations at the broadly contemporary municipium of Baelo (Bolonia), for example, have shown that by the late 2nd/early 3rd century AD, the urban

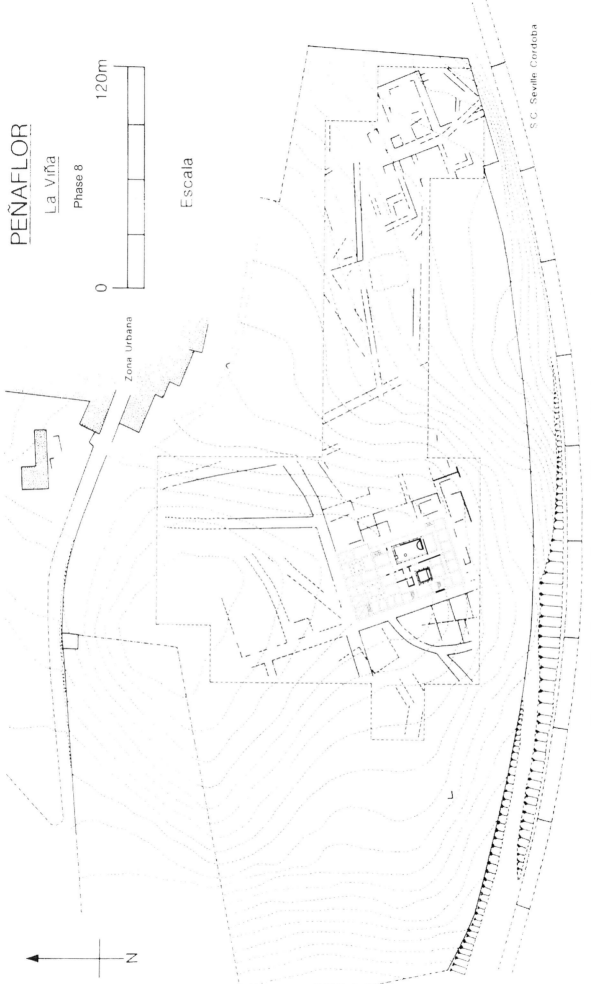

PEÑAFLOR

La Viña

Phase 8

Escala

0   120m

Zona Urbana

S.C. Seville Cordoba

N

Fig. 9.15. Phase 7a structure Reconstructed House within the Celti town plan

fabric was clearly not being maintained as it had been earlier (Sillières 1993, 147–50).

The real problem with interpreting the Phase 7a/b complex with the forum of the town, however, lies in the fact that it would probably (although not necessarily) have included a temple, which was, by definition, sacred ground. Consequently, the demolition of the forum and its replacement by a private house would necessarily have involved the ownership of the complex changing from sacred to secular. Roman legal sources imply that this was forbidden and that when it did take place, restitution would have been required:

> "The case of sacred places is different. In a sacred place, we are not only forbidden to do anything but are also ordered to make restitution: this on account of religion." (Ulpian: D. 43.8.2.19; translated by Mommsen, Kreuger & Watson 1985).

One of the few cases where this has been attested is in Asia Minor. Pliny the Younger, the governor of Bithynia, wrote to the Emperor Trajan (AD 98–117), informing him that the citizens of Nicomedia were building a new forum adjacent to their existing one, an act which necessarily involved moving the old temple of the Great Mother to a new site. Pliny asked whether this could be done without loss of sanctity, given that its original form of consecration was non-Roman (Pliny, *ep*.10.49). Trajan replied that Pliny need not worry, given that: "the soil of an alien country is not capable of being consecrated according to our laws" (Pliny, *ep*.10.50: translation in Radice 1978). In this case, therefore, it had been possible to move the temple. At Celti, however, this would have been more problematic since it was a Roman temple that would have to have been moved.

While it is clear, therefore, that there are some archaeological and architectural grounds for identifying the Phase 7a/b complex at Celti as a forum, there are quite strong legal grounds for suggesting that its demolition and replacement by a private house would not have been permitted. If this is in fact what did take place, it suggests that little attention was paid to the pre-requisites of Roman law in the heart of Roman Baetica in the late 2nd/early 3rd centuries AD. The replacement of the forum by houses in this way would not have been a symptom of urban decline, since the later 2nd and earlier 3rd centuries AD seem to have been a period of economic "boom"(see Chapter 10), but rather an index of a changing urban environment. The decision to replace the forum would have been taken by the *ordo* of the town in the later 2nd century AD. Their reasoning may have been because the current space of the forum was too small for the *dignitas* or requirements of the town and that its site should be turned over to private use and rent charged, while another sector of urban land be set aside for a larger forum. This might have been on lower-lying land to the east – possibly on the low saddle immediately to the west of the Ermita de la Encarnación and south of the Calle San Pedro. Systematic surface survey of this part of the site in 1991 revealed a high density of column segments running in a roughly north–south direction (Chapter 2), suggesting that it was shut off on its western side by a portico.

The other alternative is that the Phase 7a/b structure was not the forum of the town, but that it should be interpreted instead as a non-canonical kind of public building. There are some similarities, for example, between the Phase 7a/b structure and the second monumental esplanade complex which lies to the south of the forum and to the west of the theatre at Bulla Regia (Beschaouch, Hanoune & Thébert 1977 Fig. 105). This would make the change of ownership and function much less conflictive. In the final instance, the only solution to the problem will be to undertake further excavation at the site at some time in the future, in the hope that this will provide a clearer understanding of the complex.

Chapter 10
Celti: An Archaeological History

Simon Keay

Abstract

This Chapter uses the archaeological evidence to write an archaeological history of ancient Celti. The results from the survey and excavation are combined with the specialist reports and the epigraphic record and are integrated to trace the development of a major settlement in southern Spain from the 9th century BC to the 5th century AD. Great care has been taken to place the site in its full regional context. The survival of the evidence means inevitably that some periods are better understood than others. Thus, the archaeological record for the Bronze and Iron Age (Turdetanian) periods is not as full as that for the later periods. There is little doubt that the greatest contribution of the site is to our understanding of urban development at the Neronian/Early Flavian period (Phase 7). The evidence from Celti shows how profoundly the topography, economy, society and culture of the town was changing at the time that it was probably granted municipal status, a picture which may prove to be true of other Flavian municipia in Baetica. It also suggests that the full integration of the town into the economic, political and cultural life of the province and the Empire as a whole was not complete until the early third century AD (Phase 8). The early 5th century AD (Phase 9) clearly marked a major watershed in the history of the town, with the apparent breakdown of the earlier urban fabric and its replacement by a new urban landscape (Phase 10). This took place at a time while Roman control was ceded to the Vandals, Suevi and Visigoths although the reasons for this change are not clear.

Objectives

The aim of this final Chapter is to put the results of the survey, excavations and finds analyses into their broader regional context. It takes the form of a discussion, which is essentially a narrative history of the site and draws upon the project results and those of other scholars work. The emphasis is primarily archaeological, although historical and epigraphic data are addressed when relevant.

The survey and excavations at Peñaflor were intended to shed light on the development of ancient Celti from the protohistoric to late antique period. This is a deeply stratified site and there was every hope that the results of the project might perhaps enable Peñaflor to stand as an urban type-site for the lower Guadalquivir valley. Seven key themes were identified:

1. The date and cultural context for the first establishment of the site.
2. The date by which the settlement began to assume urban planning and functions.
3. The regional context of the site and its relationship to contemporary Phoenician and Carthaginian settlements.
4. The impact of Rome upon the town following the conquest of southern Spain in the later the 3rd and earlier 2nd centuries BC.
5. The Romanization of the town during the late Republican and early imperial periods.
6. The role of the town in the economy of the province, with particular respect to the production and export of olive oil in Dressel 20 amphorae.
7. The ways in which the town may have responded to the broader social, cultural and economic

transformation of the province during the late Roman and germanic periods.

Overall, the twin strategy of surface survey combined with open-area excavation proved crucial in maximising our understanding of the site during what was, in effect, a relatively short project. The topographic and surface survey provided a clear understanding of the character of the site and its broader chronological development. This was essential in deciding where to excavate and providing a background for the interpretation of the results. At the same time, the excavation provided one of the first major structural sequences within a Roman town in the lower Guadalquivir valley. Its chronological sequence can be summarised as follows:

Phase 1: Undiagnostic layers dating to some time before the late Bronze Age (9th century BC).

Phase 2: Two parallel walls belonging to a structure built at some time during the Late Bronze Age period (9th century BC).

Phase 3: The construction of a small hearth between the 9th and 6th/5th centuries BC

Phase 4: The construction of postholes during the 6th/5th BC.

Phases 5, 6 and 6a: The construction of a number of walls of uncertain function during the Augustan period.

Phases 6c and 6d: Modifications to one of the existing structures, possibly during the Julio-Claudian period.

Phases 6c/7a and 7a: Demolition of all earlier structures and the construction of a major public building in the Neronian/Flavian period.

Phase 8: Transformation of the earlier complex into two houses or one large *domus* with two gardens in the earlier 3rd century (*8a*); subsequent elaboration of the complex (*8b*).

Phase 9: Demolition of the whole area at some time after the early 5th century AD.

Phase 10: Construction of a new building on a different alignment on the same site some time after the early 5th century AD.

Phase 11: Undefined activity some time after the early 5th century AD.

The ways in which the site developed during the Roman and post-Roman periods and the manner of its survival into more recent periods has meant that more was learned about some of these themes than others. For example, the monumentality of the mid/late 1st century (Phase 7a/b) structures largely obscured layers of the pre-Roman and Roman Republican period, which were only accessible through small sondages. At the same time, the constant robbing and ploughing of the site down to the present day has ensured that most late antique levels have been removed.

Location of the Town

The position of ancient Celti ensured that it was well placed to play a dominant role in the economic, social, political and cultural life of the lower Guadalquivir valley. It was located on a small prominence on the north bank of the river, which provided good visibility north towards modern Constantina and the Sierra Morena, eastwards towards its intersection with the river Genil, and westwards along the valley as far as Setefilla and the Mesa de Lora (ancient Oducia).

In the first instance, Celti was well-located with respect to important transport nodes. Its precise relationship to the Guadalquivir throughout antiquity is unclear, since the course of the latter has varied quite considerably (Chapter 1). There is little doubt, however, that proximity to the river was a major factor in its economic development during the later Bronze, Iron Age and Roman periods, as Celti developed into a major stopping point on the river between Hispalis and Corduba. This was boosted by its proximity to the intersection of the Genil and the Guadalquivir, which today lies immediately to the south of Palma del Río. The Genil rose in the Sierra Nevada and was, thus, a major natural routeway which connected linked the key centres of Granada (Iliberris), and Écija (Astigi) with Celti. To the north of the town, this was continued as a land route which followed the Retortillo, through the Sierra Morena to Regina and, ultimately, the river Guadiana in the vicinity of Emerita Augusta (modern Mérida).

Celti was also able to draw upon rich natural resources in its region. In antiquity, as today, the site lay on the southern edge of rich agricultural land which sloped gently southwards from the Sierra Morena down to the Guadalquivir, and bordered the alluvial soils of the valley bottom. This was capable of supporting a varied economy, such as olive groves and cereal crops (Chapter 1). In addition, Celti lay on the line of a key transhumance route linking the Sierra Morena and the valley below (Remesal 1978a). The settlement was also well-located for some important metal reserves, even though the main precious metal sources in the region lay much further to the west, to the north of Huelva and to the east, near Córdoba. Ancient workings have been found at El Galayo, some 3.5km to the north-west of modern Puebla de los Infantes, and approximately 10km to the north-east of Celti (Domergue 1987, 480, SE: 14) and it has been suggested that copper and possibly silver and gold may have been mined here. Further to the north west, ancient copper workings have been found at Gibla, 9km to the south-east of Constantina (Domergue 1987, 475, SE: 7).

Site Topography and Area

The site of ancient Celti has a very distinctive topography although it is difficult to know when this developed and to ascertain how much can be ascribed to either natural or cultural formation processes, or both. Given that there have been only a few excavations, it is difficult to be precise about the depth of stratigraphy across the town, rates of erosion and, ultimately, the morphology of the site where the ancient settlement developed. There is good reason to believe that like many sites in the region, much was formed from an accumulation of structures and cultural material throughout antiquity. In this sense it resembles a middle-eastern tell. As it survives today, the site takes the form of a natural theatre, defined by the river to the south and by high-rising ground to the west, north and east (Fig. 1.1c). This arrangment is not unique to Celti and can be paralleled at a number of sites in the region, such as La Torre de Aguila (ancient Siarum: Utrera, Sevilla), El Casar (ancient Salpensa: El Coronil, Sevilla), Cabezas de San Pedro (Fuentes de Andalucía, Sevilla), El Gandul (Alcalà de Guadaira, Sevilla) and Castulo (Linares, Jaén). Similarly, the area of the site, 26.3Ha, is well within the range of other ancient settlements in the region (Fig. 10.1), which oscillated between about 5.01 (ancient *Oducia* ?: Mesa de Lora, Sevilla), 22.2 (Cerro de San Pedro, Sevilla), 32.4 (ancient Obulcula: La Monclova, Sevilla) and exceptionally 115.5 (ancient Urso: Osuna, Sevilla).

The Pre-Roman Settlement (Phases 2–4)

Introduction (Fig. 10.1)

The region of Celti was in the heartland of the cultural complex known as Tartessos, the focus of which lay in the mineral-rich lands to the north of Huelva. A key feature of this and many ancient towns in southern Spain is their longevity of occupation. Sondages at a number of key sites in the middle and lower Guadalquivir valley in recent years have underlined this (summarised in Escacena Carrasco 1987a; id. 1989; Murillo Redondo 1994, 63–231). It is clear that some sites, like Sevilla, El Gandul (Sevilla), Carmona (Sevilla), the Colina de los Quemados (Córdoba) and Teba

la Vieja (Córdoba: ancient Ategua) were continuously occupied between the late Bronze Age and the Roman period. There were also sites like Setefilla (Sevilla) and Montemolín (Sevilla) which began in the later Bronze Age but which \were abandoned at around the 6th and 5th centuries BC. Others, such as the settlement beneath Santiponce (Sevilla: ancient Italica) first appear in the 4th century BC but continue into the Roman period. Since many excavations took the form of sondages, it is also difficult to say very much about the character of the settlements themselves and the degree to which they might be considered urban settlements.

Consequently, our understanding of settlement patterns in the lower Guadalquivir valley is very incomplete. Surveys have shown that the region was densely occupied during the first half of the 1st millennium BC but that only a small minority have been excavated (Ruíz Delgado 1985, 83–123; Amores Carredano 1982, 85–121; López Palomo 1981; Fernández Caro 1992, 180–4). It is thus difficult to make any sense of settlement patterns in the period prior to the arrival of Rome in the late 3rd century BC. Nevertheless, it has been suggested that the disintegration of Tartessos at the end of the 6th century BC brought about a major crisis with the abandonment of sites with predominately livestock and agricultural economies in the Sevillan campiña, while those settlements along the Guadalquivir river seemed to have been largely unaffected. Thereafter there is a broad continuity in settlement patterns down to the Roman period. Roman authors suggest that the main people in the region between the 6th century BC and the Roman conquest were the Turdetanians (Strabo 3.2.1; Keay 1992). Despite attempts to see a distinctive Turdetanian identity in the material culture of sites in the region (particularly the *cerámica fina ibérica*), there is no evidence that the Turdetanians were a distinct ethnic group (see Downs 1998; *pace* Escacena and Belén 1998). Immediately prior to the arrival of Rome, the Carthaginian interlude (227/226–205BC) seems to have made little impact, apart from the walling of Carmona (Jiménez 1989) in the lower Guadalquivir valley and the Castillo de Doña Blanca on the northern side of the Bahía de Cádiz.

The results from Celti and their implications

In this context, therefore, there were expectations that the survey and excavation work at Celti might shed light upon a key point in the development of the urban tradition in the lower Guadalquivir valley. In reality, however, restricted access to the pre-Roman levels of the site made it difficult to

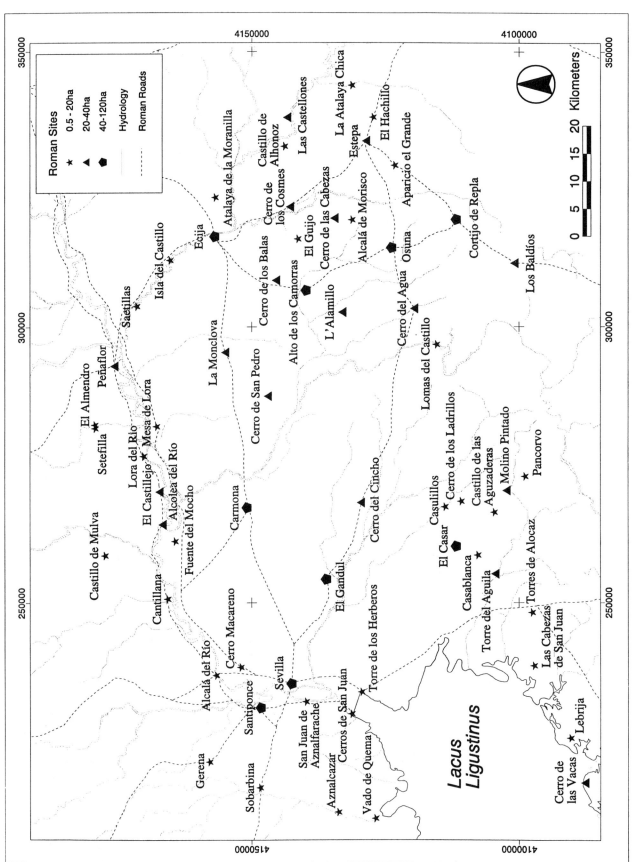

Fig. 10.1. Map showing the distribution of Roman urban settlements in the province of Sevilla

gain a clear understanding of the development and spatial organization of the settlement prior to the Roman period. Pottery from the Phase 2 context at the site suggests that the site was first established in the 9th century BC (Chapter 3), and that it continued in uninterrupted occupation through the 6th/5th centuries BC (Phase 4) down to the Augustan period. In other words, there is a fully representative range of ceramics from the 9th to late 3rd century BC period, although the nature of the archaeological record is such that there is no evidence that the site was not abandoned at any one time. The only material missing which is present at other contemporary sites like Setefilla and Carmona, is the imported Phoenician red-gloss pottery and other artefacts; but then again, the sample of material from pre–late 1st century AD contexts is comparatively small. Similarly, Carthaginian material is completely absent.

The excavations and survey tell us very little about the character and layout of the settlement during the pre-Roman period. However, consideration of the fairly wide distribution of surface materials of late Bronze and Iron Age date (Fig. 2.13 and 14) as well as the date of the earliest deposits in excavations in both the Pared Blanca and La Viña, suggest that the full 26.3 Ha was occupied, although the density or character of that occupation is unknown. At the same time excavations undertaken by Pérez Paz on the northern edge of the site suggest that the settlement may have been walled as early as the 7th and 6th centuries BC (Chapter 1), and perhaps again at a later stage (infra). It would perhaps be a mistake to assume that the site was densely or regularly occupied from inception. It is quite possible that early occupation may have been based upon small family groups occupying distinct foci within the broader site area. This seems to have been the case at settlements, such as Tejada la Vieja, Torre de Doña Blanca (Cádiz), Acinipo (Málaga) and Plaza de Armas de Puente Tablas (Jaén: Ruiz Rodríguez 1996), which were characterized by a lack of fortifications, circular houses and a predominance of handthrown pottery.

Analogy with sites like Tejada la Vieja, Plaza de Armas de Puente Tablas and others, suggests that a more intensive and organized use of internal space may have coincided with the walling of the site. This is certainly what seems to have happened in the province of Jaén in upper Andalucía, with the emergence of walled "oppida", like Torreparedones and Porcuna in the later 7th century BC (Ruiz Rodríguez 1996). However, confirmatory evidence from the site is lacking. The structures uncovered by excavation were simply too fragmentary to make

any sense. Again, analogy with sites with no later, Roman, structures like Tejada La Vieja (Huelva), Torre de Doña Blanca (Cádiz), Alhonoz (Herrera, Sevilla) and Cerro de la Cruz, (Almedinilla, Córdoba), suggests that the enclosed area of Celti may have been divided up into small irregular blocks composed of simple family-based houses. Public buildings were probably also absent, apart from the possibility of larger structures, which have been identified as "aristocratic houses". Prior to the Roman period, nothing is known about the location of cemeteries at Celti. Rich elite late Bronze Age tumulus burials of the type discovered at Setefilla and Carmona appear to be absent. Similarly, nothing is known of Iron Age burials. This is not altogether surprising, since there is so little evidence for any Iron Age cemeteries in the lower Guadalquivir valley. This is probably because the character of site of Iron Age cemeteries does not readily make them susceptible to archaeological detection. Some scholars, however, have gone as far as to suggest that this may be a cultural characteristic of the Turdetanian people (Escacena 1989; Escacena and Belén 1998).

If one accepts the premise that the Peñaflor site is to be identified with Celti, the etymology of the name, Celti, could be taken to suggest that there was some connection between the site and the settlements in northern Spain, where Celtic toponyms, anthroponyms and aspects of "Celtic" material culture were widespread (see for example Almagro Gorbea 1993). However, there was absolutely no evidence for the latter and, consequently, there would be little justification for suggesting that Celti was founded by "Celtic" populations moving southwards. Instead, the material culture of protohistoric Celti seems to have been entirely regional in character. Most of it is comprised by ceramics, with the exception of a single bronze brooch of Tartessian date (Chapter 5). Analysis of the former suggests that the inhabitants shared in well-developed regional traditions. In the later Bronze and early Iron Age transition, the inhabitants used and possibly manufactured a range of plain and burnished hand-thrown bowls, followed by burnished wheel-turned pottery, and richly painted wheel-turned vessels. Contrary to what had been anticipated not one single piece of red-slipped Phoenician pottery was found: its presence was characteristic of the Phoenician coastal colonies of the Gadir and the Mediterranean coast and it has also been found at neighbouring inland sites like Setefilla and Carmona (Belén 1986, 265). During the Iron Age, the inhabitants used a very full range of bowls, platters, casseroles and jars that were both plain and painted with simple horizontal black, red and brown lines. Analysis of all this material suggests that at least some of this was local, while much was manufactured somewhere in the region. Imports from further afield are rare (generally, see Chapter 4). The same can be said of the amphorae, which were in the Phoenicio-Punic tradition, and the contents of which are difficult to establish.

There is little known about the settlement pattern of which Celti was a part. Analogy with recent surveys undertaken in different parts of upper and lower Andalucía suggests that much of the population of the lower Guadalquivir valley was focused upon large settlements akin to the "oppida" of upper Andalucía. The position, regional resources and strategic location of Celti, suggest that it must have played a fairly key role in the region. It is highly possible that it had a notional territory that was defined by the Sierra Morena to the north, the Guadalquivir to the south, the river Guadalvacar to the west and the Retortillo to the east. Celti is the only major settlement within this area. However, there are a number of important neighbouring sites. On the north side of the river to the west lay Setefilla (Ponsich 1979, 79; Aubet Semmler *et alii* 1983) and the Mesa del Almendro (Ponsich 1979, 80; Bonsor 1931, 26) near the head of the Guadalvacar, and the Castillo de Lora (Ponsich 1974, 173). On the south side of the river lay the Mesa de Lora (Ponsich 1979, 35), to the south-west, and Saetillas (Stylow 1988) to the south-east. The nearest important site east of Celti on the north side of the river was Almodovar del Río (Ponsich 1979, 175). The survey of this region undertaken by Ponsich (1979) revealed no small "rural" sites. While it is possible that it may have missed some smaller pre-Roman sites, this apparent absence of smaller sites can be paralleled in other parts of the Guadalquivir valley. At face value, this may be taken to suggest that there was very little rural settlement in this area prior to the Roman period and that during the protohistoric period Celti may have acted as an agro-town, with its agricultural lands being worked by people who lived in the settlement itself. Analysis of the seed data from the excavations at Celti (Chapter 6) suggests that cereal production (grain and pulses) was the principal agricultural product of the region, with occasional vineyards and olive groves.

The Emergence of the Roman Town: the late 3rd century BC to the mid 1st century AD (Phases 5–6d)

Introduction

Until comparatively recently, it was generally believed that the Roman conquest ushered in a period of radical political, economic, social and cultural change in southern Spain. After the expulsion of Carthage in 206/205 BC and the creation of the *provincia* of Hispania Ulterior in 197 BC (Livy 32.27.6), Roman power is seen to have developed around an urban framework in the course of the later 3rd and 2nd centuries BC. This often tends to give the impression that the impact of Rome was sudden and deeply penetrating.

In reality, however, this view does not stand up to scrutiny. In the Guadalquivir valley, which lay at the heart of the Roman province of *Ulterior*, the Roman settlement pattern does not become firmly established until the middle and later 1st centuries BC. Prior to this date, centres of Roman power were established at Italica (Santiponce, Sevilla) and Corduba (Córdoba). The former was a settlement of Italic veterans at a pre-existing native settlement in 206 BC (Appian, *Ib*. 38. 153; Keay 1997), while the latter was a *colonia* comprising a mixed settlement of Romans and natives adjacent to a pre-existing native settlement in 169 or 152 BC (Strabo 3.2.1: Ventura *et alii* 1998, 88–91). In addition, a Roman sponsored settlement was established at Iliturgis (Cerro de Maquiz, Jaén: Arteaga & Blech 1987) in the upper Guadalquivir valley in 180–179BC. Apart from these, the literary sources allude to a number of settlements with Latin names, such as Castra Decuma and Castra Calpurniana. Many of these were probably military locations in native settlements created in the context of the raids by Lusitanians and other conflicts in the region during the 2nd century BC (Knapp 1977, 21–9).

It should be appreciated that these towns and other settlements would only have housed a relatively small population and that of this only a part would have been of Italic or Roman origin (generally, see comments in Keay 1995, note 22). The majority of the population would have continued to live in much the same way that they had done before the Roman conquest (see discussion in Keay 1998, 65). In those regions, like the upper and parts of the lower Guadalquivir valley, which were dominated by the so-called "oppida", populations would have continued to live in agro-towns. In other, more marginal areas, a significant proportion of the urban populations would have lived in small farmsteads (see for example the region around Siarum and Salpensa: Ruíz Delgado 1985). Nevertheless there is evidence that even these communities were gradually being brought into a closer economic relationship with Rome in the course of the 2nd and earlier 1st centuries BC. Towards the end of the 2nd century BC, a range of native towns issued bronze coins bearing the name of their community in Latin, Punic and southern Iberian alphabets (Villaronga 1994; Chaves 1998). These played some kind of role in tributary exchanges between native communities and Rome at a time when the monetization of the economy of the region had hardly begun. The appearance of imported italic black gloss pottery and Dressel 1 wine amphorae at Italica (Keay 1997 cit.) and particularly at Corduba (Murillo and Vaquerizo 1996) was also symptomatic of tributary exchanges and growing trade networks.

A much greater change in the urban structure of the region was initiated from the middle to later 1st century BC onwards. This was a period that saw the urban communities of the lower Guadalquivir valley being brought into a more systematically organized political, social, economic and cultural relationship with Rome. Following the conclusion of the Civil Wars, Roman colonies were established in the Guadalquivir valley and adjacent lands by Caesar and Augustus at Hispalis (Sevilla), Astigi (Écija), Urso (Osuna, Sevilla), Corduba (Córdoba), Itucci (?Torreparedones, Córdoba), Ucubi (Espejo, Córdoba) and Tucci (Martos, Jaén). At the same time municipal status was granted to a range of native towns in the region (see summary in Keay 1988, 85–6). All of these changes took place within a newly defined provincial framework, Hispania Ulterior Baetica, whose communities were linked together by a comprehensive road system and organized into four assize districts: the *conventus* hispalensis, cordubensis, gaditanus and astigitanus.

However, the total number of new Roman towns and their enhanced native counterparts was still low when compared to the majority of settlements in the region, whose populations must initially have been unaffected. This is borne out by an analysis of the archaeological evidence for the formalization of urban landscapes and the construction of public buildings in the Roman fashion at native towns in the province prior to the late 1st century AD (Keay 1988, 68–74). It suggests that it was piecemeal and that the transformation of urban landscapes did not really take place until the later 1st century AD.

The results from Celti and their implications

It is against this background that one needs to understand the results of the excavations at Celti. For this period, however, the remains are particularly difficult to interpret. In the excavated area, the Republican levels had been removed altogether. The only evidence for their existence comes in the form of abundant Turdetanian ceramics in later residual contexts and whose chronology covers the period between the 6th/5th and later 1st centuries BC. The survival of layers and structures of Augustan date (Phases 6 and 6a) was only marginally better, while virtually nothing survives of the period down prior to the middle/late 1st century AD (Phases 6c and 6d). All of this destruction must have taken place during the demolition and levelling-up that preceded the construction of the Phase 7a/b building. Notwithstanding this, however, there is enough circumstantial evidence to suggest that Rome's impact on the social, economic and cultural life of the Turdetanian town may have been both limited and gradual.

Celti is one of the many sites that are known to have produced bronze coins towards the later 2nd/earlier 1st centuries BC. It has long been suspected that the coins with the latin legend CELTITAN and image of a boar on the obverse (Villaronga 1994, 389) should be ascribed to Celti and, ultimately, to the site at Peñaflor. Although none were found during the excavations discussions with locals from the modern village made it clear that quite a few examples had been found by metal-detectors in the immediate vicinity of the site (Hoyuelos 1990, 530). Recent enquiries (J. Carranza, personal communication) suggest that they are most frequently found up to a distance of 200m away from the site on its north and west sides. These coins must be indicative of a response to the presence of Rome, both in the sense that they played some limited role in the financial reorganization of the region by Rome and in that they reflect a choice by the inhabitants to express their identity in Latin (see Chaves 1998, 167–9 and Keay 1996, 155–60) for alternative interpretations of the significance of these coins).

The absence of the stratigraphic record for the Republican period *per se* at the excavations means that it is impossible to know whether the internal organization of the site changed as a consequence of the advent of Roman control in the region. However, there is some limited evidence that the town was re-walled during the later Turdetanian or Roman Republican period. The cyclopean structure at the south-eastern corner of the site known as El Higuerón (Fig. 1.6) has been interpreted in a number of different ways, as part of the infrastructure for a bridge (Verdugo 1980, 204 note 10), the remains of a defensive structure (Chapter 1) or possibly even as platform for a crane (Amores & Keay 1999, 245 note 28). The character of the monument, as well as its position, suggests that it was most probably a defensive bastion, although this has not been firmly dated and cannot be related to any other stretch of wall along the southern part of the site.

Within the site, the excavations are our only real source of information. The only piece of evidence that might be significant consists of two column drums that were incorporated into a Phase

7b wall (E.36). This clearly belonged to a building of some pretensions but could just as well have belonged to buildings of Augustan (Phases 5, 6 and 6a), or Julio-Claudian date (Phases 6c and d), as to the Republican period. One argument in favour of the latter comes in the form of fragments of plain coloured wall-plaster from Phase 6d deposits (560) and (561). Indeed, it is only with the Augustan period that we really have any firm structural evidence, comprising two small and discrete groups of walling which may or may not have been related. The function of these cannot be readily gauged. However, it is possible that the sequence of walls at the eastern edge of the site (Area B: 562 and 568) and the large stone slab (561) may at some stage have formed part of a small tomb. The bones of a foetus were found mixed up in an adjacent context (299) which was created when the overlying 7a complex was built (Chapter 6). If this interpretation is correct, it is unclear whether this tomb belonged to the pre-7a phase of occupation or whether it was deliberately established as a ritual act immediately prior to the construction of the Phase 7a/b structure. Since infant burials are known in Iberian contexts in south-eastern Iberia (Guérin and Martínez Valle 1987–8), it seems reasonable to suggest that this was an indigenous tradition. Moreover, the presence of infant burials below the floors of houses are known from a number of Hispano-Roman towns (Celsa, Uxama Argaela and Ilerda) in north and eastern Hispania as late as the 1st century AD (García Merino and Sánchez Simón 1996; Mínguez 1989–90; Lorencio *et alii* 1987). This implies that continuation of the ritual into the Imperial period was quite common.

Virtually nothing is known of the location of the cemeteries that must have existed during this period. However, it is probable that they lay to the north and west of the site. As regards the former, an unpublished rescue excavation uncovered a cremation burial adjacent near the Polideportivo on the Carretera de La Puebla de los Infantes in 1990. This consisted of a painted terracotta funerary casket placed with a large *cerámica fina ibérica* bowl (Type 7), whose chronology extends into the Roman Republican period. In the field known as El Camello, to the west, a number of Turdetanian and Roman finds have come from here across the years (Chapter 1) and it seems likely probable that it was frequented in the Roman Republican period. One important piece of evidence consists of a stone lion which was discovered somewhere on the site and which is now conserved in the Museu Arqueològic de Barcelona. This type of sculpture draws upon deep-seated regional artistic traditions but probably dated to within the Roman Republican period (Fig.

1.9; Chapa 1984, 112–4, 148). It would have decorated the high-status tomb of some member of the town elite at this time.

It was only from the Augustan period onwards that there is any firm archaeological evidence for changes in the material culture of the town. It has already been made clear (Chapter 4) that the ceramic assemblage from the Augustan and later phases contains much residual material from the Iron Age and Republican periods. Within this, however, the imported italic Dressel I amphorae and black-gloss pottery characteristic of the 2nd and earlier 1st centuries BC only occurs in very small quantities. This is similar to the situation at the native settlement of the Cerro de la Cruz (Almedinilla, Córdoba: Vaquerizo Gil 1990). However, it stands in sharp contrast to the situation at Corduba (Ventura 1996) and both Roman centres and native sites along the eastern coast of Spain (see Carreté, Keay & Millett 1995, 257–9). For the Augustan and Julio-Claudian periods, by contrast, imported finewares, such as *terra sigillata italica*, South Gaulish *sigillata* and *sigillata hispanica* become more common. However, they were matched by the continued production of a limited range of *cerámica fina ibérica*, side-by-side with larger-scale imitations of *terra sigillata italica*. In other words, even though imports were available, the population at Celti had a clear preference for local interpretations of foreign forms. The same was true of some coarsewares: local or regional copies of *rojo pompeiano* were preferred over imported varieties.

These comments suggest that there was perhaps a degree of cultural conservatism amongst the population at Celti. The foundation of the Roman colonies at Hispalis, Astigi and Corduba may have introduced a range of new cultural forms and practices to the region. However, prior to the mid/later 1st century AD, the populations of native towns like Celti seem to have been reluctant to embrace them without question. This is particularly true of the practice of setting up inscriptions on stone to commemorate the achievement of local elites, the imperial house or Roman deities. It was integral to the spread of the Roman way of life at Roman *and* native towns during the course of the imperial period. In Baetica, the practice really begins under Augustus (Stylow 1998), and a number of inscriptions of Augustan and Julio-Claudian date have been found in both Roman colonies and Hispano-Roman towns. At Celti, however, the earliest inscriptions date to the late 1st century AD possibly reflecting a conscious choice not to adopt this very Roman form of public commemoration until comparatively late.

The picture that we have of Celti, therefore, suggests that there was little change in the internal organization and material culture of the site down to the Augustan period, with only limited cultural changes from that point onwards. By contrast, the evidence for the agricultural economy of the town does suggest that more deep-seated changes were afoot by the Augustan and Julio-Claudian periods. The presence of carbonized seeds from Augustan contexts (Chapter 6) indicates that olives and vines were being produced in the vicinity of the town and consumed at the town. This apparent change in the agricultural regime of the region can be equated with the first appearance of rural sites in the territory of Celti (Fig. 10.2; Ponsich 1979, 77–143) and in the neighbouring region to the southeast (Carrillo Diaz-Pines & Hidalgo Prieto 1990, Figs 4 and 5). In general terms, this is symptomatic of the appearance of rural sites throughout western Baetica, particularly in the hinterland of the newly established *colonia* of Hispalis (Sevilla), Astigi (Écija) and Corduba (Córdoba). However, they are still quite rare although it is possible that they have been under-represented. Archaeologists have tended to overlook rural sites with late *cerámica fina ibérica* and to rely solely upon *terra sigillata italica* as a way of characterizing them in field-surveys (Keay 2000).

Many of these farms were to become involved in the production of olive oil for markets at Rome, the frontiers and elsewhere in the Western Empire down until the middle of the 3rd century AD. This was carried in locally manufactured amphorae: initially the Oberaden 83 and later the Dressel 20. Some would also have been involved in the production of wine, although for a shorter period of time. It was transported in Haltern 70 amphorae, which were prolific at military and civil sites across the Western Empire until the Flavian period. The Haltern 70 was the more common of the two in pre-Phase 7a/b contexts at the site. Although a kiln site for these in the territory of Celti has yet to be found, the fact that they were produced at La Catria, near the neighbouring town of Oducia (Mesa de Lora, Lora del Río), suggests that one will soon be found. By contrast, Dressel 20s were rarer. Only a few fragments were discovered in Phase 7a/b contexts, suggesting that they were used and discarded at some time before the mid to late 1st century AD. On present evidence it seems likely that these were imported to the site from somewhere away from Celti, since local production of the container seems to have been largely a phenomenon of the 2nd and earlier 3rd centuries AD (see below).

Non-agricultural evidence for this period is scarcer. An analysis of animal bones from Phase 6 contexts at the site suggests that oxen were relatively rare and that sheep/goat and pig occurred in roughly equal proportions. If this sample is representative, it suggests that some dietary preferences at Celti during the Augustan and Julio-Claudian period were still largely unchanged and that Italian dietary habits had not yet begun to gain currency. One final characteristic of the site at this period is the occurrence of small nodules of iron-ore (Appendix 3). These are presumably symptomatic of small-scale iron-working at the site and were probably mined from deposits in the Sierra Morena, at some distance to the site. The nearest ancient sources of iron ore are to be found at the Cerro del Hierro (Domergue 1987, SE 6), in the vicinity of the ancient town of Munigua (Mulva: Domergue 1987, SE 15), and in the vicinity of the peak of La Lima (El Pedroso), to the north of Munigua (Domergue 1987, SE 11). At Celti, these iron-nodules are first documented during Phase 6. While it might be tempting to suggest that exploitation and working of iron-ore might be characteristic of this period, the smallness of pre-Phase 6 deposits means that one must not exclude the possibility that, given a larger sample, they might have been found in earlier periods. Recent work at Munigua, for example, has shown that iron-ore was being exploited here between the 4th and 2nd centuries BC (Domergue 1987, 480–1).

The Maturity of Roman Celti: The late 1st to the early 3rd centuries AD (Phases 7a and 8a/8b)

Introduction

It has long been recognized that this period was of key importance to the Roman province of Baetica. Drawing upon the developments that took place under Caesar and Augustus, the later 1st and 2nd centuries AD saw the extension of the Roman urban type across the province. In large measure, this was the result of a single political act under the Flavians: the grant of *ius latii* to all free communities in the province (and the rest of Hispania). In theory at least, this meant that every community was now recognized as a legally constituted municipality with the right to run its own affairs without direct intervention by Rome. Moreover, all magistrates and their families gained the Roman Citizenship after completion of their term of office. The reasons behind this concession are not clear and a range of different opinions have been voiced (discussed in Haley 1996 and Keay 1998, 62–3). The towns enfranchised at this time, together with the *colonia* and *municipia* of the Caesarian and Augustan periods, became the key nodes in an urban network that continued

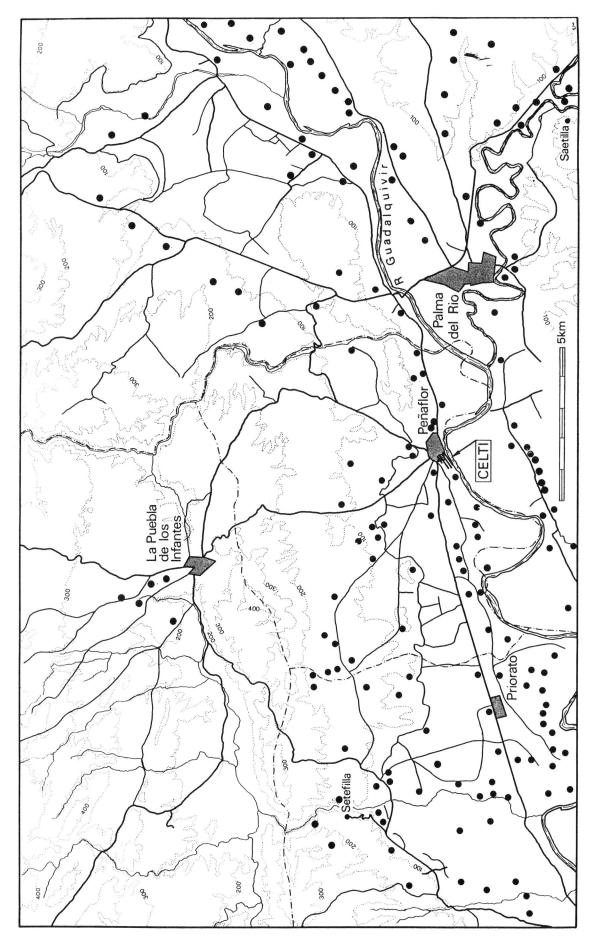

Fig. 10.2. Map showing the distribution of Roman rural settlements around Celti

largely without change down until the 3rd century AD.

In practice, however, there are a number of unresolved problems concerning these towns. In the first instance, it is not clear how many communities actually became *municipia*. Our only source of information for answering this question comes from inscriptions, whose discovery is fortuitous and the interpretation of which is often fraught with difficulties. This means that the total of Flavian *municipia* in Baetica is not known, but is continually rising as new inscriptions are discovered on new or known sites (see Keay 1998, 85–6 for an approximate list of currently known sites). Secondly, although the charters which laid down the rules for the running of these towns are now well understood (most recently, see the *lex irnitana*: González 1986), very little is actually known about the layout of the towns themselves. It is sometimes assumed that there would have been a simultaneous transformation of the topography of a particular town, or that it would have romanized its layout to the point where it was considered to have had sufficient *urbanitas* for it to warrant municipal status. So far, however, it has yet to be shown that this was generally the case. The only evidence comes from two sites: the Claudian *municipium* of Baelo and the Flavian *municipium* of Munigua. In both cases, municipal status seems to have anticipated or coincided with the monumentalization of each town along Roman lines (Sillières 1997 and Hauschild 1991 respectively). In other words, therefore, there is a clear need to establish how far the grant of municipal status to a community necessarily implied the romanization of the layout of the town and its material culture.

Another key feature of this period was the development of the Baetican olive oil industry. Ponsich (1974, 1979, 1987 and 1991) has clearly shown that in the course of the first two centuries AD, Roman rural settlement spread widely throughout the lower Guadalquivir valley, particularly on lower-lying agricultural lands between Hispalis and Isturgi (Andújar). A key product was olive oil. Some 100 kilns for the manufacture of Dressel 20 amphorae to carry the olive oil were produced on estates along the Guadalquivir between Hispalis and Corduba, and down the Genil as far as Astigi. The Guadalquivir river-ports of Ilipa Magna (Alcalá del Río), Arva (El Castillejo), Naeva (Cantillana), Canama (Alcolea del Río), Axati (Lora del Río), Celti, Detumo (Posadas ?) and Carbula (Almodovar del Río) were key centres in their export, finally leaving the province through Hispalis. Analyses of their stamps and several inscriptions have shown that estates on which the oil and amphorae were produced were owned by senators, some of whom had extensive social links to urban elites in the region. Analyses of the distribution of amphorae, their stamps and *tituli picti* around the Empire, show that the manufacture and export of olive oil began under Augustus and Tiberius, grew in the course of the 1st century AD and continued in strength down to the middle of the 3rd century AD. Estates in Baetica supplied Rome, the frontiers and a range of civil markets across the Empire (most recently, Remesal 1999 and Domergue 1999 for two opposing interpretations of the evidence).

Apart from Ponsich's great survey, and the excavation of a few kiln sites near the towns of Axati (Romo Salas and Vargas Jiménez [in press]) and Arva (Remesal *et alii* 1997), most research into the Baetican olive oil industry has either focused upon the analysis of individual Dressel 20 kilns, the distribution of their stamps and tituli picti in the lower Guadalquivir valley, or across the Empire (most recently: Monte Testaccio at Rome: Blázquez, Remesal & Rodríguez 1994, 12–3; the German Limes: Remesal 1997, 29–51; the British Limes: Carreras Monfort & Funari 1998, 257–68; the Spanish Mediterranean coast: Millet 1997, 76–98). There are thus a number of key issues in the relationship between Roman towns and olive oil production which remain unresolved. The most important of these concerns the relationship between individual towns and the 'industry' as a whole, rather than that between specific kilns or groups of kilns and the 'industry'. How important was the production, processing and export of olive oil in the economy of the river-ports along the Guadalquivir ? How far do the peaks and troughs in the supply of Dressel 20 and their stamps match rises and falls in the economic life of these towns ? In other words, how closely were the economic fortunes of Baetican towns tied to the commercialization and export of olive oil ?

The Results from Celti and their implications

It will be clear that answers to the questions posed above can only really come from an analysis of the archaeological evidence from the towns themselves. The importance of the results from Celti is that, for the first time, they provide us with the opportunity to do so. They allow us to explore a range of questions generated by analyses of a disparate range of sources of evidence from both within the province and outside. However, as in the analyses of previous periods, the archaeological evidence has some limitations. The manner in which the structures for the two key phases for the period in question (Phases 7a and 8) have survived is such that in neither case is their precise character clear. In the southern part of the excavated area, Phase 7b structures have been removed down to below floor level by sustained ploughing in recent years, while in the northern area they are masked by Phase 8 structures. This means that only the south of the Phase 7a/b and the north of the Phase 8 buildings survive, making their interpretation and relationship to one another difficult to understand. A consequence of this is that all traces of occupation debris between Phase 7a/b and 8 have been removed.

THE MID TO LATE 1ST CENTURY AD (PHASE 7A/B)

This period saw an important transformation of the western sector of the town (La Viña). Earlier structures were demolished and a large new complex was laid out just below the highest point of the site looking southwards over the river Guadalquivir (Fig. 9.10). Geophysical survey of this part of the site suggests that it was part of a fairly radical replanning of the area, with the new building being central to a new rectilinear street plan which contrasted with the alignment of other, presumably earlier, streets. The incompleteness of the archaeological evidence has meant that the definitive interpretation of this building has proved elusive. The surviving remains consist of an axially planned square building with a minimum width of 28.50m. Its southern side was defined by a series of rooms of which at least two provided communication between the street immediately to the south and the enclosed area beyond. At the centre of the south side was a larger room that was fronted by two columns. Within, the southern range of rooms opened onto an enclosed peristyle 24m wide by at least 24m long. Small rooms ran up the inside of the western side of the peristyle, while the arrangement to the east was less clear. For reasons discussed above the arrangement of space to the north was unclear.

The identification of this building was fraught with problems owing to the incompleteness of the evidence. One possibility is that this be identified with a large axial-peristyle building, while another is that it be identified with a major public building, possibly the forum of the town. The balance of the archaeological and architectural evidence tends to suggest the latter, even though there are some major objections from a legal standpoint (Chapter 9). This is not least because of the dominant position of the complex overlooking the river, the large scale of the terracing and construction involved and because there are few parallels for axial-peristyles in town houses in this part of Hispania on this scale and at this early date. The two alternative reconstructed fora suggested for this building suggested that it consisted of either

an *aula*, plaza, temple, basilica and tabernae, or, more simply, a temple, plaza and basilica. In the latter scenario, it is the large room fronted by two columns which is identified with the temple and analogy with other sites suggests that if this were correct then it might be identified with an *aedes augusti* and, consequently, identified with a cult of the Emperor.

If future work confirms that this was the forum of the town, it was clearly small. However, in terms of this and its reconstructed plan, it invites parallels with the smaller Flavian forum at Munigua and the larger Claudian forum at Baelo (Bolonia). Little is known about its internal decoration, since all the contemporary floors and walls above foundation level had been removed.

Apart from the changes in the western part of the town, little else is known about the topography of the town at this time. The geophysics indicates that the street-plan in the lower-lying areas further east was on a different alignment and thus suggests that either this part of the town was unaffected by major topographic changes at this date or that it underwent significant changes at a later date. Nothing is known about the location of any other public buildings that might have been constructed at this or later dates, such as public baths or a theatre. However, unpublished work immediately in front of the pig-sties in El Calvario to the north and in the Huerta de Pepe Higueras to the east of La Viña, suggests that these areas at least were residential zones. Finally, the systematic surface survey of the greater part of the urban area suggests that if it had not happened before, the late 1st century AD onwards saw most of its 26.3Ha in occupation. Nothing is known about the pre-Roman defences of the town, which one must have assumed to have lapsed by this date.

There were a number of other important changes in the cultural lives of the inhabitants that seem to have been simultaneous with this development. In the first instance, the elite at Celti chose this time to begin commemorating aspects of their lives in a public way by the erection of stone-cut inscriptions. In some ways, this is not surprising since the adoption of monumental writing was very much part of the Roman urban cultural package (Woolf 1996), and really only made sense once the town was organized and run along Roman lines. Thus several inscriptions dating to the later 1st century AD have come to light at Peñaflor through the years (Chapter 8). Another change which may be significant was in the nature of the animal bone assemblage at the site. This shows a lowering of the percentage of sheep and goat in favour of ox and pig, a dietary balance which is closer to that of central Italy than it had been in earlier periods

(Chapter 6), even if the proportion of ox was on the high side. At the same time, the population was also showing an increasing preference for fine table-wares imported from southern Gaul, Tarraconensis and eastern Baetica.

It will be clear from the above that the mid/late 1st century AD represented a major step along the road to the romanization of Celti. However, while the community may have felt the need to express their aspirations to *urbanitas* through the creation of the infra-structure necessary to support an active political and religious life along the Roman model, it is not absolutely clear that the town was also granted municipal status at this date. It is sometimes suggested that Celti must have been a *municipium* because it is cited first in a list of place names in the conventus hispalensis (Pliny *NH* 3, 11). However this is not a founded argument or a particularly reliable source of evidence for this kind of problem (see, for example, Mayer 1989). Although there is no unequivocal epigraphic evidence that Celti achieved municipal status in the Flavian period, there is indirect evidence that that this was probably the case. Stylow (1995) has recently suggested this on the basis of the evidence provided by the tombstone of Caius Licinius Lupus (Chapter 8: no. 23). This individual is recorded as a Roman citizen enrolled in the *Galeria* voting tribe. Stylow argues that while this is frequently taken to signify an Augustan date, it was quite common in some Flavian *municipia* in the more landlocked regions of Baetica, such as Celti, Iliturgicola (Cerro de las Cabezas, Córdoba) and Ilugo. Thus it could instead be an indication that the citizen community obtained municipal status during the Flavian period.

However, even if Celti did become a *municipium* at this time and there was a broadly simultaneous transformation in the organization of its urban space, the archaeological evidence does not necessarily support the notion that there was a wholesale trans-formation of other aspects of daily life in the town. For example, it is possible that the Phase 6 structure at the eastern end which was interpreted as a possible child-burial (supra: 200) was not an earlier burial which was destroyed upon the construction of the Phase 7a/b complex, but was instead a ritual burial contemporary with its construction. If so, this would suggest a foundation ritual for a Roman-style public building which had its origins in the pre-Roman Iron Age. Alternatively, in terms of the material culture of the site, the ceramic assemblage from the dump levels which were deposited during the construction of the Phase 7a/b complex was still dominated by native *cerámica fina ibérica*. While some forms were undoubtedly residual, others seem to have been new, indicating a preference for native styles well into the imperial period.

The transformation of the urban structure of Celti coincides with a major change in its agricultural economy, as the town becomes more integrated into a closer economic relationship with the rest of the province, and the Western Empire as a whole. This is most noticeable in the countryside. While there is no firm evidence for the extent of the territory of the town during this, or indeed, any other time in its history, it seems reasonable to suggest that, as in earlier periods, it may have lain between the river Retortillo to the east and the river Guadalvacar to the west (Fig. 10.2). An analysis of the chronology of settlements within this area mapped during Ponsich's survey of the region (1979, 76–143) suggests that there was a significant jump in the number of new rural sites in the period after AD 50. The figures are as follows:

Date at which site begins	Percentages
Turdetanian	3.26
Republican	1.08
Augustan	1.08
Augustan–AD50	6.52
AD 50+	11.95
4th century AD	7.60
Undated	68.47
N=75	

Although these figures are by no means exact, they are similar to those of a survey undertaken in the vicinity of neighbouring Palma del Río to the east (Carrillo Díaz-Pines & Hidalgo Prieto 1990, 52–55 and Fig. 6), an area which overlaps with the eastern sector of the proposed territory of Celti. Little is known about the character of the sites, since few have been excavated. However, recent rescue work at the 1st century AD site of Brazatortas (Alcalá de Guadaira), suggests that they were probably small farms (Romero Moragas 1991, Site 10). As one would expect, they occupy the rich soils of the vega, which would have been well-suited to a range of crops (see Chapter 1). The seed evidence from the excavations, however, suggests that olives and vines were now being produced on a much larger scale than before, possibly at the expense of cereals. Both were imported for domestic con-sumption at the town, although this does not preclude them also having been used for the production of olive oil for both domestic con-sumption and export. This rise in cash crops is paralleled by a decline in the presence of sheep/goat detected at the site. This may well reflect an intensification of the cash-cropping of olives and vines in the region, which would have involved sheep being pushed onto more distant and mar-ginal territory, with goats being kept nearby for meat and milk.

This evidence suggests that the mid/late 1st

century AD saw Celti intensifying is production of cash crops, presumably in an attempt to profit from the growing need of the Roman state for wine and particularly olive oil. This impression is consistent with that from other Flavian *municipia* in the conventus astigitanus to the south-east and could have been a consequence of the granting of municipal status to the town (see the evidence reviewed in Haley 1996). The traffic in wine, which had been underway since at least the Augustan period, was perhaps better developed with Type 14/Haltern 70 wine amphorae being particularly abundant in Phase 7a levels at the site. Type 20/ Dressel 20 amphorae are still rare at this point, perhaps because exploitation of olive oil was still on a relatively small scale in the territory of this particular town. Indeed, of at least eight Type 20/ Dressel 20 amphora kilns known from the proposed territory of Celti, only two had begun to function by this date:

1) *El Berro II* (Ponsich 1979, 91) was producing amphorae for export with the stamp LFS (Callender 1965, no. 857: Carreras Monfort & Funari 1998, no. 208: between AD 61 and 65)
2) *Cortijo de Mallena* (Ponsich 1979, 83) produced amphorae for export stamped AVIHR (Callender 1965, no. 164; Carreras Monfort & Funari 1998, no. 514: Flavian to Trajanic periods).

Although production was on a relatively small scale it was still in sufficient volume to reach markets in Britain. Aside from these important changes to the agricultural economy of the site, there is also evidence for the continued processing of iron-ore at the site at this period. One must also assume that this was the period when marble from the local quarries would have been exploited. One of these lay at Mayoraja (Ponsich 1979, 39), within the postulated territory of Celti but close to its western edge. The marble attributed to the Celti region is a distinctive limestone, pink/grey in colour with grey veins. It was used for inscriptions and altars at this site and elsewhere in the lower Guadalquivir valley (Amores Carredano & Keay 1999, 245).

THE LATE 1ST TO LATE 2ND CENTURY AD
The excavations provide no evidence for the development of the town during this period. The re-habilitation of the Phase 7a/b public building in the later 2nd/early 3rd centuries AD (Phase 8a) entailed the demolition and robbing of whatever archaeological evidence there might have been, a situation further exacerbated by late antique demolition and more recent plough-damage. There is little doubt, however, that occupation within the urban area of the site would have continued. The systematic surface-survey revealed that materials

of the 2nd and 3rd centuries, such as *sigillata clara A* and local imitations, local coarsewares and amphorae imported from the south coast of Baetica, and southern Gaul, were present across most of the site, while in the excavations they often appeared as residual material in later contexts. Moreover, unpublished excavations in the Huerto de Pepe Higueras, to the east of La Viña, uncovered part of a domus with impluvium (F. Fernández, personal communication) which may well date to this same period. Similarly, an unpublished decorated mosaic floor which may also date to this period has been found in front of the pig-sties at the south end of El Calvario.

Even though the evidence from the built-up part of the town is very thin, this can be supplemented in the first instance by that provided by burials found on the west, north and eastern sides of the town. Since none of these have been published in any form, it is very difficult to say how far these were simply occasional burials on roads leading out of the town, or whether they were rather more dense and merit the term cemetery. To the west of the town in the El Camello field, behind the Cuartel of the Guardia Civíl, there are reports of the discovery of 'cajas' (boxes – and presumably coffins or sarcophagi of some kind) of stone, marble and lead; some of these must date to the late imperial or Visigothic periods. To the north, most burials have been unearthed during works along the road from Peñaflor to La Puebla de los Infantes. Roman tombs of unknown type were recorded during the construction of the Polideportivo, about half a kilometre to the north of the site of Celti, while lead coffins were discovered another half a kilometre further north. Others, together with tegula burials, were discovered about 100m to the west of the Polideportivo. There are also reports of the discovery of a mausoleum and crypt in a field about 150m due north of the Calle Calvario at the northern edge of Celti.

The best known cemetery lies beneath modern Peñaflor, immediately to the east of the ancient town. The two fixed-points are the mausolea which still survive today. The better known of the two is that known as the Cortinar de las Cruces and which is to be found in the Calle Blas Infante at the eastern edge of the village. Less well known is that which survives as the Ermita de los Mártires, in the Calle Blancaflor. Both of these are unpublished but are probably of early imperial date. This seems to be confirmed in the case of the latter, given that it has been suggested that the inscription of Licinia Mancina (Chapter 8. no. 23) originated here. Less well known are the many tombs which are only known to us from their surviving inscriptions, which have been collected by different people in the village over the years. Indeed, most of the surviving inscriptions from Celti seem to have derived from this cemetery, thus providing us with a sample of the names and aspirations of some of the elite of Celti. The Fabii and the Aelii were amongst the leading families in the town. The latter were a particularly important clan in Baetica (Chic 1992) and one of those at Celti, Quintus Aelius Optatus (Chapter 8: no. 3), was involved in the production and shipping of olive oil. The Aemilii, Annii, Brutii, Caesii, Fulvii, Licinii, Lurii and Sempronii were less well represented on inscriptions. Like many Baetican towns, there was also evidence for some degree of social mobility between towns in the region, with individuals from Corduba (Córdoba: Chapter 8: no. 29) and Detumo (?Posadas: Chapter 8, no. 40) being commemorated. It is also quite significant that by the 2nd century, the inhabitants of Celti had developed a sufficiently strong sense of civic identity to have their *origo* at Celti preserved in their own *cognomina*, Celtitanus (Chapter 8: no. 5) and Celtitana (Chapter 8: no. 14). None of the inscriptions from the cemetery area or elsewhere in the town date to any later than the end of the 2nd century and many, curiously enough, seem to have been recut on earlier inscriptions and architectural fragments.

The main development in the history of Celti during the 2nd century, was its increased involvement in the production and commercialization of olive oil. Many of the rural sites which appeared after c. AD 50 will have continued in occupation and have concentrated upon the cash-cropping of olives, probably at the expense of vines. Our main source of evidence for this comes from an analysis of the distribution of Type 20/Dressel 20 amphora kilns in the territory of the town and the chronology and distribution of stamped Type 20/Dressel 20 amphorae. This suggests that between roughly the 140s and 180s AD the production of olive oil from the *territorium* of Celti was at its height, reaching a range of civil and military markets in North Africa, Italy, Gaul, Germany and Britain. It should be stressed, however, that Celti never seems to have achieved the kind of prominence in this trade that was enjoyed by other neighbouring towns, such as Arva and, to a lesser extent, Axati. It is probable that other economic activities, which leave a less distinct archaeological trace – such as the processing and export of iron ore and the distribution of marble – may have been an important supplement to its economy.

At least eight Dressel 20 have been found so far in the territory of the town. The most important group is to be found at El Cortijillo (Embarcadero) (Ponsich 1979, 102; Chic 1985, 53–54; Blanco Ruiz 1987), on the banks of the Guadalquivir at the south-western corner of the town. The kilns here produced a range of stamped amphorae dating to around the middle of the 2nd century AD, some of which were quite common, such as those of Q(uintus) F(ulvius) C(arisianus) (Callender 1965, no. 1449: Carreras Monfort & Funari 1998, no. 195: AD 149), and G(...) N(...) AC(...) (Callender 1965, no. 401; Carreras Monfort & Funari 1998 no. 327: AD 142–65), while others were rarer, such as OTV, CIB and SFE.

In the *territorium* of Celti, seven Dressel 20 kilns were in use during the 2nd century AD. Two, which had already begun in the later 1st century AD, continued. These were:

1) *Cortijo de Mallena* (Ponsich 1979, 83): this now produced amphorae stamped LFFV (Callender 1965, 853d: AD 140/180) and possibly GRVMESE (Callender 1965, 467: later 2nd/early 3rd century AD).
2) *El Berro II* (Ponsich 1979, 91): this now manufactured amphorae stamped DIA (Callender 1965, no. 535: Remesal 1997, no. 157: mid 2nd century AD).

During the 2nd century AD, new kilns were located at the following sites:

1) *La Botica* (Ponsich 1979, 99): this produced the stamp IVL V IRBIC (Callender 1965, 778)
2) *Cortijo de María* (Ponsich 1979, 85): this produced amphorae stamped DIA (Callender 1965, no. 535 = Remesal 1997, no. 157: mid 2nd century AD), and possibly MST/// (Callender 1965, no. 1181, pre-dating the end of the Antonine period) and QCCH (Callender 1965, no. 1428b: AD 80–130).
3) *Cortijo de María NE* (Ponsich 1979, 86): this produced amphorae stamped VIG, BROITAITAE (Callender 1965, no. 206) and ATITTAE (Callender 1965, 1547: second half of the 2nd century AD).
4) *El Tesoro* (Ponsich 1979, 71): this produced amphorae stamped QIC and HOPL.
5) *Cortijo del Instituto* (Ponsich 1979, 109): this produced the stamp L ATECTREIN (ATE and EIN ligatured).

There is as yet no consensus as to the significance of the names represented on the stamps of the Dressel amphorae. One school of thought suggests that they refer to the owner of the olive oil carried in the amphora (Remesal 1998, 190). In this context, the stamping of the vessel was the first stage in the monitoring of olive oil by the Roman State in order to ensure a steady supply to Rome and the frontiers (Remesal 1997). An alternative and less *dirigiste* model suggests that the stamps alluded to someone involved in the manufacture of the amphora itself (Domergue 1998, 210–11), and that stamping was part of the commercialization of the oil on open markets within the Empire. Either way, the individuals named on the stamps are a clue as to the status of individuals who probably held agricultural or commercial interests in the region of the town. However, one cannot be sure that Celti was necessarily the *origo* of all of them. Quintus Fulvius Carisianus, whose stamped products (QFC) were manufactured at El Cortijillo, was probably a resident of neighbouring Arva, given that on an inscription from that town he is named as both its patron and pontifex (CIL II 1064=CILA 2: no 119[AD 149]). Alternatively, there is the case of Quintus Aelius Optatus (Chapter 8: no. 3), one of the most well-known people to have been commemorated on inscriptions from Celti (Thevenot 1952), and who was involved in the commercialization of olive oil from Baetica to Narbo (Narbonne) and Rome. It is likely that Celti was his *origo*, although one cannot be certain, given that the Aelii Optati were an extensive family and are attested at a number of towns in the region (Chic 1992). Nevertheless, assuming that he was, it is interesting to note that stamped amphorae bearing his name (Q.AE OPTATI and Q AE OPCOL) were not manufactured in the hinterland of Celti, but at the kilns of La Catria and El Castillejo in the hinterland of the neighbouring town of Oducia instead. This suggests that, as in other parts of the Roman world, the property of Celtitanian elites like Quintus Aelius Optatus could be spread over quite a wide geographical area.

THE LATE 2ND TO EARLY 3RD CENTURIES AD (PHASES 8A AND B)

At some time around the late 2nd/early 3rd centuries AD, the Phase 7a/b public building in La Viña underwent a major transformation. One imagines that a number of structures must have been demolished while others would have been retained. The 28.50m wide building lot was then divided into two roughly equal zones by a north–south dividing wall and it is clear that each of these was now occupied by a private domus. In the house to the west (House A) the space which had been occupied by the colonnaded square of the Phase 7a/b building was now given over to a small square courtyard surrounded by rooms immediately to the west and north. Little is known about the arrangement to the south, owing to the destruction of everything down to Phase 7a/b foundations. However, one imagines that the Phase 7a/b rooms must have rehabilitated in some way, possibly with a view to making them axial along an axis running north–south through the centre of

the peristyle. In the house to the east (House B), the site of the colonnaded Phase 7a/b square was filled by a larger rectangular peristyle. This was surrounded by a passage to the east, rooms to the north and a simple colonnade to the west: one imagines that the arrangement of rooms to the south was similar to that of House A. Nothing is known of the layout of the northern sector of the house. Little survives of the internal decoration of the house. There is some evidence that one or both were graced with a mosaic floor, while an analysis of the wallplaster suggests that they were also decorated with some sophistication, including panels that imitated African marble and Egyptian porphyry.

If one assumes for a moment that the Phase 7a/b structure had been a large axial peristyle house, then this development represents the re-development of a large residential property by a member of the elite at Celti. It implies a change in ownership and considerable outlay by the new owner(s). Indeed, it is even possible that this was one single house with two peristyles rather than two houses each with their own peristyle. If, however, it proves to have been the forum or another important public building (Chapter 9), it points to a major re-planning of the town centre at this time.

Either way, the archaeological evidence from within the town, implies that in economic terms, Celti was flourishing well into the 3rd century AD. This can be supported by the ceramic evidence, with imported and locally produced *sigillata clara* C and African amphorae of 3rd to 4th century AD date appearing in residual Phase 9 contexts. An analysis of animal bones suggest that by this date also, the dietary preferences of the population had changed quite considerably, with pig now dominating the assemblage in proportions not dissimilar to those on contemporary Italian sites. An alternative, and less preferred, interpretation would be that the construction of the houses in Phase 8a marked an important stage in the decline of civic consciousness at a time when the export of olive oil from the *territorium* of Celti had peaked. This could be supported by the absence of any inscriptions at the site dating to after the end of the 2nd/beginning of the 3rd centuries AD. However, it should be remembered that the sample of inscriptions was small and that since most were derived from the eastern cemetery, it was not representative of the full chronological range of inscriptions from the town.

An important support to the notion of continued urban vitality at Celti until at least the middle of the 3rd century AD is implied by one piece of epigraphic evidence. One of the latest inscriptions from the site was the tombstone of Fabia Sempronia Aciliana Celtitana, daughter of Marcus (Chapter 8: no. 14). In

Chapter 8 it was suggested that her father may have been the Marcus Fabius Basileus Celtitanus who dedicated an inscription to his son Marcus, a *flamen divorum augustorum provinciae Baeticae*, in the provincial forum at Corduba in AD 215 or 216 (CIL II ²/₇, 295). The link between father, daughter and the town of Celti is clear and provides an index of the powerful social and political heights that the Fabii from the town had achieved by the earlier 3rd century AD. This interpretation is reinforced by the suggestion that the distinguished senator L. Fabius Cilo Septiminus Catinius Acilianus Lepidus Fulcinianus (Caballos 1990, 132–5) may well have had a Baetican origin and that he may have been a member of the family of Fabia Sempronia Aciliana Celtitana. Some kind of close family connection seems to be implied by the discovery of Dressel 20 amphora stamps L(ucius) F(abius) C(ilo) C(larissimus) V(ir) (Callender 1965, 851; Remesal 1997, 112) from the Cerro de les Pesebres (=Ponsich 1979, no. 152: Cortijo bajo del Serno; =Chic 1985: no. 26: El Molino). This man had led a very full and distinguished career under Marcus Aurelius and Commodus, becoming consul *designatus* in AD 192 and consul *suffectus* in AD 193 and subsequently playing an important role in imperial affairs under Septimius Severus; he died a few years after AD 212. This epigraphic evidence for the importance of the Fabii, when taken in conjunction with the suggested significance of the construction of the Phase 8 house, suggests that Celti was an active municipality with some economic weight in the province during the early 3rd century AD.

There is little support, therefore, for the idea that Celti was in decline at this date. From as early as the late 1st century AD, the production and commercialization of olive oil had come to play an important, although not exclusive, role in its economy. This reached a high point in the later 2nd century and probably continued into some time after the first quarter of the third century AD. Unfortunately some of the evidence from rural surveys in the region is not susceptible to the sufficiently fine analysis necessary to confirm or deny this interpretation. Nevertheless, there is little that argues to the contrary.

Celti in Late Antiquity

Introduction

In common with many other parts of the Western Roman Empire, the period between the early 3rd and 7th centuries AD witnessed a number of profound changes in the administrative, political and economic life of Baetica. One of the oldest provinces of the Roman west was gradually marginalized and transformed from being a key player in the political and economic life of the Empire into a relative backwater for whose control there were eventually power struggles between Rome, Germanic kings, regional leaders and the Byzantine Empire.

The first blow to Baetica's primacy came towards the middle of the 3rd century AD when, for reasons that are still unclear, it ceased to be the chief supplier of olive oil to Rome and the frontiers (Padilla Monje 1989, 31–7). Later, as a consequence of the reorganization of the Hispanic provinces by Diocletian (AD 284–305), Corduba was passed over as the capital of the *diocesis hispaniarum* in favour of Emerita Augusta, the capital of Lusitania (Arce 1988). In the disorder following the invasion of the Alans, Sueves and Vandals into Hispania in AD 409, Baetica soon passed out of Roman control. It was first seized by the Siling Vandals (between AD 409–411), then the Hasding Vandals (AD 421–9), and the Suevi (AD 446–458/9), before being integrated into the Visigothic Kingdom in AD 458–459 (Hydatius, *Continuatio*, 192). Visigothic control of the province was not fully consolidated until the reign of King Leovigild (AD 569–586), and the province was the scene of wars between rival Visigothic factions and between Visigoths and the Hispano-Roman population (generally, see Salvador Ventura 1990, 24–74). It was as a result of one of these internal feuds that southern Baetica was eventually conquered by the Byzantines in AD 551 and remained a Byzantine province until AD 624.

One of the key issues over this 400 year period is the changing nature of Hispano-Roman towns. Owing to a dearth of archaeological research into the late antique period in Baetica, most of what is known has been derived from an analysis of the historical and epigraphic sources (Padilla Monge 1989; Salvador Ventura 1990). These make it clear that the autonomous network of towns that had developed in the course of the early imperial period underwent some fairly radical changes as the administrative structure of the Roman Empire itself changed. Essentially, however, it remained intact so that by the Visigothic period the Hispano-Roman towns still formed the framework through which the Visigothic Kingdom governed the region. Archaeological research has begun to shed light on aspects of this process. At Baelo and Munigua, for example, it has showed how the character and function of both towns had begun to change by the later 2nd and 3rd century AD (Sillières 1993). On a broader scale, an analysis of the available archaeological and historical sources has highlighted displacement of some towns by large villas as alternative centres of power in an increasingly ruralized and regionalized province (Padilla Monge 1989). However, many other questions remain. For example, little is known about the extent to which Hispano-Roman towns remained centres of population through into the Visigothic period. Very little is known about their physical appearance, apart from the more obvious observation that their classical topography gradually ceded place to one dominated by Christian basilicas and eccelesiastical buildings. Even less is known about the ways in which the passage of Roman, to Suevic, Visigothic and Byzantine control in the province might have had an impact upon the cultural, economic and social lives of the Baetican towns. Finally, the little that is known about the economy of towns is gleaned from the Visigothic Laws and literary sources like St Isidore of Seville.

The Results from Celti and their Implications

The archaeological evidence from Celti has the potential to shed light on some of these issues. For the first time in the lower Guadalquivir valley, a sequence of deposits and structures dating to between the 3rd and at least the 5th centuries have been excavated in open-area in an attempt to understand something of the nature of the late Roman and Visigothic town. These have revealed an important abandonment sequence and some key ceramic deposits have been found at the northern part of the site. However, as with previous phases, the interpretation of these has been complicated by post-depositional processes and the character of the surviving evidence. Very extensive stone robbing in the medieval and post medieval periods as well as heavy ploughing and further robbing in recent years has removed much of the site down to Phase 7a/b foundations in the southern and central parts of the site.

EARLY 3RD TO EARLY 5TH CENTURIES AD
The systematic surface-survey of most of the site (La Viña and El Calvario fields) suggests that by the 5th century AD the occupied surface area of the site may have contracted quite significantly: there is no evidence for the rewalling of the town. Ceramics (*sigillata Clara C, D* and amphorae), dating to between the 3rd and 5th centuries AD, were found over a much more restricted area than under the early Empire. A similar development has been recorded in the *nova urbs* of Italica (Rodriguez Hidalgo, Keay, Jordan & Creighton 1999). While it is tempting to equate this with a more restricted area of activity on the site, it should be remembered that the level of pottery supply in the late antique period was much lower than

during the early Empire (Carreté, Keay & Millett 1995, 52–62). More recent research suggests that, in turn, this may be due to the changing nature of fineware types and the ways in which surface material should be quantified (Hawthorne 1998).

Within this more restricted area of activity, the excavations were the only source of evidence. They suggest that the Phase 8a house continued in occupation throughout this period without interruption. There was no accumulation of 3rd or 4th century occupation debris, which indicates that the peristyles, and some of the rooms must have been in constant use and kept clean. On the other hand, there were indications of major structural changes, which point to the changing tastes and requirements of the owner. At some time during the 3rd and 4th century AD, for example, two water tanks were added to the eastern peristyle and another one to its western counterpart (Phase 8b). Surface indications on the semi-circular tank suggest that here at least there were successive *opus signinum* relinings of the interior and successive painted and marble surfaces of the exterior. There were also indications that the inter-columnar screens were restored and re-surfaced with new layers of plaster several times in the course of the 3rd and 4th centuries AD. At some time later (Phase 8c) the drainage system at the eastern edge of the eastern peristyle was modified.

Although it is limited, this evidence argues for continuity of occupation within a changing urban milieu rather than decline. This is buttressed by the presence of sherds of 3rd and 4th century finewares, amphorae and coarseware which appear in residual 5th century contexts, and show that the town continued to form part of broader commercial networks in the province (Chapter 4). Towards the middle of the century, Celti, like many municipalities along the Guadalquivir, would have been affected to some degree by the disappearance of the Dressel 20 and large-scale Baetican olive oil export in the western Empire. For example, it is recorded that the Dressel 20 amphora kiln of El Cortijillo at Celti was abandoned in the mid 3rd century AD (Blanco Ruiz 1987). However, the significance of this can be over-estimated when it is remembered that oil production continued on a lesser scale into the 4th century and beyond and was transported in smaller Dressel 23 and similar amphorae (Keay 1984). Moreover, the excavations at Celti revealed African amphorae being imitated locally. There is no evidence as yet for these being manufactured at any of the old Dressel 20 kilns in the *territorium* of Celti. It would be interesting to see whether there was evidence for production of this form at Celti itself, given that an example was found in a residual early 5th century AD context

(Phase 9) and that the excavations of the El Cortijillo kiln have yet to be published.

THE EARLY 5TH CENTURY AD ONWARDS (PHASES 9 AND 10)

At some time in the early 5th century AD for the Phase 8 house was abandoned. Evidence for this was found throughout the building. Along the eastern portico of the eastern peristyle, the roof fell in leaving a dense spread of tiles spilling over the inter-columnar screen into much of the eastern side of the garden area. Phase 8a drains and some of the Phase 8b water-tanks show evidence of filling with sediment as they were not cleaned and maintained. At the same time, or subsequently, a process of fairly systematic robbing affected much of the building. For example, the western portico of the eastern house was completely robbed away, leaving a long north–south robber trench. Within the garden of the eastern peristyle, much of the *opus signinum* surfacing was robbed away, while within the semi-circular tank lead fittings were robbed out. Much of this and other robbed debris, including *opus spicatum* flooring, wall-plaster, ceramics, mud-brick, brick, tile and occasional pieces of glass and metalwork were then dumped into the old Phase 7a/b deep rooms, which ran along the south side of the building. There is evidence that this was done systematically, with building and domestic rubble being tipped into Room 7 and wallplaster into Rooms 4 and 5.

The effect of this whole process was to level the surface of the Phase 8 house to create some kind of building platform. In other words, although it involved the destruction of the house, it was undertaken in order to prepare the site for a new role. In our present state of knowledge it is impossible to discover what this may have been. All that can be said is that at some time after the house had been demolished, a new building was constructed (Phase 10). This was recorded in the north-western part of the site where it overlaid part of the Phase 8 building. However, it owed little to this in either construction technique or orientation. It is very likely that it continued over much of the rest of the Phase 8a house to the east, but removal of the upper layers of this by ploughing have destroyed all evidence. This building cannot be dated chronologically, as there were no associated ceramic deposits. Nor is it possible to know how long it remained in use – although the latest pottery from the site dates to the 6th or 7th century AD.

The structural evidence, therefore, points to a significant break in Roman cultural traditions at the site. The meaning of this is hard to interpret. It would be all too easy to ascribe it to the advent of germanic influence. After all, Celti was very close to at least one important historical event. Between AD 438 and 448, there was a major conflict in the vicinity of the river Genil between the Suevi led by King Rechila and an army led by Andevotus, a rich regional landowner (Isidorus, *Historia Suevorum* 85; García Moreno 1979). While it is tempting to relate this to the archaeological evidence, the link is far too tenuous and it is difficult to see any causal relationship. It should also be pointed out that there is as yet no evidence for Visigothic material culture at the site, whether it be inscriptions, metalwork, coins or ceramics. Instead, the material culture from the site points towards a continuity of the late Roman tradition. It suggests that as in earlier periods, Celti was still integrated into the broader commercial circuits of the province as a whole. Small quantities of African *sigillata clara D* and African amphorae were present. At the same time, however, local potters were producing copies of these side by side with a range of local coarseware types. Some of these were apparently still inspired by the *cerámica fina ibérica* tradition of the pre-Roman and Roman Republican periods. Similarly, changes in the animal bone assemblage which see a recovery in the proportion of sheep/goat to pig, can be paralleled at a number of late Roman sites in Baetica and in other parts of the late Roman west Mediterranean (Chapter 6).

There is virtually no evidence for the nature of the rural economy at this time. The level of recording on rural surveys was not really sensitive enough to allow more than note the presence of 4th or 5th century AD *sigillata clara* at occasional sites in the *territorium* of Celti (Ponsich 1979). At the same time, the animal bone assemblage at the site suggests that in the surrounding countryside, cash-cropping may have declined in favour of ranching, pasturing and, by implication, a return to the increased cultivation of grain. There is no evidence for the production or export of olive oil. It is also very difficult to get any clear idea of the longevity of occupation of those rural sites documented in the 4th and 5th centuries. It seems likely, however, that they may have continued into at least the early 7th century AD, given the reference to what must have been a rural church in the II Hispalensian Council of AD 619 (see Chapter 1).

Bibliography

This bibliography includes references to works which are cited in W/Chapters 1–3.

Abbreviations

AE: *L'Annee Epigraphique.* Paris (1888 onwards)

Atlante I: Carandini, A. and Tortorella, S. *Atlante delle forme ceramiche I. Cerámica fine romana nel bacino mediterraneo (medio e tardo impero). Enciclopedia dell'arte antica.* Roma (1981).

Atlante II: Hayes, J. Mezquiriz, M.A., Mazzeo Saracino, L. M., Ricci, A. and Pucci, P. *Atlante delle forme ceramiche II. Ceramica fine Romana nel bacino Mediterraneo (tardo ellenismo e primo imperio). Enciclopedia dell'arte antica.* Roma (1985).

CIL II: Hübner, E. *Corpus Inscriptionum Latinarum, Volumen Secundum. Inscriptiones Hispaniae Latinae.* Berlin (1869).

CIL II Suppl: Hübner, E. *Corpus Inscriptionum Latinarum, Voluminis Secundi Supplementum. Inscriptionum Hispaniae Latinarum Supplementum.* Berlin (1892).

CIL II ^{2}/7: Stylow, A. (ed.), *Corpus Inscriptionum Latinorum. Volumen Secundum. Inscriptiones Hispaniae Latinae Editio Altora. Pars VII. Conventus Cordubensis* (CIL II ^{2}/7). Berlin (1995)

CILA 2.1: González Fernández, J. *Corpus de Inscripciones Latinas de Andalucía.* Volumen II: Sevilla. Tomo I. *La Vega (Hispalis).* Sevilla (1991).

CLE: *Carmina Latina Epigraphica.* Leipzig (1895–7).

HAE: *Hispania Antiqua Epigraphica.* Madrid (1953 onwards)

HEp: *Hispania Epigraphica.* Madrid (1989 onwards).

IGME: *Instituto Geológico y Minero de España. Mapa Geológico de España. E. 1:200,000. Síntesis de la cartografía existente. Córdoba. Segunada Edición.* Madrid (1980).

ILER: Vives, J. *Inscripciones Latinas de la España Romana* (2 vols). Barcelona (1971–1972).

LRBC: Carson, R., Hill, P. and Kent, J. *Late Roman Bronze Coinage,* London (1976).

RIC III: Mattingly, H. and Sydenham, E. *The Roman Imperial Coinage. Antoninus to Commodus,* London: 1930.

RIC IV.I: Mattingly, H. and Sydenham, E., *The Roman Imperial Coinage. Valerian to Florian,* London (1927).

RRC: Crawford, M. *The Roman Republican Coinage* (2 vols). Cambridge (1974).

Abad Casal, L. *El Guadalquivir, via fluvial romana.* Sevilla (1975).

Abad Casal, L. "Estratigrafía en la "Casa de las columnas," in AAVV, Italica (Santiponce Sevilla). Excavaciones Arqueológicas en España 121(1982): 133–203.

Abad Casal, L. *Pintura Romana en España.* Seville and Alicante (1982a).

Adam, J-P. *Roman Building: materials and techniques.* London (1994).

Aguarod Otal, C. *Ceramica Romana importada de cocina en la Tarraconense.* Zaragoza (1991).

Alarcão, J. Mayet, F. and Moutinho, A. *Fouilles de Conimbriga VI: Ceramiques diverses et verres.* Paris (1976).

Alarcão, J. de and Etienne, R. *Fouilles de Conimbriga. I. Architecture.* Paris (1977).

Alarcão, A., Étienne, R. & J. Colvin J. Cl., 1997, "Le forum de Conimbriga: réponse à quelques contestations," in R. Étienne & F. Mayet (eds). *Itineraires Lusitaniennes. Trente années de collaboration archéologique luso-frncaise.* Paris (1997): 49–68.

Albertos Firmat, Mª L. (1964). "Nuevos antropónimos hispánicos," *Emerita* 32 (1) (1964): 209–52.

Allen, K. M. Green, S. W. & Zubrow, E. B. W. (eds.) *Interpreting Space: GIS and Archaeology.* London (1990).

Almagro Gorbea, M. "Los Celtas en la Península Ibérica: orígen y personalidad cultural," in M. Almagro Gorbea and G. Ruiz Zapatero (eds.), *Los Celtas: Hispania y Europa.* Madrid (1993): 121–73.

Alonso de la Sierra, J. "Cerámicas africanas en Munigua y el valle del Guadalquivir," *Madrider Mitteilungen* 39 (1998): 239–97.

Altuna, J. and Mariezkurrena, K. "Estudio arqueológico de los restos oseos hallados en las excavaciones romanas de Lugo," in A. Rodríguez Colmenero (ed.), *Lucus Augusti, el almanecer de una ciudad.* Coruña (1996): 55–106.

Alvarez Saénz de Buruaga, J. "Una casa romana con valiosas pinturas, de Mérida," *Habis* 5 (1974): 169–87.

Amberger, G. "Tierknochenfunde vom Cerro Macareno/Sevilla." *Studien über frühe Tierknochenfunde von der Iberischen Halbinsel* 9 (1985): 76–105.

Ambrosio de Morales, A. *Antigüedades de las ciudades de España.* Archivo de la Real Academia de la Historia (undated).

Amores Carredano, F. *Carta arqueológica de los Alcores.* Seville (1982).

Amores Carredano, F. & Keay, S. "Producciones tipo Peñaflor," in M. Roca Roumens & M. I. Fernández García, *Terra Sigillata Hispánica. Centros de fabricación y producciones altoimperiales.* Málaga (1999): 235–52.

Anon. *Informe sobre la afectación del nuevo trazado del F.C. Córdoba-Sevilla en el Bien de Interés Cultural "Ciudad Romana de Celti" Peñaflor.* Sevilla (undated).

Armitage, P., and Chapman, H. "Roman mules," *London Archaeologist* 3 (1979): 339–46.

Aranegui, C. 1980, "Contribución al estudio de las Urnas de tipo Cruz del Negro." *Saguntum* 15 (1980): 99ff.

Arce, J. "Mérida tardorromana (284–409 d.c.)," in J. Arce, *España entre el mundo antiguo y el mundo medieval.* Madrid (1988): 190–210.

Arteaga, O. "Excavaciones arqueológicas en el Cerro del Mar (Campaña del 1982)," *Noticiario Arqueológico Hispánico* 23 (1985): 195–233.

Arteaga, O. & Blech, M. "La romanización en las zonas de Porcuna y Mengíbar (Jaén)," in AAVV, *Los asentamientos ibéricos ante la romanización.* Madrid (1986): 89–99.

Arthur, P. and Williams, D. 1981, " 'Pannonische Glasierte Keramik': An assessment," in A. C. Anderson and A. S. Anderson (eds.), *Roman Pottery Research in Britain and North-West Europe. Papers presented to Graham Webster.* British Archaeological Reports International Series 123 (ii). Oxford (1981): 481–510.

Atienza Páez,R. "Inscripciones funerarias latinas en la Alcazaba de Málaga," *Málaga* 11 (1971): 31–48.

Atencia Páez, R. and Serrano Ramos, E. "El taller antikariense de terra sigillata hispánica," in AAVV, *Figlinae Malacitanae. La producción de céramica romana en los territorios malacitanos.* Málaga (1997): 177–215.

Aubet Semmler, M. E. "La Mesa de Setefilla: la sequencia estratigráfica en corte 1," in M. E. Aubet Semmler (ed.), *Tartessos. Arqueología protohistórica del bajo Guadalquivir.* Sabadell (1989): 297–338.

Aubet Semmler, M. E. "La cerámica púnica de Setefilla," *Studia Archaeologica* 42. Valladolid (1976).

Aubet Semmler, M. E. "La cerámica a torno de la Cruz del Negro (Carmona, Sevilla)," *Ampurias* 38–40 (1976–1978): 267–87.

Aubet Semmler, M. E., Serna, M. R., Escacena, J. L. and Ruiz, M. M. *La Mesa de Setefilla. Lora del Rio (Sevilla). Campaña de 1979.* Excavaciones Arqueológicas en España 122. Madrid (1983).

Bailey, O. M. *Catalogue of Lamps in the British Museum. Volume II.* London (1980).

Bailey, O. M. *Catalogue of Lamps in the British Museum. Volume III.* London (1988).

Balil, A. "Sobre la arquitectura doméstica en Emerita," *Augusta Emerita. Actas del Bimilenario de Mérida.* Madrid (1976): 85–90.

Baldomero, A., Corrales, P., Escalanate, Ma. M., Serrano, E. and Suárez, J. 1997, "El alfar romano de la Huerta del Rincón: síntesis tipológica y momentos de producción," in AAVV, *Figlinae Malacitanae. La producción de céramica romana en los territorios malacitanos.* Málaga (1997): 147–76.

Bandera, M. de la, Romo Salas. A., Sierra, F. y Vargas, J.M. "Cerro Gordo, un yacimiento orientalizante de la sierra sur sevillana (Gilena, Sevilla)," *Habis,* 20 (1989): 293–306.

Barker, G. "The animal bones," 81–91 in D. Whitehouse, G. Barker, R. Reece and D. Reese., "The Schola Praeconum I; the coins, Pottery lamps and fauna." *Papers of the British School at Rome* 50 (1982): 54–101.

Barbet, A. "Le troisième style de Pompéi: perspectives nouvelles," in *Peinture Murale en Gaule: Actes des Séminaires 1979 organisés par l'Association Française pour Peinture Mural Antique et le Centre d'Etudes des Peintures Murales Romaines.* Dijon (1980a): 29–50.

Barbet, A. "Le quatrième style de Pompéi," in *Peinture Murale en Gaule: Actes des Séminaires 1979 organisés par l'Association Française pour Peinture Mural Antique et le Centre d'Etudes des Peintures Murales Romaines.* Dijon (1980b): 65–82.

Barbet, A. (ed.) *La Peinture Murale Romaine dans les Provinces de l'Empire.* British Archaeological Reports International Series 165. Oxford (1983).

Barbet, A., Fuchs, M., Tuffeau-Libre, M. "Diverses utilisations des pigments et leurs contenants," in H. Béarat, M. Fuchs, M. Maggetti and D. Paunier (eds.), *Roman Wall Painting: Materials, Techniques, Analysis and Conservation. Proceedings of the International Workshop, Fribourg 7–9 March 1996.* Fribourg (1997): 35–62.

Barruol, G. & Marichal, R. "Le forum de Ruscino," in C. Aranegui (ed.), *Los foros romanos de las provincias occidentales.* Madrid (1987): 45–54.

Béarat, H. "Quelle est la gamme exacte des pigments romains? Confrontation des résultats d'analyse avec les textes de Vitruve et de Pline," in H. Béarat, M. Fuchs, M. Maggetti and D. Paunier, (eds.) *Roman Wall Painting: Materials, Techniques, Analysis and Conservation. Proceedings of the International Workshop, Fribourg 7–9 March 1996.* Fribourg (1997a): 11–34

Béarat, H. "Les pigments verts en peinture murale romaine: bilan analytique," in H. Béarat, M. Fuchs, M. Maggetti and D. Paunier (eds.) *Roman Wall Painting: Materials, Techniques, Analysis and Conservation. Proceedings of the International Workshop, Fribourg 7–9 March 1996.* Fribourg (1997b): 269–286.

Belchior, C. *Lucernas Romanas de Conimbriga.* Conimbriga (1969).

Belén, M. "Importaciones fenicias en Andalucía occidental," in G. del Olmo Lete and M. E. Aubet Semmler (eds.), *Los fenicios en la Península Ibérica. Volumen II.* Sabadell (1986): 263–78.

Belén, M., Fernández-Miranda, M. & Garrido, J.P. "Los orígenes de Huelva. Excavaciones en Los Cabezos de San Pedro y La Esperanza," *Huelva Arqueológica* III. (1977).

Belén, M., Fernández-Miranda, M., and Garrido, J. P. "Analisis de la fauna del sondeo M, zona 1," in M. Belén, M. Fernández Miranda and J. P. Garrido (1977a): 208–12.

Belén, M. and Fernández-Miranda, M. "La Tiñosa (Lepe, Huelva)," *Huelva Arqueológica* IV. (1978): 197–297.

Belén, M. y Pereira J. "Cerámicas a torno con decoración pintada en Andalucía," *Huelva Arqueológica* VII. (1985): 307–60.

Beltrán Lloris, M. *Las ánforas romanas en España.* Zaragoza (1970).

Beltrán Lloris, M. "Problemas de la morfologia y del concepto histórico-geográfico que recubre la noción tipo. Aportaciones a la tipologia de las ánforas béticas," in G. Vallet (ed.), *Méthodes classiques et méthodes formelles dans l'étude des amphores.* Collection de l'École Française de Rome 32. Paris (1977): 97–131.

Beltrán Lloris, M. *Guía de la cerámica romana.* Zaragoza (1990).

Beltrán Martínez, A. *Curso de numismática.* Cartagena (1950).

Bémont, C. and Jacob, J. P. (eds), *La terre sigillée gallo-romaine. Lieux de production du Haut Empire: implantations, produits, relations.* Documents d'Archéologie Francaise No. 6. Paris (1986).

Bendala Galán, M. *La necrópolis romana de Carmona* (2 vols). Seville (1976).

Bendala, M. "Excavaciones en el Cerro de los Palacios," *Italica (Santiponce, Sevilla).* Excavaciones Arqueológicas en España 121. Madrid (1982): 29–74.

Benet I Arqué, C. and Subias Pascual, E. "Els vidres," in TED'A, *Un abocador del segle V. d.c. en el forùm provincial de Tàrraco.* Memòries d'Excavaciò. Tarragona (1989).

Benito, M., "La fauna de la rabita califal de las Dunas de Guardamar," in R. Azuar *et alii., La Rabita Califal de Las Dunas de Guardamar (Alicante).* Alicante (1989): 153–61.

Berlanga, M. Rodríguez de. *Catálogo del Museo Longriniano.* Málaga (1903).

Bernal Cassola, D. "Las producciones anfóricas del bajo imperio y la Antigüedad tardía en Málaga: estado actual de la investigación e hipótesis de trabajo," in AAVV, *Figlinae Malacitanae. La producción de céramica romana en los territorios malacitanos.* Málaga (1997): 233–59.

Beschaouch, A. Hanoune, R. and Thébert, Y. *Les ruines de Bulla Regia.* Rome (1977).

Bintliff, J. and Snodgrass, A. "Mediterranean Survey and the City," *Antiquity* 62 (1988a): 57–71.

Bintliff, J. and Snodgrass, A. "The end of the Roman Countryside: a view from the east," in R. Jones, J. Bloemers, S. Dyson, S. and M. Biddle (eds.) (1988b).

Blanco Frejeiro, A and Luzón, J.Mª. "Mineros antiguos españoles," *Archivo Español de Arqueología* 39 (1966), 73–88.

Blanco Freijeiro, A. "Epigrafía en torno al acueducto de Segovia," *Symposium de arqueología romana*. Barcelona (1977): 131–46.

Blanco Ruiz, A. "Limpieza y excavación de un horno cerámico en 'El Cortjillo' (Peñaflor)," *Anuario Arqueológico de Andalucía 1986/III. Actividades de Urgencia*. Seville (1987): 413–5.

Blasco, F. "Factores condicionantes de la composición de la cabaña ganadera de la II Edad del Hierro en la mitad norte de la Península Ibérica," in F. Burrillo (ed.) *IV Simposio sobre Celtíberos. Economía*. Zaragoza (1999): 149–56.

Blázquez y Delgado Aguilera, A., "Vias romanas de la provincia de Ciudad Real," *Boletín de la Real Sociedad de Geografía* 32 (1892): 366–382.

Blázquez, A. "Epigrafía romana," *Boletín de la Real Academia de la Historia*, 77 (1920): 539–40.

Blázquez Martínez, J. Mª. "La exportación del aceite hispano en el Imperio romano. Estado de la cuestión," in J. M. Blázquez (ed.), *Producción y comercio del aceite en la antigüedad. Primer Congreso Internacional*. Madrid (1980): 19–46.

Blázquez Martínez, J. M., Remesal Rodríguez, J. and Rodríguez Almeida, E. 1994. *Excavaciones arqueológicas en el Monte Testaccio (Roma). Memoria Campaña 1989*. Madrid (1994).

Blázquez Martínez, J. Mª y Remesal Rodríguez, J. *Estudios sobre el monte Testaccio (Roma) I*. Col.leció Instrumenta 6. Barcelona (1999).

Boessneck, J. and Driesch, A. von den. "Knochenfunde aus dem römischen Munigua (Mulva), Sierra Morena," *Studien über frühe Tierknochenfunde von der Iberischen Halbinsel* 7 (1980): 160–85.

Bonneville, J. N. "Le support monumental des inscriptions: terminologie et analyse," *Épigraphie hispanique: Problèmes des methodes et d'edition*. Bordeaux 1981. Paris (1984): 117–52.

Bonneville, J.-N., Didirejean, F., Le Roux, P. Rouillard, P. and Sillères, P. "La seizième campagne de fouilles de la Casa de Velázquez à Belo en 1981 (Bolonia, province de Cadix)," *Mélanges de la Casa de Vélazquez* XVIII/2 (1983): 5–65.

Bonsor, G. "Les Colonies agricoles pre-romaines de la vallée du Bétis," *Révue Archéologique* 35 (1899): 1–143.

Bonsor, G. "Los pueblos antiguos del Guadalquívir y alfarerías romanas," *Revista de Archivos, Bíbliotecas y Museos* VI (1901): 837–57.

Bonsor, G. *The Archaeological Expedition along the Guadalquivir*. New York (1931).

Bull, G. and Payne, S. "Tooth eruption and epiphysial fusions in pigs and wild boar," in B. Wilson, C. Grigson and S. Payne, S. (eds.) 1982: 55–71.

Bullock, D. and Rackham, J. "Epiphysial fusion and tooth eruption of feral goats from Moffatdale, Dumfries and Galloway, Scotland," in B. Wilson, C. Grigson and S. Payne, S. (eds.) 1982: 73–80.

Burroughs, P. A. *Principles of Geographical Information Systems for Land Resource Assessment*. Oxford (1986).

Caamaño Gesto, J. M. "Los aelii de la península ibérica," *Boletín del Seminario de Arte y Arqueología* 38 (1972): 133–6.

Caballos Rufino, A. *Los senadores hispanorromanos y la romanización de Hispania (siglos I–III). I. Prosopografía (vol 1)*. Seville (1990).

Callender, M. *Roman Amphorae*. London (1965).

Calvani, C. *Veleia. Guida*. Parma (1975).

Campos, J. *Excavaciones arqueológicas en la ciudad de Sevilla. El orígen prerromano y la Hispalis romana*. Seville (1986).

Campos Carrasco, J., Vera, M. and Moreno, M. T. *Protohistoria de la ciudad de Sevilla. El corte estratigráfico de San Isidoro 85–6*. Seville (1988).

Cano García, D. G. *Naturaleza de Andalucía (8 Tomos). Tomo 1. Naturalez y especios Andaluces*. Seville (1998).

Caro, A. *Cerámica gris a torno tartesia*. Servicio de Publicaciones Universidad de Cádiz. Cádiz (1989a).

Caro, A. "Consideraciones sobre el Bronce Antiguo y Pleno en el Bajo Guadalquivir," in M. E. Aubet (ed.) *Tartessos. Arqueología Protohistórica del Bajo Guadalquivir*. Sabadell (1989b): 85–120.

Carriazo, J. M. and Raddatz, K. "Primicias de un corte estratigráfico en Carmona," *Archivo Hispalense* 103–104 (1960): 12–49.

Carreras Monfort, C. "Haltern 70: a review," in *Roman Amphorae*. R. Symonds (ed.), Problems of Identification and Methodology. London 1994 (forthcoming).

Carreras Monfort, C. and Funari, P. P. A. *Britannia y el Mediterráneo. Estudios sobre el abastecimiento de aceite bético y africano en Britannia*. Col.leció Instrumenta 5. Barcelona (1998).

Carreté, J. M. Keay, S. and Millett, M. *A Roman Provincial Capital and its Hinterland. The Survey of the Territory of Tarragona, Spain 1985–1990*. Journal of Roman Archaeology Supplementary Series Number Fifteen. Michigan (1995).

Carrillo Díaz-Pines, J. and Hidalgo Prieto, R. "Aproxcimación al estudio del poblamiento romano en la comarca de Palma del Río (Córdoba): La implantación territorial," *Ariadna* 8 (1990): 37–68.

Casariego, A., Cores, G. and Pliego, F. *Catálogo de plomos monetiformes de la Hispania antigua*, Madrid (1987).

Castaños, P. M., 1981, 'Estudio de los restos oseos,' 275–86. in F. Burillo, "Poblado de San Esteban (El Poyo del Cid, Teruel)," *Noticiario Arqueologio Hispanico* 12 (1981): 187–290.

Ceán Bermúdez, J. A. *Sumario de las antigüedades romanas que hay en España, en especial las pertenecientes a las Bellas Artes*. Madrid (1832).

Cepas Palanca, A. *Crisis y continuidad en la Hispania del siglo III*. Anejos de Archivo Español de Arqueología XVII. Madrid (1997).

Cereijo, M. A. and Patón, D., "Estudio sobre la fauna de vertebrados recuperada en el yacimiento tartesico de la Calle de Puerto 6 (Huelva). Primera parte: mamiferos," in J. Fernández Jurado. Tartessos y Huelva. *Huelva Arqueologica* 10/11 part 3 (1989): 215–44.

Cereijo, M. A. and Patón, D., 'Informe sobre la fauna de vertebrados recuperada en Puerto-29 (Huelva): mamiferos', 79–95 in J. Fernández Jurado et al., "Excavacion arqueologica en el solar no 29 de la Calle Puerto de Huelva," *Huelva Arqueológica* 12 (1990): 9–166.

Chapa Brunet, T. *La escultura ibérica zoomorfa*. Madrid (1985).

Chaves Tristán, F. "Iberian and early Roman coinage of Hispania Ulterior Baetica," in S. Keay (ed.), *The Archaeology of Early Roman Baetica*. Journal of Roman Archaeology Supplementary Series Number Twenty-Nine. Portsmouth R.I. (1988): 147–70.

Chaves Tristán, F. and de la Bandera Romero, M.L. "Figurlich verzierte keramic aus dem Guadalquivir-geviet," *Madrider Mitteilungen* 27 (1986): 117–150.

Chic García, G. "Inscripciones de Peñaflor," *Habis* 6 (1975): 357–363.

Chic García, G.. "Consideraciones sobre la navegabilidad del Guadalquivir en epoca romana," *Gades* 1 (1978): 7–20.

Chic García, G. *Epigrafía anforica de la Bética I. Los sellos*. Seville (1985)

Chic García, G. *Epigrafía anforica de la Bética II. Los rótulos pintados sobre ánforas olearias. Consideraciones sobre la annona*. Seville (1988).

Chic García, G. "Los Aelii en la producción y difusión del aceite bético," *Münstersche Beiträge z. antiken Handelsgeschichte, Band XI, Heft 2* (1992): 1–22.

Clapham, Jones, and Tenas, in press "The plant remains from Villaricos, Almeria Province"

Clark Maxwell, W.G. "The Roman towns in the valley of the Baetis between Cordoba and Sevilla," *Archaeological Journal* LVI (1899): 262–305.

Crawford, M. (ed.) *Roman Statutes I*. London (1996)

Crook, J. "Classical Roman Law and the Sale of Land," in M. Finley (ed.), *Studies in Roman Property*. Cambridge (1976): 133–36.

Collins, R. *Early Medieval Spain. Unity in Diversity, 400–1000*. London (1983).

Colls, D. Etienne, R. Lequément, R. Liou, B. & Mayet, F. *L'Épave Port-Vendres II et le commerce de la Bétique à l'époque de Claude*. *Archeonautica I*. Paris (1977).

Correa, J. A. "Dístico elegiaco en una inscripción de Peñaflor (Sevilla)," *Habis* 7 (1976): 367–69.

Corzo Sánchez, R. and Jiménez, A. "Organización territorial de la Baetica," *Archivo Español de Arqueología* 53 (1980): 21–47.

De Frutos Reyes, G. & Muñoz Vicente, A. "Hornos púnicos de Torre Alta," in AAVV, *Arqueologia en el entorno del Bajo Guadiana*. Huelva (1994): 393–414.

De Gusseme, T. A. Noticias pertenecientes a la historia antigua y moderna de la villa de Lora del Río en Andalucía. *Real Academia Sevillana de Buenas Letras*. Seville (1773): 237.

De la Rosa, D. and Moreira, J. M. *Evaluación ecológica de recursos naturales de Andalucía. Aproximación al conocimiento necesario para planificar el uso y protección de las tierras*. Seville (1987).

De la Sierra, J. A. "Cerámicas africanas en Munigua y el valle del Guadalquivir," *Madrider Mitteilungen* 39 (1998): 238–97.

De Ruyt, C. *Macellum. Marché alimentaire des romains*. Louvain-La-Neuve (1983).

Del Rivero, C.M., *El lapidario del Museo Arqueológico de Madrid*. Valladolid (1933).

Delgado, A. *Nuevo método de clasificación de las medallas autónomas de España*, 3 Vols. Seville (1871–6).

Deneauve, J. *Lampes de Carthage*. Paris (1969).

Domergue, C. "La campagne de fouilles 1966 a Bolonia (Cádiz)," *X Congreso Nacional de Arqueología*. Zaragoza (1969): 442–56.

Domergue, C. "A view of Baetica's external commerce in the 1st c. A.D. based on its trade in metals," in S. Keay (ed.), *The Archaeology of Early Roman Baetica*. Journal of Roman Archaeology Supplementary Series Number Twenty Nine. Portsmouth R.I. (1999): 201–15.

Domergue, C. *Catalogue des mines et des fonderies antiques de la Péninsule Ibérique*. Publications de la Casa de Velázquez. Serie Archéologique VIII (2 tomes). Madrid (1987).

Domínguez de la Concha, M. C., Cabrera Bonet, P. and Fernández Jurado, J. "Cerro de la Cabeza (Santiponce, Sevilla)," *Noticiario Arqueológico Hispánico* 30 (1988): 119–186.

Downs, M. "Cultural identity in Iberian and Early Roman Baetica," in S. Keay (ed.), *The Archaeology of Early Roman Baetica*. Journal of Roman Archaeology Supplementary Series Number Twenty Nine. Portsmouth, R.I. (1998): 39–53.

Drain M. Lhénaff, R. and Vanney, J.-R. *Le Bas Guadalquivir. Introduction géographique: le milieu physique*, Paris (1971).

Driesch, A. von den. *A Guide to the Measurement of Animal Bones from Archaeological Sites*, Cambridge, Mass (1976).

Driesch, A. von den, and Boessneck, J., "Kritische Anmerkungen zur Widerristhöhenberechnung aus Langenmassen vor- und frühgeschichtlicher Tierknochen," *Saugetierkundliche Mitteilungen* 22 (1974): 325–48.

Driesch, A. von den, and Boessneck, J., 1976, "Die Fauna vom Castro do Zambujal," *Studien über frühe Tierknochenfunde von der Iberischen Halbinsel* 5 (1976): 4–129.

Durán Cabello, R. M. "La técnica constructiva de la llamada "Casa-Basílica" de Mérida," in M. Beltrán Lloris (ed.) *La casa urbana hispanorromana*. Zaragoza (1991): 359–69.

Escacena Carrasco, J. L. "La cerámica ibérica de la Mesa de Setefilla (Sevilla)," *Pyrenae* 15–16 (1979–80): 181–210.

Escacena Carrasco, J. L. *Cerámicas a torno pintadas andaluzas de la Segunda Edad del Hierro* (microfichas CA-311–87). Cádiz (1987).

Escacena Carrasco, J. L. "El problamiento inérico en el bajo Gauadalquivir," in A. Ruiz and M. Molinos (eds.), *Iberos. Actas de las I Jornadas sobre el Mundo Ibérico/Jaén 1985*. Seville (1987a): 273–97.

Escacena Carrasco, J. L. "Los Turdetanos o la recuperación de la identidad perdida," in M. E. Aubet Semmler (ed.), *Tartessos. Arqueología protohistórica del bajo Guadalquivir*. Sabadell (1989): 433–76.

Escacena Carrasco, J. L. y Belen, M. "Sobre la cronología del horizonte fundacional de los asentamientos tartésicos," *Cuadernos del Suroeste* 2 (1991), 9–42.

Escacena Carasco, J. L. and Belén, M. "Pre-Roman Turdetania," in S. Keay (ed.), *The Archaeology of Early Roman Baetica*. Journal of Roman Archaeology. Supplementary Series Number Twenty Nine Portsmouth, R.I. (1998): 23–37.

Escacena Carrasco, J. L. and Frutos, G. de, "Estratigrafía de la Edad del Bronce en el Monte Berrueco (Medina Sidonia, Cádiz," *Noticiario Arqueológico Hispánico* 24 (1985): 7–90.

Estévez, J., "La fauna del corte 3: aproximación a la fauna del yacimiento de Setefilla," in E. Aubet Semmler Aubet Semmler, M. E., Serna, M. R., Escacena, J. L. and Ruiz, M. M. *La Mesa de Setefilla, Lora del Rio (Sevilla), Campaña de 1979*. Excavaciones Arqueologicas en España 122 (1983): 158–68

Estévez, J. "Dynamique des faunes préhistoriques au N–E de la péninsule ibérique," *Archaeozoologia* 1, 2: 197–218.

Ettlinger, E., Hedinger, B., Hoffmann, B., Kenrick, P. M., Pucci, G., Roth-Rubi, K., Schneider, G., Von Schnurbein S., Wells, C.M., Zabehlicky-Scheffenegger, S. *Conspectus Formarum Terrae Sigillatae Italico Modo Confectae*. Bonn (1990).

Fabre, G. Mayer, M. and Rodà, I. "Inscripciones 'alienae' en museos y colecciones de la provincia de Barcelona,"*Ampurias* 44 (1982): 185–240.

Fazekas, I. G. and Kosa, F. *Forensic Foetal Osteology*. Akademai Kiako. Budapest (1978).

Fernández Caro, J. J. *Carta arqueológica del término de Fuentes de Andalucía*. Écija (1982).

Fernández Casanova, A. *Catálogo monumental de la provincia de Sevilla*. Seville (1909).

Fernández Chicarro, C. "Adquisiciones del Museo Arqueológico Provincial de Sevilla durante el año 1946," *Memorias de los Museos Arqueológicos Provinciales* 7 (1946): 118–28.

Fernández-Chicarro y de Dios, C., *El Museo Provincial de Sevilla*. Madrid (1951).

Fernández Chicarro, C. and Fernández Gómez, F. *Catálogo del Museo Arqueológico Provincial de Sevilla*. (3ª Ed.). Seville (1980).

Fernández, F. and Verdugo, J. "Peñaflor," Memoria de las actuaciones programadas en el año 1979. *Arqueologia 79*. Madrid (1980): 204–5.

Fernández, F. and Verdugo, J. "Peñaflor," Memoria de las actuaciones programadas en el año 1979. *Arqueologia 80*. Madrid (1981): 133.

Fita, F. "Excursiones epigáfricas," *Boletín de la Real Academia de la Historia* 25 (1894): 43–136.

Fita, F. "Inscripciones romanas de Peñaflor en la provincia de Sevilla, y de Quintanaélez en la de Burgos," *Boletín de la Real Academia de la Historia* 69 (1916): 114–25.

Fleischer, R. *Die Römische Bronzen aus Österreich*. Mainz (1967).

Flórez, E. *España Sagrada IX*. Madrid (1754).

Florido, C. "Anforas prerromanas sudibéricas," *Habis* 15 (1984): 419–36.

Fortea, J. and Bernier, J. *Recintos y fortificaciones ibéricos en la Bética*. Memorias del Seminario de prehistoria y arqueología de Salamanca II. Salamanca (1970).

Francia Somalo, R. "Notas de antroponimia al Thesaurus Linguae Latinae," *Analecta Malacitana* XI/1 (1988): 11–24.

Frutos, G., Chic García, G. and Berriatua, N. "Las ánforas de la factoría prerromana de salazones de "Las Redes" (Puerto de Santa María, Cádiz)," in *Actas del I Congreso Peninsular de Historia Antigua. Santiago de Compostela, 1986.* Santiago de Compostela (1988): 295ff

Frizot, M. *Mortiers et enduits peints antiques: étude technique et archaeologique.* Dijon (1984).

Furtwängler, A. *Königliche Museen zu Berlin. Beschreibung der Geschnitenen Steine in Antiquarium.* Berlin (1896).

Gamer, G. *Formen römischen Altäre. Madrider Beiträge* 12 (1989).

García, E., Mora, M. and Ferrer, E. "Estudios sobre cerámicas ibéricas andaluzas: Montemolín (Marchena, Sevilla)," *Habis* 20 (1989): 217–43.

García Barquero López. *Geografía física y humana de Andalucía.* Madrid (1990).

García y Bellido, A. "Parerga de arqueología y de epigrafía hispano-romana," *Archivo Español de Arqueología* XXXIII (1960): 191–92.

García y Bellido, A. *Los hallazgos cerámicos del área del templo romano de Córdoba.* Anejos de Archivo Español de Arqueología V. Madrid (1970).

García Merino, C. and Sánchez Simón, M. "Enterramiento infantil bajo un pavimento de la Casa de los Pintos de Uxama," *Celtiberia* 90 (1996): 203–14.

García Moreno, L. "Andalucía durante la antigüedad tardía (ss. V–VII). Aspectos socio-económicos," in *I Congreso de Historia de Andalucía. Diciembre 1976.* Córdoba (1979): 297–307.

García Sandoval, E. *"Informe sobre las casas romanas de Mérida y excavaciones en la casa del Anfiteatro,"* Excavaciones Arqueológicas en Espana. Madrid (1966).

García Vargas, E. "La producción anfórica en la bahía de Cádiz durante la Republica como índice de romanización," *Habis* 27 (1996): 49–57.

Garnsey, P. "Appendix. Demolition of houses and the law," in M. Finley (ed.), *Studies in Roman Property* Cambridge (1976): 133–36.

Gáspár, D. Römische kästchen aus Pannonien. *Antaeus* 15 (2 vols). Budapest (1986).

Gettens, R. J., and Stout, G. L. *Painting materials; a short encyclopaedia.* New York (1966).

Gettens, R. J., Feller, R. L., and Chase, W. T. "Vermilion and cinnabar," in A. Roy (ed.) *Artists' Pigments. A handbook of their History and Characteristics. Volume 2.* Washington (1993): 159–182.

Gil Farres, O. *La moneda hispanica en la edad antigua.* Madrid (1966).

Gimeno Pascual, H. *Historia de la investigación epigráfica en España en los ss. XVI y XVII.* Zaragoza (1997).

Gimeno Pascual, Y. H. and Stylow, A. U., "Analecta epigraphica hispanica: manuscritos,calcos, dibujos, duplicaciones," *Sylloge Epigraphica Barcinonensis* III (1999): 85–112.

González Fernández, J. "The Lex Irnitana: a new copy of the Flavian municipal law," *Journal of Roman Studies* 76 (1986): 147–243.

González Fernández, J. *Corpus de Inscripciones Latinas de Andalucía. Volumen II: Sevilla. I. La Vega.* Seville (1991).

González Jiménez, M. *En torno a los orígenes de Andalucía.* Seville (1988).

Grigson, C. "Sex and age determination of some bones and teeth of domestic cattle: a review of the Literature," in B. Wilson, C. Grigson, and S. Payne (eds.) (1982): 7–23.

Grissom, C. "Green earth," in R. L. Feller (ed.) *Artists' Pigments: A handbook of their History and Characteristics Vol 1.* Washington (1986): 141–67.

Gros, P. *L'Architecture romaine. 1. Les monuments publics.* Paris (1996).

Guadán, A. M. de. *Numismática ibérica e ibero-romana.* Madrid (1969).

Guérin P. and Martínez Valle, R. "Inhumaciones infantiles en

poblados ibéricos del área valenciana," *Saguntum* 21 (1987–8): 231–65.

Gutiérrez Mendez, M. "Hallazgos de época visigoda en Antequera (Malaga)," *II Congreso Andaluz de Estudios Clasicos* (1987): 268–55.

Haley, E. "Rural settlement in the conventus astigitanus (Baetica) under the Flavians," *Phoenix 50* (1996): 283–303.

Hayes, J. *Late Roman Pottery.* London (1972).

Hidalgo, R. Alarcón, F. J. del Camino Fuertes, Ma del, González, M. and Moreno, M. 1996, *El criptopórtico de Cercadilla. Análisis arquitectónico y sequencia estratigráfica.* Córdoba (1996).

Harcourt, R., "The dog in prehistoric and early historic Britain," *Journal of Archaeological Science* 1 (1974): 151–75.

Hawthorne, J. "Pottery and Paradigms in the Early Western Empire," in C. Forcey, J. Hawthorne and R. Witcher (eds.), *TRAC. Proceedings of the Theoretical Roman Archaeology Conference. Nottingham 1997.* Oxford (1998): 160–72.

Hauschild, T. "Munigua. Excavaciones en el muro de contención del foro 1985," *Anuario Arqueológico de Andalucía 1989/II. Actividades sistemáticas.* Seville (1991): 171–84.

Hebblethwaite. *The Faba bean (Vicia faba L.): a basis for improvement.* London (1983).

Hesnard, A. "Un dépot Augustéen d'amphores à La Longarina, Ostie," in J. H. D'Arms and E.C. Kopff (eds.), *The Seaborne Commerce of Ancient Rome. Studies in Archaeology and History. Memoirs of the American Academy at Rome XXXVI.* Rome (1980): 141–156

Hochuli-Gysel, A. *Kleinasiatische glasierte Reliefkeramik (50 v. Chr. bis 50 n. Chr.) und ihre oberitalischen Nachahmungen.* Bern (1977).

Hopf M. 1991 "South and Southwest Europe," in W. van Zeist et alii (eds.) *Progress in Old World Palaeoethnobotany.* Rotterdam (1991): 241–77.

Hoyo, J. del, "Joyas en la Andalucía romana. Documentación epigráfica," *Actas del II Congreso de Historia de Andalucía. Vol 3. Historia Antigua. Córdoba 1991.* Córdoba (1994): 419–29.

Hoyuelos, E. L. "Actividades arqueológicas en el bien de interes cultural 'Ciudad Romana de Celti," Peñaflor. Sevilla," *Anuario Arqueológico de Andalucía 1987/III. Actividades de Urgencia.* Seville (1991): 526–30.

Huntley, B. and Birks, H. J. B. *An atlas of past and present pollen maps for Europe 0–13,000 years ago.* Cambridge (1983).

Isings, C. *Roman Glass from Dated Contexts.* Gröningen (1957).

Jiménez, A. 1975, "De Vitruvio a Vignola: autoridad de la tradición," *Habis* 6 (1975): 253–93.

Jiménez, A. *La puerta de Sevilla en Carmona.* Seville (1989).

Jansen, G. C. M. "Water Systems and Sanitation in the Houses of Herculaneum," *Mitteilungen Leichtweiss Institut* 117: 450–68.

Jones, M. & Reed, J. "Agricultural evidence from charred seeds and fruits," in B. Cunliffe & M. C. Fernández Castro, *The Guadajez Project. Andalucía in the First Millennium BC. Volume 1. Torreparedones and its Hinterland.* Oxford (1999): 403–7.

Jones, R., Bloemers, J., Dyson, S. and Biddle, M. (eds.), *First Millennium Papers.*, British Archaeological Reports International Series 401. Oxford (1988).

Jourdan, L. *La Faune du Site gallo-romain et paléochrétien de la Bourse (Marseille),* Paris (1976).

Kajanto, I. *The Latin Cognomina.* Helsinki (1965).

Keay, S. J. *Late Roman Amphorae in the western Mediterranean. A Typology and Economic Study.* British Archaeological Reports International Series 196 (2 vols). Oxford (1984).

Keay, S. J. *Roman Spain.* London (1988).

Keay, S. 1992. "The romanization of Turdetania," *Oxford Journal of Archaeology* 11.2: 275–315

Keay, S. "Innovation and adaptation: the contribution of Rome to urbanism in Iberia," in B. Cunliffe and S. Keay (eds.),

Social Complexity and the development of towns in Iberia. Oxford (1995): 291–337.

Keay, S. "La romanización en el sur y el levante de España hasta la época de Augusto," in J. Blázquez Martínez and J. Alvar Ezquerra (eds.), *La romanización en occidente.* Madrid (1996): 147–77.

Keay, S. "Early Roman Italica and the Romanization of western Baetica. " in A. Caballos and P. León (eds.), *Itálica MMCC. Actas de las Jornadas del 2200 aniversario de la fundación de Italica.* Seville (1997): 21–47.

Keay, S. "The development of towns in Early Roman Baetica," in S. Keay (ed.), *The Archaeology of Early Roman Baetica.* Journal of Roman Archaeology. Supplementary Series Number Twenty Nine. Portsmouth, R.I. (1998): 55–86.

Keay, S. "African Amphorae," in L. Saguì (ed.) *Cerámica in Italia: VI–VII secolo. Atti del Coloquio in onore di John W. Hayes. Roma, 11–13 maggio 1995.* Vol. I. Rome (1998): 141–55.

Keay, S. "Ceramic chronology and Roman rural settlement in the lower Guadalquivir valley during the Augustan period," in R. Frankovich & H. Patterson (eds.) *Extracting Meaning from Ploughsoil Assemblages. The Archaeology of Mediterranean Landscapes* 5, 163–73. Oxford (2000).

Keay, S., Creighton, J. and Jordan, D. "Sampling Ancient Towns," *Oxford Journal of Archaeology* 10.3 (1991): 371–83.

Keay, S. and Jones, R. "Differentiation of early imperial amphora production in Hispania Tarraconensis," in I. Freestone *et alii* (eds.), *Current Research in Ceramics. The British Museum Seminar 1980.* Occasional Paper 32: 45–61. London (1980).

Keay, S., Wheatley, D. and Poppy, S. "The Territory of Carmona during the Turdetanian and Roman periods: Some preliminary notes on visibility and urban location," in A. Caballos (ed.) *II Congreso de Historia de Carmona. Carmona Romana.* Seville (forthcoming 2001).

King, A. C. "I resti animali: i mammiferi, i rettili e gli anfibi," in A. Ricci (ed.), *Settefinestre. Una Villa Schiavistica nell'Etruria Romana, III,* Modena (1985): 278–300.

King, A. C. "Estudi de les restes faunistiques," in A.Roure i Bonaventura, S. Keay, J. M. Nolla Brufau and J. Tarrús, *La Vil.la Romana de Vilauba (Camós).* Girona (1988): 95–6.

King, A. C., "Animal bones," pp. 247–58 in E. Fentress (ed.), *Fouilles de Sétif 1977–1984.* Algiers (1990): 247–58.

King, A. C., "Mammiferi," in P. Arthur (ed.), *Il Complesso Archeologico di Carminiello ai Mannesi, Napoli (Scavi 1983–1984).,* Galatina (1994): 367–406.

King, A. C., "Mammals," in W. Jashemski (ed.) *The Natural History of Pompeii and the Vesuvian Sites* (forthcoming).

King, A. "Diet in the Roman world: a regional inter-site comparison of the mammal bones," *Journal of Roman Archaeology* 12 (1999): 169–202.

Knapp, R. *Aspects of the Roman Experience in Iberia, 206–100 B.C.* Valladolid (1977).

Knowles, K. "The Lamps," in M. G. Fulford and D. P. S. Peacock (eds.), *Excavations at Carthage. The Circular Harbour, North Side.* Vol II, 2. London (1994): 23–41.

Kvamme, K. L. "GIS Algorithms and their Effects on Regional Archaeological Analyses," in Allen, Green and Zubrow (eds.) 1990: 112–126.

Ladero Quesada, M. A. *Andalucía en el siglo XV.* Madrd (1973).

Ladero Quesada, M. A. and González Jiménez, M. "La orden militar de San Juan en Andalucía," *Archivo Hispalense* LIX.180 (1976): 129–37.

Ladrón, I. *et alii,* "Materiales inéditos de Setefilla (Lora del Río, Sevilla)," *Spal* 1(1993): 293–312.

Lamboglia, N. "Nuovi osservazione sulla 'terra sigillata chiara'," *Rivista di Studi Liguri* XXIV (1963): 145–212.

Lancha, J., Le Roux, P. and Rouillard. "La dix-septième campagne de fouilles de la Casa de Velázquez à Belo en 1982 (Bolonia,

province de Cadix)," *Mélanges de la Casa de Vélazquez.* XIX (1983): 401–32.

Larrey Hoyuelos, E. "Actividades arqueológicas en el 'Bien de Interés Cultural Ciudad Romana de Celti' Peñaflor, Sevilla," *Anuario Arqueológico de Andalucía 1985/III. Actividades de Urgencia.* Seville (1987): 526–30.

Laubenheimer, F. *La production des amphores en Gaule Narbonnaise.* Paris (1985).

Lineros Romero, R. and Domínguez Mora, F. "Excavaciones arqueológicas de urgencia en Carmona," *Anuario Arqueológico de Andalucía 1985/III. Actividades de Urgencia.* Seville (1987): 326–9

Ling, R *Roman Painting.* Cambridge (1991).

Loeschcke, S. *Lampen aus Vindonissa.* Zurich (1919).

López Mullor, A. "Notas para una clasificación de los tipos más frecuentes de la cerámica vidriada romana en Cataluña," *Ampurias* 43 (1981): 201–15.

López Mullor, A. Las cerámicas romanas de paredas finas en Cataluña. *Quaderns Científics I Tècnics (Vol.I and II).* Barcelona (1989).

López Palomo, J. A. "Alhonoz: Excavaciones de 1973 a 1978," *Noticiario Arqueológico Hispánico* 11 (1981): 33–187,

López Roa, C. "Las cerámicas alisadas con decoración bruñida," *Huelva Arqueológica.* IV (1978): 145–80.

Lorencio, C., Puig, F. and Juliá, M. "Enterramientos infantiles a l'edifici imperial de la Magdalena (Lleida)," *Pre-Actes de las I Jornadas internacionals de arqueología romana. Homenatje a Josep Estrada I Garriga.* Granollers (1987): 274–83.

Luzónnogué, J. M. *Excavaciones en Itálica. Estratigrafía en el Pajar de Artillo (Campaña 1970).* Excavaciones Arqueológicas en España 78. Madrid (1973).

Luzónnogué, J. M. and Ruiz, D. *Las raíces de Córdoba. Estratigrafía de la colina de los Quemados* Córdoba (1973).

Maldonado de Saavedra, J. *Discurso Geográfico de la villa antigua de Peñaflor que consulta a los peritos en esta materia, sobre su antiguo, y verdadero nombre Don, noble sevillano.* Sevilla (1673).

Mar, R. and Ruiz de Arbulo, J. "La basílica de la colonia Tarraco. Una nueva interpretación del llamado foro bajo de Tarragona," in C. Aranegui (ed.), *Los foros romanos de las provincias occidentales.* Madrid (1987), 31–44.

Mariezkurrena, K., and Altuna, J. "Arqueozoología de la villa romana del Alto de la Cárcel, Arellano (Navarra)," *Trabajos de Arqueología Navarra* 11 (1994): 109–25.

Márquez, C. *Capiteles romanos de Corduba Colonia Patricia.* Córdoba (1993).

Martin T. "Montans," in C. Bémont and J. P. Jacob (eds.), *La terre sigillée gallo-romaine. Lieux de production du haut empire: implantations, produits, relations.* Documents d'Archéologie francaise n. 6 Paris (1986): 58–72.

Martin-Kilcher, S. "Les amphores romaines à huile de Bétique (Dressel 20 et 23) d'Augst (Colonia Augusta Rauricorum) et Kaiseraugst (Castrum Rauracense). Un rapport préliminaire," in J. M. Blázquez Martínez and J. Remesal Rodríguez (eds.), *Producción y comercio del aceite en la antigüedad. Segundo congreso Internacional.* Madrid (1983): 337–47.

Marín Jordá, C., Piá Brisa and Rosselló I Mesquida, M. *El foro romano de Valentia.* Valencia (1999).

Martín Roldán, R., "Estudio anatómico de los restos procedentes de la excavaciones arqueológicas en el Cerro de 'El Carambolo' (Sevilla)," *Anales de la Universidad Hispalense* 19 (1959): 11–47.

Martínez Rodríguez, F. *Análisis y personalización de un grupo cerámico de barniz rojo de imitación propio de la Bética romana altoimperial. Memoria de Licenciatura.* Seville (1987).

Mayet, F. *Les céramiques a parois fines dans la péninsule ibérique.* Paris (1975).

Martínez Rodríguez, F. "Las cerámicas béticas de imitación tipo Peñaflor: bases para el estudio de un nuevo grupo cerámico de época altoimperial," *Boletín de la Asociación Española de Amigos de la Arqueología*, no. 26 (1989): 60–5.

Mayet, F. *Les céramiques sigillées hispaniques. Contribution à l'histoire économique de la péninsule ibérique sous l'empire romain* (2 vols) Paris (1983).

Mayer, M. "Plinio el viejo y las ciudades de la *Baetica*. Aproximación a un estado actual del Problema,"in J. González (ed.), Estudios sobre Urso. Colonia Iulia Genetiva. Seville (1989): 303–33.

Melchor Gil, E. "La élites municipañes de Hispania en el alto imperio: un intento de aproximación a sus fuentes de riqueza," *Florentia Iliberritana* 4–5 (1993–1994): 335–49.

Meyer, K. E. "Axial peristyle houses in the western empire," *Journal of Roman Archaeology* 12 (1999): 101–21.

Mezquiriz de Catalán, M. A. *Terra sigillata hispanica* (2 vols) Valencia (1961).

Mezquiriz de Catalán, M. A. "Terra sigilata ispanica," in AAVV, *Atlante delle forme ceramiche II*. Roma (1985): 99–183.

Miguel, J. de, and Morales, A. "Informe sobre los restos faunisticos recuperados en la excavación de la Muralla de Tiermes,"in J. L. Argente, C. Casa, de la, *et alii., Tiermes II: campañas de 1979 y 1980*. Excavaciones Arqueologicas en España 128 (1984): 292–309.

Millet, B. *Las ánforas de aceite de la Bética y su presencia en la Cataluña romana*. Col.lecció Instrumenta 4. Barcelona (1997).

Mínguez Morales, J. A. "Enterramientos infantiles domésticos en la Colonia Lepida Celsa (Velilla de Ebro, Zaragoza)," *Caesaraugusta* 66–67 (1989–1990): 105–22.

Miró i Miró, J. M. "La fauna," in TED'A. *Un Abocador del Siglo V d.c. en el Fòrum Provincial de Tàrraco*. Memories d'Excavació 2. Tarragona (1989): 403–14.

Molero, G. "Informe sobre los restos óseos hallados en el poblado de La Muela de Cástulo (Linares – Jaén)," in J. M. Blázquez Martínez, M. P. García Gelabert and F. López. *Castulo V*. Excavaciones Arqueologicas en España, 140 (1985): 305–14.

Molina Vidal, J. *La dinámica comercial romana entre Italia e Hispania Citerior*. Alicante (1997).

Mommsen, T., Kreuger, P. and Watson, A. (eds.), *The Digest of Justinian. Vol. IV*. Philadelphia (1985).

Montero, A., "Análisis osteológico de los restos exhumados en el Cerro de la Cruz, Sector B, campaña de 1985," in D. Vaquerizo Gil, *El Yacimiento Ibérico del Cerro de la Cruz (Almedinilla, Córdoba)*, Córdoba (1990): 175–80.

Mora Serrano, B. and Corrales Aguilar, P. "Establecimientos salsarios y producciones anfóricas en los territorios malacitanos," in AAVV, *Figlinae Malacitanae. La producción de céramica romana en los territorios malacitanos*. Málaga (1997): 27–59.

Morales, A. de *Las antigüedades de las ciudades de España*. Alcalá de Henares (1575; Republished in 1577; Edition of Benito Cano: Madrid 1792).

Morales, A. *et alii, Inventario artístico de Sevilla y su provincia*. Madrid (1982).

Morales, A., Cereijo, M., Brännström, P., and Liesau, C. "The mammals," in E. Roselló and A. Morales (1994a): 37–69.

Morales, A., Chamorro, J., Moreno, R., Roselló, E., *et alii*, "The biological evidence in a wider Context," in E. Roselló and A. Morales (1994b): 201–17.

Morel, J. P. *Céramique Campanienne*. Bibliothéque des École Francaises d'Athènes et de Rome, Fascicule 244. Rome (1981) (2 vols).

Moreno Almenara, M. *La villa altoimperial de Cercadilla (Córdoba). Análisis arqueológico (Córdoba)* Seville (1997).

Moreno Almenara, M. and Alarcón Castellano, F. "Producciones de cerámicas locales y regionales de época tardía en Colonia Patricia Corduba. El yacimiento de Cercadilla," *XI Convegno Internazionale di Studi sull'Africa Romana*. Tunis (1994).

Moreno Almenara, M. "Materiales de época romana. La cerámica," in R. Hidalgo, F. Alarcón, Ma. del Camino Fuertes and M. Moreno. *El criptoportico de Cercadilla. Análisis arquitectónico y secuencia estratigráfica*. Seville (1996): 69–112.

Murillo Redondo, J. F. *La cultura tartésica en el Guadalquivir medio*. Ariadna 13–14 Córdoba (1994).

Murillo Redondo, J. F. and Vaquerizo Gil, D. "La Córdoba prerromana," in P. León (ed.), *Colonia Patricia Corduba, una reflexion arqueológica. Coloquio internacional*. Seville (1996): 37–47.

Navarro Luengo, I., Fernández Rodríguez, L. E. and Suárez Padilla, J. "Cerámicas comunes de época tradorromana y bizantina en Málaga," in AAVV, *Figlinae Malacitanae. La producción de céramica romana en los territorios malacitanos*. Malaga (1997): 79–93.

Nieto. J. Kover, A., Izquierdo, P., Puig. A., Alaminos, A., Martín, A. and Pujol, M. *Excavacions Arquològiques subaquàtiques a Cala Culip. Vol. I*. Girona (1989).

Oswald, F. and Pryce, T. D. *An Introduction to the Study of Terra Sigillata*. London (1966).

Padilla Monge, A. *La provincia romana de la Bética*. Écija (1989).

Panella, C. "Appunti su un gruppo di anfore della prima, media e tarda età imperiale,"*Ostia III. Studi Miscellani* 21. Roma (1973): 460–633.

Panella, C. "Mercato di Roma e anfore galliche nella prima età imperiale," in F. Laubenheimer (ed.), *Les amphores en Gaule. Production et circulation*. Paris (1992): 185–206.

Parsons, J. J. "The acorn-hog economy of the oak woodlands of southwestern Spain," *Geographical Review* 52 (1962): 211–35.

Pascual Madoz. *Dicionario geográfico-estadístico-histórico de España y sus posesiones de ultramar. Tomo XII*. Madrid (1849).

Passelac, M. Sabrié, R. & Sabrié, M. "Centre de production de Narbonne," in C. Bémont and J. P. Jacob (eds.), *La terre sigillée gallo-romaine. Lieux de production du haut empire: implantations, produits, relations*. Documents d'Archéologie Francaise n. 6. Paris (1986): 52–55.

Payne, S., "Kill-off patterns in sheep and goats: the mandibles from Asvan Kale," *Anatolian Studies* 23 (1973): 281–303.

Peacock, D. "Pompeian Red Ware," in D. Peacock (ed.) *Pottery and Early Commerce. Characterization and Trade in Roman and Later Ceramics*. London (1973): 147–62.

Peacock, D. P. S. and Williams, D. F. *Amphorae and the Roman Economy*. London (1986).

Pellicer, M. "El Bronce Reciente y los inicios del Hierro en Andalucía Occidental," in M. Aubet Semmler (ed.), *Tartessos. Arqueología Protohistórica del Bajo Guadalquivir*. Sabadell (1989): 147–87.

Pellicer, M., Hurtado, V. and de la Bandera, M. L. "Corte estratigráfico de la casa de la Venus," *Italica* (Santiponce, Sevilla). Excavaciones Arqueológicas en España 121. Madrid (1982): 11–28.

Pellicer, M. and Amores, F. "Prehistoria de Carmona. Cortes estratigráficos CA80-A y CA80-B," *Noticiario Histórico Hispánico* 22 (1985): 55–195.

Pellicer, M., Escacena Carrasco, J. L. and Bendala, M. *El Cerro Macareno*. Excavaciones Arqueológicas en España 124. Madrid (1983).

Perdigones Moreno, L. and Muñoz Vicente, A. "Excavaciones arqueológicas de urgencia en los hornos púnicos de Torre Alta, San Fernando, Cádiz," *Anuario Arqueológico de Andalucía 1988/ III. Actividades de Urgencia*. Seville (1990): 106–112.

Perdiguero López, M. *Aratispi (Cauche el Viejo, Antequera). Investigaciones Arqueológicas*. Malaga (1995).

Pereira, J. "La cerámica ibérica de la cuenca del Guadalquivir I. Propuesta de clasificación," *Trabajos de Prehistoria* 45 (1988): 143–73.

Pérez-Minguez, F., "El castillo de los Marqueses de la Navas," *Boletín de la Real Academia de la Historia* 97 (1930): 745–816.

Pérez Paz, A. *Peñaflor 89.* Unpublished Manuscript. Delegación Provincial de Cultura. Seville (1989).

Pieksma, E. J. *A Petrological Study of Dressel 20 Amphora,* unpublished M.Sc. dissertation, University of Southampton (1982).

Piernavieja, P. *Corpus de las inscripciones deportivas de la España romana.* Madrid (1977).

Piganiol, A., *Les documents cadastraux de la colonie romaine d'Orange. XVIe suplément de Gallia* (1962).

Ponsich, M. *Implantation rurale antique sur le bas-Guadalquivir. Tome 1.* Paris (1974).

Ponsich, M. *Implantation rurale antique sur le bas-Guadalquivir. Tome 2.* Paris (1979)

Ponsich, M. *Implantation rurale antique sur le bas-Guadalquivir. Tome 3.* Paris (1987).

Ponsich, M. *Implantation rurale antique sur le bas-Guadalquivir.* Tome 4. Paris (1991).

Price, J. and Cottam, S. *Romano-British Glass Vessels: A Handbook. Practical Handbooks in Archaeology.* The Council for British Archaeology. London (1998).

Puertas Trias, R. *Excavaciones arqueológicas en Lacipo (Casares, Málaga). Campañas de 1975 y 1976.* Excavaciones Arqueológicas en España 125. Madrid (1982).

Puertas Trias, R. "Los hallazgos arqueológicos de Torreblanca del Sol (Fuengirola)," *Mainake VIII–IX* (1986–1987): 145–200.

Quirós, A., Romo, A. and Vera, M. "Intervención arqueológica en la Plaza Virgen de los Reyes," *Anuario Arqueológica de Andalucía 1997/III. Urgencias.* Seville (in press).

Radice, B. *The Letters of the Younger Pliny.* London (1978)

Ramírez y Las Casas-Deza, L. M. "Descubrimientos de Peñaflor," *Semanario Pintoresco Español. Tercera Serie. Tomo II* (1874): 371–73.

Ramón Torres, J. *Las ánforas fenicio-púnicas del Mediterraneo central y occidental.* Col.lecio Instrumenta 2. Barcelona (1995).

Remesal, Rodríguez, J. "Les lampes à huile de Belo," *Melanges de la Casa de Velazquez* X (1974): 561–74.

Remesal Rodríguez, J. "Cerámicas orientalizantes andaluzas," *Archivo Español de Arqueología* 48 (1975): 3–21.

Remesal Rodríguez, J. "Algunos datos sobre las dos útimas campañas de excavación en Belo (Bolonia, Cádiz)," *XIV Congreso Nacional de Arqueología.* Zaragoza (1975a): 1161–86.

Remesal Rodríguez, J. "Economía oleícola bética. Nuevas formas de análisis," *Archivo Español de Arqueología 50/51* (1978): 87–142.

Remesal Rodríguez, J. "Gerión et Argantonius et le peuplement protohistorique de l'Adalousie," *Caesarodunum* 13 (1978): 194–205.

Remesal Rodríguez, J. (ed.). *Thomás Andrés de Gusseme. Noticias pertecenientes a la historia antigua y moderna de Lora del Río, Alcolea del Río, Setefilla y Arva, en Andalucía.* Lora del Río (1981).

Remesal Rodríguez, J. "Tres nuevos centros productores de ánforas Dressel 20 y 23. Los sellos de Lvcivs Fabivs Cilo," *Ariadna* 6 (1989): 119–53.

Remesal Rodríguez, J., "Sextus Iulius Possessor en la Bética,"' in *Alimenta, Estudios en homenaje al Dr. Michel Ponsich. Gerión, Anejos III* (1991): 281–95.

Remesal Rodríguez, J. "Mummius Secundinus. El Kalendarium Vegetianum y las confiscacones de Severo en la Bética," *Gerión* 14 (1996): 195–221.

Remesal Rodríguez, J. "Evergetismo en la Bética, nuevo documento de un municipio ignoto (= ¿Oducia?)," *Gerión* 15 (1996): 283–95.

Remesal Rodríguez, J. *Heeresversorgung und die wirtschaftlichen Beziehungen zwischen der Baetica und Germanien. Landesdenkmalamt Baden-Würtemburg.* Stuttgart (1997).

Remesal Rodríguez. J. "Baetican oilve oil and the Roman economy," in S. Keay (ed.), *The Archaeology of Early Roman Baetica.* Journal of Roman Archaeology Supplementary Series Number Twenty Nine. Portsmouth R.I. (1998): 183–99.

Remesal Rodríguez, J. "Cuatrocientos años de historia e historiografía a través de la inscripción de C. Iuventus Albinus (CIL II, 1054). La labor de Tomás Andrés de Gusseme en Lora del Río (Sevilla)," *Gerión 16* (1998a): 223–53.

Remesal Rodríguez, J., Revilla Calvo, V., Carreras Monfort, C. and Berni Millet, P. "Arva: Prospecciones en un centro productor de ánforas Dressel 20 (Alcolea del Río, Sevilla)," *Pyrenae* 28 (1997): 151–78.

Renfrew, J. *Palaeoethnobotany: the prehistoric food plants of the Near East and Europe.* London (1973).

Ribera, A. *Las anforas prerromanas valencianas (Fenicias, ibéricas y púnicas). Servicio de Investigaciones Prehistóricas, Serie de trabajos varios varios núm 73.* Valencia (1982).

Ricci, A. "Ceramica a pareti sottili" in AAVV *Atlante delle forme ceramiche* II, 231–363.

Riederer, J. "Egyptian blue," in E. West Fitzhugh, E., (ed.) *Artists' Pigments: A handbook of their History and Characteristics* Vol 3. Washington (1997): 23–45.

Riveiro, Casto Maria, del, *La colección de monedas ibéricas de M.A.N.* Madrid (1923).

Rivero, C. M. del. *El Lapidario del Museo Arqueológico de Madrid.* Valladolid (1933).

Richardson, L. *Pompeii. An Architectural History.* London (1988).

Roca Roumens, M. *Sigillata Hispanica producida en Andújar* (Jaén). Jaén (1976).

Roca Roumens, M. "A propósito de ciertas formas, en T.S.H., fabricadas en el centro de producción de los villares de Andújar," *Cuadernos de Prehistoria de Granada* (1991–1992): 389–400.

Roca Roumens, M. & Fernández García, Ma. I. *Terra Sigillata Hispánica. Centros de fabricación y producciones altoimperiales.* Malaga (1999).

Rodrigo Caro, D. *Antigüedades y principado de la ilustrissima ciudad de Sevilla y chrorographia de su convento iurudico, o antigua chancilleria.* Seville (1634).

Rodríguez Hidalgo, J. M. "Dos ejemplos domésticos en Traianopolis (Itálica): Las casas de los Pájaros y de la Exedra," in M. Beltrán Lloris (ed.) *La casa urbana hispanorromana.* Zaragoza (1991): 291–302.

Rodríguez Hidalgo, J. M., Keay, S. Jordan, D. and Creighton, J. "La Itálica de Adriano. Resultados de las prospecciones arqueológicas 1991 y 1993," *Archivo Español de Arqueología* 72 (1999): 73–96.

Rodríguez Moñino, A. R. "Arqueología extremeña," *Revista del Centro de Estudios Extremeños 14* (1940): 44–5.

Rodríguez Oliva, P. "Los hornos romanos de Torrox," in AAVV, *Figlinae Malacitanae. La producción de céramica romana en los territorios malacitanos.* Malaga (1997): 271–303.

Roldán Gómez, L. *Técnicas constructivas romanas en Carteia (San Roque, Cádiz).* Monografías de arquitectura romana 1. Madrid (1992).

Roldán Gómez, L., Bendala Galán, M., Blánquez Pérez, J. and Martínez Lillo, S. *Carteia.* Madrid (1998).

Roldán Hervas, J. M. *Itineraria hispana. Fuentes antiguas para el estudio de las vías romanas en la península ibérica.* Valladolid/Granada (1975).

Romero Moragas, C. "Un horno de cerámica común romana en Marchena (Sevilla)," *XVIII Congreso Nacional de Arqueología.* Zaragoza (1987): 207–18.

Romero Moragas, C. *Instrumento para el etsudio del poblamiento rural antiguo en la campiña sevillana. Estudio arqueológico de la obra del gasoducto Sevilla-Madrid en el tramo correspondiente a la provincia de Sevilla.* Seville (1991: Unpublished Document),

Romero Moragas, C. and Campos, J. "La villa Romana del

Cortijo de Miraflores," *Anuario Arqueológico de Andalucía 1986/III. Urgencias.* Seville (1987): 321–28.

Romo Salas, A. "El sondeo estratigráfico de la Plaza Virgen de los Reyes (Sevilla). El registro deposicional," *Anuario Arqueológico de Andalucía, III/1994. Urgencias.* Sevilla (in press).

Romo Salas, A. and Vargas Jiménez, J. M. "Azanaque. Evidencias arqueológicas de un centro de producción anfórica," in *Congreso Internacional. Ex Baetica Amphorae. Conservas, aceite y vino de la Betica en el imperio Romano. Diciembre de 1998.* Seville (in press).

Romo Salas, A. "Intervención en el yacimiento de Itálica: el inmueble de C/- Silio No. 12 (Santiponce, Sevilla)," *Anuario Arqueológico de Andalucía 1996/III. Urgencias.* Seville (in press).

Roos, A. Mª. "Acerca de la antigua cerámica gris a torno en la Península Ibérica," *Ampurias* 44 (1982): 43–70.

Roselló, E. and Morales, A., (eds.), *Castillo de Doña Blanca: archaeo-environmental investigations in the Bay of Cádiz, Spain (750–500 BC).* British Archaeological Reports International Series 593. Oxford (1994).

Roth Congès, A. "Nouvelles fouilles à Glanum (1982–1990)," *Journal of Roman Archaeology* 5 (1992): 39–55.

Rufete Tomico, P. "La cerámica con barniz rojo de Huelva," in M. E. Aubet Semmler (ed.) *Tartessos. Arqueología protohistórica del bajo Guadalquivir.* Sabadell (1989): 375–94.

Ruiz Delgado, M. M. *Carta arqueológica de la campiña sevilla. Zona Sureste I.* Sevilla (1985).

Ruiz Delgado, M. M. *Fíbulas Protohistóricas en el Sur de la Península Ibérica.* Seville (1989).

Ruiz Mata, D. "Huelva: un foco temprano de actividad metalúrgica durante el Bronce Final," in M. E. Aubet Semmler (ed.) *Tartessos. Arqueología Protohistórica del Bajo Guadalquivir.* Sabadell (1989): 209–43.

Ruiz Mata, D. "La colonización fenicia en la Bahía de Cádiz a través del Castillo de Doña Blanca," *Anuario Arqueológico de Andalucía 1990/II. Actividades sistemáticas.* Seville (1992): 291–300.

Ruiz Mata, D. "Castillo de Doña Blanca: resultados de las investigaciones," *Anuario Arqueológico de Andalucía 1990/II. Actividades sistemáticas.* Seville (1992a): 301–3

Ruiz Mata, D. "Las cerámicas del Bronce Final. Un soporte tipológico para delimitar el tiempo y el espacio tartésico," in *Tartessos. 25 Años después. 1968–1993. Jérez de la Frontera. Actas del Congreso Conmemorativo del V Symposium Internacional de Prehistoria Peninsular.* Jérez de la Frontera (1995): 265–313.

Ruiz Rodríguez, A. "Desarrollo y consolidación de la ideología aristocrática entre los iberos del sur," in R. Olmos Romera and J. A. Santos Velasco (eds.), *Iconografía Ibérica. Iconografía Itálica. Propuestas de interpretación y lectura (Roma 11–13 Nov. 1993).* Serie Varia 3. Coloquio Internacional. Madrid (1996): 61–71.

Ruiz Solva, S. "El estudio de la macrofauna del yacimiento de Atxa," in E. Gil Zubillaga (ed.), *Atxa: Memoria de las excavaciones arqueológicas 1982–1988.* Vitoria-Gasteiz (1995): 385–420.

Saavedra, E., 1862, *Discursos leidos ante la Real Academia de la Historia en la recepción pública de Don Eduardo Saavedra el día 28 de diciembre de 1862. Madrid 2ª ed.* Madrid (1914).

Saénz Preciado, M. P. and Saénz Preciado, C. S. "Estado de la cuestión de los alfares riojanos: La terra sigillata Hispánica altoimperial," in M. Roca Roumens and M. I. Fernández García (eds.), *Terra Sigillata Hispánica.* Malaga (1999): 61–136.

Salvador Ventura, F. *Hispania meridional entre Roma y el Islam.* Granada (1990).

Sánchez Sánchez, Ma A. "Producciones importadas en la vajilla culinaria romana del bajo Guadalquivir," in X. Aquilué and M. Roca (eds.) *Ceràmica comuna romana d'època alto-imperial a la penìnsula ibèrica.* Monografíes Emporitanes VIII. Barcelona (1995): 251–79.

Sanmartí Grego, E. "Nota acerca de una imitación de la sigillata aretina detectada en Emporion," *Ampurias* 36–37 (1974–975): 251–61.

Santos Retolaza, M. "Distribución y evolución de la vivienda urbana tradorrepublicana y altoimperial en Ampurias," in M. Beltrán Lloris (ed.) *La casa urbana hispanorromana.* Zaragoza (1991): 19–34.

Sayas Abengochea, J. J. and García Moreno, L. *Romanismo y germanismo. Despertar de los pueblos hispánicos (ss. IV–X).* Barcelona (1982).

Schiffer, M. B. *Behavioural Archaeology.* New York (1976).

Sealey, P. R. *Amphoras from the 1970. Excavations at Colchester Sheepen.* British Archaeological Reports. British Series 142. Oxford (1985).

Serrano Ortega, M. *Guía de los monumentos históricos y artísticos de los pueblos de la provincia de Sevilla.* Seville (1911).

Serrano Ramos, E. and Atienza, R. *Inscripciones latinas del museo de Málaga.* Madrid (1981).

Serrano Ramos, E. "Imitaciones de cerámica aretina procedentes de yacimientos arqueológicos malagueños," *Mainaké X* (1988): 83–9.

Serrano Ramos, E. "Producciones de cerámicas comunes locales de la Bética," in X. Aquilué and M. Roca Roumens (eds.) *Ceràmica comuna romana d'època alto-imperial a la península ibèrica.* Monografíes Emporitanes VIII. Barcelona (1995): 227–49.

Serrano Ramos, E. "La producción cerámica de los talleres romanos de la Depresión de Antequera," in AAVV. *Figlinae Malacitanae. La producción de céramica romana en los territorios malacitanos.* Malaga (1997): 217–32.

Serrano Ramos, E. and Atencia Paez, R. "Un centro productor de sigillata Hispánica en Singilia Barba (Antequera, Málaga)," *Baetica* 6 (1983): 175–92.

Serrano Ramos, E. Gómez Valero, A. and Castaños Alés, C. "Informe sobre las excavaciones de urgencia en el yacimiento romano de la "Fábrica"(Teba, Málaga)," *Anuario Arqueológico de Andalucía 1992/III. Actividades de Urgencia.* Seville (1995): 540–44.

Sillières, P. *Les voies de communication de l'Hispanie meridionale.* Paris (1990).

Sillières, P. "Vivait-on dans des ruines au IIe siècle ap. J.-C.? Approche du paysage urbain de l'Hispanie d'après quelques grandes fouilles récentes," in J. Arce and P. Le Roux (eds.) *Ciudad y comunidad cívica en Hispania (siglos II y III d.C.).* Madrid (1993): 147–52.

Sillières, P. *Baelo Claudia. Una ciudad romana de la Bética.* Madrid (1997).

Silver, I. A. "The ageing of domestic animals," in D. Brothwell and E. Higgs (eds.), *Science in Archaeology*, 2nd ed. London (1969): 283–302.

Sotomayor, M. "Excavaciones en la Huerta de Facultad de Teologia de Granada," *Noticiario Arqueológico Hispánico* VIII–IX (1964–1965). Madrid (1966): 193–9.

Stevenson, A. C. "Studies in the Vegetational History of SW Spain. I. Modern Pollen Rain in the Doñana National Park, Huelva," *Journal of Biogeography* 12(3) (1985): 243–68.

Stevenson, A. C. "Studies in the Vegetational History of SW Spain. II. Palynological Investigations at Laguna de las Maedres, Huelva," *Journal of Biogeogrpahy* 12(4) (1985a): 293–314.

Stevenson, A. C. & Moore, P. D. "Studies in the Vegetational History of SW Spain IV. Palynological Investigations at El Acebrón, Huelva," *Journal of Biogeography* 15(2) (1988): 339–61.

Stevenson, A. C. & Harrison, R. J. "Ancient Forests in Spain. A Model for Land-use and Dry Forest Management in Southwestern Spain from 4000 BC to 1900 AD," *Proceedings of the Prehistoric Society* 58 (1992): 227–47.

Stylow, A. 1988. "Epigrafía romana y paleocristiana de Palma del Río. Córdoba," *Ariadna* 5: 113–50.

Stylow, A. "Apuntes sobre las *tribus* romanas en Hispania," *Veleia* 12 (1995): 105–23.

Stylow, A. "The beginnings of Latin epigraphy in Baetica: the case of the funerary inscriptions," in S. Keay (ed.) *The Archaeology of Early Roman Baetica*. Journal of Roman Archaeology Supplement Number Twenty Nine. Portsmouth R.I. (1998): 111–21.

Tchernia, A. *Le vin de l'Italie romaine*. Paris (1986).

Thevenot, E. "Una familia de negociantes en aceite establecida en la Baetica en el siglo II: los Aelii Optati," *Archivo Español de Arqueología XXV* (1952): 225–30.

Thompson, E. A. *The Goths in Spain*. Oxford (1969).

Thouvenot, E. *Essai sur le province romaine de Bétique*. Paris (1940: 2nd Edition 1973).

Tovar, A. *Iberische Landeskunde. Zweiter Teil: Die Völker und die Städte des antiken Hispanien. Band I. Baetica*. Baden-Baden (1974).

Trillmich, W., Hauschild, T., Blech, M., Niemeyer, H.G., Nünnerich-Asmus, A. and Kreilinger, U. *Hispania Antiqua. Denkmäler der Römerzeit*. Mainz (1993).

Uerpmann, H.-P. and Uerpmann, M., "Die Tierknochenfunde aus der phönizischen Faktorei von Toscanos," *Studien über frühe Tierknochenfunde von der Iberischen Halbinsel* 4 (1973): 35–65.

Vanney, J. R. *L'hydrologie du bas-Guadalquivir*. Paris (1970).

Vargas Jiménez, J. M. and Romo Salas, A. *Memoria de la intervanción arqueológica de urgencia en la Plaza de España de Écija. Fase 1. 1988*. Seville (Unpublished).

Vaquerizo Gil, D. *El Yacimiento Ibérico del Cerro de la Cruz (Almedinilla, Córdoba)*. Cordoba (1990).

Vegas, M. *La cerámica común romana del Mediterráneo Occidental*. Barcelona (1973).

Ventura, A., León, P. & Márquez, C. 1998, "Roman Córdoba in the light of recent archaeological Research," in S. Keay (ed.), *The Archaeology of Early Roman Baetica*. Journal of Roman Archaeology Supplementary Series Number Twenty Nine. Portsmouth R.I. (1998): 87–108.

Ventura, J. J. "El orígen de la Córdoba romana a través del estudio de las verámica de barniz negro," in P. León Alonso (ed.), *Colonia Patricia Corduba. Una reflexión arqueológica*. Seville (1996): 49–62.

Vernhet, A. "Centre de production de Millau. Atelier de la Graufesenque," in C. Bémont and J.-P. Jacob (eds.) *La terre sigillée gallo-romaine. Lieux de production du Haut Empire: implantations, produits, relations*. Documents d'Archéologie Francaise No. 6. Paris (1986): 96–103.

Vidal, J. "Restos oseos de fauna (estrato III A/B)," in M. Beltrán, M., Sánchez Nuviala, J. J., Aguarod Otal, M. C. and Mostalac Carrillo, A. *Caesaraugusta I (Campaña 1975–1976)*. Excavaciones Arqueologicas en España 108 (1980): 101–3.

Villacavallos, P. de, *Explanación antiquo-lapidea, inscripcional del Museo de D. Pedro de Villa y Zeballos natural de Córdoba, fixado, y establecido en el Patio primero de sus Casas principales de ella, y del Señor Dn. Raphael su Padre Caballero de Santiago en la calle de las Pabas, Calleja de su apellido, y Collación de la Cathedral. Año 1740*. (Real Academia de Historia No. 9–5770 nº 2). Madrid (1740).

Villaronga, L. *Numismatica antigua de Hispania*. Barcelona (1979).

Villaronga, L. *Corpus nummorum Hispniae ante Augusti aetatem*. Barcelona (1994).

Vitruvius *The Ten Books of Architecture (trans Hicky Morgan, M.)*. New York (1960).

Vives, A. *La moneda hispánica*. (4 vols) Madrid (1924–26).

Vives, J. *Inscripciones cristianas de la España romana y visigoda*. Barcelona (1942).

Vives, J. *Concilios visigóticos e hispanorromanos*. Barcelona (1963).

Ward Perkins, J. *Roman Imperial Architecture*. Harmondsworth (1981).

Walker, L. "Survey of a settlement: a strategy for the Etruscan site of Doganella," in C. Haselgrove, M. Millett and I. Smith (eds.) *Archaeology from the Ploughsoil*. Sheffield (1985): 87–94.

Walker M. J. "Nuevos datos acerca de la explotación de la vid en el Eneolitico español," *Cuadernos de Prehistoria y Arqueologia* 11–12 (1984–5): 163–82.

Will, E. "Greco-Italic amphoras," *Hesperia* 51 (1982): 338–56.

Wilson, B., Grigson, C., and Payne, S. (eds.) *Ageing and Sexing Animal Bones from Archaeological Sites*. British Archaeological Reports 109. Oxford (1982).

Wolf, K. B. *Conquerors and Chroniclers of Early Medieval Spain*. Liverpool (1990).

Woolf, G. "Monumental Writing and the Expansion of Roman Society in the Early Empire," *Journal of Roman Studies* 86: 22–39.

Zanker, P. *The Power of Images in the Age of Augustus*. Ann Arbor (1983).

Zemer, A. *Storage jars in ancient sea trade*. Haifa (1978).

Zevi, F. "Appunti sulle anfore romane," *Archeologia Classica 18* (1966): 207–47.

Appendix 1
Pottery Counts Quantification (SK)

For Key to Ceramic Abbreviations see p. 69

CONTEXT / FASE	414 / 2	431 / 2	432 / 2	TOTAL / 2	428 / 3	433 / 3	TOTAL / 3	419 / 4	420 / 4	TOTAL / 4	401 / 5	405 / 5	TOTAL / 5	403 / 6	404 / 6	417 / 6
Brunida	1	6	0	7	1	3	4	18	0	18	20	3	23	8	21	0
A Torna Brunida	1	0	0	1	0	0	0	24	0	24	6	3	9	4	9	1
A Mano	3	0	10	13	3	4	7	34	2	36	1	1	2	0	0	2
Ceramica Fina Iberica (P)	0	0	0	0	1	5	6	42	0	42	43	11	54	17	18	5
Ceramica Fina Iberica (L)	0	0	0	0	0	1	1	45	0	45	43	32	75	27	12	3
Gria Emporitana	0	0	0	0	0	0	0	0	0	0	0	0	0	0	0	0
Anfora Prerromana	0	0	0	0	0	0	0	0	0	0	0	0	0	0	0	0
Campaniense	0	0	0	0	0	0	0	0	0	0	2	3	5	0	0	0
Campaniense regional	0	0	0	0	0	0	0	0	0	0	0	0	0	0	1	1
Anfora Republicana	0	0	0	0	0	0	0	0	0	0	0	0	0	0	0	0
Anfora Punica	0	0	0	0	0	0	0	0	0	0	1	0	1	1	0	0
CC ITAL	0	0	0	0	0	0	0	0	0	0	0	0	0	0	0	0
Lamp	0	0	0	0	0	0	0	0	0	0	0	0	0	0	0	0
TSI	0	0	0	0	0	0	0	0	0	0	0	0	0	0	0	0
TSI Local	0	0	0	0	0	0	0	0	0	0	0	0	0	0	0	0
TSSG	0	0	0	0	0	0	0	0	0	0	0	0	0	0	0	0
TSH	0	0	0	0	0	0	0	0	0	0	0	0	0	0	0	0
Rojo Pompeiano	0	0	0	0	0	0	0	0	0	0	0	0	0	0	0	0
Paredes Finas	0	0	0	0	0	0	0	0	0	0	0	1	1	0	0	0
Anfora Halt. 70	0	0	0	0	0	0	0	0	0	0	0	1	1	0	0	0
Anfora Dr. 20	0	0	0	0	0	0	0	0	0	0	0	0	0	0	0	0
Anfora Dr. 2-4	0	0	0	0	0	0	0	0	0	0	0	0	0	0	0	0
Anfora Dr. 28	0	0	0	0	0	0	0	0	0	0	0	0	0	0	0	0
Anfora Garum	0	0	0	0	0	0	0	0	0	0	0	0	0	0	0	0
Anfora Gaul 4	0	0	0	0	0	0	0	0	0	0	0	0	0	0	0	0
Anfora Otra	0	0	0	0	0	0	0	0	0	0	0	0	0	0	0	0
Anfora Egipcia	0	0	0	0	0	0	0	0	0	0	0	0	0	0	0	0
TSCLA	0	0	0	0	0	0	0	0	0	0	0	0	0	0	0	0
TSCLA IMIT	0	0	0	0	0	0	0	0	0	0	0	0	0	0	0	0
TSCLC	0	0	0	0	0	0	0	0	0	0	0	0	0	0	0	0
TSCLC IMIT	0	0	0	0	0	0	0	0	0	0	0	0	0	0	0	0
TSCLD	0	0	0	0	0	0	0	0	0	0	0	0	0	0	0	0
TSCLD IMIT	0	0	0	0	0	0	0	0	0	0	0	0	0	0	0	0
TSCL	0	0	0	0	0	0	0	0	0	0	0	0	0	0	0	0
Misc. TS	0	0	0	0	0	0	0	0	0	0	0	0	0	0	0	0
Vidriada	0	0	0	0	0	0	0	0	0	0	0	0	0	0	0	0
CCA	0	0	0	0	0	0	0	0	0	0	0	0	0	0	0	0
CCA IMIT	0	0	0	0	0	0	0	0	0	0	0	0	0	0	0	0
Anfora Gaza	0	0	0	0	0	0	0	0	0	0	0	0	0	0	0	0
Anfora Bajo Imperial	0	0	0	0	0	0	0	0	0	0	0	0	0	0	2	0
C. Comun	0	0	0	0	0	0	0	0	0	0	5	4	9	5	0	0
Dolia	0	0	0	0	0	0	0	0	0	0	0	0	0	0	0	0
Sin Identificar	0	0	0	0	0	0	0	7	0	7	4	5	9	3	0	0
TOTAL	5	6	10	21	5	13	18	170	2	172	125	63	188	65	63	12

CONTEXT	421	569	296	551	560	564	567	575	577	TOTAL	172	173	262	263	299	335	336
FASE	6	6a	6c	6c	6d	6d	6d	6d	6d	6	7a	7a	7a	7a	7a	7a	7a
Brunida	3	4	0	0	13	0	2	2	0	53	0	0	31	20	1	1	6
A Torna Brunida	14	1	0	5	21	0	1	1	1	58	0	0	13	0	0	0	0
A Mano	0	9	0	6	28	0	0	1	1	47	4	1	69	6	3	2	3
Ceramica Fina Iberica (P)	14	38	72	66	50	2	3	3	4	292	12	24	116	80	45	6	34
Ceramica Fina Iberica (L)	14	92	24	268	132	26	7	1	0	606	16	132	213	336	173	35	193
Gria Emporitana	0	0	0	0	0	0	0	0	0	0	0	0	1	0	0	0	0
Anfora Prerromana	0	0	0	0	11	0	0	0	0	11	0	3	3	3	1	0	1
Campaniense	0	0	0	0	0	0	0	0	0	2	0	0	1	0	0	0	1
Campaniense regional	0	0	0	0	0	0	0	0	0	0	0	0	0	0	1	0	0
Anfora Republicana	0	0	0	0	1	0	0	0	0	1	0	0	0	1	0	0	0
Anfora Punica	0	0	0	0	0	0	0	0	0	0	0	0	14	0	0	0	1
CC ITAL	0	0	0	0	0	0	0	0	0	0	0	0	1	1	0	0	0
Lucerna	0	0	0	0	0	0	0	0	0	0	0	2	0	0	0	0	2
TSI	0	0	1	5	0	0	0	0	0	6	0	0	4	24	8	1	0
TSI Local	0	3	1	5	0	1	0	0	0	11	1	14	10	0	0	1	14
TSSG	0	0	0	0	0	0	0	0	0	0	0	0	0	0	0	0	0
TSH	0	0	0	0	0	0	0	0	0	0	0	0	0	0	0	0	0
Rojo Pompeiano	0	0	0	1	0	0	0	0	0	1	0	2	2	2	0	0	0
Paredas Finas	0	2	1	4	0	0	1	0	0	8	1	1	6	4	5	1	3
Anfora Halt. 70	0	4	3	7	1	5	0	1	0	21	1	1	109	95	27	0	1
Anfora Dr. 20	0	0	0	0	0	0	0	0	0	0	0	0	0	0	0	1	3
Anfora Dr. 2-4	0	0	0	0	0	0	0	0	0	0	0	0	0	0	0	0	0
Anfora Dr. 28	0	0	0	0	0	0	0	0	0	0	0	0	0	0	0	0	1
Anfora Garum	0	0	0	2	0	0	0	0	0	2	0	0	0	12	0	0	0
Anfora Gaul 4	0	0	0	0	0	0	0	0	0	0	0	0	0	0	0	1	0
Anfora Otra	0	1	6	5	0	0	0	0	0	12	0	0	11	0	17	0	2
Anfora Egipcia	0	0	0	0	0	0	0	0	0	0	0	0	0	0	0	0	0
TSCLA	0	0	0	0	0	0	0	0	0	0	0	0	0	0	0	0	0
TSCLA IMIT	0	0	0	0	0	0	0	0	0	0	0	0	0	0	0	0	0
TSCLC	0	0	0	0	0	0	0	0	0	0	0	0	0	0	0	0	0
TSCLC IMIT	0	0	0	0	0	0	0	0	0	0	0	0	0	0	0	0	0
TSCLD	0	0	0	0	0	0	0	0	0	0	0	0	0	0	0	0	0
TSCLD IMIT	0	0	0	0	0	0	0	0	0	0	0	0	0	0	0	0	0
TSCL	0	0	0	0	0	0	0	0	0	0	0	0	0	0	0	0	0
Misc. TS	0	0	0	0	0	0	0	0	0	0	0	0	0	0	0	0	0
Vidriada	0	0	0	0	0	0	0	0	0	0	0	0	0	0	0	0	0
CCA	0	0	0	0	0	0	0	0	0	0	0	0	0	0	0	0	0
CCA IMIT	0	0	0	0	0	0	0	0	0	0	0	0	1	0	0	0	0
Anfora Gaza	0	0	0	0	0	0	0	0	0	0	0	0	0	0	0	0	0
Anfora Bajo Imperial	0	2	0	0	0	0	0	0	0	2	0	0	0	0	0	1	0
C. Comun	9	34	5	93	5	1	5	9	9	177	27	100	216	90	32	9	53
Dolia	0	0	0	0	15	0	0	0	0	15	0	0	2	3	0	0	0
Sin Identificar	2	1	0	27	4	0	1	4	0	42	23	30	0	44	24	6	39
TOTAL	56	191	112	494	281	35	20	22	15	1366	85	310	823	721	336	64	357

CONTEXT / FASE	406 7a	410 7a	411 7a	413 7a	415 7a	416 7a	642 7a	645 7a	647 7a	652 7a	276 7c-8c	TOTAL 7	337 7a-9	TOTAL 7a-9	271 8	TOTAL 8
Brunida	0	1	8	3	2	0	0	3	21	2	0	99	3	3	0	0
A Torna Brunida	3	0	5	4	0	0	0	6	20	0	0	51	2	2	0	0
A Mano	36	0	0	4	0	8	0	4	10	1	0	151	1	1	2	2
Ceramica Fina Iberica (P)	51	37	26	10	2	9	16	6	160	19	10	663	11	11	0	0
Ceramica Fina Iberica (L)	223	82	53	18	14	22	28	1	339	45	6	1929	80	80	24	24
Gria Emporitana	0	0	0	0	0	0	0	0	0	0	0	1	0	0	0	0
Anfora Prerromana	10	0	0	0	0	0	0	0	0	0	0	20	0	0	0	0
Campaniense	2	1	0	0	0	0	0	0	1	0	1	8	0	0	0	0
Campaniense regional	0	0	0	1	0	0	0	0	0	0	0	0	0	0	0	0
Anfora Republicana	0	0	1	0	0	0	1	0	0	0	1	4	0	0	0	0
Anfora Punica	0	0	0	0	0	0	0	0	0	0	0	15	0	0	0	0
CC ITAL	0	0	0	0	0	0	0	0	0	0	0	2	0	0	0	0
Lucerna	0	0	0	0	0	0	1	0	1	0	0	6	0	0	0	0
TSI	0	0	0	0	0	0	0	0	0	0	0	4	0	0	0	0
TSI Local	26	0	0	0	0	0	2	1	17	4	0	122	2	2	0	0
TSSG	0	0	0	0	0	0	0	0	0	0	0	0	0	0	0	0
TSH	0	0	0	0	0	0	0	0	0	0	1	1	0	0	0	0
Rojo Pompeiano	0	1	0	0	0	0	0	0	0	0	0	9	1	1	0	0
Paredas Finas	18	1	1	1	0	0	0	0	2	0	0	44	0	0	7	7
Anfora Halt. 70	2	17	0	0	7	0	0	0	27	7	1	295	1	1	3	3
Anfora Dr. 20	0	0	0	0	0	0	0	0	2	0	0	4	7	7	0	0
Anfora Dr. 2-4	0	0	0	0	0	0	0	0	0	0	0	0	1	1	3	3
Anfora Dr. 28	0	0	0	0	0	0	0	0	0	0	0	1	0	0	0	0
Anfora Garum	0	3	0	0	0	0	0	0	7	1	2	25	1	1	8	8
Anfora Gaul 4	0	0	0	0	0	0	0	0	0	0	0	1	0	0	0	0
Anfora Otra	0	0	0	0	0	0	0	0	0	0	1	31	0	0	0	0
Anfora Egipcia	0	0	0	0	0	0	0	0	0	0	0	0	0	0	0	0
TSCLA	0	0	0	0	0	0	0	0	0	0	0	0	1	1	0	0
TSCLA IMIT	0	0	0	0	0	0	0	0	0	0	0	0	0	0	0	0
TSCLC	0	0	0	0	0	0	0	0	0	0	0	0	0	0	0	0
TSCLC IMIT	0	0	0	0	0	0	0	0	0	0	0	0	0	0	0	0
TSCLD	0	0	0	0	0	0	0	0	0	0	0	0	0	0	0	0
TSCLD IMIT	0	0	0	0	0	0	0	0	0	0	0	0	0	0	0	0
TSCL	0	0	0	0	0	0	0	0	0	0	0	0	0	0	0	0
Misc. TS	0	0	0	0	0	0	0	0	0	0	0	0	0	0	0	0
Vidriada	0	0	0	0	0	0	0	0	0	0	0	0	0	0	0	0
CCA	0	0	0	0	0	0	0	0	0	0	0	0	0	0	0	0
CCA IMIT	0	0	0	0	0	0	0	0	0	0	0	1	0	0	0	0
Anfora Gaza	0	0	0	0	0	0	0	0	0	0	0	0	0	0	0	0
Anfora Bajo Imperial	0	0	0	0	0	0	0	0	0	0	0	1	0	0	0	0
C. Comun	66	22	15	12	9	6	29	5	71	4	2	768	44	44	50	50
Dolia	0	0	0	0	0	0	0	0	1	0	0	6	1	1	0	0
Sin Identificar	35	7	8	4	2	1	5	0	20	8	0	256	25	25	3	3
TOTAL	472	172	117	57	36	46	82	26	699	91	25	4518	181	181	100	100

CONTEXT	245	246	247	252	253	254	264	265	553	554	555	557	630	705	707	723
FASE	9	9	9	9	9	9	9	9	9	9	9	9	9	9	9	9
Brunida	4	3	10	13	1	0	8	7	2	0	2	4	0	1	0	0
A Torna Brunida	0	0	1	1	0	0	1	3	0	1	0	0	0	0	1	0
A Mano	0	3	4	7	2	1	1	2	0	3	3	1	0	0	2	0
Ceramica Fina Iberica (P)	0	3	2	5	1	1	9	8	11	2	1	1	20	0	7	1
Ceramica Fina Iberica (L)	19	7	4	33	0	1	9	10	49	35	0	2	2	110	36	13
Gria Emporitana	0	0	0	0	0	0	0	0	0	0	0	0	0	0	0	0
Anfora Prerromana	0	0	0	0	0	0	0	0	0	0	0	0	0	0	0	0
Campaniense	0	0	0	0	0	0	0	1	0	0	0	0	0	0	1	0
Campaniense regional	0	0	0	0	0	0	0	0	0	0	0	0	0	0	0	0
Anfora Republicana	0	0	0	0	0	0	0	0	0	0	0	0	0	0	0	0
Anfora Punica	0	0	0	0	0	0	0	0	0	0	0	0	0	0	0	0
CC ITAL	0	0	0	0	0	0	2	0	1	0	0	0	0	0	0	1
Lucerna	0	0	0	1	1	0	2	7	0	0	0	0	1	0	1	0
TSI	0	0	0	0	1	0	6	0	1	0	0	0	0	0	0	0
TSI Local	0	2	5	10	0	1	2	4	4	0	0	3	1	0	1	1
TSSG	0	0	1	2	1	1	5	1	2	0	0	0	0	0	0	0
TSH	1	2	1	3	1	2	1	5	3	0	1	6	0	0	1	1
Rojo Pompeiano	2	2	0	1	0	3	2	14	3	0	0	2	0	0	0	1
Paredes Finas	0	0	0	0	0	0	1	1	0	0	3	0	0	0	2	0
Anfora Halt. 70	34	8	7	22	2	1	26	1	19	8	3	0	0	31	34	92
Anfora Dr. 20	0	0	0	0	0	0	0	30	0	0	0	0	0	0	0	0
Anfora Dr. 2-4	0	0	0	0	0	0	0	0	0	0	0	0	0	0	0	0
Anfora Dr. 28	53	5	6	25	0	2	8	0	5	1	0	0	0	0	5	12
Anfora Garum	7	0	0	5	0	61	0	16	7	0	0	0	0	0	0	0
Anfora Gaul 4	2	2	0	4	0	0	0	3	0	4	0	14	0	4	0	0
Anfora Otra	2	0	0	0	0	0	0	26	0	0	0	0	0	0	0	0
Anfora Egipcia	2	0	1	1	2	0	4	0	0	0	0	1	0	0	1	0
TSCLA	7	0	0	3	0	0	1	2	0	4	0	2	1	0	0	0
TSCLA IMIT	0	0	0	0	2	0	0	12	0	0	0	0	1	0	0	2
TSCLC	0	0	0	1	0	0	0	0	1	0	0	0	0	0	5	8
TSCLC IMIT	0	0	2	0	0	0	0	0	0	0	0	1	0	0	8	0
TSCLD	0	0	0	0	0	0	0	3	1	0	0	0	0	1	0	0
TSCLD IMIT	0	0	0	0	2	0	0	0	0	0	0	0	0	0	0	0
TSCL	0	0	2	0	1	0	0	0	0	0	0	0	0	0	0	0
Misc. TS	0	0	0	0	0	0	0	0	0	0	0	0	0	0	0	0
Vidriada	0	0	0	0	0	0	5	0	0	0	0	0	0	0	1	0
CCA	0	0	0	0	6	0	0	4	0	0	0	3	0	0	0	0
CCA IMIT	0	0	0	24	0	0	0	25	0	0	0	1	0	4	1	3
Anfora Gaza	0	0	0	0	0	0	0	0	0	0	0	1	0	0	0	0
Anfora Bajo Imperial	0	0	0	0	0	0	0	0	1	0	0	0	0	0	6	4
C. Comun	279	22	56	153	31	24	237	586	55	38	8	5	63	172	71	277
Dolia	0	0	0	0	0	0	0	0	0	2	0	0	0	0	0	0
Sin Identificar	66	12	5	37	2	3	0	0	1	0	0	2	6	55	6	18
TOTAL	476	71	107	351	56	101	330	771	165	98	21	49	93	378	181	433

CONTEXT FASE	741 9	762 9	788 9	TOTAL 9	153 12	256 12	257 12	260 12	412 12	TOTAL 12
Brunida	0	13	0	68	7	2	0	1	0	10
A Torna Brunida	0	2	0	10	3	0	0	0	0	3
A Mano	0	17	0	46	20	0	0	1	1	22
Ceramica Fina Iberica (P)	0	11	1	84	153	0	3	0	0	156
Ceramica Fina Iberica (L)	4	120	25	479	692	23	12	1	9	737
Gria Emporitana	0	0	0	0	0	0	0	0	0	0
Anfora Prerromana	0	0	0	0	12	0	0	2	0	14
Campaniense	1	0	0	3	0	0	0	0	0	0
Campaniense regional	0	0	0	0	0	0	0	0	0	0
Anfora Republicana	0	0	0	0	4	1	2	2	0	9
Anfora Punica	0	0	0	0	0	0	0	0	0	0
CC ITAL	0	0	0	1	0	0	0	0	0	0
Lucerna	0	1	0	12	1	0	1	0	0	2
TSI	0	0	0	6	1	0	0	0	1	2
TSI Local	4	6	0	45	23	0	8	4	1	36
TSSG	3	3	0	17	0	0	9	2	0	11
TSH	3	4	3	39	0	3	16	2	0	21
Rojo Pompeiano	0	5	2	36	10	0	1	10	1	22
Paredas Finas	0	2	3	16	5	0	1	0	0	6
Anfora Halt. 70	3	0	0	5	3	0	0	0	0	3
Anfora Dr. 20	9	3	35	364	1	12	0	3	0	16
Anfora Dr. 2-4	0	0	0	0	0	0	1	1	0	2
Anfora Dr. 28	0	0	0	0	0	0	1	0	0	1
Anfora Garum	2	14	0	154	41	10	16	8	0	75
Anfora Gaul 4	0	4	0	83	2	1	2	0	0	5
Anfora Otra	76	0	0	136	2	0	0	1	0	3
Anfora Egipcia	0	0	0	0	0	1	0	0	0	1
TSCLA	3	1	2	20	1	0	12	9	0	22
TSCLA IMIT	0	0	0	30	0	3	1	0	0	4
TSCLC	0	0	0	4	0	0	0	2	0	2
TSCLC IMIT	0	0	0	14	0	0	0	0	0	0
TSCLD	1	2	0	10	0	0	1	2	0	2
TSCLD IMIT	0	1	0	2	0	0	1	0	0	0
TSCL	0	1	0	5	0	0	0	0	0	0
Misc. TS	0	0	0	1	0	0	0	0	0	0
Vidriada	0	0	0	0	0	0	0	0	0	0
CCA	8	1	5	26	0	0	4	5	0	9
CCA IMIT	0	15	2	81	0	3	19	0	0	22
Anfora Gaza	0	0	0	0	0	0	0	0	0	0
Anfora Bajo Imperial	1	136	0	148	0	0	0	0	0	0
C. Comun	230	263	125	2695	189	58	167	59	2	475
Dolia	0	0	0	2	0	0	0	0	0	0
Sin Identificar	7	25	80	325	121	10	11	3	3	148
TOTAL	355	650	283	4969	1291	127	287	118	18	1841

Appendix 2
Pottery Weights (grams) Quantification (SK)

CONTEXT / FASE	414 / 2	431 / 2	432 / 2	TOTAL / 2	428 / 3	433 / 3	TOTAL / 3	419 / 4	420 / 4	TOTAL / 4	401 / 5	405 / 5	TOTAL / 5	403 / 6	404 / 6	417 / 6
Brunida	50	115	0	165	40	80	120	390	0	390	380	80	460	260	265	0
A Torna Brunida	40	0	0	40	0	0	0	430	0	430	240	80	320	120	120	40
A Mano	120	0	605	725	80	90	170	885	100	985	40	40	80	0	0	80
Ceramica Fina Iberica (P)	0	0	0	0	40	165	205	1080	0	1080	775	325	1100	290	310	120
Ceramica Fina Iberica (L)	0	0	0	0	0	40	40	955	0	955	1015	445	1460	170	260	80
Gria Emporitana	0	0	0	0	0	0	0	0	0	0	0	0	0	0	0	0
Anfora Prerromana	0	0	0	0	0	0	0	0	0	0	100	300	400	0	0	0
Campaniense	0	0	0	0	0	0	0	0	0	0	0	0	0	0	40	40
Campaniense regional	0	0	0	0	0	0	0	0	0	0	0	0	0	0	0	0
Anfora Republicana	0	0	0	0	0	0	0	0	0	0	0	0	0	0	0	0
Anfora Punica	0	0	0	0	0	0	0	0	0	0	40	0	40	0	0	0
CC ITAL	0	0	0	0	0	0	0	0	0	0	0	0	0	0	0	0
Lamp	0	0	0	0	0	0	0	0	0	0	0	0	0	0	0	0
TSI	0	0	0	0	0	0	0	0	0	0	0	0	0	0	0	0
TSI Local	0	0	0	0	0	0	0	0	0	0	0	0	0	40	0	0
TSSG	0	0	0	0	0	0	0	0	0	0	0	0	0	0	0	0
TSH	0	0	0	0	0	0	0	0	0	0	0	0	0	0	0	0
Rojo Pompeiano	0	0	0	0	0	0	0	0	0	0	0	0	0	0	0	0
Paredas Finas	0	0	0	0	0	0	0	0	0	0	0	0	0	0	0	0
Anfora Halt. 70	0	0	0	0	0	0	0	0	0	0	0	40	40	0	0	0
Anfora Dr. 20	0	0	0	0	0	0	0	0	0	0	0	0	0	0	0	0
Anfora Dr. 2-4	0	0	0	0	0	0	0	0	0	0	0	0	0	0	0	0
Anfora Dr. 28	0	0	0	0	0	0	0	0	0	0	0	0	0	0	0	0
Anfora Garum	0	0	0	0	0	0	0	0	0	0	0	0	0	0	0	0
Anfora Gaul 4	0	0	0	0	0	0	0	0	0	0	0	0	0	0	0	0
Anfora Otra	0	0	0	0	0	0	0	0	0	0	0	0	0	0	0	0
Anfora Egipcia	0	0	0	0	0	0	0	0	0	0	0	0	0	0	0	0
TSCLA	0	0	0	0	0	0	0	0	0	0	0	0	0	0	0	0
TSCLA IMIT	0	0	0	0	0	0	0	0	0	0	0	0	0	0	0	0
TSCLC	0	0	0	0	0	0	0	0	0	0	0	0	0	0	0	0
TSCLC IMIT	0	0	0	0	0	0	0	0	0	0	0	0	0	0	0	0
TSCLD	0	0	0	0	0	0	0	0	0	0	0	0	0	0	0	0
TSCLD IMIT	0	0	0	0	0	0	0	0	0	0	0	0	0	0	0	0
TSCL	0	0	0	0	0	0	0	0	0	0	0	0	0	0	0	0
Misc. TS	0	0	0	0	0	0	0	0	0	0	0	0	0	0	0	0
Vidriada	0	0	0	0	0	0	0	0	0	0	0	0	0	160	80	0
CCA	0	0	0	0	0	0	0	0	0	0	0	0	0	0	0	0
CCA IMIT	0	0	0	0	0	0	0	0	0	0	0	0	0	0	0	0
Anfora Gaza	0	0	0	0	0	0	0	0	0	0	0	0	0	0	0	0
Anfora Bajo Imperial	0	0	0	0	0	0	0	0	0	0	0	0	0	0	0	0
C. Comun	0	0	0	0	0	0	0	0	0	0	170	160	330	160	80	0
Dolia	0	0	0	0	0	0	0	0	0	0	0	0	0	120	0	0
Sin Identificar	0	0	0	0	0	0	0	200	0	200	280	205	485	120	0	0
TOTAL	210	115	605	930	160	375	535	3940	100	4040	3040	1675	4715	1160	1075	360

CONTEXT	421	569	296	551	560	564	567	575	577	TOTAL	172	173	262	263	299	335	336
FASE	6	6a	6c	6c	6d	6d	6d	6d	6d	6	7a	7a	7a	7a	7a	7a	7a
Brunida	120	40	0	0	275	0	20	40	0	1020	0	0	860	900	50	140	395
A Torna Brunida	200	10	0	45	550	0	10	10	40	1145	0	0	170	0	0	0	0
A Mano	0	120	0	40	525	0	0	75	20	860	100	40	2050	300	50	140	145
Ceramica Fina Iberica (P)	460	410	525	1135	800	20	30	30	50	4180	710	1280	2075	1660	1060	200	455
Ceramica Fina Iberica (L)	170	1320	875	1820	1475	1000	90	10	0	7270	250	3460	3650	7420	2490	410	2030
Gria Emporitana	0	0	0	0	0	0	0	0	0	0	0	0	0	0	0	0	0
Anfora Prerromana	0	0	0	0	500	0	0	0	0	500	0	300	150	200	0	0	85
Campaniense	0	0	0	0	0	0	0	0	0	80	0	0	10	0	50	0	40
Campaniense regional	0	0	0	0	0	0	0	0	0	0	0	0	0	0	0	0	0
Anfora Republicana	0	0	0	0	0	0	0	0	0	0	0	0	0	150	0	0	0
Anfora Punica	0	0	0	0	150	0	0	0	0	150	0	0	0	0	0	0	40
CC ITAL	0	0	0	0	0	0	0	0	0	0	0	0	700	0	0	0	0
Lamp	0	0	0	0	0	0	0	0	0	0	0	0	50	50	0	0	80
TSI	0	0	100	120	0	0	0	0	0	220	0	80	80	0	0	0	0
TSI Local	0	30	50	80	0	50	0	0	0	250	40	200	200	975	290	40	280
TSSG	0	0	0	0	0	0	0	0	0	0	0	0	0	0	0	0	0
TSH	0	0	0	0	0	0	0	0	0	0	0	0	0	0	0	0	0
Rojo Pompeiano	0	0	0	10	0	0	0	0	0	10	0	0	100	100	0	0	0
Paredas Finas	0	20	25	30	0	0	10	0	0	85	40	40	40	100	150	40	40
Anfora Halt. 70	0	1750	450	250	50	575	0	30	0	3105	40	40	5600	6200	1500	0	150
Anfora Dr. 20	0	0	0	0	0	0	0	0	0	0	0	300	0	0	0	40	370
Anfora Dr. 2-4	0	0	0	0	0	0	0	0	0	0	0	0	0	0	0	0	0
Anfora Dr. 28	0	0	0	0	0	0	0	0	0	0	0	0	0	0	0	0	40
Anfora Garum	0	0	0	150	0	0	0	0	0	150	0	0	0	1150	0	0	0
Anfora Gaul 4	0	0	0	0	0	0	0	0	0	0	0	0	0	0	0	40	0
Anfora Otra	0	20	180	110	0	0	0	0	0	310	0	0	2150	0	180	0	510
Anfora Egipcia	0	0	0	0	0	0	0	0	0	0	0	0	0	0	0	0	0
TSCLA	0	0	0	0	0	0	0	0	0	0	0	0	0	0	0	0	0
TSCLA IMIT	0	0	0	0	0	0	0	0	0	0	0	0	0	0	0	0	0
TSCLC	0	0	0	0	0	0	0	0	0	0	0	0	0	0	0	0	0
TSCLC IMIT	0	0	0	0	0	0	0	0	0	0	0	0	0	0	0	0	0
TSCLD	0	0	0	0	0	0	0	0	0	0	0	0	0	0	0	0	0
TSCLD IMIT	0	0	0	0	0	0	0	0	0	0	0	0	0	0	0	0	0
TSCL	0	0	0	0	0	0	0	0	0	0	0	0	0	0	0	0	0
Misc. TS	0	0	0	0	0	0	0	0	0	0	0	0	0	0	0	0	0
Vidriada	0	0	0	0	0	0	0	0	0	0	0	0	0	0	0	0	0
CCA	0	0	0	0	0	0	0	0	0	0	0	0	0	0	0	0	0
CCA IMIT	0	0	0	0	0	0	0	0	0	0	0	0	20	0	0	0	0
Anfora Gaza	0	0	0	0	0	0	0	0	0	0	0	0	0	0	0	40	0
Anfora Bajo Imperial	0	20	0	0	0	0	0	0	0	20	0	0	0	0	0	0	0
C. Comun	200	420	100	585	150	10	70	90	80	1945	620	3745	3905	2275	480	360	1035
Dolia	0	0	0	0	300	0	0	0	0	300	0	0	650	400	0	0	0
Sin Identificar	80	10	0	560	600	0	50	80	0	1500	1110	2520	0	2475	1730	320	1850
TOTAL	1230	4170	2305	4935	5375	1655	280	365	190	23100	2910	12005	22460	24355	8030	1770	7545

| CONTEXT | 406 | 410 | 411 | 413 | 415 | 416 | 642 | 645 | 647 | 652 | 276 | TOTAL | 337 | TOTAL | 271 | TOTAL |
FASE	7a	7a	7a	7a	7a	7a	7a	7a	7a	7a	7c-8c	7	7a-9	7a-9	8	8
Brunida	0	40	100	140	80	0	0	140	500	50	0	3395	125	125	0	0
A Torna Brunida	80	0	80	80	0	0	0	200	140	0	0	750	80	80	0	0
A Mano	750	0	0	190	0	210	0	50	195	50	0	4270	40	40	20	20
Ceramica Fina Iberica (P)	1190	1500	660	250	40	225	605	100	4140	500	150	16800	240	240	0	0
Ceramica Fina Iberica (L)	5755	2480	1480	520	320	750	560	50	8140	1405	150	41320	1060	1060	175	175
Gria Emporitana	0	0	0	0	0	0	0	0	0	0	0	20	0	0	0	0
Anfora Prerromana	1255	0	0	0	0	0	0	0	0	0	0	1990	0	0	0	0
Campaniense	80	40	0	0	0	0	0	0	10	0	50	280	0	0	0	0
Campaniense regional	0	0	0	75	0	0	0	0	0	0	0	0	0	0	0	0
Anfora Republicana	0	0	60	0	0	0	200	0	0	0	50	460	0	0	0	0
Anfora Punica	0	0	0	0	0	0	0	0	0	0	0	740	0	0	0	0
CC ITAL	0	0	0	0	0	0	0	0	0	0	0	100	0	0	0	0
Lamp	0	0	0	0	0	0	10	0	10	0	0	180	0	0	0	0
TSI	0	0	0	0	0	0	0	0	0	0	0	80	0	0	0	0
TSI Local	380	0	0	0	0	0	20	50	160	200	0	2835	80	80	0	0
TSSG	0	0	0	0	0	0	0	0	0	0	0	0	0	0	0	0
TSH	0	0	0	0	0	0	0	0	0	0	50	50	0	0	0	0
Rojo Pompeiano	0	40	0	0	0	0	0	0	100	0	0	380	40	40	125	125
Paredes Finas	170	40	40	40	0	0	0	0	10	0	0	730	0	0	30	30
Anfora Halt. 70	275	1520	0	0	550	0	0	0	2250	350	50	18785	105	105	0	0
Anfora Dr. 20	0	0	0	0	0	0	0	0	0	0	0	410	2065	2065	650	650
Anfora Dr. 2-4	0	0	0	0	0	0	0	0	0	0	0	0	100	100	0	0
Anfora Dr. 28	0	0	0	0	0	0	0	0	0	0	0	40	0	0	0	0
Anfora Garum	0	360	0	0	0	0	0	0	1050	50	50	2660	0	0	850	850
Anfora Gaul 4	0	0	0	0	0	0	0	0	0	0	0	40	40	40	0	0
Anfora Otra	0	0	0	0	0	0	0	0	0	0	50	2890	0	0	0	0
Anfora Egipcia	0	0	0	0	0	0	0	0	0	0	0	0	0	0	0	0
TSCLA	0	0	0	0	0	0	0	0	0	0	0	0	0	0	0	0
TSCLA IMIT	0	0	0	0	0	0	0	0	0	0	0	0	40	40	0	0
TSCLC	0	0	0	0	0	0	0	0	0	0	0	0	0	0	0	0
TSCLC IMIT	0	0	0	0	0	0	0	0	0	0	0	0	0	0	0	0
TSCLD	0	0	0	0	0	0	0	0	0	0	0	0	0	0	0	0
TSCLD IMIT	0	0	0	0	0	0	0	0	0	0	0	0	0	0	0	0
TSCL	0	0	0	0	0	0	0	0	0	0	0	0	0	0	0	0
Misc. TS	0	0	0	0	0	0	0	0	0	0	0	0	0	0	0	0
Vidriada	0	0	0	0	0	0	0	0	0	0	0	0	0	0	0	0
CCA	0	0	0	0	0	0	0	0	0	0	0	0	0	0	0	0
CCA IMIT	0	0	0	0	0	0	0	0	0	0	0	20	0	0	0	0
Anfora Gaza	0	0	0	0	0	0	0	0	0	0	0	0	0	0	0	0
Anfora Bajo Imperial	0	0	0	0	0	0	0	0	0	0	0	40	0	0	0	0
C. Comun	1825	850	370	510	260	160	710	150	2010	175	100	19540	1580	1580	1635	1635
Dolia	0	0	0	0	0	0	0	0	50	0	0	1100	510	510	0	0
Sin Identificar	1555	1470	460	140	80	60	460	0	1450	650	0	16330	1370	1370	210	210
TOTAL	13315	8340	3250	1945	1330	1405	2565	740	20215	3430	700	136235	7475	7475	3695	3695

CONTEXT	245	246	247	252	253	254	264	265	553	554	555	557	630	705	707	723
FASE	9	9	9	9	9	9	9	9	9	9	9	9	9	9	9	9
Brunida	40	140	250	345	40	0	200	200	30	0	50	80	0	20	0	0
A Torna Brunida	0	0	40	40	0	0	10	70	0	10	0	0	0	0	50	0
A Mano	0	120	60	190	105	40	30	150	0	50	60	100	0	0	100	0
Ceramica Fina Iberica (P)	0	80	40	160	40	80	100	170	80	40	50	50	250	4890	250	10
Ceramica Fina Iberica (L)	250	240	90	1030	0	40	275	530	800	280	0	110	30	0	500	150
Gria Emporitana	0	0	0	0	0	0	0	0	0	0	0	0	0	0	0	0
Anfora Prerromana	0	0	0	0	0	0	0	0	0	0	0	0	0	0	0	0
Campaniense	0	0	0	0	0	0	0	20	0	0	0	0	0	0	50	0
Campaniense regional	0	0	0	0	0	0	0	0	0	0	0	0	0	0	0	0
Anfora Republicana	0	0	0	0	0	0	0	0	0	0	0	0	0	0	0	0
Anfora Punica	0	0	0	0	0	0	0	0	0	0	0	0	0	0	0	0
CC ITAL	0	0	0	0	0	0	0	0	10	0	0	0	0	0	0	0
Lamp	0	0	0	40	40	0	10	70	10	0	0	0	0	0	50	10
TSI	0	0	0	200	40	0	30	0	10	0	0	0	10	0	0	0
TSI Local	0	80	160	80	0	0	100	90	40	0	0	60	0	0	0	0
TSSG	0	0	40	120	40	40	30	50	30	0	50	90	0	0	10	0
TSH	40	80	40	40	40	40	60	110	60	0	50	90	0	0	0	10
Rojo Pompeiano	40	100	0	0	0	80	30	410	20	0	0	0	0	0	0	20
Paredas Finas	0	0	0	0	0	80	10	10	0	0	150	0	0	0	100	0
Anfora Halt. 70	0	0	0	0	0	0	300	30	0	0	0	0	0	0	0	0
Anfora Dr. 20	6545	1710	1055	2785	150	45	4550	4300	1660	1150	100	0	0	14400	10510	20100
Anfora Dr. 2-4	0	0	0	0	0	0	0	0	0	0	0	0	0	0	0	0
Anfora Dr. 28	0	0	0	0	0	0	0	0	0	0	0	0	0	0	0	0
Anfora Garum	6745	640	490	2060	0	380	400	1350	620	100	0	0	0	0	640	1200
Anfora Gaul 4	640	0	0	100	0	9365	0	400	275	0	0	0	0	0	0	0
Anfora Otra	300	40	0	315	0	0	0	1540	0	500	0	1500	0	460	0	0
Anfora Egipcia	0	0	0	0	0	0	0	0	0	0	0	0	0	0	0	0
TSCLA	80	0	40	40	40	0	70	20	0	0	0	40	0	0	50	0
TSCLA IMIT	260	0	0	80	0	0	30	145	0	60	0	20	20	0	0	0
TSCLC	0	0	0	0	60	0	0	0	0	0	0	0	0	0	0	50
TSCLC IMIT	0	0	0	40	0	0	0	0	0	0	0	0	0	0	0	160
TSCLD	0	0	50	0	40	0	0	0	0	0	0	10	0	30	150	0
TSCLD IMIT	0	0	0	0	0	0	0	0	0	0	0	0	0	0	0	0
TSCL	0	0	40	0	40	0	0	0	0	0	0	0	0	0	0	0
Misc. TS	0	0	0	0	0	0	0	0	0	0	0	0	0	0	0	0
Vidriada	0	0	0	0	0	0	0	0	0	0	0	0	0	0	50	0
CCA	0	0	0	300	80	0	100	80	0	0	0	60	0	0	0	0
CCA IMIT	0	0	0	0	0	0	0	475	0	0	0	10	0	60	50	90
Anfora Gaza	0	0	0	0	0	0	0	0	0	0	0	40	0	0	0	0
Anfora Bajo Imperial	0	0	0	0	0	0	0	0	150	0	0	0	0	0	390	1350
C. Comun	8675	565	1165	4075	1420	590	5030	14250	2050	700	300	610	940	2570	1630	11255
Dolia	0	0	0	0	0	0	0	0	0	350	0	0	0	0	0	0
Sin Identificar	6410	675	435	2095	60	260	0	0	50	0	0	210	630	8500	670	2325
TOTAL	30025	4470	3995	14135	2235	11040	11365	24490	5895	3240	760	3080	1880	30930	15250	36730

| CONTEXT | 741 | 762 | 788 | TOTAL | 153 | 256 | 257 | 260 | 412 | TOTAL |
FASE	9	9	9	9	12	12	12	12	12	12
Brunida	0	250	0	1645	240	40	0	40	0	320
A Torna Brunida	0	100	0	320	140	0	0	0	0	140
A Mano	0	400	0	1405	360	0	0	55	40	455
Ceramica Fina Iberica (P)	0	175	50	1625	3610	0	120	0	0	3730
Ceramica Fina Iberica (L)	30	975	200	10420	15125	730	340	40	170	16405
Gria Emporitana	0	0	0	0	0	0	0	0	0	0
Anfora Prerromana	0	0	0	0	1195	0	0	150	0	1345
Campaniense	10	0	0	80	0	0	0	0	0	0
Campaniense regional	0	0	0	0	0	0	0	0	0	0
Anfora Republicana	0	0	0	0	400	260	290	150	0	1100
Anfora Punica	0	0	0	0	0	0	0	0	0	0
CC ITAL	0	0	0	10	0	0	0	0	0	0
Lamp	0	10	0	140	40	0	0	0	0	80
TSI	0	0	0	170	50	0	40	0	40	90
TSI Local	50	125	0	915	325	0	0	0	40	605
TSSG	20	55	0	395	0	0	160	80	0	160
TSH	30	75	150	955	365	120	80	80	0	370
Rojo Pompeiano	0	50	100	1020	240	0	210	40	40	585
Paredes Finas	0	50	100	500	250	0	40	140	0	280
Anfora Halt. 70	260	0	5650	590	100	0	40	0	0	250
Anfora Dr. 20	505	600	0	75815	0	770	0	0	0	1650
Anfora Dr. 2-4	0	0	0	0	0	0	530	780	0	680
Anfora Dr. 28	0	0	0	0	0	0	40	150	0	40
Anfora Garum	350	800	0	15775	10100	2070	3015	630	0	15815
Anfora Gaul 4	0	0	0	10780	60	40	40	0	0	140
Anfora Otra	3100	700	0	8455	100	0	0	40	0	140
Anfora Egipcia	0	0	0	0	0	100	0	40	0	0
TSCLA	135	10	50	575	50	0	130	0	0	260
TSCLA IMIT	0	0	0	615	0	90	40	80	0	130
TSCLC	0	0	0	110	0	0	0	0	0	40
TSCLC IMIT	0	0	0	350	0	0	0	40	0	0
TSCLD	10	0	0	100	0	0	0	0	0	80
TSCLD IMIT	0	10	0	40	0	0	0	80	0	0
TSCL	0	0	0	90	0	0	0	0	0	0
Misc. TS	0	10	0	40	0	0	0	0	0	0
Vidriada	0	0	0	0	0	0	0	0	0	0
CCA	200	0	0	640	0	0	0	0	0	0
CCA IMIT	0	50	150	1465	0	0	120	80	0	200
Anfora Gaza	0	350	50	0	0	50	150	0	0	200
Anfora Bajo Imperial	50	13850	0	15790	0	0	0	0	0	0
C. Comun	3035	4185	1885	64930	7070	2160	2845	1855	40	13970
Dolia	0	0	0	350	0	0	0	0	0	0
Sin Identificar	480	1100	5200	29100	10055	1210	1175	450	165	13055
TOTAL	8265	23930	13585	245300	49875	7640	9405	4960	535	72315

Appendix 3
Small Finds Quantification (SK)

Phase	Context	Nail	Window Glass	Tin	Bronze	Iron	Iron Nodules	Stone Vessel	Stone Mortarium	Copper	Whetstone	Counter	Loom	Lead	Glass	Phase Total
5	163						1									
Total		0	0	0	0	0	1	0	0	0	0	0	0	0	0	1
6	403					1										
Total		0	0	0	0	1	0	0	0	0	0	0	0	0	0	1
6a	569					1						1				
Total		0	0	0	0	1	0	0	0	0	0	1	0	0	0	2
6c	551					2										
Total		0	0	0	0	2	0	0	0	0	0	0	0	0	0	2
6d	560	1				1										
Total		1	0	0	0	1	0	0	0	0	0	0	0	0	0	2
7	148					4										
Total		0	0	0	0	4	0	0	0	0	0	0	0	0	0	4
7a	31						1								1	
7a	128					2					1					
7a	159						1									
7a	172					1										
7a	186										1					
7a	262														1	
7a	299											1		1		
7a	336	1			2		1							1		
7a	406						1									
7a	413					1										
7a	416				1											
7a	642											2				
7a	647					5	9									
Total		1	0	0	3	9	13	0	0	1	1	3	0	2	2	35
7a-9	609													1		
7a-9	623				1											
7a-9	641														1	
Total		0	0	0	1	0	0	0	0	0	0	0	0	1	1	3
7b	37					2										
7b	233		1													
7b	319														1	
Total		0	1	0	0	2	0	0	0	0	0	0	0	0	1	4
7b-8a	20					4									2	
Total		0	0	0	0	4	0	0	0	0	0	0	0	0	2	6
7b-9	348						1									
Total		0	0	0	0	0	1	0	0	0	0	0	0	0	0	1
7c-8c	276											1			2	
Total		0	0	0	0	0	0	0	0	0	0	1	0	0	2	3
7d-8a	123						28									
Total		0	0	0	0	0	28	0	0	0	0	0	0	0	0	28
8	271				3	1									3	
Total		0	0	0	3	1	0	0	0	0	0	0	0	0	3	7
8a	28					2									1	
8a	60					2	7								1	
8a	61						3									
8a	68					2	1								5	
8a	119				1											
8a	516				1											
Total		0	0	0	2	6	11	0	0	0	0	0	0	0	7	26

Phase	Context	Nail	Window Glass	Tin	Bronze	Iron	Iron Nodules	Stone Vessel	Stone Mortarium	Copper	Whetstone	Counter	Loom	Lead	Glass	Phase Total
8b	19				1											
8b	204													1		
8b	728														13	
Total		0	0	0	1	0	0	0	0	0	0	0	0	1	13	15
9	32					1				1						
9	53					6	14								1	
9	62														1	
9	63														4	
9	65					2										
9	71					1										
9	100					1	2									
9	127					2										
9	129					5									4	
9	136					1	1							1		
9	149					1									3	
9	154				1											
9	208					1									4	
9	219														1	
9	222														3	
9	247														1	
9	252					2				1					4	
9	253	2												1	2	
9	254	12	2												4	
9	264														4	
9	265	6				1						1			27	
9	324	2				5	3							4		
9	350														1	
9	354				1	1									1	
9	380														2	
9	508	1														
9	529	1														
9	550													1		
9	553	3														
9	554				1											
9	555														2	
9	557					13									6	
9	630									1		1				
9	653	1														
9	704	5		1											5	
9	705											1				
9	707				1	89			1							
9	724	4				5										
9	741								1							
9	749	1				3									2	
9	755				1											
9	758														2	
9	762					5						1		1		
9	788														1	
Total		38	2	1	5	145	20	0	2	3	0	4	0	8	85	313
11	51				1	4	11								2	
11	714						1									
Total		0	0	0	1	4	12	0	0	0	0	0	0	0	2	19
12	1	1			1	11	8							1	7	
12	13				1	1	4			1						
12	15					2	15									
12	16					1				1						
12	21					2				1						
12	24					1				1						
12	27					1									2	
12	50													1		
12	145													1	2	

Phase	Context	Nail	Window Glass	Tin	Bronze	Iron	Iron Nodules	Stone Vessel	Stone Mortarium	Copper	Whetstone	Counter	Loom	Lead	Glass	Phase Total
12	153					1	1						1		1	
12	236	1												1	11	
12	250													2		
12	256									6						
12	257	9			3					1					10	
12	260	7			2	1				2				2	25	
12	305														1	
12	306					1	1							1		
12	315				1										2	
12	323													1	4	
12	326						1							1	1	
12	343	1														
12	349					2										
12	366		1											1	1	
12	513				1	15										
12	518					1									2	
12	519													2		
12	523														4	
12	530					1										
12	543					2										
12	602	4												1		
12	605														1	
12	628	1														
12	650	1														
12	700				7		2								7	
12	701														3	
12	702	1					1								3	
12	761	1				1									2	
12	763	1														
12	765				1										1	
12	766	3			1	2									1	
12	767	1		1		5		1								
Total		32	1	1	18	51	33	1	0	13	0	0	1	15	91	257

Appendix 4
Data from Animal Bones and Comparative Data
(ACK)

Phase	2–5	6	7	8	9	11	12	Sub-total
Species								
Ox (*Bos taurus*)	2	5	52	21	62	1	77	220
Sheep/Goat (*Ovis aries/Capra hircus*)	3	13	38	34	163	6	75	332
Pig (*Sus scrofa*) **	1	13	51	42	90	15	64	276
Horse (*Equus caballus*)			19	2	4		6	31
Donkey (*Equus asinus*)							2	2
Dog (*Canis familiaris*)			6	7	223*		19*	255
Red Deer (*Cervus elaphus*)			2	2	4		4	12
Rabbit (*Oryctolagus cuniculus*)	1	3	11	6	21		1	43
Hare (*Lepus europaeus*)			1					1
Wood Mouse (*Apodemus sylvaticus*)			3					3
Tortoise (*Testudo* sp.)			3					3
Ribs: large (ox, horse size)			9	5	8		4	26
" : small/very small (pig or smaller)	2	7	25	8	40	4	22	108
Vertebrae: large			8	2	17		2	29
" : small	1	2	4	3	7	1	5	23
Long bone fragments: large		11	32	16	89	2	91	241
" : small	5	29	51	44	125	9	85	348
Other fragments: large		1	2	4	12	1	3	23
" : small			12	8	19	1	11	51
Unidentified small mammal size							1	1
Unidentified fish bone					1			1
Sub-Total:	15	84	329	204	885	40	472	
							Total:	2029

* includes partial skeletons
** all domestic pig, except the following, which are large enough to be wild boar: 2 (phase 6); 2 (phase 7); 1 (phase 8)

Table 1 Mammal Bones: numbers of fragments by phase

Phase		Ox	Sheep/Goat	Pig	Horse	Dog
2–5	BN	2	3	1		
	MN	1	1	1		
6	BN	5	13	13		
	BN%	16.1	41.9	41.9		
	MN	1	1	1		
	BN:MN	5:1	13:1	13:1		
7	BN	52	38	51	19	6
	BN%	36.9	27.0	36.2		
	MN	4	3	2	1	1
	BN:MN	13:1	13:1	26:1		
8	BN	21	34	42	2	7
	BN%	21.6	35.1	43.2		
	MN	1	3	2	1	1
	BN:MN	21:1	11:1	21:1		
9	BN	62	163	90	4	7
	BN%	19.7	51.7	28.6		
	MN	3	7	5	1	2
	BN:MN	19:1	23:1	18:1		
11	BN	1	6	15		
	MN	1	1	2		
12	BN	77	75	64	6	9
	BN%	35.6	34.7	29.6		
	MN	3	4	3	1	3
	BN:MN	26:1	24:1	21:1		

Table 2 Domestic species represented, (a) by fragment count (BN) adjusted to count articulated skeletons as a nominal two bones each, (b) by percentage of BN for ox, sheep/goat and pig, (c) by minimum number of individuals (MN) and (d) by BN:MN ratio

		Ox			Sheep/Goat				Pig			
		7	9	12	7	8	9	12	7	8	9	12
I	scap	4	1	5	1	1	2		1	4		1
	hum		8	8	1	2	12	5	4	2	2	2
	pelv	2	4	3	2	2	1		2	2	4	1
	fem	1	1	2	3	2	9	4	1	3	5	3
II	rad	5	6	5	4	3	13	4	5	2		8
	uln			2	2		3		2		3	
	tib	6	3	4	3	6	11	5	2	2	11	7
III	cran	3		1	3	1		2	1	2	2	3
	max		1				1	1	2		6	
	mand	6	1	1	2	3	11	2	3	3	6	4
	teeth	9	11	10	4	8	67	37	16	6	31	18
	core			1	2	1						
IV	metac	2	2	4	1	2	10	2	3	5	5	5
	metat	3	5	7	6	1	7	6	4	4	6	4
	calc		4						2	2	1	1
	astrag	1	1	1	1			1	1			1
	carp/tars			4					1			
	phal I-III	4	4	5			3	3	1	4	2	1
	others/frs	6	5	13	5	1	14	5	2	3	7	4
Total	I	7	14	18	7	7	24	9	8	11	11	7
	II	11	9	11	9	9	27	9	9	4	14	15
	III	9	2	2	5	4	12	5	6	5	14	7
	IV	10	16	21	8	5	20	9	12	15	14	12
	I %	19	34	35	24	28	29	28	23	31	21	17
	II %	30	22	21	31	36	33	28	26	11	26	37
	III %	24	5	4	17	16	15	16	17	14	26	17
	IV %	27	39	40	28	20	24	28	34	43	26	29
T/B	T/B	9:43	11:46	10:66	4:36	8:27	67:97	37:37	16:37	6:38	31:60	18:45
	%	20.9	23.9	15.2	11.1	29.6	69.1	100.0	43.2	15.8	51.7	40.0

Table 3 Parts of the carcass represented for ox, sheep/goat and pig by phase, grouped according to the scheme of Barker 1982. The numbers of teeth and the tooth:bone ratio are also given.

Ox	phase	7		8		9		12	
	mo.	F-NF	%F	F-NF	%F	F-NF	%F	F-NF	%F
scap	10	4-0		1-0		2-0		4-1	
pelv	10	2-0		1-0		4-0		3-0	
hum d	12–18	-	100	-	100	4-0	100	1-0	91
rad p	12–18	-		1-0		3-0		1-0	
ph II	15–18	1-0		1-0		2-0		1-0	
ph I	20–24	2-0		3-0		4-0		4-0	
tib d	24–30	3-0	100	-	100	2-0	89	-	100
mc d	24–30	-		-		1-0		-	
mt d	24–30	-		-		1-1		1-0	
calc	36	-		-		3-1		-	
hum p	42–48	-		-		1-0		-	
rad d	42–48	1-0	100	-	-	1-0	86	1-0	100
fem p	42–48	-		-		-		-	
fem d	42–48	-		-		-		-	
tib p	42–48	-		-		1-0		-	

Sheep/Goat	phase	7		8		9	
	mo.	F-NF	%F	F-NF	%F	F-NF	%F
hum d	< 12	-		-		1-0	
rad p	< 12	1-0		-		1-0	
scap	12	1-0	100	1-0	100	2-0	100
pelv	12	2-0		1-0		1-0	
ph I	14–35	-		1-0		3-0	
ph II	14–35	-		2-0		-	
tib d	35	1-0	100	-	100	2-0	100
fem p	36	-		-		-	
mc d	47	-		-		-	
mt d	47	1-0		-		0-1	
fem d	48	-	100	-	-	-	0
tib p	48	-		-		-	
calc	48–60	-		-		-	
rad p	48–60	-	-	-	-	-	-
hum p	48–60	-		-		-	

Pig	phase	7		8		9		12	
	mo.	F-NF	%F	F-NF	%F	F-NF	%F	F-NF	%F
scap	7–11	1-0		2-2		-		1-0	
pelv	7–11	2-0		1-0		3-0		0-1	
rad p	11	1-0	83	-	71	-	75	2-0	80
hum d	11+	1-1		-		0-1		-	
ph II	11+	-		2-0		-		1-0	
tib d	19–23	0-1		1-0		3-1		3-2	
mc d	19–23	-		0-2		0-2		0-3	
mt d	19–23	2-1	60	0-1	50	0-5	38	0-1	33
ph I	19–23	1-0		2-0		2-0		-	
calc	31–35	1-1		0-2		1-0		0-1	
fem p	31–35	-		-		-		-	
hum p	31–35+	-		-		-		-	
rad d	31–35+	-	67	-	0	-	100	1-0	50
uln	31–35+	1-0		-		1-0		-	
fem d	31–35+	-		-		-		-	
tib p	31–35+	-		-		-		-	

Table 4 Fusion of epiphyses for pig, sheep/goat and ox. The number fused (F) and not fused (NF) is given for each group of bones, together with the group's percentage fused (i.e. surviving to be older than the approximate ages given for each group). Adapted from Bull and Payne 1982 for pig, Silver 1969 and Bullock and Rackham 1982 for sheep/goat, and Grigson 1982 for ox.

Ox

phase	no. mandibles	tooth wear
5	1	elderly, c. 5 yrs + (M1/2 worn almost to alveolus)
7	3	one young adult, c. 2 yrs (M2 just wearing); two adult, c. 3 yrs + (one with P2,P3 worn, one with M1 very worn)
8	1	adult, c. 4 yrs + (M3 worn/very worn)
12	1	adult, c. 4 yrs + (M3 worn/very worn)

Sheep/Goat

phase	no. mandibles	tooth wear
2	1	adult/elderly (M3 very worn)
7	1	juvenile of c. 18 mo. (m3 very worn)
8	2	both adult (one with P1-M1 very worn, one with M3 in wear)
9	9	one at c. 36 mo. (M3 first cusp just coming into wear); four at c. 42-48 mo. (M3 coming into wear); two adult (M3 in wear); two adult/elderly (very worn cheek teeth)
12	5	one at c. 36 mo. (P2 erupting); four adult (worn or very worn M3)

Pig

phase	2 mo	6-10 mo	1 yr (-)	1½/1¾	3 +
6	-	-	-	1	-
7	-	2	-	-	-
9	3	1	-	-	-
11	-	-	1	-	-
12	-	-	-	-	1

Table 5   Summary of age-at-death from mandible tooth wear. Approximate ages for pig from Bull and Payne 1982, for sheep/goat from Bullock and Rackham 1982 and for ox from Grigson 1982.

	bone	meas.	value (m)	ratio	height (cm)	phase
Ox	mt	GL	211	5.45	115	9
	mt	GL	220	5.45	120	12
Sheep/Goat	astr	GLl	25	22.68	57 (sheep)	12
	astr	GLl	28	22.68	64 (goat)	7
	astr	GLl	28	22.68	64 (sheep)	5
Pig	astr	GLl	38	17.90	68	7

Dog skeleton 1 (phase 12)

bone	meas.	value (mm)	ratio (v.d.D & B)	height (cm)	ratio (H)	height (cm)
rad	GL	175	3.22	56.4	3.18 + 19.51	57.6
fem	GLC	177.5	3.01	53.4	3.14 - 12.96	54.4

Dog skeleton 3 (phase 9)

bone	meas.	value (mm)	ratio (v.d.D & B)	height (cm)	ratio (H)	height (cm)
hum	GL	164	3.37	55.3	3.43 - 26.54	53.6
hum	GL	164	3.37	55.3	3.43 - 26.54	53.6
rad	GL	163	3.22	52.5	3.18 + 19.51	53.8
fem	GLC	177	3.01	53.3	3.14 - 12.96	54.3
tib	GL	186	2.92	54.3	2.92 + 9.41	55.3
tib	GL	187	3.01	54.6	2.92 + 9.41	55.5
Average for skeleton 3				54.2		54.4

Table 6   Calculations of withers heights, using the ratios of von den Driesch and Boessneck 1974, and Harcourt 1974 (for dog). The measurements are taken from Table 8.

Site/phase	Date	Type	Ox %	Sh/Gt %	Pig %	Total	Reference
Celti							
phases 2 to 6	Iberian-eC1	urb.	18.9	43.2	37.8	37	this report
phase 7	eC1-C2	urb.	36.7	27.0	36.2	141	"
phase 8	lC2	urb.	21.4	35.1	43.2	97	"
phase 9	mC4-eC5	urb.	19.7	51.7	28.6	315	"
phases 11 and 12	C5 +	urb.?	32.7	34.0	33.2	238	"
Contemporary sites in the region							
Munigua	C2	urb.	40.7	19.1	40.2	1380	Boessneck &
Munigua	C3-C4	urb.	21.3	46.6	32.0	178	Driesch 1980
Cerro Macareno (1980)	Iberian	sett.	46.1	31.5	22.4	553	Amberger 1985
Cerro Macareno (1985)	Iberian-Rom	sett.	53.2	20.7	26.1	111	"
Toscanos	C1-C4	sett.	10.0	51.1	38.9	90	Uerpmann 1973
Other Roman sites in Spain							
Lugo (Gal)	C1-C2	urb	84.1	5.7	10.2	703	Altuna & Mariezkurrena 1996
Lugo (Gal)	C1-C2	urb	65.9	13.5	20.6	223	Altuna & Mariezkurrena 1996
Lugo (Gal)	C1-C2	urb	73.1	5.0	21.9	160	Altuna & Mariezkurrena 1996
Tiermes (Soria)	C1-C3	urb.	22.8	57.5	19.7	351	Miguel & Morales 1984
Zaragoza	lC4-eC5	urb.	20.3	62.3	17.4	69	Vidal 1980
Tarragona	mC5	urb.	26.6	52.0	21.3	342	Miró 1989
Vilauba 2/3 (Gir.)	C2-C4	villa	32.3	24.6	42.9	350	King 1988
Vilauba 4/5	mC4-lC6	villa	38.5	26.9	34.6	312	"
Vilauba 6	lC6-eC7	villa	29.2	36.9	34.0	312	"
Arellana (Nav.)	C1-C2	villa	22.4	63.1	14.5	290	Mariezkurrena &
Arellana	C3-C4	villa	38.6	50.8	10.6	746	Altuna 1994
San Esteban (Ter.)	e-mC1	sett.	8.5	73.1	18.4	305	Castaños 1981
Atxa (Nav)	LC1	mil	17.3	60.8	21.9	612	Ruiz 1995

Table 7   Comparison of the main domestic mammal species representation (by fragment count) with other assemblages from Spain of the Roman period.

Ox (*Bos taurus*)

Mand   (10) 38.5 × 17 [153; 12]
Scap   GLP 82, LG 68, BG 51 [153; 12]
    GLP 50, LG 39, BG 35.5 (epi. prox.) [256; 12]
    LG 54, BG 45 [723; 9]
    SLC 52, LG 59, BG 44 [766; 12]
mc   Bd62 [136; 9]
    Bp 57, SD 38 [262; 7a]

ph 1 ant
	Glpe	Bp	SD	Bd	
	64	35	32	33	[24; 12]
	60.5	29	24.5	26	[60; 8a]
	62	-	25	29	[149; 9]
	61.5	36	30	-	[153; 12]
	57	29	25	26.5	[186; 7a]
	62	32	26	31	[265; 9]
	61	29	24	29	[299; 7a]
	-	32	28	32	[403; 6]

pelv   LA 63, LAR 54* [326; 12]
tib   Bd 61* [336; 7a]
    Bd 60 [410; 7a]
    Bd 65 [724; 9]
astr   GLl 65, GLm 60, Dl 36, Dm 35, Bd 43.5 [151; 7a]
    GLl 66, GLm 61, Dl 37, Dm 36, Bd 41 [564; 6d]
    GLl 66, Dl 37, Bd 42 [724; 9]
    GLl 53, GLm 48, Dl 30, Dm 31, Bd 34 [763; 12]
nav-cub GB 55 [700; 12]
mt   Bp 15 [15; 12]
    GL 220, Bp 51.5, SD 29, DD 25, Bd 63 [326; 12]
    GL 211, Bp 42*, SD 27, Bd 53 [723; 9]

ph 2
	GL	Bp	SD	Bd	
	43	31	25	25	[24; 12]
	44	31	25	26	[68; 8a]
	43	29	23	24	[724; 9]

Sheep/Goat *Ovis/Capra*

mand   (10) 18 × 7 [13; 12]
    (7)75, (8)53, (9)25, (10)20.5* × 7, (15b)22, (15c)17 [53; 9]
    (10) 22.5 × 9 [149; 9]
    (7) 76, (8) 54, (9) 25, (10) 21.5 × 8.5, (15b) 23, (15c) 17.5 [208; 9]
    (10) 22 × 9 [265; 9]
    (10) 22 × 7.5 [354; 9]
    (10) 19.5 × 7 [431; 2]
    (10) 21 × 8 [554; 9]
    (10) 21 × 8 [723; 9]
    (10) 22 × 8 [767; 12]
rad   Bp 28, BFp 25 [762; 9]
uln   LO 40, DPA 26, SDO 22.5, BPC 17 [128; 7a]
mc   Bp 23 [37; 7b]
    Bp 24 [156; 8b]
    Bp 24, SD 14 [767; 12]
pelv   LA 30, LAR 25* [186; 7a]
tib   Bp 35 [1; 12]
    SD 14, Bd 27 [337; 7a-9]

astr
	GLl	GLm	Dl	Dm	Bd	
	25	23.5	13	14	16.5 prob. Ovis [13; 12]	
	28	26	14	16	17 prob Capra [148; 7]	
	28	26	15	15	17 def. Ovis [163; 5] *Cont'd p.240*	

Table 8   Bone measurements, given in mm using the scheme and abbreviations of von den Driesch 1976. * estimated measurement. The context number and phase are given in brackets at the end of each entry.

mt   SD 13, DD 11, Bd 25 [415; 7a]

ph 1 | Glpe | Bp | SD | Bd | |
       |------|----|----|----|----|
       | 37 | 13 | 11 | 12 | def. Ovis [53; 9] |
       | 34.5 | 13.5 | 11 | 13 | prob. Capra [60; 8a] |
       | 40 | 13 | 10 | 12 | def. Ovis post. [612; 9] |

ph 2 | GL | Bp | SD | Bd | |
       |----|----|----|----|----|
       | 20 | 13 | 11 | 11 | [502; 8b] |
       | 23 | 13 | 10 | 10 | [632; 8c] |

Pig (*Sus scrofa*)

mand   (9) 50, (9a) 34, (16c) 45.5 [153; 12]
rad   Bp 28 [27; 12]
uln   BPC 20 [31; 7a]
       BPC 19 [51; 11]
       BPC 20 [254; 9]
mc III GL 64, Bp 16, Bd 18 [27; 12]
pelv   LAR 28 [264; 9]
tib   Bd 27 [13; 12]
       Bd 29 [260; 11]
       SD 16, Bd 27 [623; 7a-9]
       Bd 26 [630; 9]
astr   GLl 38, GLm 34, DL 19, Dm 21, Bd 22 [415; 7a]
mt II GL 58, Bd 9 [31; 7a]

ph 1 | GLpe | Bp | SD | Bd | |
       |------|----|----|----|----|
       | 35 | 16 | 13 | 15 | [265; 9] |
       | 45 | 17 | 15 | 17 | prob. wild boar [728; 8b] |

ph 2 | GL | Bp | SD | Bd | |
       |----|----|----|----|----|
       | 27.5 | 13 | 10 | 10 | [27; 12] |
       | 22 | 14 | 12 | 13 | [271; 8] |
       | 30 | 14 | 9 | 11 | [828; 8a] |

Horse (*Equus caballus*)

mand   (14) 27 × 12 poss. E. asinus [628; 12]
hum   BT 77 [252; 9]
calc   GH 58 [1; 12]
ph 1   GL 83 [700; 12]
       GL 81, Bp 53, BFp 49, Dp 34, SD 31, Bd 44, BFd 41
       [723; 9]
ph 2   GL 41*, SD 38, Bd 40 [1; 12]

Dog (*Canis familiaris*)

mand   (11) 25, (12) 22, (13) 16 × 6, (14) 15.5, (20) 12, (21) 28
       {141; 7b]
       (13) 21 × 8 [276; 7c-8c]
       (13) 21 × 8, (14) 20, (15) 9 × 7, (19) 22 [723; 9]
       (5) 128, (7) 84, (8) 81, (9) 75, (10) 39, (11) 44, (12) 38,
       (14) 20, (15) 9 × 7, (17) 11, (19) 24, (20) 19, (24) 186.88,
       (26) 190.9 [801; 8c]
fem   Bd 30 [324; 9]

dog skeleton I [1; 12]
hum   Bd 33, SD 13.5
rad   GL 175, Bp 17, SD 12, Bd 21
mc II GL 61, Bd 10
mc V   GL 57.5, Bd 10
fem   GLC 177.5, Bp 38, DC 16.5, SD 12, Bd 28

dog skeleton II [1; 12]
scap   GLP 31, SLC 26.5, LG 26, BG 18.5
rad   Bp 18

dog skeleton III [758; 9]
l. cran   (16) 19, (18) 19, (18a) 9, (19) 18, (20) 13 × 14, (21) 8 × 9
r. cran   (16) 19, (18) 19, (18a) 9, (19) 17, (20) 13 × 14, (21) 8 × 9

l. mand (7) 79, (8) 71, (9) 67, (10) 34, (11) 40, (12) 35, (13) 20 ×
         9, (14) 19, (15) 9 × 7, (16) 5 × 4, (17) 9, (19) 20, (20) 15,
         (21) 37, (26) 161.9
r. mand (4) 116, (5) 108, (6) 114, (7) 78, (8) 72, (9) 66, (10) 34,
         (11) 40, (12) 33, (13) 20 × 8, (14) 19, (15) 9 × 7, (17) 9,
         (19) 20, (20) 15, (23) 158.92, (24) 157.68, (26) 164.8
l. scap DHA 127, SLC 23, GLP 30, LG 26, BG 18
r. scap SLC 22, GLP 29, LG 26, BG 18
l. hum   GL 164, GLC 158, Dp 40, SD 12, Bd 32
r. hum   GL 164, GLC 159, Dp 39, SD 12, Bd 32
l. rad   GL 163, Bp 18, SD 12, Bd 23
r. rad   Bp 18, SD 12, Bd 23
l. uln   DPA 23, SDO 20, BPC 17
r. uln   DPA 23, SDO 19, BPC 17
sacr (3 segments)
         GL 40, PL 37, GB 47, BFcr 24, HFcr 11
l. pelv LAR 22, SH 19, SB 8
r. pelv GL 152, LAR 21, SH 19, SB 8, LFo 29
l. fem   Bp 37, DC 18, Bd 31
r. fem   GLC (=GL) 177, Bp 38, DC 18, SD 12, Bd 31
pat   GL 18, GB 10
l. tib   GL 186, SD 12, Bd 21
r. tib   GL 187, Bp 32, SD 12, Bd 21
l. astr GL 27
r. astr GL 27
l. calc GL 44, GB 17
r. calc GL 43, GB 17

mt | | l. | II | III | V | r. II | III | IV | V |
    |----|----|----|-----|---|-------|-----|----|---|
    | GL | 63 | 71 | 66 | 64 | 71 | 74 | 65 | |
    | Bd | 8 | 9 | 7 | 8 | 9 | 8 | 8 | |

ph   not measured

Red Deer (*Cervus elaphus*)

hum   GLC 237*, SD 23, Bd 57, BT 48 [60; 8a]
rad   GL 295*, Bp 52, BFp 47, SD 30, BFd 46.5 [53; 9]
uln   BPC 28.5 artic. to previous [53; 9]
mc   Bp 34.5, SD 21 [410; 7a]
ph 1   GLpe 50.5, Bp 16.5, SD 13.5, Bd 17 [1; 12]
       SD 14, Bd 17 [50; 12]

Hare (*Lepus europaeus*)

tib   Bp 15.6, SD 6.3 [262; 7a]

Rabbit (*Oryctolagus cuniculus*)

cran   (9) 17.3, (16) 41* [265; 9]
mand   (2) 13.2 [63; 9]
hum   GL 55.5, GLC 54.9, Dp 11.6, SD 3.8, Bd 7.8 [37; 7b]
       GL 56.0, GLC 55.6, Dp 12.3, SD 3.7, Bd 6.8 [560; 6d]
rad   Bp 7.4, SD 3.8, Bd 9.7 [63; 9]
       Bp 8.0, SD 4.6 [233; 7b]
       Bp 6.1, SD 3.2 [252; 9]
uln   DPA 7.1, SDO 6.6, BPC 5.4 [222; 9]
       GL 56.1, DPA 6.0, SDO 6.0, BPC 5.0 artic. to hum
       from 560 above [560; 6d]
pelv   LAR 6.7, LFo 15.1 pathological wear on acet. rim [647;
       7a]
       LAR 8.5, LFo 15.5 [788; 9]
fem   GL 77.7, GLC 74.0, Bp 15.1, BTr 13.4, DC 6.1, SD 5.6,
       Bd 12.0 [161; 7a]
       Bd 11.8 [306; 12]
       GL 75.4, GLC 72.4, Bp 14.8, BTr 14.2, DC 6.2, SD 6.2,
       Bd 12.5 poss. modern [551; 6c]
tib   Bd 10.7 [53; 9]
       SD 5.1, Bd 10.7 [265; 9]

Table 8 Continued.

Appendix 5
Construction Material (SK)

Tile and Brick

See W/Appendix 3.

Painted Wallplaster

See list in Appendix 7.

Ceramic Column Segments

Layer	Phase	Number
E.337	7a-9	2
E.723	P.9	1
E.21	P.12	1
E.24	P.12	1
E.38	P.12	1
E.145	P.12	1
E.153	P.12	1
E.322	P.12	1

Opus Signinum Fragments

Layer	Phase	Number
E.428	P.3	2
E.567	P.6d	2
E.263	P.7a	1
E.623	P.7a-9	1
E.641	P.7a-9	4
E.276	P.7c-8c	1
E.728	P.8b	1
E.632	P.8c	3
E.95	P.9	2
E.99	P.9	4
E.246	P.9	4 blocks*
E.264	P.9	1
E.265	P.9	3
E.550	P.9	1
E.553	P.9	3
E.612	P.9	2
E.614	P.9	2
E.705	P.9	3
E.723	P.9	1
E.724	P.9	1
E.741	P.9	1
E.756	P.9	2
E.714	P.11	1
E.1	P.12	8
E.246	P.12	1
E.295	P.12	2
E.518	P.12	2
E.519	P.12	1
E.523	P.12	4
E.530	P.12	5
E.600	P.12	1
E.602	P.12	7
E.628	P.12	11
E.700	P.12	3
E.701	P.12	1
E.702	P.12	2
E.761	P.12	1
E.763	P.12	4
E.766	P.12	1

* Including many fragments

Opus Spicatum Bricks

Layer	Phase	Number
E.262	P.7a	4
E.246	P.9	Large number
E.264	P.9	1
E.553	P.9	2
E.705	P.9	2
E.707	P.9	1
E.741	P.9	1
E.723	P.9	15
E.762	P.9	2
E.628	P.12	1

Marble Fragments

Layer	Phase	Number
E.428	P.3	3
E.31	P.7a	1
E.299	P.7a	1
E.334	P.7a	4
E.728	P.8b	1
E.56	P.9	1
E.219	P.9	1
E.252	P.9	1
E.707	P.9	2
E.723	P.9	2
E.762	P.9	1
E.714	P.11	1
E.14	P.12	1
E.21	P.12	1
E.24	P.12	1
E.31	P.12	1
E.145	P.12	1
E.260	P.12	1
E.306	P.12	1
E.307	P.12	1
E.360	P.12	1
E.602	P.12	4
E.650	P.12	1
E.700	P.12	2
E.701	P.12	1
E.778	P.12	2

Mosaic Tesserae

Layer	Phase	Number
E.569	P.6a	1
E.641	P.7a-9	1
E.271	P.8	2
E.569	P.9	1
E.63	P.9	2
E.704	P.9	1
E.705	P.9	1
E.707	P.9	2
E.749	P.9	1
E.714	P.11	2
E.153	P.12	1

Appendix 6
Seeds (MJ)

Phase No:	1	1	3	3	3	3	3	3	4	4	6	6	6
Sample No.	439/1	439/2	428/1	428/2	428/3	428/4	433/1	433/2	419/1	419/2	417	421/1	421/2
Consolida sp.					2								
Papaver sominferum						1							
Caryophyllaceae indet.					1								
Chenopodium indet.					1	1							
Chenopodium album													
Cruciferae indet.													
Erica sp.					4								
cf. Prunus communis													
Lens culinaris													
Fabaceae indet.				3	60	6		3				1	
Vicia sp.													
Vicia sativum													
Vicia/Lathyrus			1										
Vicia cf.tetrasperma													
Trifolium /Medicago sp.													
Myrtus communis						1							
Vitis vinifera			4										
Apiaceae indet.					1								
Pistacia sp. (terebinthus / atlantica)										1			
Plantago sp. (coronopus / maritima)					3								
Olea europea													
Galium sp.					3								
Anthemis/Metricaria sp.													
Poaceae sp.					32	5							2
Poaceae indet.			26	4	36	5	3	6	2	2		1	
cf. Festuca													
Lolium sp.				1	31					1			
cf. Phalaris sp.					32								
Bromus sp.													
Hordeum sp.													
Hordeum sp. (murinum / hystrix)													
H. vulgare (six-rowed)													
H. sativum			30			1				2		1	
Triticum sp.	1												
T. aestivum / compactum													
T. dicoccum			21										
Cereal indet.													
Seed indet.		2				2							
Unidentified fruitstone													
Unidentified kernel			1										

Phase No:	6a	6c	6c	6c	6d	6d	6d	7a	7a	7a	7a	7a	7a	7a	7a-9
Sample No.	569	296	551	552	560	567	577	172/1	172/2	182	263	226/1	336/2	642	641
Consolida sp.															
Papaver sominferum															
Caryophyllaceae indet.															
Chenopodium indet.															
Chenopodium album										1					
Cruciferae indet.															
Erica sp.															
cf. Prunus communis															
Lens culinaris	1														
Fabaceae indet.															
Vicia sp.				1							1				
Vicia sativum															
Vicia/Lathyrus															
Vicia cf.tetrasperma															
Trifolium /Medicago sp.															
Myrtus communis															
Vitis vinifera				1	2		2	120							
Apiaceae indet.															
Pistacia sp. (terebinthus / atlantica)															
Plantago sp. (coronopus / maritima)															
Olea europea				3f					1f					2f	2f+1w
Galium sp.															
Anthemis/Metricaria sp.															
Poaceae sp.				2		1									
Poaceae indet.									1	1					
cf. Festuca															
Lolium sp.															
cf. Phalaris sp.															
Bromus sp.					1										
Hordeum sp.		2				1									
Hordeum sp. (murinum / hystrix)															
H. vulgare (six-rowed)													1		
H. sativum															
Triticum sp.						2	1								
T. aestivum / compactum											1				
T. dicoccum															
Cereal indet.	2	2		3		3	1								
Seed indet.						1							1		
Unidentified fruitstone															
Unidentified kernel															

Phase No:	8	8a	8a	8b	8c	9	9	9	9	9	9	9	9	9
Sample No.	365	657/1	657/2	728	632	99	100/1	100/2	100/3	222/1	222/2	252/1	252/2	254/1
Consolida sp.														
Papaver sominferum														
Caryophyllaceae indet.														
Chenopodium indet.														
Chenopodium album														
Cruciferae indet.		1												
Erica sp.														
cf. Prunus communis														
Lens culinaris														
Fabaceae indet.												5		1
Vicia sp.		1												
Vicia sativum														
Vicia/Lathyrus														
Vicia cf.tetrasperma			1											
Trifolium /Medicago sp.				1										
Myrtus communis														
Vitis vinifera														
Apiaceae indet.														
Pistacia sp. (terebinthus / atlantica)														
Plantago sp. (coronopus / maritima)														
Olea europea	78f	4f	1f	1f	91f				1f	6f	11f		21f	
Galium sp.														
Anthemis/Metricaria sp.			1											
Poaceae sp.		1												
Poaceae indet.												6		
cf. Festuca														
Lolium sp.														2
cf. Phalaris sp.		1												
Bromus sp.														
Hordeum sp.			1								1			
Hordeum sp. (murinum / hystrix)														
H. vulgare (six-rowed)														
H. sativum														
Triticum sp.											2			
T. aestivum / compactum										1				
T. dicoccum														
Cereal indet.	3	8	8		1	1					2			
Seed indet.								1				1		
Unidentified fruitstone					1									
Unidentified kernel														

Phase No:	9	9	9	9	9	9	9	9	9	9	9	9	9
Sample No.	254/2	254/3	354	395	550	553	554	555/1	555/2	556	557	558	653
Consolida sp.													
Papaver sominferum													
Caryophyllaceae indet.													
Chenopodium indet.													
Chenopodium album			1										
Cruciferae indet.													
Erica sp.													
cf. Prunus communis												2	
Lens culinaris													
Fabaceae indet.		1											
Vicia sp.													
Vicia sativum													
Vicia/Lathyrus													1
Vicia cf.tetrasperma													
Trifolium /Medicago sp.													
Myrtus communis													
Vitis vinifera										1			
Apiaceae indet.													
Pistacia sp. (terebinthus / atlantica)													
Plantago sp. (coronopus / maritima)													
Olea europea	8f	3f+1h		23f+1h	7f	19f		34f+1h	45f+1w	110f+2w	29f+2h	36f+1h+1w	33f
Galium sp.													
Anthemis/Metricaria sp.													
Poaceae sp.													
Poaceae indet.			1										
cf. Festuca				1							1		
Lolium sp.													
cf. Phalaris sp.													
Bromus sp.													
Hordeum sp.					1								
Hordeum sp. (murinum / hystrix)													
H. vulgare (six-rowed)													
H. sativum													
Triticum sp.													
T. aestivum / compactum									1				
T. dicoccum													
Cereal indet.				1				2		1	1		2
Seed indet.													
Unidentified fruitstone													
Unidentified kernel													

Phase No:	9	9	9	9	9	9	9	9
Sample No.	724	749	754	756	757	758	788	793
Consolida sp.								
Papaver sominferum								
Caryophyllaceae indet.								
Chenopodium indet.								
Chenopodium album								
Cruciferae indet.								
Erica sp.								
cf. Prunus communis								
Lens culinaris	1							
Fabaceae indet.								
Vicia sp.								
Vicia sativum	1							
Vicia/Lathyrus								
Vicia cf.tetrasperma								
Trifolium /Medicago sp.								
Myrtus communis								
Vitis vinifera								
Apiaceae indet.								
Pistacia sp. (terebinthus / atlantica)								
Plantago sp. (coronopus / maritima)								
Olea europea		7f	1f				242f+3h	
Galium sp.								
Anthemis/Metricaria sp.								
Poaceae sp.								
Poaceae indet.								
cf. Festuca								
Lolium sp.								
cf. Phalaris sp.								
Bromus sp.								
Hordeum sp.								
Hordeum sp. (murinum / hystrix)								
H. vulgare (six-rowed)								
H. sativum								
Triticum sp.								
T. aestivum / compactum								
T. dicoccum								
Cereal indet.								
Seed indet.								
Unidentified fruitstone								
Unidentified kernel								

Appendix 7
Wallplater: Catalogue (EP)

Phase	Context	Approx no. frags	Plaster type	Colours	Design
6d	560	9		red, green, white	plain
6d	561	1		red	plain
7a	262	7		red, yellow	plain
7a	263	1		dark red	plain
7b	342	1	C	cinnabar, green	The red and black scheme
7a–9	348	80+	C	cinnabar, black, green	The red and black scheme
	601	7	C	yellow, dark red, white	The yellow +dark red scroll scheme
7a–9	609	7	C	yellow, dark red, white	The yellow +dark red scroll scheme
7a–9	641	29	C	mustard yellow, dark purple-red	The yellow +dark red scroll scheme
7c–8c	276	2		white with black and yellow marbling	plain, marbling
8	365	9		red, and some black, green, white	plain /border
8	748	1		red	plain
8a	537	30	A	dark red, black, blue/grey	plain
8a	636	2		unpainted	rendering
8a	796	11	C	red, curved	The red column rendering
8b	300	sample	F	unpainted	rendering
8b	389	7	C	red, including one curved fragment	The red column rendering
8b	525	sample	E	unpainted	rendering
8b	728	54		red, white, grey (?blue) , black	plain
8b	752	sample	E	unpainted	rendering
8b	797	25	C	red, all curved	The red column rendering
9	95 Deep rm	30		yellow, red	plain
9	95 Deep rm	sample	D	unpainted	stucco
9	99 Deep rm	50	B	red, blue, white	plain/borders
9	100 Deep rm	200	B	red, blue, white, possibly related to red and white borders (see below)	plain/borders
9	100 Deep rm	30		red, grey? (possibly originally blue)	plain/borders

Phase	Context	Approx no. frags	Plaster type	Colours	Design
9	100 Deep rm	125	A	grey (originally blue), orange	The blue/grey +orange scheme
9	100 Deep rm	200	A or B	red over yellow: possibly two types, some plain red, some marbled red on yellow; much of the red damaged and flaking	plain and/or marbled
9	100 Deep rm	150	B	yellow, purple-red, green, grey, red, white	The marble scheme
9	100 Deep rm	85	B	plain red, red border with double white line, associated with the marble scheme (some red very damaged)	plain, border of the marble scheme
9	136	7	?C	black, white	? The red and black scheme
9	222	1		dark red	plain
9	246	85+		red, green, white	plain/borders
9	254	40+		red, blue, white (double line), one fragment with green	plain/borders
9	254	3	B	yellow, purple-red, green, grey, red, white	The marble scheme
9	264	20	B	white, dark red, purple, red	plain
9	264		D	unpainted	stucco
9	265	15		white, green, black, red	plain/borders
9	265	3		possible ceiling or stucco	? stucco
9	345	17	C	cinnabar, black, green, white	The red and black scheme
9	354	84		red, yellow, white, green,	plain/borders
9	354	4	D	possible ceiling or stucco	stucco
9	553	5		white, red, grey	plain/borders
9	554	3		yellow, dark red	plain
9	566	50		red, some white	plain
9	612	3		red, white	plain
9	614	1		red	plain
9	653	100	? A	yellow, red, white, black, pink	plain/borders marbling
9	705	7		red	? rendering
9	707	20		white, 1 frag dark red	rendering
9	723	2		red, white	plain/borders
9	724	70		red, green, white, yellow	plain/borders
9	724	7		unpainted	stucco
9	741	1		red	plain
9	762	10		unpainted	rendering

Phase	Context	Approx no. frags	Plaster type	Colours	Design
12	1	1		pink	plain
12	11	26		red, blue, white	plain/borders
12	257	6		dark red	plain
12	295	1		red	plain
12	306	8	C	cinnabar, black, green, white	The red and black scheme
12	343	6		black	?The red and black scheme
12	513	16		red, yellow	plain
12	515	1		red	plain
12	517	2		red	plain
12	518	15		white, red	plain
12	523	2		red	plain
12	530	1		red	plain
12	543	2		red, white	plain
12	600	5	A	yellow, red, white, grey, pink	plain/border
12	602	14		yellow, grey, red, black, blue	plain/border
12	605	5		yellow, red, white, green, including 1 frag with possible design of red on green	plain/border; possible design on one frag
12	628	15		grey, red, purple	plain/border
12	651	48		yellow, red, white, black	plain/border
12	700	60		dark red, white	plain/border
12	700	2		unpainted	stucco
12	701	1		red, white	plain
12	702	2		white	plain
12	766	3		white, red, yellow	plain/border
12	768	8		white, red	plain

Appendix 8
Wallplaster: excavation and conservation (EP)

Aims

The aims of the work on site were to record the position of the plaster fragments in the ground, to remove them from the deposit without damage and without losing the relationship between them. Once extracted the aim was to clean them, elucidate the design and rejoin fragments wherever possible.

Methods

1. Excavation

Initially groups or spreads of fragments were planned at a scale of 1:10; groups were given a muslin facing attached with a polyvinyl acetate emulsion adhesive in order to keep the fragments together during removal; isolated fragments were removed individually.

Unfortunately the 1:10 plans were not accurate enough to be useful during reassembly (this was largely due to the fact that details were obscured in the ground by a slurry of deteriorated mud-brick). Subsequently all fragments were planned or traced at a scale of 1:1 on transparent plastic sheet and this proved to work very well. Working plans could be amended and added to as excavation progressed and a neater plan prepared once all fragments in a group had been uncovered and removed from the ground.

The groups lifted using a muslin facing were difficult to retrieve without some surface damage because the plaster was in poor condition, and where possible fragments were subsequently lifted without adhesive and facing. Each group was recorded and placed in a shallow box using the 1:1 tracing as a guide.

Removing fragments from the ground was difficult where the clay (deteriorated mud-brick) had hardened in the sun. Areas were prepared for excavation by laying dampened foam plastic sponges over the surface to soften the clay and thus reduce the stress on the fragments during the excavation process. This problem would have been minimised if the deposit had been kept covered or shaded from the time of its discovery.

2. Cleaning and elucidation

The fragments in poor condition were soft and crumbly; the painted surface of most of the fragments was obscured by a deposit of clay resulting from the deterioration of the mud-brick, a few had isolated hard encrustations of insoluble salt crystals on their surfaces.

The clay was easily softened using distilled water but the painted surface was affected by attempts to remove the softened clay. Other solvents such as alcohol and acetone did not offer much improvement. Mechanical cleaning using a scalpel was reasonably effective but could damage the vulnerable surface below, and was very slow. The most effective and least damaging method involved the use of a poultice of sepiolite (magnesium silicate) mixed with distilled water (or water and alcohol, or acetone), applied to the surface, covered with food wrap or aluminium foil, or left in a sealed polythene bag for 15 to 20 minutes, and then gently peeled off, while still damp, using a scalpel. With this method the clay came away cleanly from the painted surface and the process caused minimal disruption to the paint. Other poultice materials such as cotton-wool were also effective. The poultice was used without a protective layer of tissue to ensure full contact between the poultice and the clay.

3. Consolidation and reconstruction

A few of the very fragile fragments from the upper

levels of the deposit were consolidated with an acrylic polymer (Paraloid B72) in acetone. Joins were made with adhesive only where it was possible to assemble small fragments into a coherent larger group, and these groups were kept to a handleable size (no more than 150 to 200 mm across). Cellulose nitrate adhesive was used because of its good performance in the high temperatures experienced during the summer in southern Spain (as high as 45 C). Joins in weak and crumbling fragments were reinforced with a proprietary plaster-based filler (Polyfilla).

4. Packaging

The plaster was packed for storage in shallow fruit crates to minimise the number of superimposed layers of fragments, and each layer was padded with plain white paper. Assembled groups were laid out in specially constructed wooden trays.

Appendix 9
Wallplaster: methods of analysis (EP)

with analytical work by Maria Mertzani

Aims

The aims of the analysis were to study the structure and raw materials of the plaster, and to identify the pigments and pigment combinations.

Methods

1. Analysis of the plaster

When possible, each sample fragment was cut in half. One half was used for preparing a polished section and the other half was used to analyse the proportion of filler to lime.

PREPARATION OF POLISHED SECTIONS

Each sample was mounted using Tiranti's embedding resin. The resin was left to fully set, then the sample was sectioned and polished. The sections were examined microscopically under reflected light to study the structure of the layers, and the relationship of the pigment to the plaster. The sections were also used to examine some of the pigments using Electron Probe Microanalyser (EPMA) (see below).

SEPARATING FILLER FROM PLASTER

Hydrochloric acid was used on a range of samples to dissolve the calcium carbonate and to establish the ratio of filler to lime. This is a simple and quick method for separating the filler from the lime, but its disadvantage is that the acid will dissolve some types of filler such as marble-powder.

The lime surface layer (a) was removed (if present) using a scalpel, then the resulting sample was divided into its component layers and each was analysed separately. Each was weighed, dissolved in concentrated hydrochloric acid and the insoluble fraction left to dry out on filter paper. Once dry, the insoluble filler was removed, using a brush, and weighed again.

2. Analysis of the pigments

Laboratory examination of the pigments employed polarising light microscopy (PLM), supported by elemental analysis using a Scanning Electron Microscope with Energy Dispersive Spectrometer (SEM EDS) (Hitachi 5570 with Link AN 10000 EDS Analyser) or, in some cases, Electron Probe Microanalyser (EPMA) (Jeol Superprobe JXA8600 with Wavelength Dispersive Spectrometers and Link AN 10000 EDS Analyser).

Microscope slides were prepared after removing a small sample of pigment from the surface of the painted plaster, dispersing it on a glass slide and mounting with Meltmount (n = 1.662); the prepared samples were examined under a polarising microscope and compared with a pigment reference collection. For SEM EDS a small portion of the pigment was removed and mounted on a stub. Cross sections already prepared to study the nature of the plaster were examined microscopically or with EPMA.